The Apocalyptic Vision
in America

Interdisciplinary Essays on Myth and Culture

Edited and with an introduction by

Lois Parkinson Zamora

WITHDRAWN
Rock Valley College
Educational Resources
Center

Bowling Green University Popular Press
Bowling Green, Ohio 43403

To Robert and Amy Parkinson,
in appreciation

Copyright © 1982 Bowling Green University Popular Press

Library of Congress Catalog Card No.: 81-85524

ISBN: 0-87972-190-1
      0-87972-191-X

Acknowledgements

This collection of essays had its inception in an interdisciplinary course at George Mason University in Fairfax Virginia: to the administration and the faculty at George Mason University who supported that course I owe thanks. I am also grateful to the University of Houston, George Mason University, and Clemson University for their financial support, to Kay Knight, Leah Alexander, Deborah Fant, Diane McManus and John Hohlt for their assistance in the preparation of the manuscript, and to Lucille McCarthy for the idea which led to this volume. To my colleagues in this enterprise for their patience and cooperation I want to express my special appreciation.

Lois Parkinson Zamora
Houston, June 1982

Contents

	Introduction	1
I.	*Philosophy:*	
	The Apocalyptic Meaning of History	11
	Debra Bergoffen	
II.	*Religion:*	
	Waiting for the End: The Social Context of American Apocalyptic Religion	37
	Charles H. Lippy	
III.	*History:*	
	The Development of America's Sense of Mission	64
	Ernest Cassara	
IV.	*Literature:*	
	The Myth of Apocalypse and the American Literary Imagination	97
	Lois Parkinson Zamora	
V.	*Art:*	
	The American West as Millenial Kingdom	139
	Dawn Glanz	
VI.	*Popular Culture:*	
	The Apocalyptic Vision in American Popular Culture	154
	John Wiley Nelson	
VII.	*Biology and Ecology:*	
	The Evolution and Imminent Extinction of an Avaricious Species	183
	Michael Emsley	
VIII.	*Economics:*	
	Apocalypse Yesterday	206
	Thomas R. DeGregori	
	Appendix:	
	The Revelation of St. John	222
	General Bibliography	242
	Notes on the Contributors	255
	Index	256

And I saw a new heaven and a new earth: for the first heaven and the first earth were passed away; and there was no more sea. And I John saw the holy city, new Jerusalem, coming down from God out of heaven, prepared as a bride adorned for her husband. And I heard a great voice out of heaven saying, Behold, the tabernacle of God is with men, and he will dwell with them, and they shall be his people, and God himself shall be with them, and be their God. And God shall wipe away all tears from their eyes; and there shall be no more death, neither sorrow, nor crying, neither shall there be any more pain; for the former things are passed away.

And he that sat upon the throne said, "Behold, I make all things new." And he said unto me, "Write: for these words are true and faithful." And he said unto me, "It is done. I am Alpha and Omega, the beginning and the end."

Revelations 21:1-6

Our universe is the best possible because it can contain no Promised Land; no point where we could have all we imagine. We are designed to want: with nothing to want, we are like windmills in a world without wind.

John Fowles, The Aristos

Introduction
Lois Parkinson Zamora

AMERICA has long been the source and focus of a powerful apocalyptic vision, at first millennial but becoming by our century unmistakably cataclysmic in nature. At the earliest intimations of a vast land beyond the circumscribed *orbis terrarum* of the fifteenth century, Europe endowed America with its millennial hopes. Columbus, reaching the coast of South America, quoted passages from Revelation and Isaiah which tell of "a new heaven and a new earth," and he wrote to his royal patrons, "I deeply feel within me that there, where I have said, lies the Terrestrial Paradise."[1] In his journal, the explorer explained that the world is pear-shaped like a woman's breast and that the Terrestrial Paradise lies on the spot corresponding to the nipple, from whence flow the waters of the Rivers of Eden. Citing scripture and his own observations, Columbus at length concluded that his voyage and God's historical purpose were one.[2] The New World's promise exerted irresistible attraction upon many Europeans who came to convert the Indians, to find that golden New Jerusalem called El Dorado, to exercise the religious, political, and economic freedom impossible in the Old World. Until relatively recently, America seemed to offer what the rest of the world never could, a place without a past, a place with only a future.

In the past two or three decades and in fact during much of this century, however, America's sense of its apocalyptic historical destiny has become almost universally pessimistic in outlook. In our time, millennial optimism seems to have been transformed into a foreboding suspicion of the imminence of great cosmic disaster in which the world may be annihilated, with no possibility of anything beyond the cataclysm. Our modern sense of apocalypse is less religious than historical, the cataclysm resulting from the events of recent history and man's own capacities for self-destruction. The current pessimism about our collective future has its basis in the cataclysmic side of apocalypse as surely as our earlier national optimism proceeded from its millennial vision. The essays in this collection, each according to the methods of its own discipline, deal with the apocalypse and the manifestation of that myth in American culture. But before proceeding further, we will do well to stop for some definitions.

The word "apocalypse" comes from the Greek word *apokalupsis,* to uncover or reveal (the root is *kalupto,* to cover or conceal), and is eschatological in nature (the root here being *eschatos,* furtherest or uttermost), concerned with final things, with the end of the present age, the Day of Judgment, and the age to follow. Apocalypse is a revelation of spiritual realities in the future, realities which are given temporal sequence and historical embodiment by the apocalyptist. This projection of the way in which time will progress toward its end is essentially linear, describing one event after another, each event belonging to a definite pattern of historical relationships which will not repeat itself in the cyclical manner of oriental myth but will move toward its goal which lies at the end of history.[3] Thus "apocalypse" is a synonym for "revelation" (*not* for "disaster," though it is frequently misused as such), and the essays that follow are not mere prophecies of doom, but attempts to understand a complex myth and its influence on our American way of seeing the world.

The basic mode of apocalypse began to develop from the Judaic prophetic tradition during the century or so preceding Christ. With the growth of the great empires of Persia, Greece, Rome and the consequent political powerlessness of the Hebrew people, the contradiction between prophetic ideals and the actual experience of the nation became more and more apparent. The prophets' vision of their history as moving toward the establishment of a community based on a special relationship with Yahweh seemed less and less likely in view of their contemporary historical situation. The apocalyptists began to replace the prophets, insisting on a radical change or break in history, when the present age would end and only the righteous would survive the eschatological revolution. Where prophecy focuses on the earthly destinies of men and on their specific behavior as they attempt to fulfill their appointed role as God's chosen people, apocalypse emphasizes future events and exhorts men to endure their present suffering with the assurance of a blessed future life. Both prophecy and apocalypse look forward to the future, but the prophet sees the future as arising out of the present, whereas the apocalyptist sees the future as breaking into the present.[4] The beleaguered early Christians found the apocalyptic mode suitable for the expression of their oppressive earthly situation as had the Hebrews. Indeed, it is quite likely that to some extent Christ's great appeal has been his assurance, first to his disciples and then to all his followers, that the end of this world and the beginning of his Messianic kingdom are near. Thus, there are many apocalypses in both the Hebrew and Christian canon: The Book of Daniel and The Revelation of St. John are, by most judgments, the most complete and the finest of traditional apocalyptic writing; the Revelation of St. John is included in the Appendix of this collection.[5]

Apocalypse is concerned with the nature of history and the nature of time itself. The apocalyptist stands outside of time, recounting the past, present and future from an atemporal point of view beyond the end of time. In Revelation, St. John responds to God's urgent command, "Write the things which thou has seen, the things which are, and the things which shall be hereafter" (Rev. 1:19). The events he describes include a catalogue of natural disasters and civil chaos, a thousand-year reign by Christ and his martyred followers, a "last loosing" of Satan from the bottomless pit where Christ had cast him, the final triumph of Christ and the Last Judgment, the ultimate destruction of this world and the descent of the eternal city, the New Jerusalem. For the traditional apocalyptists, the future is recounted as if it were past: thus St. John describes the projected end of time in a strange mixture of tenses, for the rest of history lies revealed before him: "And I saw the holy city, New Jerusalem, coming down from God out of heaven prepared as a bride adorned for her husband. And I heard a great voice out of heaven saying, Behold, the tabernacle of God is with men, and he will dwell with them, and they shall be his people, and God himself shall be with them, and be their God" (Rev. 21:2-3). Thus apocalypse projects the patterns of creation, growth, decay, renewal, catastrophe onto history, encompassing the beginning and the end of time within its vision.[6] Time itself becomes a vehicle of divine purpose.

Apocalyptic thinking is fundamentally dualistic, envisaging human history as a kind of dialectic between two opposing forces, both personal and cosmic in character, which vie for control of the world; although malign powers are now considered to be in control of this evil, temporal, limited age, they are soon to be overcome by the direct intervention of God. This age will end abruptly, and God will then initiate a timeless kingdom which will be perfectly righteous. The progression of events within this historical dialectic may vary from one apocalypse to another, but all describe the alternation of evil and good as the forces of the Antichrist and those of God engage in their cosmic battle for ultimate supremacy. This dualism of ethical forces, of ages, of worlds, implies the view that history is radically discontinuous: after the final cosmic struggle between Satan's forces and God's, time will cease, heaven and earth will become one for eternity, and the faithful will enter the holy city. If the end of time is catastrophic for some, it is a glorious consummation of God's plan for those who have faithfully maintained their eschatalogical conviction. Thus, it should be clear that the current use of the word "apocalypse" as a synonym for "disaster" or "cataclysm" is only half correct: the myth comprehends both cataclysm *and* millennium, tribulation *and* triumph, chaos *and* order, and it is the creative tension, the dialectic, between these opposites that explains, in part, the myth's enduring relevance. The extent to which various ages have emphasized the pessimistic or the optimistic side of apocalypse differs greatly, of course: that our own age has focused primarily upon the cataclysmic side of the myth is made evident in several of the essays that follow.

Apocalyptic thinking is also fundamentally deterministic: the apocalyptist, speaking from a point beyond the future, reveals a definite time schedule which God Himself has predetermined. The vision of things to come, listed in apocalyptic literature, provides a metaphoric itinerary for God's inevitable victory over evil. But despite the assumption of a predetermined progression of events toward a given end, man's actions are not necessarily predetermined: apocalypse developed out of the Judaic prophetic tradition as a mode of exhortation, of encouragement to those suffering persecution. It urges struggle, will, tenacity, loyalty, even martyrdom for the cause of God's kingdom; it promises reward to the faithful and vengeance to the wicked, those who fail to act for the achievement of the kingdom of God.

Thus, apocalypse describes men's actions and God's reactions: it is this expression of confident expectation of His justice that has given apocalypse its great appeal during periods of oppression, affliction and persecution. So it is that visions of apocalypse appear to the Puritans fighting for justice as they understood it four hundred years ago; to Gabriel Garcia Marquez as he portrays the terrors of a Latin American dictatorship in his novel, *The Autumn of the Patriarch;* to Russian dissident Andrei Sinyavsky, who hid the hand-copied pages of Revelations in his boot for six years in a Soviet labor camp.[7]

Apocalyptic visions are often expressed in hermetic symbols and coded references: addressing himself to a minority who was suffering political and religious persecution, the apocalyptist was forced to use a kind of cryptic language, allusive and obscure. It is this political expedient that explains in part the rich poetic content of apocalyptic archetypes, allusions and symbolic patterns.[8] Again, The Revelation of St. John provides our best example, with its extensive symbolism, beginning with the vision of God and the Lamb on the throne, surrounded by four beasts and a sea of glass like crystal, from which issue lightning and thunder and voices. There are the visions of the seven seals on the book of destiny or doom, which when broken produce the four horsemen of the apocalypse (war, oppression, famine and death), the cosmic woes of the earthquakes, falling stars, a blackened sun and a bloody moon, the seven trumpet woes, the swarms of locusts, the red dragon with seven heads and ten horns, the whore of Babylon—all expressing man's awe of divine retributive power. Such visions of violence have always exerted an intense fascination: the relation between eschatological insight and private fantasies of vengeance is profound and unsearchable. And the visions of Christ Triumphant upon a white horse with a vesture dipped in blood, the triumphant songs in heaven, and the vision of the New Jerusalem, with its pure river of the water of life, its tree of life with leaves for the healing of the nations, express man's most ardent hopes for the realization of God's just rule on earth. The imagery, drawing on Psalms and Isaiah and many other Old Testament sources, is set in resounding phrases of great liturgical power: "Alleluia: for the Lord God Omnipotent reigneth" (Rev. 19:6). "And I saw heaven opened, and behold a white horse; and he that sat upon him was called Faithful and True ... and he treadeth the wine-press of the fierceness and wrath of Almighty God. And he had on his vesture a name written, KING OF KINGS, AND LORD OF LORDS" (Rev. 19: 11, 15, 16). With such symbols and phrases as these, the apocalyptists attempted to understand and communicate the spiritual purpose in history.

Against the background of Europe's eschatological conceptions of America as an innocent new world where man might begin again, Americans have frequently drawn upon the myth of apocalypse as we have sought to understand what we consider to be our special relation to history. The myth's application has by no means been limited to a religious context: in our history and literature, apocalypse has been secularized in order to explain our individual and collective destinies. The end of time is by now less a chronological fact for most of us (after all, the world has defied all apocalyptic calculations,) than it is a fact of the imagination, necessary to our thinking about our national and our personal identities. As the following essays will suggest, apocalypse, one of our most basic yet least understood myths, has always been essential to America's conception of itself.

Because each of the following essays is concerned with the nature of apocalypse, each author will develop a definition of the word according to the usage of his or her discipline: there will, of course, be both convergences and divergences among the various definitions and disciplines. Furthermore, the essays tend to be broad in their focus rather than narrow, because our concern is the influence of the myth of apocalypse during the entire course of America's history rather than just during our own own times and its influence, furthermore, on many cultural levels.

Debra Bergoffen lays the foundations for an understanding of American apocalyptic attitudes by discussing the philosophical bases of apocalyptic eschatology, the inclusion, after the dispersion of Israel, of Greek and cosmic temporal motifs within the Biblical sense of history, and on the other hand, the exclusion of certain prophetic and tragic motifs. She then applies this philosophical definition to contemporary American attitudes toward history, analyzing the implications of our current emphasis on the cataclysmic dimension of apocalypse.

Charles Lippy, in his essay on apocalyptic attitudes in American religious thought, begins by examining the Puritans' emphatic sense that they had been chosen to fulfill God's historical purpose in the New World. The apocalyptic mentality of the Puritans—their strong dualism, their emphasis on retributive justice, their faith in the direct proportions of God's grace to success, their conviction that every detail of human reality is part of a historical pattern governed by God's will, their belief in the imminent end of the present age—initiated what seem to be permanent visions of apocalypse in North America. The extent to which such visions inhere in North American religious attitudes is witnessed by the fact that its major indigenous religious movements—Seventh-Day Adventists, the Church of Jesus Christ of Latter-Day Saints, Jehovah's Witnesses, and the recent "Jesus movement"—are based on apocalyptic expectations, on an urgent sense of the end of this world and the initiation of God's promised kingdom. Professor Lippy looks beyond White Christian America to the apocalyptic elements in the native American religious ritual and in Black American sects as well.

The role of the myth of apocalypse in American intellectual history is traced by Ernest Cassara. Professor Cassara describes the apocalyptic impulse which motivated the settlement of America, the universal goal of creating a haven in the New World where history might begin again, a goal which motivated much of the nation's westward expansion as well. Apocalyptic attitudes, furthermore, explain in part why America has traditionally seen the world as morally dualistic, a mentality that has turned our wars into crusades and which, since World War II, has led us to express our relations with global adversaries in the most cataclysmic of terms. Thus, from an historical and political perspective, Professor Cassara proposes a continuity of attitudes which he calls the American ideology, a "sense of mission" which can be related to our apocalyptic tradition.

North American literature has constantly reflected the historical pressure inherent in the American experience, the apocalyptic view of the New World as a special place with a special role to play in the regeneration of the Old World. In the seventeenth and eighteenth centuries, expression of America's apocalyptic role was largely discursive and declamatory; in the first half of the nineteenth century, our great writers, conditioned by their Puritan backgrounds and their awareness of the seemingly limitless expanses of the frontier, produced visions of freedom from social constraint, visions of inexhaustible potential for selfhood, whether social, economic or metaphysical. After the Civil War, however, this confidence seems to have shifted to pessimism, the gleam of American millennialism all but extinguished in the literature of our own century. I will discuss several American authors in the context of their apocalyptic stance, beginning with our earliest writers and proceeding to the present, considering the temporal patterns in which they organize their works and their urgent sense of aesthetic as well as historical ultimacy.

The apocalyptic vision of history, at once terrifying and captivating, has frequently inspired the imagination of painters, engravers, sculptors. Dawn Glanz discusses the artistic embodiment of the myth of apocalypse which reinforces visually the ideas, trends, attitudes which have been discussed in preceding essays. In particular, she describes the mural by Emanuel Leutze called "Westward the course of Empire takes its way," painted in 1862 in the United States Capital building, and relates it to America's sense of its millennial destiny at a time of national upheaval.

John Wiley Nelson directs his attention to the manifestations of the myth of apocalypse in American popular culture. He discusses the works of Hal Lindsey (*The Late Great Planet Earth, The Terminal Generation*, and others), and numerous films and television programs which suggest a veritable "boom in doom" in these media. Indeed, film and television seem to have replaced the medieval triptych as the visual repository of apocalyptic anxiety of the twentieth century: there has been a recent rash of disaster movies; television programs are often concerned with the ends of cities, countries, worlds, galaxies; science fiction frequently envisions the end of man, the transcendence or transformation of the human race. Dr. Nelson suggests that the mass media, in their preoccupation with cataclysmic endings of history, point to an apocalyptic mentality in America which has never been stronger.

Michael Emsley, biologist and ecologist, discusses apocalypse not in philosophical terms but in scientific ones. He traces the history of our universe from its beginning to its projected end as did the ancient apocalyptists, but uses scientific method rather than inspired revelation as the basis for his predictions. He looks at the implications of dietary contaminants, topical toxins, air and water pollution, energy shortages, population pressure, and global famine due to changing weather patterns, all results of the tremendous acceleration in technological change in our recent history. While technology has undeniably created great problems for man, economics professor Thomas DeGregori argues that technology also possesses the means to correct those problems. Professor DeGregori questions some of the best known of recent scientific doomsaying and finds that there is in fact reason to view the future with optimism rather than despair.

Of course, predictions of apocalypse have been proved wrong time and again, and by now most of us do not take altogether seriously predictions of the imminent end of time, even in the face of nuclear warfare, ecological disaster, the population bomb. And certainly we are far more cynical than our Puritan forefathers about the possibility of a new heaven on earth. Nevertheless, the mythic dimensions of apocalypse provide for the modern secular imagination a means of thinking about time: as Frank Kermode says in *The Sense of an Ending*, "Crisis, however facile the conception, is inescapably a central element in our endeavors toward making sense of our world."[9] Apocalypse satisfies our need for the wholeness of beginnings and endings, our need for a view of the world which places our brief individual span in the context of the longer span of world history. Thus it provides a mythic conjunction of biography and history, a conjunction of the "immanent time of the flow of consciousness" of the individual and "world time," to use the terms of the phenomenologist Edmund Husserl.[10]

Husserl, who knew that time is the most subjective of experienced phenomena, wrote that all "sensed temporal data ... are charged with characters of apprehension...;" these "characters of apprehension," our internal time consciousness, create objective temporal orders of one sort or another "in which all things and events—material things with their physical properties, minds with their mental states—have their definite temporal positions which can be measured by chronometers."[11] Surely this process, described by Husserl, accounts for the continuing relevance of the apocalyptic myth. Apocalypse responds to our internal time consciousness, orders and unifies our "characters of apprehension" with its specific temporal content, and gives significance to our very temporal human condition.

Notes

[1]Christopher Columbus, *The Four Voyages of C. Columbus*, trans. J.M. Cohen (Baltimore: Penguin Books, 1969), pp. 265 (Letter to Doña Juana de la Torre), 222, 224; Edmundo O'Gorman, *The Invention of America: An Inquiry into the Historical Nature of the New World and the Meaning of its History* (Bloomington: Indiana University Press, 1961), p. 99. This is a fascinating study of the impact of the idea of America on Renaissance Europe, and the difficulty of reconciling a new world with the Catholic conception of one world in which all men are descended from Adam. O'Gorman writes that the very idea of a new world was heretical, and shows how Christopher Columbus attempted to avoid heresy when he began to suspect that he had indeed come upon a new world. In Columbus' time, the word "world" referred to the *orbis terrarum*, "the Island of the Earth, that portion of the globe occupied by Europe, Asia, and Africa, which had been assigned to man by God as a place for him to live in, to the exclusion of any other portion of the universe" (pp. 113-114). The possibility of inhabitants in a new world "was inadmissible to Christians, not only because it attacked the dogmatic idea of humankind as having descended from a

single couple, but because it posed an additional difficulty in that the Antipodeans (granting that they might be descendants of Adam) could not possibly have received the Gospel. This ran counter to the Holy Writ, where it is stated that the teachings of Christ and His Apostles had reached the very ends of the earth" (p. 55). Thus, despite his quoting from Revelations and Isaiah, Columbus never definitely concludes that he has discovered a new land mass, but dies thinking—indeed, insisting—that he has reached the east coast of Asia.

[2] Christopher Columbus, pp. 217-218 ("Narrative of the Third Voyage of Christopher Columbus to the Indies").

The most complete discussion of Columbus' apocalypticism is in John Leddy Phelan, *The Millennial Kingdom of the Franciscans in the New World,* 2nd ed. (Berkeley: University of California Press, 1970), pp. 17-29.

[3] Carl Jung, in comparing the occidental temporal sense to the oriental, points to the end-dominated, goal-oriented nature of western myth: "The mythic needs of the Occidental call for an evolutionary cosmogony with a *beginning* and a *goal* . . . . [He cannot accept the idea of a static, self-contained, eternal cycle of events. The Oriental, on the other hand, seems able to come to terms with this idea . . . . [The succession of birth and death is viewed as an endless continuity, as an eternal wheel rolling on forever without a goal." C.G. Jung, *Memories, Dreams, Reflections* (New York: Vintage Books, 1965), pp. 316-317 (emphasis Jung's), 316.

[4] See H.H. Rowley, *The Relevance of Apocalyptic: A Study of Jewish and Christian Apocalypses from Daniel to the Revelation,* (New York: Association Press, 1963), pp. 1-65.

[5] Apocalypses written before Christ include The Book of Daniel, I Enoch, The Book of Jubilees, The Testament of the Twelve Patriarchs, the Sibylline Oracles, The Psalms of Solomon, The Zadokite Work, The Qumran Scrolls; in the first century after Christ, there are The Assumption of Moses, II Enoch, IV Ezra, The Apocalypse of Baruch, the Ascension of Isaiah, The Apocalypse of Abraham, The Testament of Abraham, The Revelation of St. John, etc. For a complete discussion of these apocalypses, see R.H. CHarles, *Eschatology: The Doctrine of a Future Life in Israel, Judaism, and Christianity; A Critical History* (1899; rpt. New York: Schocken Books, 1963).

[6] Frank Kermode, *The Sense of an Ending: Studies in the Theory of Fiction* (New York: Oxford University Press, 1967), p. 29.

[7] Gabriel García Márquez, *The Autumn of the Patriarch,* trans. Gregory Rabassa (New York: Harper and Row, 1976); see, in this regard, my article, "The Myth of Apocalypse and Human Temporality in García Márquez's *Cien años de soledad* and *El otoño del patriarca, Symposium* 32, iv (1978), 341-355; Abram Tertz (Andrei Sinyavsky), *A Voice from the Chorus* (New York: Farrar, Straus and Giroux, 1976).

[8] D.H. Lawrence argues that the real value of the myth is the "imaginative infusion" which it provides into our perception of space. It is a "magnificent cosmic and starry drama" which opens up the heavens for the reader as it did for St. John, and "lets out the spirit into a new world, even it if is a very old world!" For Lawrence, the spirit of apocalypse is primarily a presentation of the "live space" of the ancient zodiacal heavens. D.H. Lawrence, "Apocalypse" in *Phoenix: The Posthumous Papers of D.H. Lawrence,* ed. Edward D. McDonald (New York: Viking Press, 1964), p. 301.

[9] Kermode, p. 94.

[10] Edmund Husserl, *The Phenomenology of Internal Time Consciousness,* ed. Martin Heidegger, trans. James S. Churchill (Bloomington: Indiana University Press, 1964), p. 23.

[11] Husserl, p. 26.

I.
The Apocalyptic Meaning of History
Debra Bergoffen

I. *Introduction*

PEOPLE are taking note of America's emergent doomsday mentality, calling this mentality apocalyptic. Commentators, assuming either that we are already familiar with the meaning of apocalypse or that a few words will suffice to articulate its meaning, are concerned with showing how this mentality is manifest in the various segments of American life. From their perspectives, the meaning of apocalypse appears to be either obvious and in need of no discussion, or easily defined as an orientation toward the world which anticipates its imminent and cataclysmic end. For the philosopher, however, meanings which appear to be obvious or simple often conceal more accurate and complete meanings which are essential for adequate intelligibility. As the essence of the task of philosophy is clarification, this essay, a philosophical inquiry into apocalypse, will explore the hidden sources and complex meanings of the apocalyptic sense of history.

We begin by accepting apocalypse as a symbol of time which articulates a people's experience of their being-in-the-world. Experiences give rise to symbols, and symbols allow us to reflect upon the meaning of our experiences, for though experiences are fleeting, the symbolic articulations of them are not. The symbol gives us the opportunity to explore the experience at our leisure, to look at it again and again. In this looking, we become aware of the meaning of the experience, and of the ways in which the symbol, in reifying the experience, influences our attitudes toward being. Symbols are not static until they have dropped out of use. A living symbol is layered with meanings. As the symbol orients us to the world, new experiences of the world are integrated within the original symbol. A complete understanding of any living symbol may be impossible, but it remains a goal nonetheless. With due and realistic humility regarding the attainment of this goal, I will attempt in this essay to understand the symbol of apocalypse.

As a living and ancient symbol of temporality, apocalypse can be neither reduced to, nor severed from, its biblical roots. Becoming aware of the meaning of the apocalyptic experience will require a patient and sympathetic unraveling of the layers of the symbol. Our efforts will, I hope, have practical as well as purely philosophical consequences. One of the philosophical results of the inquiry will be a clarification of the essential complexity of the apocalyptic experience: we will discover that the apocalyptic symbol cannot be understood simply as a symbol of anxiety or doom, for there are important differences between the apocalyptic and doomsday attitudes. Applying our philosophical insights to the practical questions of the American experience will allow us to see whether the contemporary American mood is genuinely apocalyptic or whether, in referring to the contemporary mentality as apocalyptic, we are misinterpreting the American attitude toward being.

II: *Methodology*

This essay examines the meaning of apocalypse from an existential-phenomenological perspective. From this perspective, apocalypse articulates a living, existential relationship between human consciousness and time; it has unique structures and meanings which distinguish it from other attitudes toward time and is a significant symbol of a specific relationship between human and temporaral being.

Without going into detail, and without attempting to be exhaustive, I want to say a few words about the existential-phenomenological approach. The critical feature of this approach is the assertion that human consciousness neither passively receives meaning from the world, nor absolutely imposes its truth on the world; consciousness and the world exist in active relationship with each other. Without consciousness there could be no meaningful realm of being; without being, consciousness would be incapable of articulating meaning. There is therefore no objective truth, truth inherent in the object only; nor is there subjective truth, truth created by the subject absolutely; rather, there is only relational truth, truth encountered in the interaction between being and consciousness.

With respect to the issue of apocalypse, this means that answering the question, "What is the meaning of the apocalyptical symbol?" requires the acknowledgment that apocalypse is a particular way of relating to historical temporality. Historical temporality, however, is not a fact, that is, something already there waiting to be found: it is something chosen. Understanding the meaning of this choice is essential. This understanding involves perceiving the distinction between the historical and the non-historical choice. It requires the recognition that consciousness need not understand itself as an historical being and that if consciousness chooses to be related to being historically, it need not choose the apocalyptic perspective. Though the non-historical, the Greek historical, and the biblical historical meanings of time are not the subject of this essay, the basic features of these temporalities will be surveyed in order to delineate the horizon from which the apocalyptic choice emerges and to appreciate the significance of the apocalyptic perspective.

I must emphasize that we are concerned with the meaning, not the accuracy, of the apocalyptic attitude. We are not asking whether the apocalyptic interpretation of the historical process is a verifiable description of the course of historical events. There is one sense in which the correctness of the apocalyptic orientation cannot be ascertained: if the apocalypse occurred, we would not be here to verify it. In another sense, however, it is accurate to say that the apocalyptic vision has been refuted innumerable times. Many predicted ends of the world have passed without having been fulfilled. These "falsifications" of the apocalyptic concept have proved, however, to be powerless against the meaning of the idea. That people continue to orient themselves toward history in the apocalyptic tradition despite the repeated failure to predict accurately the date of the world's end indicates that though it may be a poor indicator of the *when* of the end of history, it is a meaningful articulation of the *why* of history. All of which brings us back to a basic concept of the existential-phenomenological method: historical events are not objectively meaningful but become meaningful only in the encounter between human consciousness and being. As a meaning of being, the apocalyptic tradition cannot be nullified by inaccurate mathematical computations. So long as it remains a viable way of articulating the sense of history, it must be considered to be truthful in the phenomenological sense.

III. *Apocalypse: Its Horizons and Structures*

The apocalyptic concept of time is an anti-historical structuring of history. It is anti-historical in two respects: 1) it assesses the course of history negatively (history is the time of sin and evil which will ultimately be destroyed and transcended), 2) it does not allow human decisions to affect the process of history (history is determined by God). In the first evaluation of history, apocalypse resembles the anti-historicism of the Greeks save for the fact that crises of history are not seen as tragedies, but as opportunities for salvation; in the second, it is similar to the anti-historicism of archaic peoples, except that history is not thought to repeat itself in changeless cycles but to proceed in a linear process toward a final goal. The anti-historical motifs of apocalypse, therefore, are neither pessimistic (as in the Greek) nor unhistorical (as in the archaic). Apocalypse is distinguished from other symbolizations of historical temporality in being an optimistic, historical, anti-historicism. Its uniqueness stems from the fact that, in response to the dispersion of Israel and the emergence of Christianity, it brought Greek and archaic motifs to the biblical tradition without negating the meaning of the biblical sense of history. An adequate understanding of the apocalyptic perspective, therefore, requires some prior appreciation of the archaic and Greek attitudes toward history; this will allow us to see the way in which apocalypse draws on these perspectives without becoming assimilated by them.

Archaic temporality. The anti-historicism of archiac peoples may be termed unhistorical or cosmic: archaic peoples perceive themselves as being part of a cosmic process over which they have no control. They interpret their lives as following preordained patterns of existence: these patterns, or archetypes, are divinely determined. Their permanence is guaranteed by their having been created by the gods and by periodic ritualistic observances. This archaic cosmic orientation is not a sign of an unawareness of the historical dimension of time, but rather reflects a choice against the becoming of history. The difference between the cosmic and the historical perspectives is that the cosmic chooses to acknowledge as meaningful only those aspects of human life which reflect the cosmic repetitive structure of time, whereas the historical chooses to accept as meaningful only those aspects of human life which are distinguishable from cosmic processes, that is, those dimensions of life which are unique and individual.[1] In the same way that historical peoples are aware of the recurrence of life-cycle events such as birth and death but devaluate the cosmic dimensions of those experiences, cosmic people are aware of the unique, or choice,

The Apocalyptic Meaning of History

dimensions of their lives but negate the historical motifs of these events. Where historically oriented persons will focus on the fact that their marriage is a consequence of the unique decision to marry and the individual choice of a specific person, cosmically oriented people will perceive their marriage as fulfilling the requirements of a particular stage in the process of life. But, just as historically oriented people are aware of the cosmic dimensions of marriage, cosmically-oriented people are aware of the historical aspects of marriage.

Students of primitive cultures agree that ancient people, like their modern counterparts, experienced the temporality of their lives as being distinct from the time of nature. Stanley Diamond, for example, writes: "Primitive peoples have strong canons and perceptions of personal growth or progress as the individual journeys through society ... on what the Winnebago call the 'road of life and death.' The concrete idea of personal growth saturates primitive society."[2] Unlike contemporary cultures, however, which choose to focus on the experience of progress, archaic communities chose to incorporate the experience of progress within the experience of cosmic recurrence. Using the symbol of the cosmic myth, historical reality is negated as all temporal becoming is subordinated to the pattern of seasonal recurrence.

The cosmic myth is an unhistorical negation of history because it negates the existence as well as the value of history. By interpreting all critical human experiences according to the archetype of seasonal renewal, it refuses to acknowledge the reality or possibility of genuine change. This is made clear when we note that even the gods of the myth are bound by the structures of the myth. Though the organized cosmos of our experience is said to have been created by the unique acts of the gods, the gods are not interpreted as having the power to disrupt the natural order of being. They too are bound by the rhythm of recurrence.

In subordinating all experiences to the archetype of seasonal recurrence, the cosmic myth denies the possibility of unique human activity. For historical peoples there are at least two, and often three, dimensions of time. There is the cosmic time of natural activity, the historical time of human action and sometimes the divine time of God. For unhistorical people, however, there are only two structurings of time, the sacred and the profane. The times when the gods structured the cosmos are the sacred times of the gods; the structured time of the cosmos is the profane time of being. Unlike historical consciousness which identifies certain temporal possibilities as being unique to human becoming, cosmic consciousness refuses to distinguish human from cosmic temporality. There is the sacred time of the gods and the profane time of the cosmos, but there is no time of humanity *per se*: human time is cosmic.

The basic distinctions between cosmic and historical consciousness must be kept in mind in this discussion of apocalypse in order that the anti-historicism of the apocalyptic tradition not be mistakenly seen as an unhistorical relationship to being. Apocalyptic anti-historicism is quite different from cosmic anti-historicism insofar as it recognizes the existence of history, the time of human activity within which change is possible. Unlike the anti-historicism of the cosmic myth which chooses against history by not allowing it to come into being, the apocalyptic anti-historicism chooses against history by attending to its negative reality and asserting that it will be destroyed and transcended. Whereas from the archaic perspective history is continuously being absorbed and destroyed by the cosmic archetype so that it never clearly emerges as a unique dimension of time, from the apocalyptic view, history emerges as the time of the profane which will be ultimately absorbed and destroyed by the sacred time of God.

The Greek sense of time. The anti-historicism of apocalypse bears some resemblance to the anti-historical motifs found in the Greek symbols of time. Unlike the cosmic vision of being which denies the reality of history and assumes the eternal continuance of cosmic temporality, the Greek and apocalyptic orientations toward being acknowledge the reality of historical becoming. Further, both of these world views perceive the process of history as essentially degenerative. History is the time within which existence deteriorates and is ultimately destroyed. What distinguishes the apocalyptic from the Greek interpretation of history, however, is the meaning each gives to its experience of the destructive effects of history. Whereas the Greeks anticipate the cataclysmic end of history within the context of the tragic symbol, those whose perspective is apocalyptic anticipate the terrible end of history through the messianic symbol. Understanding the meaning of this distinction reveals that apocalypse cannot be reduced to the attitude which believes that history will end cataclysmically.

Hesiod's story of the five ages of man is generally accepted as marking the transition in Greek culture from the cosmic to the historical world view. Hesiod is anti-historical but not unhistorical. Though history is not disengaged from mystical motifs, it is recognized as a unique dimension of time.[3] Cosmic patterns of season renewal do not define humanity. Human existence is conditioned by the particular historical age within which one lives. Each of the five ages of man has a unique archetype, and each archetype is a consequence of the point in time of the age. Ages further from the beginning are necessarily older and inferior to those which are closer to the beginning, but these ages do not grow out of each other: nothing in one age is responsible for the inferior conditions of the next. History is simply the process of deterioration and growing disorder. Hesiod's Age of Iron, the age in which we are said to live, is described as ending in chaos. The people who are to be destroyed at the end of the Age of Iron are tragic figures in the sense that they are in no way responsible for the crisis of their age and powerless to avert it. Their situation is necessitated by an incomprehensible law of fate. Though history exists as a human dimension of time, it is a dimension over which human beings have no control. From Hesiod's perspective, human life is determined by an archetype. Though the archetype is not that of cosmic recurrence but of historical degeneration, it remains a deterrent to the possibility of human activity influencing the reality of human life.

The Greek historians Herodotus and Thucydides articulate a more ambivalent attitude toward history. In stating that their purpose in recording the events of their times is to save them from being forgotten or falsified, they are, like Hesiod, expressing a negative orientation toward historical becoming: history is seen to be responsible for either the loss or distortion of the truth. In choosing to write their histories, however, they show how human action can counteract the negative effects of time. The truth of events may be preserved if one chooses to record them in writing.

Herodotus and Thucydides are not merely antiquarians. Because they perceived the past as being causally and morally related to the present, they believed that preserving the facts of history would enable us to understand the present better and anticipate the future.[4] In place of Hesiod's disjointed ages of man, Herodotus and Thucydides envision an historical continuum where the present is an outgrowth of the past. Where for Hesiod one could understand one's existence in the world merely by being aware of one's present age, for the historians, one could not understand one's present without understanding the past from which that present emerged. Though the historians do not go so far as to sever the processes of history from the cosmic laws of fate, they do allow that we may, through a proper understanding of history, make decisions which can improve our individual and collective lives. Thus we are no longer seen as passive, tragic figures caught in the grip of history. Our tragic condition is attributed more to our ignorance of the past and its bearing on our lives than to the necessities of history.

Plato echoes the historians' ambivalent attitude toward history and their attribution of our tragic condition to ignorance in his discussion (*Republic*, Book VIII) of the effect history will have on the ideal state. Having provided us with a blueprint for the perfect society, Plato advises us at the end of Book VII that his vision of the just community is not a mere dream but a realistic ideal which, though difficult, is not impossible to attain. This, I believe, is his way of indicating that once we establish and become committed to clear goals, it is within our power to realize them. Fate does not condition our existence in the world.

In Book VIII he clarifies his position regarding the relationship between knowledge, fate and human destiny. There he assumes that the ideal republic has been realized and questions whether its existence can be sustained. The Muses, Plato suggests, would answer his question in a "lofty, tragic vein," saying:

A city which is thus constituted can hardly be shaken; but seeing that everything which has a beginning has also an end, even a constitution such as yours will not last forever but will in time be dissolved. And this is the dissolution:—In plants that grow in the earth as well as in animals that move on the earth's surface, fertility and sterility of soul and body occur when the circumferences of the circles of each are completed.... But to the knowledge of human fecundity and sterility all the wisdom and education of your rules will not attain; the laws which regulate them will not be discovered by an intelligence which is alloyed with sense, but will escape them, and they will bring children into the world when they ought not.[5]

Without denying that human beings can engage in purposeful activity within the context of their historical condition, Plato indicates that cosmic necessities affect the historical process. Fate remains a factor within history. Unlike Hesiod, who attributed our historical misfortunes to the laws of fate themselves, Plato attributes our historical degeneration to a combination of factors. The first factor is the basic law of becoming, the law that all beginning must have an end; the second is our ignorance of the laws of regeneration. Here, again, our situation is tragic. We are, it seems, barred by the fact of our human condition from understanding and acting in accordance with those laws which govern the continued existence of the ideal state. Our situation is neither entirely determined nor entirely free. As the dimension of history is not subordinated to the cosmic archetypes, we are free to gain knowledge of the ideal human community and free to realize that ideal within the context of history. Our human condition, however, limits our capacity for knowledge. We lack the knowledge necessary for perpetuating the ideal, so that it will necessarily deteriorate and ultimately be destroyed.

This overview of the Greek sense of time indicates that the Greeks did not perceive history to be essentially teleological. Though they acknowledged that certain historical events and realities were to be understood as the consequence of human, purposeful action, they did not see the overall processes of history as being meaningful or purposeful *per se*. History is the time of beginnings and ends.

The biblical prophetic perspective. The clear, unambiguous depiction of history as the inherently meaningful time of human choice and action is unique to the biblical world view. As a specific form of the biblical sense of time, apocalypse cannot be described merely in terms of its crisis mentality or anti-historicism. There are significant differences between the Greek attitude, which focuses primarily on the deteriorating effects of history, and the apocalyptic concept of time. The following investigation of the biblical perspective, the soil within which apocalypse is rooted, is intended to clarify these distinctions.

The unique feature of the biblical attitude toward history is not that it recognized the distinction between cosmic processes and historical occurrences—the Greeks, as we have seen, also made this distinction—but that it chose to place significant, positive value on historical existence. This choice is articulated in the biblical doctrines of revelation and covenant. Though all specifications of the biblical attitude contain these ingredients, different interpretations of the content of the revelation or the meaning of the covenant relationship account for the distinctions between apocalyptic and other (for example the prophetic) biblical orientations toward history.

The concept of revelation is the central doctrine of the scriptures.[6] It is, in a literal sense, the original doctrine of the Jewish people. Abraham is considered to be the first Jew not simply because he rejected polytheistic idolatry and chose to believe in one, non-anthropomorphic God, but more fundamentally because he believed that God was capable of endowing his life with a unique historical purpose. Abraham believed that God had chosen him to fulfill a critical historical mission. God revealed Himself to Abraham in a specific moment of time and in this revelation disclosed His decision to make Abraham a great nation. Following Abraham's God means accepting the fact that He is capable of changing reality. It required Abraham to accept the idea that God had the power to transform a single man into a great nation; it required the Israelites in Egypt to believe that the time of slavery would be transformed into the time of freedom; it requires all believers to view history as a time within which genuine, even radical change is possible.

Unlike the Greeks who perceived history as the time of degeneration, the people of the biblical tradition viewed history as the time of hope. But where the Greeks attributed the ill effects of historical being to the inherent process of historical becoming, biblical peoples did not attribute the hopefulness of historical being to the process of historical temporality *per se*. It is not history itself which is meaningful and promisory; it is the fact that God chooses to reveal himself in the course of historical time which makes it significant. History without God would be meaningless.

Without suggesting that God lacks power over nature (nature, being His creation, is subject to His law), the doctrine of revelation indicates that the laws of cosmic recurrence do not describe God's archetype for human life. It is within the course of history, not nature, that the meaning of humanity is found.[7] As natural as this perception of the human condition may seem to us today, the evidence of the Bible shows that human beings do not naturally perceive themselves to be historically situated. The story of the Golden Calf, the numerous accounts of Israel's straying idolatry, and the commandment to worship *only* one God, show that the Jewish community understood that they had to choose between two ways of orienting itself toward time, the cosmic or the historical, and that to choose history was not easy. Having chosen the historical world view, the people of the Bible came to articulate their historical situation as grounded in their encounter with God. The fundamental thought in the Bible is not creation, but God's care for His creation: as He reveals Himself in history, God manifests His concern for man and man's relevance to Him.[8]

The prophetic and apocalyptic traditions represent two related

The Apocalyptic Meaning of History   21

but distinct understandings of the historical dimensions of the human-divine relationship. Both the prophetic and apocalyptic attitudes see history as the time within which God reveals Himself to humanity. Further, prophetic and apocalyptic traditions are fundamentally optimistic about the course of history: history is the time within which God's plan for humanity is fulfilled. As God is by their definition all powerful and good, His plan must be good and He must have the ability to implement it. The distinction between the prophetic and apocalyptic orientations centers on their different understandings of the biblical concept of covenant.

The prophets viewed the covenant as a symbol of the promissory relationship between God and His people. God asks people to act in certain ways and promises that human beings can, by responding positively to His commandments, create the conditions necessary for realizing His purposes. God's control over history is not deterministic. He sets the teleological course of history but needs human beings, whose choices He does not control, to create the conditions which allow the teleological process to occur. The symbol of the covenant shows history to be the time of God and humanity. God promises to reward moral behavior by implementing the Messianic Age, but the people must choose whether or not to be moral. God cannot guarantee human righteousness. From the prophetic perspective, the divine promise is the revelation of a possible future, not a necessary one. Humanity's participation in the covenant is the precondition of the fulfillment of God's plan. The complexity of the prophetic tradition is a consequence of its insisting on these two dimensions of the covenant relationship: neither God nor humanity alone can redeem the world, but in partnership with each other they can inaugurate the age of the Messiah.[9]

This dialectical sense of covenant focuses the prophet's attention on the human dimensions of the historical process. As history is the realm of human action, the prophets are in no position to predict the future. The future is inherently unpredictable because it depends on the choices people make in the present. Instead of claiming to know the future, the prophets assert their knowledge of the future consequences of present choices. They predict that unfaithful choices will bring punishment and that faithful ones will bring rewards. The essence of the prophetic mission is to convince people of the need to choose differently:

> Return, faithless Israel, says the Lord,

> I will not look on you in anger,
> For I am merciful, says the Lord.
>
> **Jeremiah 3:12**

The prophets urge their people to choose the path of righteousness. They sense that the people will reject them, but as they believe that it is possible that their message will alter human decisions and thereby the course of history, they continue to preach. And when they become discouraged, when they take a deterministic, people-will-never-change-their-mind attitude, God Himself rebukes them.

Like the Greek historians who perceived history to be a causally related continuum, the prophets acknowledged the reality of historical causality. Instead, however, of seeing the present merely as an outgrowth of the past, they interpreted the present as the occasion for a new beginning. The present is the time within which the causal sequence of the past may be broken and a new line of causality established. History is the time of causality and freedom.

In our unreflective understanding of prophecy, we are over-impressed with the fact that the prophets predicted the destruction of Israel, and tend to equate prophecy with an ability to foresee the future. The distinguishing feature of the prophets, however, was not so much their clear vision of the future as their accurate perception of the present. God revealed the meaning of their contemporary situation in order that they might show their people that continuing in their present choices would be destructive, and that it was possible to choose differently and thereby avoid disaster. If the future were predictable in the sense of being already closed (determined), the prophetic mission would be meaningless: urging people to reorient themselves is absurd if such reorientation is understood to be impossible. Even when the situation seemed to be closed, the prophets perceived themselves to be bound, under the symbol of the covenant, to remind their people that alternative choices were always possible and that God was always waiting to respond to human awakenings. Theologian Abraham Heschel explains: "the prophets discovered the problem of history as a tension between what happens now and what may happen next. The future is no simple continuation of the present. Just as the present, in their eyes, represented a violation of what was established in the past (Israel's commitment to God), so may the future overturn the seeming solidity of what is being done in the present."[10]

The Apocalyptic Meaning of History   23

It is by focusing on the centrality of the covenant to the prophetic mission that Buber distinguishes between the true and the false prophet. The false prophet, according to Buber, is one who, in opposition to the dialectical sense of covenant, claims to be able to predict the future. Instead of insisting on the openness of the future and on the need to change directions, the false prophet insists that the future of Israel is secured and secure. The critical difference between the true and the false prophet is not that one's predictions came to pass while the other's did not, but that one did not claim to be certain about the future whereas the other did. Using Buber's criteria, it is possible to view the apocalyptic writers as successors to the false prophets. Seeing them in this perspective is useful in that it focuses our attention toward the way in which diverse interpretations of the covenant account for some of the distinctions between the prophetic and apocalyptic traditions.

The prophetic tradition perceives the covenant as a promissory relationship between God and the nation of Israel and between God and the individual Jew. Individual choices affect national choices and national choices affect the course of history. The individual must respond to the demands of the covenant in order that the nation may respond properly, but ultimately it is the national, not the individual, response which determines the historical future. So long as the nation exists, history remains a partnership between God and humanity; and so long as an optimism regarding the willingness of the individual and the nation to make moral choices exists, prophecy remains a viable tradition.

The prophetic response to the destruction of Israel was to refuse to identify the nation with its geographical boundaries and to insist that as long as the people existed the nation existed. The prophets said that the continued existence of the people provided the opportunity for choices which would inaugurate the Messianic Age. Thus, after witnessing the fall of Jerusalem, Jeremiah declares that "the people of Israel and the people of Judah shall come together" (Jeremiah 50:4) and that the rule of Babylon will pass:

> It is a time of distress for Jacob;
> Yet he shall be saved out of it....
> Then fear not, O Jacob My Servant, says the Lord,
> Nor be dismayed, O Israel;
> For lo, I will save you from afar,
> And your offspring from the land of captivity
> Jacob shall return and have quiet and ease

> And none shall make him afraid,
> For I am with you to save you, says the Lord.
>
> **Jeremiah 20:7, 10-11**

The biblical apocalyptic perspective. The apocalyptic response to the fall of Israel is different from the prophetic: the apocalyptist viewed the destruction as the end of the covenant between God and the nation. Though a covenant between God and the individual was still said to exist, this covenant was not seen as affecting the course of history. The end of history is inevitable, but the meaning of history is to be found in each individual who chooses to exist for the glory of God.[11] Like the false prophets who competed with the true prophets for the attention of Israel, the apocalyptic writers saw the historical process as determined. In the same way that the false prophets assured the Israelites that God would never allow His nation to be destroyed, the apocalyptic writers assured their audiences that God would never allow this evil history to continue. The ultimate destruction of the world and thus God's justice is, from their perspective, assured.

The deterministic sense of history is intimately related to the apocalyptic vision of the Messianic Age. Again, some comparisons with prophecy are useful. From the prophetic perspective it is not history *per se* which is evil, but human choices within history which make it evil: there is thus no inherent reason against envisioning an historical Messianic Age. The prophets linked the historical time of preparing for the Messianic Age with the Messianic Age itself. The Messianic Age was seen as the end of the history of scarcity, suffering and violence and as the beginning of the history of prosperity and peace. It represented a radical change in the content of history, but not a radical change in the temporality of history. For the prophets, the time within which God's promise was to be fulfilled was continuous with the time of making reality ready for the fulfillment.

The apocalyptic interpretation of the Messianic Age is quite different. As the course of history is not affected by human decisions, human choices cannot create the conditions for the Messianic Age: God alone will create the Messianic Age. He will affect a recreation of being whereby historical reality will be destroyed and transcended: apocalyptic writers stressed the transcendence of God and in so doing envisioned the time of divine judgment as transcending historical reality. Historical events are not seen as manifestations of the human—God relationship, but as the effects of the conflict between the Kingdom of God and the Kingdom of Satan.[12] The outcome of the conflict is determined; God will triumph. His supernatural and catastrophic intervention in history will take the form of a great historical crisis which will mark the destruction of the world as we know it.

Apocalypse is anti-historical in that it perceives history to be the time of evil. Like the Greek attitude which acknowledged the existence of history only to endow it with negative value, the apocalyptic writers depicted historical becoming as a process of degeneration. Their anti-historicism is biblical, however, not Greek, insofar as it posits the existence of a transcendent God who uses history to reveal his plan for a trans-historical era. The supernatural, anti-historical motif of apocalypse transforms the pessimistic overtones of Greek anti-historicism into an anti-historicism which is fundamentally optimistic. The crises of history are not tragedies which necessarily befall human beings; they are opportunities for salvation. In announcing the imminent end of the world, they are issuing last minute warnings to those who have not converted, telling them that the time of the end is near. These terrors of history may convince the undecided to respond to the covenant. For those who have already converted to the ways of God, the calamities of history are signs of their impending salvation. However terrible the events of history may appear, they are in reality good, for the crises of history are not the effects of the temporality of historical becoming, but the effects of divine providence.

The optimism of apocalypse differs from that of prophecy in this respect: the prophets, convinced that history is an open time of the ever possible inauguration of the Messianic Age, are optimistic regarding human nature; the human choice to live according to the covenant remains an historical possibility. The apocalyptics, however, are decided that the goodness of God lies, not in His leaving the human choice of history open, but in His determining the speedy end to the evils of history and the imminent beginning of the Messianic Age. These different motifs of optimism are reflected in the difference between the prophetic and apocalyptic vision of the role of the Messiah. The term Messiah denotes an escatological figure associated with the coming kingdom of God. In the Hebrew Scriptures, it designates an individual appointed by God to fulfill a special purpose, a king or a priest for example.[13] In prophecy it referred to the person, usually Elijah, who announced the coming of the Messianic Age. That the prophets speak of a human Messiah is indicative of their sense of history as the time of partnership between God and humanity; it is through human beings that the age of peace will be implemented. In apocalypse there is no need for a human Messiah: the coming kingdom transcends the human dimensions of being: it is the work of God Himself.[14] Though the historical motif is never completely abandoned, the prophetic task of urging human beings to translate the divine promise into historical terms is forsaken.[15]

A current of political activism runs through the prophetic tradition. The prophets speak to the people and the kings, urging them to make certain political, military and moral choices. They insist that the nation is capable of making the decisions needed to inaugurate the Messianic Age. The apocalyptic writers are non-political; despite the urgency of their message, their tone is passive. There is nothing that can be done to either hasten or prevent the coming historical disaster. Instead of taking to the streets, engaging the people in a dialogue and urging an active response, the apocalyptics take to their rooms and write. Though it is true that the political situation may have made it too dangerous to preach publicly, it is also true that their message did not require dialogue or direct confrontation. They were not asking people to alter the course of history; they were asking them to understand it.

The apocalyptics exhibit Greek and cosmic tendencies in this respect: they see the becoming of history as already determined and limit the historical role of people to that of understanding their place in the historical process.[16] The apocalyptics bring the Greek sense of historical time into the biblical tradition in their depiction of history as a temporality of degeneration. The time of history loses the salvation significance attributed to it by the prophets as events of the past are viewed as episodes in the progressive deterioration of being.[17] The Greek view of history as the time of decay is accompanied by a sense of otherworldliness which evokes cosmic themes of transformation and renewal. Whereas the cosmic myth depicted being as going through periodic destructions and renewals, the apocalyptic writers spoke of a fallen world which would be destroyed once and forever and replaced by a completely new order of being. The Greek theme of historical degeneration is linked to the cosmic themes of regeneration in a uniquely biblical way. From both the cosmic and Greek perspectives, time is itself responsible for the effects of history; from the apocalyptic perspective, God, who transcends time, uses time for His purposes. Thus the destruction and regeneration of being in fulfillment of God's promise occurs only once: endless historical and cosmic repetition is replaced by a final resolution of history.[18]

The message and tone of the apocalyptic writers reflects the altered situation of Israel after the destruction of Jerusalem. Powerless to control their national destiny and confronted by people who were intent on either destroying or assimilating them, the Jews developed the rabbinic and apocalyptic attitudes as alternative orientations toward being. Apocalyptic writers retained the visionary and promissory aspect of prophecy while the rabbis systematically developed the moral action prescribed by prophecy.[19] After about 70 A.D., apocalypse began to lose its place within mainstream Judaism. But as the Jews were losing interest in apocalypse, Christians were embracing it.[20] Though the work of Ezekiel exhibits apocalyptic motifs, apart from the Book of Daniel, the apocalyptic tradition is Christian, not Jewish. The Book of Revelation is the most significant Christian apocalypse, and though it differs from Jewish apocalypse in the meaning it gives to Jesus as the Messiah who is the meaning and end of history, it retains the familiar Jewish features of fantastic imagery and symbolic language and the Old Testament themes of resurrection and the Messianic kingdom.[21] Whether Christian or Jewish, however, apocalypse refuses to accept the appearance of historical crises as ultimate: it insists on perceiving the calamities of history as appearances of a more fundamental reality, the divine reality of the covenant between God and humanity.

In addition to destroying the reasonable optimism necessary for the political activism of the prophets, post-exilic conditions seem to have forced a re-examination of the decision to distinguish the time of humanity from cosmic time. The prophetic tradition insists that human beings are free to translate their visions of the age of peace and prosperity into mundane history because human time, unlike archaic cosmic time, is capable of becoming the time of the sacred. Instead of seeing historical events as a threat to the sacred order of being as in the cosmic tradition, the prophets made history a participant in the sacred order. The apocalyptics re-established the distinction between the secular and the sacred, believing historical time to be subsumed under the archetype of God's predestination

This was, it appears, the apocalyptics' way of maintaining an optimism toward history in times of adversity. It assures the righteous person of a unique resurrection and eternal life in the world to come. By focusing on the triumph of righteousness, apocalypse remains firmly within the biblical tradition. Though it appropriates aspects of the cosmic and Greek attitudes, it never allows the amoral or anti-moral orientation toward history of these world-views to penetrate its perspective.

Like prophecy, apocalypse is essentially ethical.[22] Based on the concept of the righteousness of God, the apocalyptic visions never ascribe ultimate significance to the evils of history. Or, perhaps it would be more accurate to say that they insist that the ultimate significance of the evils of history is the triumph of God's righteousness and the redemption of humanity. History, however terrible, remains bearable because it is conditioned by the covenant. The crises of history reflect the judgments of God in His wrath against the sinners, but they are the judgments of a God who promised that he would save those who remained faithful to Him and make them the nucleus of the Messianic kingdom.[23]

The essence of apocalypse. Apocalypse is an articulation of humanity's relationship to history which is called forth, but not determined by, times of distress and upheaval. Apocalypse is not *the* response to historical calamities: it is one possible response to difficult times. As people may relate to the historical dimensions of being cosmically, tragically, prophetically or apocalyptically, we see that the perception of history as crisis-ridden is the consequence of a choice. If we are careful to define a crisis as an event which marks a radical transition, an event which is at once an end and a new beginning, then we become sensitive to the fact that crisis is a meaning we give to history.[24] From this perspective, apocalypse is a decision to accept the upheavals of history as crises in order to invest them with meaning and hope.

Continuing the biblical tradition of accepting history as the time within which God reveals himself, apocalyptic writers insist on seeing all historical events as manifestations of God's will. Instead of saying that God sometimes breaks into mundane time to reveal Himself, the apocalyptic authors see all mundane occurrences as signs of God's presence. They are thereby able to see evil as a mere appearance, which, if properly understood, is a sign of goodness. The calamities of history only appear to be calamities; they are actually crises, times of renewal and recreation. In this way, the apocalyptist acknowledges that the evils of history have an ultimately positive significance.

This optimism of the apocalyptic perspective is directed toward God, not humanity. In reinterpreting the biblical motif of the sporadic intervention of God in history as the continuous presence of God in history, apocalyptic writers are expressing their pessimistic attitude toward history and humanity *per se.* History of itself is seen as the time of increasing evil; human beings are attracted to the City of Man; only Divine providence and grace can transform history and humanity into the time and people of the City of God. The optimism of the apocalyptic tradition cannot be separated from the vision of God as controlling history. The apocalyptist insists on the determinism of the historical process in order to assure human beings that they can be freed from the terrors of history.[25] Instead of viewing people as capable of choosing their historical destiny, apocalyptic writers deny human freedom *within* history in order to allow freedom *from* history. It is not a case of a dualistic choice between determinism or freedom but of a dialectical encounter between predestination and the destiny of freedom.

Apocalypse, like all attitudes of consciousness, represents a choice to relate to reality from a specific perspective within the horizon of being. It is a meaning by which consciousness symbolizes its relationship to the temporality of becoming. The symbols of the apocalyptic tradition are unique in the ways in which the motifs of evil, goodness, the secular, the sacred, freedom and destiny are interrelated to create a vision of history which is fundamentally ruled by the archetypes of morality and salvation.

IV. *The Contemporary Mood*

American pluralism is both a political ideal and a cultural fact: no single view of the meaning of history dominates American attitudes. We cannot, therefore, suggest that America as a whole either is or is not in an apocalyptic mood. The best we can do is examine the various perspectives of contemporary Americans to see which, if any, of them are apocalyptic. In this examination we must remain sensitive to the intricacies of the apocalyptic symbol, remembering that it is a complex interweaving of an experience of temporality which perceives:

1. that history is teleological,

2. that the teleology of history is moral,
3. that the evils of history are necessary preludes to the realization of the moral end of history,
4. that this world will be cataclysmically destroyed before the new world begins,
5. that we are living at the critical period of historical transformation,
6. that only the moral person has a place in the new world,
7. that human choices have no effect on the process of history *per se*, but they do affect the individual's own situation in the world to come.

Keeping these characteristics of apocalypse in mind reminds us that there are genuine differences between pessimistic, anxious, or alienated attitudes toward history and the apocalyptic attitude. It also shows us that the apocalyptic *vision* of the end of history is only a part of the apocalyptic *sense* of the meaning of history. Of the seven ideas that characterize apocalypse, the vision of the apocalyptic end comprise only two (numbers 4 and 5). If the vision is taken out of context, it becomes a doomsday-crisis orientation toward history and ought not be mistaken for an apocalyptic worldview. A proper understanding of the relationship between contemporary American views of history and the apocalyptic perspective requires that we remember the differences between a doomsday vision of history and a crisis vision of history, as well as the differences between *a* crisis perspective and *the* specific crisis perspective of apocalypse.

That we are living in times of rapid and difficult change is a fact. To perceive these changes as crises, that is as events marking a radical transition, is to interpret them in a unique way. Contemporary advocates of the doctrine of contingent progress (progress contingent upon human choices as opposed to necessary progress) articulate a non-apocalyptic, crisis orientation toward history.[26] Like the biblical prophets who believed that human beings could, by making certain choices, transform suffering into salvation, contemporary advocates of the idea of progress believe that the powers of reason and technology which threaten to destroy us can, if human beings make the proper decisions, become the source of a spiritual and material rejuvenation.[27] Contemporary defenders of contingent progress are, in effect, secularizing the prophetic interpretation of history. Where the prophets declared history to be the time of God's relationship to humanity and accepted the future as the time of hope because they believed in the capacity of human beings to make moral choices, proponents of the idea of progress are optimistic about the future because they believe in human rationality.

Having declared that the historical process is entirely secular, advocates of the doctrine of progress make human beings alone responsible for the course of history. In referring to these times as periods of crisis, they affirm their belief in the human ability to transform the history of scarcity and suffering into the history of utopia. If the Hebrew prophets looked forward to the Messianic Age, the secular prophets of our own times expect the realization of the American Dream, of a transformed future which reflects both human desire and human potential.[28]

Herbert Marcuse is an example of a contemporary prophet of the doctrine of progress. Like the prophets of ancient Israel, Marcuse is realistically pessimistic about the conditions of the times. He believes that we are at a pivotal point in history and that the ways in which we choose to use technology will determine the meaning of human existence in the future. He outlines the consequences of continuing to choose according to the traditional logic of our era and urges us to re-evaluate our orientation to technology and humanity. Though he doubts that people will listen to him, he continues to write and teach in the belief that some may understand his message. He predicts the end of humane humanity while insisting that the future is open to our choices.

The secular, humanistic, social-action motifs of the Marcusian type no longer seem to inspire major sectors of the American community. Though social activists, motivated by the visions of the doctrine of contigent progress still exist, their influence appears to be waning. There are interesting parallels between the historical events of the ancient world which affected the decline of the prophetic tradition and the emergence of apocalypse, and the history of our times and its effect on the viability of the doctrine of progress. In the same way that the destruction of Israel, the rise of the great empires of Persia, Greece, Rome, and the resulting political powerlessness of the Hebrew people severely weakened the people's belief that they were capable of directing history toward its Messianic goal, technological terrorism and dehumanization have placed our equation of scientific rationality and the good life in question. In both instances, the fact that people have not used their knowledge to choose morally has led to the conviction that people could not be expected to direct history to a desirable end. The apocalyptic response to this developing pessimistic view of humanity is to insist that the ultimate destiny of history is controlled by God who will inaugurate the Age of the Messiah, with or without human assistance. This response, because it emerges from a religious tradition which understands God to be revealed in history and to be good, can assume a pessimistic attitude toward humanity while maintaining an optimistic orientation toward history.

A secular response to the failure of the doctrine of progress similar to the biblical response to the failure of prophecy would have to affirm the wickedness of humanity, deny the influence of human choices on the course of history, and affirm the blessings of the end of history by interpreting the process of history as determined by itself to fulfill the moral mission of the apocalyptic ideal. Without insisting that a belief in a moral God of history is essential to the apocalyptic world view, we have stressed that the moral-dimension-of-history motif is essential to the apocalyptic vision. Secular versions of apocalypse are therefore possible only if the vision of the end of history is perceived as morally and teleologically conditioned.

Deterministic interpretations of Marx's dialectical materialism, and non-Marxist, popular versions of Hegel's dialectic of history (for example, *The Greening of America* by Charles Reich, an extraordinarily popular and influential analysis of American society in the late 1960s) have articulated a secularized apocalyptic response to the failure of the secular version of prophecy. According to these interpretations of history, we are witnessing the final crisis of history and are justified in anticipating the dawn of a new transcendent era of being. In their determinism and secularity, these attitudes toward history are essentially inversions of the Greek tragic orientation toward reality. Just as the Greeks believed that the process of history itself was responsible for the deteriorating conditions of being, these views insist that the temporality of becoming will, of necessity, effect a rejuvenation of being. Instead of believing in the goodness of the god of history, secularized apocalypse believes in the godlike goodness of history.

In the same way that our era has given rise to the belief in the godlike goodness of history, it has also given rise to a contrary belief in the malign nature of history itself. The literature of alienation, the anti-politics of powerlessness and the popularity of such fictional portrayals of the future as *1984, Fail Safe* and *On the Beach* indicate that apocalyptic *visions* of the end are not, for many Americans, linked to the apocalyptic sense of the goodness of the end. Though the deterministic motif of history is accepted, the optimism of the motif is not. We are, in short, surrounded by doomsday, not apocalyptic, understandings of history. Like the ancient apocalyptic writers who graphically depicted the terrible calamities of the end, contemporary writers warn us of "the fire next time" as they lay the horrors of racial conflict, ecological disaster or nuclear destruction before us; but the present visionaries lack an apocalyptic context for their predictions. The hope, the optimistic, anti-historical motif of apocalypse, sustained by a belief in the moral teleology of history, is reduced to a simple anti-historicism reminiscent of the tragic anti-historicism of the Greeks.

Although we can perhaps agree that the American secular mood is fundamentally gloomy, its gloominess takes different forms. Only one of these forms is apocalyptic, the others are versions of the symbols of prophecy and tragedy. There seems to be, however, a reaction to secularism taking place. America appears to be experiencing a new religious awakening. Though the new religions, like the older secularism, constitute an erosion of the influence of the biblical tradition and therefore cannot be expected to adopt the biblical symbol of apocalypse, we may find that these religions (or some of them) project a version of the apocalyptic attitude.

Like the counter-culture movements of the sixties, the new religions are negatively oriented toward the established society: they perceive it as "sunk in materialism and headed for disaster."[29] Unlike the prophetic-progress optimists of the sixties, however, who hoped and worked for radical social changes, converts to the new religions are concerned about their personal, physical and moral survival.[30] They have expressed these concerns, in many instances, in apocalyptic-millennial visions:

Viewing the present society as in the last stage of degradation before the dawning of a new era, people speak of the Aquarian Age which is about to replace the dying Piscean age. Krishna Consciousness people speak of the present as the last stage of the materialist Kali Yuga and on the verge of a new age of peace and happiness. More traditionally, biblical and expectations of the millennium are common among Jesus people.[31]

Also, like the ancient apocalyptists, devotees of the emergent religions express their negativism toward history by passively withdrawing from social action efforts. Given the calamitous history of this century, they have become skeptical of the possibility of affecting history and have preffered to "sit it out."[32] Further, as their perception of being possesses sacred as well as secular dimensions, they are able to sustain visions of the end of the world which are fundamentally optimistic: The destruction of historical reality is not equated with the end of being. This religious attitude toward the hardships of the times evidences the characteristics of a crisis mentality insofar as it interprets the coming doom as a part of the process of transformation. The fact that this religious orientation toward history is negative about history but optimistic about the end of history distinguishes it from the secular doomsday attitude and indicates its similarity to apocalypse.

There is, however, a critical difference between the historical orientations of the traditional and contemporary apocalyptic visions. The contemporary visions are essentially cosmic and non-teleological. The dualism of creator and creation which is critical to the biblical view of history, whatever its form, is absent.[33] Indeed the absence of dualism is one of the attractions of the new religious movements. Instead of declaring the otherness of God and nature, the otherness of God and history, or the otherness of God and humanity such that individuals might strive to relate to God, or that history must fulfill God's purpose, these religions speak of the identity of God, nature, history and the individual; one is God. Everything is the One.[34]

This lack of dualism in the new religions expresses a cosmic relationship to being which negates history by denying the reality of its existence. The one cosmic dimension of being renders all other dimensions illusionary. Human living, like all other living, is not historical. History is denied. Whereas from the biblical perspective, history is very real and directed by its creator to a moral end, there is, from the perspective of the new religions, either no real historical dimension, or an historical dimension which lacks moral significance. The affirmation of the reality of the moral dimension of history which is essential to the meaning of apocalypse is replaced by a cosmic negation. The anti-historical optimism of apocalypse is rejected in favor of an unhistorical optimism.

The brief comparison of the essential characteristics of the apocalyptic vision with the characteristics of contemporary

American perspectives indicates that, strictly speaking, it is inaccurate to refer to most of the present attitudes toward history as apocalyptic. The apocalyptic vision depicts in supernatural images the terrible destruction of existence as we know it. This vision cannot be lifted out of the context of the apocalyptic interpretation of the meaning of the end without losing its apocalyptic sense. Although Professor Nelson will expand this list in his essay on the manifestations of the myth of apocalypse in American popular culture, of the visions I have mentioned, only strict Marxist materialistic determism, deterministic Hegelianism, and contemporary variations of the traditional biblical motif (for example, Jesus people) synthesize the apocalyptic vision of the end with the apocalyptic interpretation of the end. That we frequently use the word apocalyptic to refer to America' sense of the imminent end of history, despite the fact that most of these versions of the end lack important ingredients of the apocalyptic perspective, may mean that we have become so estranged from our biblical roots that we no longer appreciate the essential relationship between the dual vision of cataclysm and the New Jerusalem of apocalypse. Or it may indicate that although we have *consciously* forsaken the moral optimism of apocalypse pre-consciously we have not. Our vision of ourselves as apocalyptic may indicate that we have not, despite our secular public attitudes, renounced the biblical roots of our American heritage, roots which insist on the essentially moral significance of history and history's end.

Notes

[1] For more complete discussions of the archaic sense of history see Mircea Eliade, *Cosmos and History: The Myth of the Eternal Return*, ed., Willard Trask (New York: Pantheon Books, 1954); Stanley Diamond, ed. *Primitive Views of the World* (New York: Columbia University Press, 1964); Paul Ricoeur, *The Symbolism of Evil*, trans. Emerson Buchanan (New York: Harper & Row, 1967).

[2] Stanley Diamond, "The Uses of the Primitive," in *Primitive Views of the World*.

[3] John Gunnell, *Political Philosophy and Time* (Middletown, Conn.: Wesleyan University Press, 1968), p. 95.

[4] B.A. von Groniger, *In the Grip of the Past: Essays on an Aspect of Greek Thought* (Leiden: E.J. Brill, 1953), pp. 27-30.

[5] Plato, *The Republic*, in *The Republic and Other Works*, trans. B. Jowell (New York: Dolphin Books, 1960), pp. 236-237.

[6] Emil Fackenheim, *Quest for Past and Future* (Boston: Beacon Press, 1968), p. 70.

[7] Herbert Butterfield, *Christianity and History* (New York: Scribners Sons, 1949), pp. 2-3.

[8]Abraham Heschel, *The Prophets* (New York: Jewish Publication Society of America, 1955), p. 484.
[9]Heschel, pp. 184-185.
[10]Heschel, p. 173.
[11]Butterfield, pp. 66-67.
[12]D.S. Russell, *The Method and the Message of Jewish Apocalyptic* (Philadelphia: Westminster Press, 1964), p. 106.
[13]Russell, p. 304.
[14]Russell, p. 309.
[15]Paul D. Hanson, *The Dawn of Apocalyptic* (Philadelphia: Fortress Press, 1975), p. 29.
[16]Russell, p. 231.
[17]Hanson, pp. 404-406.
[18]Hanson, p. 407.
[19]Russell, p. 84.
[20]Russell, pp. 32-33.
[21]Russell, pp. 34-35.
[22]R.H. Charles, *Eschatology: The Doctrine of a Future Life in Israel, Judaism and Christianity* (New York: Schocken Books, 1963), p. 191.
[23]Butterfield, p. 77.
[24]Frank Kermode, *The Sense of An Ending* (New York: Oxford Univ. Press, 1966), pp. 101, 96.
[25]Eliade, *Cosmos and History*.
[26]See for example Charles Frankel, *The Case for Modern Man* (Boston: Beacon Press, 1959) or Radoslav Tsanoff, *Civilization and Progress* (Lexington: Univ. Press of Kentucky, 1971).
[27]See for example B.F. Skinner, *Beyond Freedom and Dignity* (New York: Beacon Press, 1964).
[28]See Ihab Hassan, "Models of Transformation: Ideology, Utopia, and Fantasy in America," in *Paracriticisms: Seven Speculations of the Times* (Urbana: Univ. of Illinois Press, 1975), pp. 151-176. Hassan discusses briefly five such contemporary secular prophets of social transformation whom he calls "futurists": Herman Kahn, B.F. Skinner, Herbert Marcuse, R. Buckminster Fuller and Norman O. Brown.
[29]Robert Bellah, "The New Consciousness and the Crisis in Modernity" in *The New Religious Consciousness*, ed. Charles Glock and Robert Bellah, (Berkeley: Univ. of Calif. Press, 1976), p. 343.
[30]Bellah, p. 342.
[31]Bellah, pp. 343-344.
[32]Harvey Cox, *Turning East: The Promise and Peril of the New Orientalism* (New York: Simon & Schuster, 1977), p. 102.
[33]In Theravada Buddhism, for example, there is no creator god. See also "The Zen Teaching of Huang Po on the Transmission of Mind," in *The World of Zen*, ed. Nancy Wilson Ross, (New York: Vintage Books, 1960), p. 66. In discussing the Zen insistence on Enlightenment as that state of being which transcends all dualisms, we see that the idea of God as creator is rejected because "... the idea of God as the creator of the universe suggests a dualism, a distinction between creator and created."
[34]Ross, p. 66. "A Buddha's Enlightenment denotes an intuitive realization of his unity with the Absolute .... The experience commonly called entering Nirvana is, in fact, an intuitive realization of that self-nature which is the true Nature of all things." See also Harvey Cox, *Turning East*, pp. 86-87, and Jacob Needleman, *The New Religions* (New York: Doubleday, 1970), pp. 4, 23-29, 78.

II.
Waiting for the End: The Social Context of American Apocalyptic Religion

Charles H. Lippy

FROM THE PURITANS' vision of their Massachusetts settlement as a "city on a hill" to the Born Again movement's "Jesus is Coming" automobile bumper stickers, apocalyptic strains have echoed throughout American religious life. In a technical sense, apocalypticism refers to purported revelations or prophecies of a future end of time and the start of a new, divine age, usually expressed in symbolic language or an esoteric code. But more popularly, apocalyptic expressions in American religion also include fascination with the presumed "Second Coming" of Christ or the Parousia, a mythico-historical event which will mark the end of chronological time. This return of the Christ is related to the idea of the millennium, a thousand years of weal or woe for humankind (depending on whether the Parousia initiates or climaxes the period) and the anticipated rapturous reunion of believers of all generations with the Christ in celestial glory.

The apocalyptic vision need not be restricted to its variant Christian expressions. In the American context, at least, it has associations with the peculiar religious experience of particular ethnic groups as much as with the dominant Christian tradition. The Ghost Dance religion which emerged among the Plains Indians in the late nineteenth century, for example, is an apocalyptic phenomenon as much as the development of the Seventh-Day Adventists within Christian circles. What they both share is a vision of a future state of existence whose reality displaces the empirical realm as primary.

While apocalyptic concerns have a secure and continuing place in American religion, zeal for the apocalypse, Christian or otherwise, has never been constant. As Norman Cohn has persuasively argued in his important work, *The Pursuit of the Millennium*, interest in apocalyptic and millennial ideas correlates directly with social factors.¹ For the most part, strong interest in apocalypticism comes during times of social instability or transition, during times when an old order is passing and a new order has not yet appeared in established forms. It may be war, economic depression, social class conflict, or a host of other factors which prompt perception of social disintegration and appear as signals of the end. Whenever "this world" offers little security for individuals or for groups and whenever ordinary experience fits less and less into a plausible interpretive framework, then some "other world" will entice the discontent by offering hope for a more satisfying future on a higher plane of existence.²

The problem of the apocalypticist, simply put, is a gap between the perceived structures of a powerful social order which appears basically pragmatic, amoral and oriented toward individual achievement and one's own experience of the world as unjust and whimsical, if not malevolent.³ In other words, apocalyptic enthusiasm transpires with greater intensity when once-operative norms and standards no longer regulate or explain behavior. To counter this perceived trend, apocalyptic groups emerge with tight boundaries, and a strong sense of their corporate identity and distinctiveness, a view of the universe as a battleground between forces of good and evil (with evil momentarily holding the upper hand), and an intense concern to protect pure believers from constant attack by polluting forces.

While sophisticated apocalyptic thinking may come from the pen of the theologian, as it did that of Jonathan Edwards in the mid-eighteenth century, much apocalyptic thought in America has been advanced by persons who are more appropriately labelled as charismatic figures. As delineated by Max Weber, the charismatic figure (Weber preferred the term "prophet") claims authority on the basis of direct personal gifts (traditionally such abilities as divination, healing, and the like). The charismatic leader is not recognized or granted authority by established institutions, but seizes them nonetheless, usually through highly emotional preaching or oratory. In turn, those who hear and believe reinforce both the leadership of the charismatic prophet and the content of the new message promulgated simply by their acceptance of the prophet's proclamation as authoritative.⁴ In social terms, the charismatic leader, then, captures the inchoate discontent and frustrations of followers and formulates them in a coherent fashion so that adherents themselves are able to identify the sources of their difficulties. The charismatic prophet next provides an alternative to the empirical realm in a vision of a sublime future beyond history or somehow removed from history, unveiling the true order of reality in which those now outcast or ill at ease will be manifest in the glory they deserve.

In the essay which follows, I shall first examine the apocalyptic dimension in colonial Puritan thought, perhaps the most judicious strand in American apocalypticism, noting its relation to the emergence of a distinctive American identity. Then I shall look at apocalyptic expression in the nineteenth century, particularly as evinced in the utopian experiment of the Shakers, the sectarian development of the Christadelphians and the Millerites, and the move to denominational respectability with the Seventh-Day Adventists and the Jehovah's Witnesses. Apocalyptic dimensions of one aspect of Amerindian religious life, the Ghost Dance, and the lack of any pervasive chiliastic ideas in Black religious experience form the focus of the next section, while twentieth century apocalypticism, as manifested in dispensationalism and fundamentalism, the Jesus Movement, and popular Protestant piety, provide materials for analysis in the final section.

I

Millenarianism was among the cultural preconceptions which the Puritans brought from England to America in the seventeenth century.[5] But until the revivals of the eighteenth century known as the Great Awakening, most Puritan apocalyptic thought centered on rigorous exegesis of the chiliastic literature of the Bible. (The word "chiliasm," like 'millennialism," denotes a belief in the second coming and the thousand year reign of Christ on earth, deriving from the Greek "kilias," meaning one thousand, rather than from the Latin.) Such prominent Puritan divines as John Cotton, Thomas Shepard, and Increase Mather and less well-known clergy and laymen such as Ephraim Huit, William Aspinwall, and Thomas Parker all penned expositions of apocalyptic ideas in the Scriptures, but few sought to pinpoint the precise coming of the apocalypse in historical time or to locate in geographical terms the seat of the apocalyptic kingdom.[6] Cotton, for example, spoke vaguely of the apocalypse's dawning after the destruction of the Papacy, which he and numerous others believed to be the Antichrist, while Increase Mather argued that the conversion of the Jews—which he put sometime within the next one thousand years—would herald the apocalypse. Aspinwall, a layman, was among the few who attempted to fix an approximate date for the chiliastic inbreaking. While declining to select a specific year, Aspinwall suggested that the apocalypse would dawn not later than 1673.

But popular Puritan belief in the apocalypse was captured less in theological tomes than in the poetry of Michael Wigglesworth, teacher and pastor at Malden. In 1662, a year of drought in New England, Wigglesworth published two widely-read poems. One, "God's Controversy with New England," attributed Puritan misfortunes to a loss of true faith,[7] but the apocalyptic expectation came to the fore in "The Day of Doom, or a Poetical Expression of the Great and Last Judgment":

> For at midnight breaks forth a light,
>   which turns the night to day,
> And speedily an hideous cry
>   doth all the World dismay.
> Sinners awake, their hearts do ache,
>   trembling their loins surpriseth;
> Amaz'd with fear, by what they hear,
>   each one of them ariseth.
>
> They rush from beds with giddy heads,
>   and to their windows run,
> Viewing this light, which shines more bright
>   than doth the noon-day Sun.
> Straightway appears (they see't with tears)
>   the Son of God most dread,
> Who with his Train comes on amain
>   to judge both Quick and Dead.[8]

Wigglesworth's tone is consistent with the bulk of seventeenth-century Puritan apocalypticism: the end remains a future historical reality, inaugurated by the return of the Christ, an event for which Christians ought constantly to be prepared. As David D. Hall declared, "Both Calvinist and Puritan saw God as ceaselessly at work bending the course of human history toward the goal of the kingdom."⁹

In the eighteenth century, New England apocalypticism became both more specific in terms of when and where the Second Advent would transpire and more oriented to a post-millennial view of the Parousia.¹⁰ The thrust of eighteenth century apocalyptic thought was capsuled in the views of Jonathan Edwards and his ideological heirs, especially Samuel Hopkins. In the 1730s and 1740s, the revivals of the Great Awakening swept the New England colonies, leaving vast numbers of men and women aware of the precariousness of life, as revealed in the extent of human sin, and alert to the stirrings of divine grace in their souls. To Jonathan Edwards, the Awakening represented an event so miraculous as to defy classification in ordinary terms. In his *Some Thoughts Concerning the Present Revival of Religion in New England* (1742), Edwards exulted:

> 'Tis not unlikely that this work of God's Spirit, that is so extraordinary and wonderful, is the dawning, or at least a prelude, of that glorious work of God, so often foretold in Scripture, which, in the progress and issue of it, shall renew the world of mankind. If we consider how long since the things foretold, as what should precede this great event, have been accomplished; and how long this event has been expected by the church of God, and thought to be nigh by the most eminent men of God in the church; and withal consider what the state of things now is, and has for a considerable time been, in the church of God and world of mankind, we can't reasonably think otherwise, than that the beginning of this great work of God must be near. And there are many things that make it probable that this work will begin in America.¹¹

Edwards also drafted weighty expositions of biblical apocalyptic passages, but he continued to believe in the advent of the millennium in the near future.¹² In his *History of the Work of Redemption*, based on a series of sermons preached in 1739 but not published until after his death, Edward proclaimed:

> The end of God's creating the world, was to prepare a kingdom for his Son ... which should remain to all eternity. So far as the *kingdom of Christ is set up* in the world, *so far* is the world brought to its end, and the eternal state of things set up—*so far* are all the great changes and revolutions in the world brought to their everlasting issue, and all things come to their ultimate period.... So far as Christ's kingdom is established in the world, *so far* are things wound up and settled in their everlasting state, and a period put to the course of things in this changeable world, *so far* are the first heavens and the first earth come to an end, and the new heavens and the new earth, the everlasting heavens and earth established in their room.¹³

If the millennial age was soon to begin and America was to be the site of the apocalyptic kingdom, the whole nevertheless would remain a part of the inscrutable design of God and would operate according to God's providential sovereignty.[14] History itself remained important, for it was the arena where the faithful could observe the subtle work of God in bringing the world to its divinely ordained end.

What made the Awakening era open to apocalyptic thought? Why did Jonathan Edwards and others come to think that the millennium would dawn in America? In responding to these queries, it is important to recall that the Awakening itself was not only a religious movement, but a general social movement *par excellence*, signalling more than the recasting of the religious landscape: it marked the transition from a colonial identity to a national identity in American life. Indeed, some commentators have viewed the revivals associated with Edwards as the first major evidence of the Americanization of those English colonies which became the United States,[15] and one has argued that this religious earthquake made millenarianism "the common vital possession of American Christians."[16] The mid-eighteenth century possessed the conditions suggested by Norman Cohn as basic to apocalyptic enthusiasm: colonists were restless and discontented with both British control and local political structures long in the hands of a colonial power elite. Social realities no longer meshed with experience. The time was ripe for change as settlers away from the long dominant coastal areas sought social power and status equivalent to their growing importance in colonial economics and politics and as the colonies themselves sought power and status within the British imperial system equivalent to their importance. With Jonathan Edwards and others, leaders came forth who were able to focus both the discontent and the aspirations of their audiences. Adoption of apocalyptic symbols seemed a logical means to elevate those outside the circles of power to a superior status, for if the apocalypse began in America, then not only would American self-perceptions be legitimized, but also those who stood among the elect, those converted in the revivals, would share the glory of the Second Advent regardless of their social status and power. Indeed, apocalyptic strands merged with secular politics during the era of the War for Independence a quarter century later when many regarded the break with Britain and the establishment of an independent federal republic as another harbinger of the nearness of the Parousia and confirmation of the belief that the Kingdom would come first in America.[17] In the words of Ezra Stiles, the United States itself would be "elevated to glory and honor."[18] Later, in the wake of the French Revolution, some who feared that the "infidelity" of republican France would adversely influence American religious purity nevertheless regarded the attacks on the Roman Catholic Church, still popularly regarded as the Anti-Christ, as a precursor of the apocalypse.[19] American Christians disagreed about the seriousness of the threat posed by French infidelity, but one matter was certain: by the end of the eighteenth century apocalypticism had become indelibly imprinted on the fabric of American religion. Events of history would continue to prompt speculation concerning the end.

II

Apocalyptic thinking in the nineteenth century demonstrated a multi-faceted development, providing impetus for phenomena as diverse as the idea of "Manifest Destiny," the world missions movement, and frontier revivalism.[20] The nineteenth century also witnessed a new dimension in American chiliastic thought: the emergence of particular religious groups which adopted peculiar interpretations of the apocalypse as major ingredients in their ideologies. The list of such groups is long and includes the Mormons (who still believe the Kingdom will be based on the American continent) and the Oneida Perfectionists led by John Humphrey Noyes (who claimed to live in the millennial state within their communities), along with groups such as the Seventh-Day Adventists and the Jehovah's Witnesses.[21] With each, the social context at the time of the group's birth remains critical to understanding why a certain brand of apocalypticism attracted adherents. The social fluidity of westward expansion, the abolitionist movement and other efforts at social reform, and the unsteady growth of American political institutions all left a feeling of personal and social dislocation among large numbers of Americans who felt excluded from the power, prestige, and security which national leaders seemed to extol. These conditions created a setting which charismatic prophets found ripe for harvesting followers; all provided the stimulus for developing new ways of viewing present and future reality.

The Shakers are a good case in point. Technically known as the

44   The Apocalyptic Vision in America

United Society of Believers in Christ's Second Appearing, the Shakers owe their origins to the charismatic Ann Lee. In 1774 Ann Lee migrated to New York from England, where she had been part of a fringe religious circle oriented toward ecstatic experience. Ann's own religious quest involved numerous visions in which she received the teachings central to Shaker belief. Among them was the conviction that the Christ had already returned to earth in the person of Ann Lee. As Jesus represented the advent of Christ in masculine form, so Ann represented the advent of Christ in feminine form.[22] This return of Christ in feminine form brought a radical alteration in ordinary affairs, for it meant that believers were already living in the apocalyptic age. In the Shaker perspective, apocalypse and history are fused: Brothers and Sisters structured their lives in chronological time as if they were living in the consummated kingdom. In practical terms, millennial life required strict separation of the sexes, the practice of celibacy, and isolation from an impure world. Whatever might thwart the full pursuit of purity was to be abandoned.

The Shakers reached the peak of their popularity in the 1830s and 1840s, numbering around six thousand devotees in some twenty virtually self-sustaining communities. But growth brought its own problems, and the same years witnessed the outbreak of so many individual ecstatic experiences and, concomitantly, such internal chaos, that the communities had temporarily to abandon accepting converts and prohibit outsiders from visiting. When control had been re-established, the excesses had been neatly incorporated into the historical apocalypse of the Society. The era was labelled "Mother Ann's Work," and new rituals were instituted to channel the once-rampant emotionalism into acceptable outlets. One ritual especially shows the fusion of the historical and the apocalyptic in Shaker belief. It involved an apocalyptic banquet, to be held twice yearly, to which the faithful came garbed in imaginary spiritual clothes and shared an imaginary meal.[23] Clearly reminiscent of the eschatological feast expected in orthodox Christian chiliasm, the meal and its attendant ceremonies reminded the Shakers that they were not of this world, but already part of the world which most thought was yet to come.

Records suggest that at least through the period of maximum growth, the Shakers drew their adherents from among persons who had experienced much personal and social dislocation. Most came from frontier areas where the tension between the civilization left behind and the wilderness ahead produced an unsettled life at best. The Shakers, thanks to their charismatic founder, invited potential converts to share in a comprehensive alternative to empirical reality. Their sense of the world as evil and the community as pure, their aim of sexual purity, and their concern for total withdrawal from society provided the conditions which one would expect to find as a reaction to an increasingly implausible social order.

At the time of Mother Ann's Work came the inception of another sect which intertwined the historical and the apocalyptic in unusual fashion. Under the charismatic leadership of an immigrant physician from England by the name of John Thomas, the Christadelphians propagated a message which combined orthodox and heterodox apocalyptic notions.[24] Thomas, after arriving in the United States in 1830, had aligned himself with Alexander Campbell and his followers who later became the Disciples of Christ denomination. The Campbellites were primitivists in that they wished to replicate the structural patterns they believed characterized pristine New Testament Christianity. Among the early Campbellites, apocalyptic hopes ran high, and many shared the conviction that their own restitution of the ways of primitive Christianity served as a direct herald of the millennial age. Thomas numbered himself among those of Campbell's disciples who were most fascinated by millenarian thought. When he broke away from Campbell in the late 1840s, Thomas pushed Campbellite apocalypticism to its extreme. In a major treatise entitled *Elpis Israel; Being an Exposition of the Kingdom of God,* Thomas traced the Christadelphian gospel not simply to primitive Christianity but to the covenant made with Abraham recounted in Genesis.[25] The history of humankind was the saga of preparation for gospel knowledge and apostasy from true belief. With Thomas, humanity had one more opportunity to receive the truth.

Thomas gave unique contours to his apocalypticism. By linking the gospel dispensation with ancient Israel, he intimately connected the coming millennium with Judaism. Indeed, a Zionist thrust marks Christadelphian belief, for Thomas argued that the historical restoration of Israel as a nation would precede the Second Advent. But historical events themselves, especially wars, were also millennial signs for Thomas. He was convinced, for example, that every violent war brought humanity one step closer to the apocalypse. Hence Christadelphians, while avowed pacifists, nevertheless rejoiced in the outbreak of war, for each war signalled the advance of the approaching kingdom in which they would be glorified because of their pure knowledge. At one point, Thomas ventured to predict the beginning of the apocalypse proper, for he spoke of a mysterious "intervention" in human affairs due around 1866-68 which would inaugurate the chain of events immediately preceding the return of the Christ in judgment.

As had the Shakers, Thomas drew most of his followers from among the lower socio-economic ranks at first. His message that those who entered the kingdom through his teachings had the secret knowledge of ultimate truth gave Christadelphians a higher status in the cosmic scheme than they had in mundane reality, and they were careful to protect this knowledge from pollution by screening potential members carefully and sealing their entrance into the fold through a secret rite of immersion. Indeed, while the specifics of the Christadelphian vision differ markedly from those of the Shaker vision, both saw the world as fraught with evil; both sought to avoid participation in worldly affairs. But while the Shakers stepped out of history to live in the heavenly kingdom now, the Christadelphians rejoiced in the tribulations of history which advanced them toward the heavenly kingdom glimpsed in John Thomas' reconstruction of biblical teaching.

Today the Shakers number but a handful and the Christadelphians a few thousand. Though their apocalyptic hope was fervent, relatively few accepted their ways. The same cannot be said about a third chiliastic group which flourished just as the Shakers reached their numerical zenith and John Thomas was about to leave the Campbellite fold. In 1839, a student of biblical prophecy named William Miller came into contact with Joshua V. Hines, a genius at public relations and a skilled organizer. Propelling Miller into the revival and camp meeting preaching circuit, Hines ensured that the version of apocalypticism which Miller had decoded from the Book of Daniel would not go unheard. Miller proclaimed the coming of the apocalypse in 1843, later revising the date to 1844, by counting as a year each of the 2300 days mentioned in Daniel 8:14 as the time to pass before the final cleansing of the earth and by dating the original prophecy to 457 B.C.[26] Under Hines' direction, Miller's preaching drew vast audiences, and the movement garnered at least 50,000 followers by the time of the expected Parousia. But the millennial age did not commence on schedule, and many of Miller's supporters abandoned the adventist fold and returned to more mainline religious groups.[27]

Others, however, recast Miller's essential message and spoke of spiritual cleansings and spiritual advents unseen by human eyes. Indeed, Miller's legacy in generating continuing apocalyptic reflection may be more significant than his leadership of a group of disappointed disciples, for among those adventists who refused to abandon belief in the imminence of the Parousia was Ellen G. White, whose own visions provided the revelations central to the teaching of the Seventh-Day Adventists. Mrs. White was the archetypal charismatic figure. As Elmer T. Clark has recounted:

> Mrs. White's visions were received in a state of trance; after an experience of rapture and shouting she swooned, then regained her strength and in an entranced condition repeated her visions. Loughborough, an eyewitness, declared that while in that condition, at one time for six hours, *she did not breathe*, though her pulse was normal and she possessed superhuman strength; he cites other witnesses, and even medical authority, to that effect.[28]

The Seventh-Day Adventists, drawing on Millerite thinking, believed—and assert—that divine judgment commenced with the apocalyptic dramas of 1843-44. But instead of returning to established churches when a visible Parousia did not occur and revitalizing a lively apocalypticism there, Adventists who followed Mrs. White argued that such perversion of true belief and doctrine pervaded mainline Christian bodies that it was necessary to remove into a distinct group where purity could be maintained. In addition, all the biblical commandments, including the keeping of the Sabbath on Saturday, had to be observed as tokens of pure religious practice. And, as one might expect, biblical prophecies, especially those with an apocalyptic cast, became central to Seventh-Day Adventism. Indeed, the Adventists maintain that all but one of the apocalyptic prophecies have already been fulfilled: the consummation of the apocalypse awaits only the full gathering of a "prepared people" to preach the gospel of the imminent Parousia. The heirs of Ellen G. White, of course, regard themselves as the nucleus of the prepared people in question and believe their version of Christian doctrine constitutes the gospel which must be preached before the millennium begins.[29] Once the Seventh-Day Adventists' truth has spread throughout the world, history will reach its climax, the Lord will return, and time will be no more.

The same era which saw Mrs. White's revisions of the apocalyptic hope also gave birth to another movement which by the last quarter of the twentieth century ranked among the fastest growing religious groups in the United States. Founded in 1872 by former Congregationalist layman Charles Taze Russell, the Jehovah's Witnesses provide yet a different fusion of historical time and apocalyptic time.[30] According to Russell, the Second Advent occurred in 1874 with a spiritual return of the Christ to the "upper air," and the reign of the Christ began in heaven in 1914. The millennium is, then, already underway in one sense, and those who accept the Witnesses' gospel are already living in the apocalypse. But Christ's reign at present remains incomplete; its consummation awaits the annihilation of all associated with Satan—the churches, nations, and their leaders. In another sense, though, the millennium looms in the future, albeit the immediate future, for the approaching defeat of Satan's forces will inaugurate the full reign of Christ, a thousand year epoch when humanity will be offered one more chance to repent and believe. For the Jehovah's Witnesses (a name given to the group in 1931 under the leadership of Judge Joseph Rutherford, Russell's successor), the millennium both is and is not yet, history both is and is no more.

To what extent do the Millerites, Seventh-Day Adventists, and Jehovah's Witnesses fit the pattern which has been found with the other apocalyptic expression that I have discussed? All three, of course, owed their genesis to charismatic figures; all three set clear boundaries between truth and falsehood and saw the world as essentially evil territory to be shunned at all costs; all three drew from those numbered among the sociologically and psychologically unsettled masses. But the Millerite movement proper fizzled quickly when the apocalypse did not occur on schedule, while the Seventh-Day Adventists and the Jehovah's Witnesses continue to flourish. Why? I should offer two suggestions. First, the curious admixture of time and apocalypse in these latter two groups provides a means by which history itself assumes meaning. Unlike the Millerites, for whom history as *chronos* had no value since the date of the end was certain, the Adventists and the Witnesses have embued time with value. For the Adventists, time is of the essence since but one prophecy awaits fulfillment before the apocalypse comes. For the Witnesses, time is also of the essence, but for a different reason: the present is already part of the anticipated age since the Lord has already returned in the heavens. By attaching this peculiar significance to present time, both allow adherents to accept the empirical world, although they attach different significations to empirical reality than do others who are outside their respective folds. Second, the Millerites drew primarily from among rural, frontier folk. The other two, initially at least, tapped the discontented living in a rapidly urbanizing and industrializing America. As the cities grew and more and more people left behind the familiar ways of a seemingly simpler agrarian past, many experienced a strong sense of social dislocation. The Adventists and the Witnesses were able to offer a security to those alienated from the emerging urban, industrial social order with their reinterpretation of the apocalyptic hope and their new understanding of the place of history in the cosmic scheme. Their continuing attraction may well reflect their ongoing ability to offer a plausible alternate construction of "reality" to those who feel removed from the main currents of contemporary life.

III

White Christian Americans were not the only ones in the United States to experience severe social dislocation in the closing decades of the nineteenth century or the only ones to turn to charismatic leaders who invited listeners to enter a higher plane of reality through belief in an apocalyptic vision. With the acceleration, after 1840, of the movement to settle lands west of the Mississippi, native Americans—the so-called Indians—faced even more restrictive governmental control, as tribes were forced onto reservations, and even greater hostility from white Americans, who still tended to see the Indians as an uncivilized threat to their own culture and sense of superiority. The creation of the reservation system could not but upset living patterns (as had earlier programs to push Eastern and Southern tribes west of the Mississippi), destroy centuries old tribal customs and traditions, and disrupt once-established means of support offered by hunting, herding, growing crops, and the like.

In 1870, primarily among California tribes, and again in 1890, mainly among tribes—mostly Sioux—to the east, there arose a millenarian movement known as the Ghost Dance. In both cases, charismatic shamans, Tavibo in 1870 and Wovoka in 1890, attempted to recall their followers to their own history and traditions on the basis of apocalyptic revelations they had received. Wovoka described his own experience:

> When the sun died, I went up to heaven and saw God and all the people who had died a long time ago. God told me to come back and tell my people they must be good

and love one another, and not fight, or steal, or lie. He gave me this dance to give my people.[31]

Tapping a longstanding belief that the dead would return to usher in a new age of glory, both outbreaks of the Ghost Dance developed elaborate ecstatic rituals of song and dance which were signs of the coming apocalypse, if not catalysts designed to aid its dawning. But there was a new element, prominent in the later Ghost Dance, which concerned the status of the dominant white culture. Combined with the old tenet of the eventual return of the dead was the notion that white culture and white people would be destroyed in a concomitant cataclysm. As the Ghost Dance spread—and there were many different tribal variants—the imminence of the apocalypse was accented. The frenzy generated by ritual dances, the abandonment of ordinary tasks, and the defiance of United States control which accompanied the revival only fed the fears of government and military personnel and led to even more repressive actions. The culmination came in the massacre of Wounded Knee, which not only obliterated the internal integrity of tribal cultures for generations, but also destroyed the apocalyptic hopes kindled anew by the Ghost Dance.

Whether one follows James Mooney, the first serious student of the Ghost Dance, in seeing the "new" religion as the result of the extreme cultural deprivation forced on the various tribes or whether one accepts the interpretation of later scholars such as Anthony F.C. Wallace in regarding it as a revitalization effort, the Dance meets the criteria of an apocalyptic movement.[32] It revolved around strong charismatic leaders, it emerged in a time of unusual social stress, and it created a lively sense of group identity through establishing clear boundaries between Indian and white and by promoting the doctrine that the world was essentially evil. What sets the Ghost Dance apart from much other American apocalypticism is its understanding of history. The new age which would arrive, bringing the demolition of the dominant but oppressive white culture, was by no means discontinuous with the past. Rather, the return of the dead operated as a return to a past which was itself pure and undefiled. To this extent, the apocalypse of the Ghost Dance is more a restoration of a presumed golden age than the introduction of a radically new age. Nevertheless, the present was transformed, the powerless received power, and the vicissitudes of empirical reality disappeared in the vision. All are hallmarks of apocalyptic thinking.

Curiously, chiliastic expectations have not flourished among the other group of Americans, the Blacks, who have suffered as much, if not more, repression and oppression than the Indians. Perhaps because the process of enslavement frequently snuffed out obvious remnants of African tribal religious traditions (though much survived beneath the surface), Black Americans were deprived of an historical past and even of a mythological past from the time of their arrival in the New World. History and myth have generally provided the springboard for millennial dreams. At least in slave religion, the distinctly apocalyptic element was minimal.[33] And when Black Americans have clustered in pentecostal and holiness groups, similar to countless small white groups where an apocalyptic sense has often been nurtured, they have placed far greater stress on conversion, sanctification, perfection, and rigid morality than on apocalyptic hopes.[34]

The absence of a fervent apocalypticism does not mean, however, that there is no futuristic dimension in Black religious experience. Indeed, there is a lively futuristic impulse, but it has tended to focus either on chronological history (a future within time) or on life after death (a future beyond time) rather than on an apocalypse (a future which ends time). The references to freedom in many slave spirituals, for example, pointed to release from slavery within historical time as well as to release from spiritual bondage to sin. Those which spoke of future rewards in heaven likewise had a double meaning: it was necessary to prepare not only for heavenly existence after death, but also for a future on earth when the oppression of slavery would cease.[35] And, as Joseph R. Washington, Jr., has argued, once slavery was abolished but social oppression continued, the dynamic of future freedom within historical time easily became translated into the drive for justice within history, still drawing on the old metaphors of Israel in Egypt and life in heaven as models.[36]

Had American Blacks not been thrust into slavery or regarded as inferior beings by the dominant white culture, the story might have been different. If the various African cultures from which the Black population was drawn had been accepted as having their own integrity or had Blacks been allowed to remain in cultural groupings in the New World, then internal resources from the rich African religious past might well have offered themselves for adaptation or revitalization among apocalyptic or millennial lines once transported to the American context. But since such was not the case, what might have been remains sheer speculation. It is safe to conclude, however, that the apocalyptic strand in American religious life is the poorer because of the inhumane treatment of Black Americans since the arrival of the first slave ship in 1619.

IV

Urbanization and industrialization furnished a social context for the emergence of groups such as the Seventh-Day Adventists and Jehovah's Witnesses. The same milieu also set the stage for refining other variants of the apocalyptic vision which helped to assure the place of hope for a "new heaven and a new earth" within mainstream Protestantism. One constellation of apocalyptic ideas imbibed heavily from the fountains of liberal theology, Darwinian thought, and the idea of progress and was basically post-millennialist in its perspective. Another brought the pre-millennial viewpoint, with its sense of impending cataclysm, to the center, first in dispensationalism and then in fundamentalism. Both strands remain vital to the pulse of American Protestantism today.

The first matrix of ideas reached its zenith in the late nineteenth and early twentieth centuries and found its leading advocates in such persons as Walter Rauschenbusch, Washington Gladden, Richard T. Ely, George Herron, and Josiah Strong. Because their message saw human need in corporate or social terms as well as in individualistic terms and because it called for regeneration of the social order as well as the salvation of individual souls, it has become known as the Social Gospel.[37] Essentially a program of social/ethical reform designed to combat perceived urban and industrial ills, to enhance the quality of life of the laboring class, and to give renewed plausibility to a broadly defined evangelical Protestantism, the Social Gospel embraced the idea of evolutionary social progress. Human society, claimed Social Gospel exponent Josiah Strong, had progressed from an agricultural economy to an industrial economy, from rural life to urban life, from a tribal organization to organization of nation-states.[38] All such progress appeared inevitable when reviewing the facts of history; it also seemed the manifestation of the will of God for human life. Yet the world and, more particularly American society, were far from perfect. Nevertheless, humankind with its wealth and technological knowledge had the resources to rid society of its ills and social injustice. When such problems as urban poverty, labor-capital conflict, and the like were resolved, humanity would be prepared for the gradual emergence of the Kingdom of God on earth. Simply put, history would merge into the apocalypse.

Josiah Strong was likewise convinced that American Anglo-Saxon Protestants were God's chosen agents appointed to translate the Kingdom from expectant hope to historical reality.[39] But other Social Gospel leaders, while generally optimistic about the potential of human progress, were more reticent to identify the Kingdom with any strictly human possibility or people. In time, though, the Kingdom would come. Walter Rauschenbusch, perhaps the most respected of the Social Gospel advocates and one who was more cautious than Strong in equating the coming Kingdom with American evangelical Protestantism, closed his best-selling exposition of the Social Gospel program by rhapsodizing:

Last May a miracle happened. At the beginning of the week the fruit trees bore brown and greenish buds. At the end of the week they were robed in bridal garments of blossom. But for weeks and months the sap had been rising and distending the cells and maturing the tissues which were half ready in the fall before. The swift unfolding was the culmination of a long process. Perhaps these nineteen centuries of Christian influence have been a long preliminary stage of growth, and now the flower and fruit are almost here. If at this juncture we can rally sufficient religious faith and moral strength to snap the bonds of evil and turn the present unparalleled economic and intellectual resources of humanity to the harmonious development of a true social life, the generations yet unborn will mark this as that great day of the Lord for which the ages waited, and count us blessed for sharing in the apostolate that proclaimed it.[40]

The calamity of the First World War shattered the somewhat naive optimism of the Social Gospel, and the eager anticipation of gradual progress into the apocalyptic age dwindled. But the style of apocalyptic expectation which marked the Social Gospel movement left a continuing heritage in church agencies and leaders who still place social reform and social justice as the first items on any agenda which aims to bring the Kingdom of God into concrete manifestations.

The Social Gospel and its liberally oriented descendants represent an important strand in American apocalypticism. The movement in its own way drew support from an alienated segment of society, though from one which was alienated more in terms of its perceived status than its actual status. The Social Gospel attracted mainly those who came to be identified as the new urban middle class, those who were to become the dominant grouping in the American social order. When the call for a Social Gospel came forth in the late nineteenth century, this embryonic class was in the throes of making an uneasy transition from a rural, agrarian culture to an urban, industrial one. Its members felt rootless and insecure as a result of that transition. The cry to transform the very fabric of American life relied on strong, aggressive, charismatic leaders—those identified above—who wrote, spoke, and argued relentlessly for justice and reform. And although Social Gospel advocates did not see the world itself as inherently evil, they did decry a world fraught with evils and did not hesitate to identify those evils and those persons thought responsible for them—generally the wealthy capitalist class which had gained power through oppressive treatment of the urban laborer. Hence the Social Gospel evinces all the qualities expected in an apocalyptic movement.

Dispensationalists and their fundamentalist heirs, while aghast at many of the same social sores, regarded the signs of progress lauded by the Social Gospelers not as harbingers of an evolution into the Kingdom, but as omens of the decay and disaster believed attendant on the collapse of moral order which would immediately precede the return of the Christ in judgment. Dispensationalism had its origins in the thinking of an Englishman, John Nelson Darby, a leader of one faction of a movement known as the Plymouth Brethren. Darby lectured widely in North America, reacting strongly against the wave of biblical criticism which followed on the scientific and intellectual advances of the late nineteenth century. Darbyites argued that the new approaches quite simply reduced the Bible to being a book among books rather than elevating it as the Book of Books. Treating the Bible as literal, inerrant truth, and aided by the unique dating of biblical prophecies promulgated by C.I. Schofield in his annotations to the King James Version, dispensationalists maintained that the whole of history should be divided into periods ("dispensations") which transpired in a fixed order from creation to apocalypse. Many believed that the present age was the final dispensation before the end and that history would soon culminate in the Parousia.[41]

Darby's reinterpretation of history aroused much interest. A spate of conferences ensued to promote study of the Bible, a study which explored how biblical prophetic teaching and specific historical incidents could be correlated. The biblical literalism espoused at these conferences merged with a resurgent conservatism rebelling against liberal optimism to produce the style of Christianity known as fundamentalism.[42] What distinguished fundamentalist expressions of apocalyptic fervor from many earlier surges was the reluctance of believers to abandon their established religious affiliations. Most did not break away from their denominations, as many earlier apocalypticists had seemed eager to do, but remained within them, serving as leavening to raise questions of prophetic fulfillment and as a stumbling block to any who would adopt a more liberal approach to apocalyptic revelation. Hence it is impossible to speak of fundamentalists as a discrete group. Rather, one must speak of fundamentalist Baptists, fundamentalist Methodists, fundamentalist Presbyterians, fundamentalist independents, and the like. Fundamentalists may be found in all major denominations and dominate many of the smaller ones.

Fundamentalism gained credulity largely because of controversies in the early decades of the twentieth century. One dispute concerned the teaching of theories of biological evolution in the public schools of Tennessee in 1925. Another was dubbed the "Fundamentalist—Modernist Controversy" and saw Harry Emerson Fosdick, a vocal supporter of the new critical methods of analyzing biblical texts, cast out of his pulpit at New York City's First Presbyterian Chruch and, with considerable outside assistance, founding the famous Riverside Church in Manhattan. Both episodes involved outspoken rejection of the intellectual currents buttressing more liberal attitudes, the presumably decadent social trends of the 1920s, and the confidence in future progress which seemed a hallmark of much scientific and religious thought. The appeal of the fundamentalists spanned the continent, but gained an especially warm reception in the South and Southeast, stamping Southern Christianity with a conservative tone which endures to the present.

Fundamentalists, because of their affirmation of scriptural inerrancy and the literal interpretation of biblical texts, loudly reasserted orthodox apocalyptic teaching. While few responsible fundamentalist leaders rushed to set dates for the coming cataclysm, many relied heavily on the symbols of the Parousia, the sense of the shortness of time remaining before the Last Judgment, and the conviction that dire consequences awaited those who refused to believe to exhort listeners to repent. History was near its end; the Lord could return at any moment.

As a cross-denominational presence, fundamentalism gained even greater currency amid the social upheaval which swept American society in the late 1960s. In that era, its most public manifestation was the so-called Jesus Movement. Mainly attracting young adults disaffected by both mainline churches and the counterculture, the Jesus Movement dressed fundamentalism in a hip disguise. The result was a Christian alternative to the style associated with political protest, drug use, fascination with forms of Eastern religions, and so forth. More importantly, not only were these facets of counterculture life rejected by the various groups within the Jesus Movement, they were themselves interpreted as blatant signs of the nearness of the end. As Ronald M. Enroth and his collaborators reported:

> Everything in the Jesus Movement is colored by [an] apocalyptic mentality. Bumper stickers flaunt it; songs repeat it; witnessing returns to it over and over again; sermons and personal conversations are obsessed by it. Typical is Larry Norman's song "I Wish We'd All Been Ready," which envisions a married couple being separated by the rapture, since one member is saved and one is not. The standard handbill passed out on Hollywood Boulevard by the Christian Foundation team reads, "Repent Now. Jesus is coming soon." Chuck Smith, pastor of Calvary Chapel, says,
>
>> The last days are upon us, and the Spirit of God is being poured out upon us. And it's just God's plan. It's just coming to completion. The Bible is full of prophetic utterances which describe the last times, and we can see that the world's really living in a whole lot of chaotic, bad ways. You want to call it sin. That's what the Bible would call it. It's prophesied in the Bible that the Lord will pour the Spirit down upon all men, and I believe that it won't be long until we see the Second Coming of the Lord.[43]

The Jesus Movement groups, more than the fundamentalism absorbed by the denominations, exhibit all the traits of apocalypticism. Virtually every group centers around a highly charismatic, authoritarian leader or leaders. David Berg of the Children of God, Tony and Sue Alamo of the Christian Foundation, and "Daddy" Jack Sparks of the Christian World Liberation Front are only a few examples. Each has donned the prophetic mantle to proclaim a gospel of simple salvation and of impending apocalypse. Each has structured a comprehensive understanding of history and society which paints the world as evil, requires tight control of behavior, sees danger on all sides, and offers followers a secure identity only within the confines of group membership. Each has gained a hearing among those who feel out of place in mainstream society.

Billy Graham, like many fundamentalist prophets, has continually predicted the imminent end of the world: "I sincerely believe that the Lord draweth nigh." "We may have another year, maybe two years," he said in 1950, "to work for Jesus Christ, and [then], ladies and gentlemen, I believe it is all going to be over.... Two years, and it's all going to be over." Two years later he said, "Unless this nation turns to Christ within the next few months, I despair of its future."[44] Billy Graham, like revivalists from the time of Dwight L. Moody on, heavily utilizes hymns and gospel songs to implant this message in the subconscious of his audiences. Indeed, the popularity of gospel songs since the late nineteenth century may well account for the pervasive presence of apocalyptic expectation in American religion today, for many of the hymns emphasize the coming of the Lord in judgment and glory and the subsequent end of history.[45] Witness the following:

> Jesus may come today.
>   Glad day, Glad day!
> And I would see my Friend;
>   Dangers and troubles would end
> If Jesus should come today.
>   Glad day. Glad day!
> Is it the crowning day?
>   I'll live for today, nor anxious be;
> Jesus, my Lord I soon shall see.
>   Glad day. Glad day!
> Is it the crowning day?

> And, Lord, haste the day when the faith shall be sight,
> The clouds be rolled back as a scroll,
> The trump shall resound and the Lord shall descend,
> "Even so"—it is well with my soul.

> One day He's coming, for Him I am longing;
>   One day the skies with his glory will shine;
> Wonderful day, my beloved ones bringing;
>   Hope of the hopeless, this Jesus is mine.
> Living, He loved me; dying, He saved me;
>   Buried, He carried my sins far away;
> Rising, He justified, freely forever;
>   One day He's coming—O glorious day!

> When the trumpet of the Lord shall sound,
>   and time shall be no more,
> And the morning breaks, eternal, bright and fair;
>   When the saved of earth shall gather
>   over on the other shore,
> And the roll is called up yonder, I'll be there.[46]

While not suggesting a chronology for the apocalypse, these lyrics convey to the popular mind a lively awareness that the Parousia may well be at hand and that the end, whenever it comes, should generate rejoicing among believers, for they will share the glory of the Lord when he returns. The power of the hymns in perpetuating chiliastic hopes rests in their being the common property of American Protestants, particularly of those within the evangelical circle. Through repeated use, the hymn texts enter the subconscious and assume a subtle, but real, psychological authority. They represent in familiar form what preachers like Billy Graham argue in more sophisticated fashion. Because of their familiarity, the gospel songs may be a more accurate expression of religious Americans' conception of the apocalypse than the teachings of the Jehovah's Witnesses, for example, or the preaching of fundamentalist clergymen. The apocalyptic hope remains strong, its place in American religion guaranteed through popular hymnody.

V

Since the immigration of the Puritans to the New World, Americans have looked forward to an apocalyptic culmination of both their own history and the history of all mankind. The expectation has fostered much hope and much despair—hope for the glory beyond, despair at the necessary tribulations along the way. The assurance that the divine close of history is real has led thinkers of various stripes to search for signs to determine how near that end might be and where the reign of the triumphant Christ would begin. Not surprisingly, many have speculated that the United States was chosen by God to inaugurate the rule of the Lord on earth. Groups such as the Shakers have believed that the Second Coming has already occurred in some fashion and that believers were already living in the millennial kingdom. Others—individuals like William Miller and groups like the Jehovah's Witnesses—have been so caught up by apocalyptic fervor that they have worked assiduously to place human history within a time-table of biblical prophecies of the end and developed a sense of urgency to complete work on earth since time soon would be no more. Apocalypticists who fixed dates for the final cataclysm have suffered disappointment, but their followers have reorganized as frequently as they have disbanded in despair. Present day groups such as the Christadelphians, Seventh-Day Adventists, and Jehovah's Witnesses, for example, all owe their existence to leaders who were sure of how and when the Christ would return. Among the oppressed, apocalyptic hopes have occasionally helped revitalize a sense of peoplehood, as the revelation in the Ghost Dance did among the Sioux.

Not all who have awaited the coming kingdom have expected a sudden irruption in human affairs. Social Gospel leaders, among others, confidently expected progress to lead humanity gradually into the apocalyptic age. Social Gospel advocates remained within the churches, rather than splitting off into separate sects as have most of the fundamentalists, who viewed the technological and industrial developments which excited Social Gospelers as a sure sign of the decay which would precede the sudden return of the Christ. More recently, younger fundamentalists who have called themselves Jesus People have also found decay and corruption wherever they looked, thus forming small enclaves under authoritarian leaders in order to remain holy for that day when the Lord will appear.

Wherever apocalypticism has taken hold in American life, it has generally come from the teaching of charismatic figures who saw the world as a perpetual battleground between good and evil, who argued for the necessity of leading pure lives in anticipation of the end, and who gathered a following from among those who perceived themselves as strangers in the world around them. But it is no doubt accurate to assert that apocalyptic hope has been kept alive within the heart of American Christianity, at least in its Protestant forms, through a heritage of popular hymnody which extols the imminent Parousia. Dreams of a future when the vagaries of history will vanish and the faithful will live in rapture have inspired religious folk in America since the Puritans began to erect their "city on a hill" in seventeenth century Massachusetts. To understand the vitality of American religion, one must hear the echoes of an apocalypticism which boldly proclaims the advent of a new order and eagerly awaits its dawning.

Notes

¹Norman Cohn, *The Pursuit of the Millennium*, rev. ed. (New York: Oxford University Press, 1970).

²See also Ira V. Brown, "Watchers for the Second Coming: The Millenarian Tradition in America," *Mississippi Valley Historical Review*, Vol. XXXIX, No. 4 (December 1952), 443. Also see H. Richard Niebuhr, *The Kingdom of God in America* (New York: Harper and Brothers, 1937), pp. 127-63.

³Mary Douglas, *Natural Symbols: Explorations in Cosmology* (New York: Vintage Books, 1973). Categories developed by British anthropologist Mary Douglas also help illuminate infatuation with the apocalypse. Douglas speaks of two characteristics of societies or of identifiable clusters within them: "group" and "grid." By "group" she means quite simply group pressure or the degree to which a society or sub-society is able to enforce conformity to its own established behavioral norms. A society manifesting "high group" would have clearly delineated boundaries restricting to a minimum the range of approved behavior and the means of defining one's identity. Conversely, a society with "low group" sense would have few limits on acceptable behavior and identities and little if any pressure to conform to norms. The matter of "group" for Douglas is intimately connected with some sort of system of socially shared symbols which are used to interpret and organize one's experience as a member of society. The system of classifications of a particular society Douglas labels "grid." As with "group," "grid" may be high or low. The determinants of strength (high) or weakness (low) are the scope and coherence of the particular symbol system. The more that one's experience comes together in a meaningful whole, the higher the "grid"; while the fewer the aspects of life which are granted intelligibility or the greater the number of apparently viable symbol systems within a society, the lower will be the sense of "grid." With regard to apocalypticism, it may be claimed, in Douglas' terms, that interest in the end of chronological time and life in another realm of reality occurs when the dominant social forces exhibit a sense of "group" which is low and of "grid" which is high. In Douglas' lexicon, apocalypticism should demonstrate "high group" and "low grid," features opposite to those of a social order regarded as dominant but oppressive (pp. 77-92). Also see Sheldon R. Isenberg and Dennis E. Owen, "Bodies Natural and Contrived: The Work of Mary Douglas," *Religious Studies Review*, Vol. III, No. 1 (January 1977), 1-17.

⁴Max Weber, *Sociology of Religion*, trans. Ephraim Fischof (Boston: Beacon Press, 1964), pp. 46-59. Weber's and my use of the term charismatic differs from its less precise use among religious groups today which stress such ecstatic phenonema as speaking in tongues.

⁵See Brown, p. 444. Also see Perry Miller, "The End of the World," *William and Mary Quarterly*, 3rd Ser., Vol. VIII, No. 2 (April 1951), 171-91, and Joy B. Gilsdorf, "The Puritan Apocalypse: New England Eschatology in the Seventeenth Century (unpublished Ph.D. dissertation, Yale University, 1964).

⁶See, for example, John Cotton, *The Churches Resurrection* (London: Printed by R.O. and G.D. for Henry Overton, 1642), his *The Pouring Out of the Seven Vials* (London: Printed by R.S. for Henry Overton, 1642), and his *An Exposition Upon the Thirteenth Chapter of the Revelation* (London: Printed for Livewel Chapman, 1655); Thomas Shepard, *The Parable of the Ten Virgins Opened and Applied* (London: Printed by J.H. for John Rothwell and Samuel Thomson, 1660); Increase Mather, *The Mystery of Israel's Salvation Explained and Applied* (London: Printed for John Allen, 1669), and his *A Discourse Concerning ... the Glorious Kingdom of the Lord Jesus Christ, on Earth, Now Approaching* (Boston: Printed by B. Green, for Benj. Eliot, 1710); Ephraim Huit, *The Whole Prophecie of Daniel Explained* (London:

Waiting for the End 61

Printed for H. Overton, 1644); William Aspinwall, *A Brief Description of the Fifth Monarchy, or Kingdome That Shortly Is to Come into the World* (London: Printed by M. Simmons, 1673); and Thomas Parker, *The Visions and Prophecies of Daniel Expounded* (London: Printed for E. Paxton, 1646).

[7] Michael Wigglesworth, "God's Controversy with New England," *Proceedings of the Massachusetts Historical Society,* Vol. XII (1871-73), 83-93; reprinted in Conrad Cherry, ed. *God's New Israel* (Englewood Cliffs: Prentice-Hall, 1971), pp. 44-54.

[8] Wigglesworth, *The Day of Doom; or, a Poetical Description of the Great and Last Judgment* (New York: American News Co., 1867), pp. 22-23.

[9] David D. Hall, "Understanding the Puritans," in *Religion in American History: Interpretive Essays,* ed. John M. Mulder and John F. Wilson (Englewood Cliffs: Prentice-Hall, 1978).

[10] See James W. Davidson, *The Logic of Millennial Thought: Eighteenth-Century New England* (New Haven: Yale University Press, 1972).

[11] Jonathan Edwards, *The Great Awakening,* Vol. IV of *The Works of Jonathan Edwards,* ed. C.C. Goen (New Haven: Yale University Press, 1972), p. 353.

[12] Edwards, *Apocalyptic Writings,* Vol. 5 of *The Works of Jonathan Edwards,* ed. Stephen J. Stein (New Haven: Yale University Press, 1977).

[13] Edwards, "History of the Work of Redemption," in *The Works of President Edwards,* ed. Sereno E. Dwight (New York: S. Converse, 1928), III, 325.

[14] On the development of apocalyptic thought in the work of Edwards' disciple, Samuel Hopkins, see Samuel Hopkins, *A Treatise on the Millennium* (Boston: Isaiah Thomas and Ebenezer T. Andrews, 1793).

[15] Prominent among these interpreters are Perry Miller, Alan Heimert, Richard Bushman, J.M. Bumsted, and Dietmar Rothermund. See the excerpts from their writings in Darrett B. Rutman, ed., *The Great Awakening: Event and Exegesis* (New York: John Wiley and Sons, 1970).

[16] Niebuhr, p. 143.

[17] See Nathan O. Hatch, *The Sacred Cause of Liberty: Republican Thought and the Millennium in Revolutionary New England* (New Haven: Yale University Press, 1977). The interplay of apocalyptic expectation and nationalistic sentiment has been scrutinized in James F. Maclear, "The Republic and the Millennium," in *The Religion of the Republic,* ed. Elwyn A. Smith (Philadelphia: Fortress Press, 1971), pp. 183-216.

[18] Ezra Stiles, *The United States Elevated to Glory and Honour* (New Haven: Thomas and Samuel Green, 1783).

[19] For examples, see Timothy Dwight, *The Duty of Americans, at the Present Crisis* (New Haven: Thomas and Samuel Green, 1798), p. 31, and his *A Sermon Delivered in Boston, September 16, 1813* (Boston: S.T. Armstrong, 1813), pp. 19-20, 25-26. In the latter work, Dwight suggested that the millennium would commence "not too far from the year 2000."

[20] See Part II of Cherry's *God's New Israel;* Jedediah Morse, "An Address to the Christian Public," *Panoplist and Missionary Magazine United,* Vol. IV (November 1811), 244; Mark Hopkins, *Miscellaneous Essays and Discourses* (Boston: T.R. Marvin, 1847), pp. 442-43; and William G. McLoughlin, *Revivals, Awakenings, and Reform* (Chicago: University of Chicago Press, 1978), pp. 98-140.

[21] The apocalyptic dimension in Mormonism is noted by Fawn M. Brodie, *No Man Knows My History: The Life of Joseph Smith* (New York: Knopf, 1945), pp. 101-2, while chiliastic beliefs among utopian communalists (including the Oneida Perfectionists) are stressed in Arthur E. Bester, Jr., *Backwards Utopias: The Sectarian Origins and the Owenite Phases of Communitarian Socialism in America, 1663-1829,* 2nd ed. (Philadelphia: University of Pennsylvania Press, 1970).

[22] The most comprehensive statement of early Shaker teaching is Benjamin S. Youngs *The Testimony of Christ's Second Appearing* (Lebanon, Ohio: From the Press of John M'Clean, 1808). The standard secondary treatments include the

numerous works of Edward Deming Andrews and Faith Andrews. See, especially, Edward Deming Andrews, *The People Called Shakers*, rev. ed. (New York: Dover Publications, Inc., 1963). See also Marguerite Fellows Melcher, *The Shaker Adventure* (Princeton: Princeton University Press, 1941). The interpretation developed above is amplified in my "The Shaker Quest: On the Threshold of Purity," in *American Religion: 1974,* comp. Edwin S. Gaustad (Missoula, Mont.: Scholars' Press, 1974), pp. 18-29.

[23]Andrews, pp. 161-69.

[24]There is relatively little literature on the Christadelphians. The two most readily accessible, albeit brief, treatments are Bryan R. Wilson, *Sects and Society* (Berkeley: University of California Press, 1961), pp. 219-354, and Fred J. Powicke, "Christadelphianism," *Encyclopedia of Religion and Ethics,* ed. James Hastings, (New York: Scribner's, 1955), III, 5, 569-71. See also my "The Christadelphians in America" (unpublished M. Div. thesis, Union Theological Seminary, 1968).

[25]John Thomas, *Elpis Israel: Being an Exposition of the Kingdom of God* (From the English edition, New York: Fowlers and Wills, 1951).

[26]Miller developed his thinking most comprehensively in *Evidence from Scripture and History of the Second Coming of Christ, About the Year 1843* (Troy, N.Y.: Kemble and Hooper, 1836). Also see Edwin S. Gaustad, ed., *The Rise of Adventism* (New York: Harper & Row, 1975).

[27]Much popular mythology has the Millerites donning robes and waiting on rooftops to be whisked away into the air when the Christ appeared. No evidence supports this contention. See Whitney R. Cross, *The Burned-Over District: The Social and Intellectual History of Enthusiastic Religion in Western New York, 1800-1850* (Ithaca: Cornell University Press, 1950), p. 306, and Ira V. Brown, "The Millerites and the Boston Press," *New England Quarterly,* Vol. XVI, No. 4 (December 1943), 592-614.

[28]Elmer T. Clark, *The Small Sects in America*, rev. ed. (New York and Nashville: Abingdon Press, 1965), p. 39.

[29]John L. Shuler, *Is the End Near?* (Nashville and Atlanta: Southern Publishing Association, 1928), pp. 45-46, 80, 110.

[30]A somewhat dated, but still superb, summary of the doctrines of the Jehovah's Witnesses may be found in Chapter Ten of Charles S. Braden, *These Also Believe* (New York: Macmillan Co., 1949).

[31]Quoted in James Mooney, *The Ghost-Dance Religion and the Sioux Outbreak of 1890,* ed. Anthony F.C. Wallace (Chicago and London: University of Chicago Press, 1965), p. 2.

[32]Mooney, *passim,* and Anthony F.C. Wallace, *Religion: An Anthropological View* (New York: Random House, 1966), pp. 165, 210. Also see Paul Bailey, *Wovoka, the Indian Messiah* (Los Angeles: Westernlore Press, 1957); David H. Miller, *Ghost Dance* (New York: Duell, Sloan and Pearce, 1959); Robert M. Utley, *The Last Days of the Sioux Nation* (New Haven: Yale University Press, 1963); Weston LaBarre, *The Ghost Dance* (New York: Dell, 1972); George A. Dorsey, *The Arapaho Sun Dance* (Chicago: Field Museum of Natural History, 1903); and Joseph G. Jorgensen, *The Sun Dance Religion: Power for the Powerless* (Chicago: University of Chicago Press, 1972).

[33]The absence of any discussion of apocalypticism in Albert J. Raboteau's definitive *Slave Religion: The "Invisible Institution" in the Antebellum South* (New York: Oxford University Press, 1978), is telling. In a personal conversation, Prof. Raboteau confirmed the present writer's belief that apocalypticism was nearly nonexistent in slave religion.

[34]Joseph R. Washington, Jr., *Black Sects and Cults: the Power Axis in an Ethnic Ethic* (New York: Doubleday, 1972), pp. 58-82.

[35]Raboteau, pp. 243-66. Also see Lawrence Levine, "Songs and Slave

Consciousness," in *Anonymous Americans: Explorations in Nineteenth-Century Social History,* ed. Tamara K. Hareven (Englewood Cliffs: Prentice-Hall, 1971), pp. 99-130; LeRoy Moore, Jr., "The Spiritual: Soul of Black Religion, *Church History,* Vol. XL, No. 1 (March 1971), 79-81; and Joseph R. Washington, Jr., *Black Religion: The Negro and Christianity in the United States* (Boston: Beacon Press, 1964), pp. 206-20.

[36]The thematic idea links Washington's earlier *Black Religion* with his *Black Sects and Cults.*

[37]Standard surveys of the Social Gospel movement include C. Howard Hopkins, *The Rise of the Social Gospel in American Protestantism, 1865-1915* (New Haven: Yale University Press, 1940); Henry F. May, *Protestant Churches and Industrial America* (New York: Harper and Row, 1949); and Ronald C. White, Jr. and C. Howard Hopkins, *The Social Gospel: Religion and Reform in Changing America* (Philadelphia: Temple University Press, 1976). A fine anthology of source materials is Robert T. Handy, ed., *The Social Gospel in America, 1870-1920: Gladden, Ely, Rauschenbusch* (New York: Oxford University Press, 1966). For the Catholic story, see Aaron I. Abell, *American Catholicism and Social Action: A Search for Social Justice, 1865-90* (South Bend: University of Notre Dame Press, 1963); Robert D. Cross, *The Emergence of Liberal Catholicism in America* (Cambridge: Harvard University Press, 1958); and Thomas T. McAvoy, ed., *Roman Catholicism and the American Way of Life* (South Bend: University of Notre Dame Press, 1960).

[38]This theme is prominent in Josiah Strong, *Our Country* (1886), ed. Jurgen Horbst (Cambridge: Harvard University Press, 1963), and in his *The Twentieth Century City* (New York: Baker and Taylor, 1898).

[39]See the closing chapters of *Our Country* as well as Strong's *The New Era or the Coming Kingdom* (New York: Baker and Taylor, 1893).

[40]*Christianity and the Social Crisis,* ed. Robert D. Cross (1907; New York: Harper and Row, 1964), p. 422.

[41]A sketch of the impact of dispensationalists is provided in Robert T. Handy, *A History of the Churches in the United States and Canada* (New York: Oxford University Press, 1976), pp. 290-1.

[42]Ernest R. Sandeen, *The Roots of Fundamentalism: British and American Millenarianism, 1800-1930* (Chicago: University of Chicago Press, 1970), carefully assesses the various sources of this peculiar form of religious conservatism.

[43]Ronald M. Enroth, Edward E. Ericson, Jr., and C. Breckenridge Peters, *The Jesus People: Old-Time Religion in the Age of Aquarius* (Grand Rapids: William B. Eerdmans Publishing Co., 1972), pp. 179-80. Also see Robert S. Ellwood, Jr., *One-Way: The Jesus Movement and Its Meaning* (Englewood Cliffs: Prentice-Hall, 1973), pp. 86-96, and Lowell D. Streiker, *The Jesus Trip: Advent of the Jesus Freaks* (Nashville and New York: Abingdon Press, 1971).

[44]McLoughlin, p. 190. Also see his *Billy Graham: Revivalist in a Secular Age* (New York: Ronald Press, 1960).

[45]See Sandra S. Sizer, *Gospel Hymns and Social Religion: The Rhetoric of Nineteenth-Century Revivalism* (Philadelphia: Temple University Press, 1978).

[46]All are taken from texts found in *Billy Graham Crusade Songs,* comp. Cliff Barrows (Minneapolis: Billy Graham Evangelistic Association, 1957).

III.
The Development of America's Sense of Mission

Ernest Cassara

> This people ... is the hope of the human race.
> Turgot (1778)[1]

THE EUROPEANS who came to the "New World" brought with them intellectual as well as other kinds of baggage. Columbus, for instance, was convinced that he had reached the fabled realms of the East. A total of four voyages from Spain to the Caribbean did nothing to disabuse him of the notion that he had reached his original goal. He had not the slightest idea of what he had actually done, but attempted to fit what he saw during his several voyages into his preconceived ideas of the Orient.[2] Those who came to the New World after Columbus to take advantage of his "discovery" also brought with them preconceptions, imposing on the new hemisphere their own expectations nurtured in Europe, the product of their experience in the Old World rather than the New. Only gradually did they accept their new environment for what it was, rather than what they had projected onto it. In the course of this essay I shall examine some of the major ideas the colonists brought with them and indicate how they were altered and adapted in their new surroundings. It was in this process that we see the beginnings of what develops into an American national ideology.

America from the beginning of colonization served as a haven for groups that were unwilling to live with certain pressures in the Old World. The Puritans, who proved to be the most influential group in the formation of the American character, believed that they were in a covenantal relationship with God, and, consequently, that their community was to serve as a model to others. The idea that America was the product of divine providence was one of their bequests to future generations. This Hebraic concept of the covenant, with the passage of time, accrued to it the apocalyptic elements that have played a recurring role in Christian history. Even though these, and related ideas, have undergone mutations in

The Development of America's Sense of Mission   65

the course of three hundred years, I shall attempt to show that they have persisted and have become part of an American ideology.

Let us begin by examining the crucial role played by the Puritans who migrated to the New England shore in 1629-30. In what follows, it may appear that I am neglecting the earlier settlements of Virginia and Plymouth in choosing to concentrate on Massachusetts. Certainly the settlement and survival of Virginia encouraged other ventures in colonization. Once the gold craze had passed, Virginians accepted the reality of their physical environment. There were among them many capable men, but it is not until the eighteenth century that Virginians play an important role in the formation of the American outlook on life.

The people of Plymouth are not so much neglected in what follows as taken for granted. As the left-wing of the Puritan movement in England, as "Separatists" from the Church of England, they were a relatively small and penniless group with little influence at home or during their stay in the Netherlands. On the American side of the water they were soon overwhelmed in numbers, wealth and influence by their Massachusetts Puritan neighbors to the north. They had the satisfaction of watching as the Puritans—despite protestations to the contrary—in effect separated from the Church of England also, and adopted the congregational form of church government similar to that at Plymouth. Plymouth may have been undistinguished at the time, with relatively little influence, but it avoided the worst extremes of Puritan bigotry as it was exemplified by Massachusetts.

It is an irony of history, also, that it was from this relatively obscure and unlettered group that the first classic of American literature came. With all of the intellectual fire power of the people of the Bay and their hundreds of publications, it is Governor William Bradford's *History of Plymouth Plantation* which has captured the imaginations of the American people.[3] It is also ironical that in the minds of Americans in the process of creation of a national myth, the people of Massachusetts have been absorbed into the little group of Separatists at Plymouth and have been given the appellation used by Bradford in passing: Pilgrim. Despite this popular assumption, however, the fact of the matter is that the intellectual strivings of Massachusetts Bay were the most formative influence on the development of what became the United States and it is on that group we shall concentrate, choosing for discussion from their history those elements which were to have most influence in shaping American thought and attitudes.

The ideal for Massachusetts Bay was expressed even before the main body of the settlers arrived in 1630. On board the *Arbella* on the voyage across the ocean, John Winthrop set forth the expectations of those in control of the venture in a lay sermon, "The Modell of Christian Charity."[4] The significance of the sermon was in his formulation of the role that the colony was to play in the world. Winthrop described the obligations that various social classes owed each other. It was an ordered, stratified society that he envisaged—certainly there was no hint of the democracy that emerges later—a society in which each level acted in loving kindness toward the others and in which each knew its place. Alluding to a passage in the Sermon on the Mount he called on his fellow believers to establish "a city upon a hill"[5] which would set an example of Christian living for all the world to see, but most particularly for their fellow Puritans left behind and the Anglicans who had resisted their most persistent attempts to reform the English church.

It is difficult for us in the twentieth century to put ourselves back into the mode of thinking of a previous age and especially difficult if the age in question lies on the other side of the eighteenth-century Enlightenment which drastically altered the world view of the Western world. To enter the mind of the Puritan is to enter a vastly different cosmology, one in which it was possible for a group to conceive itself under contract with the Deity to follow a particular mode of life and be rewarded for it. Obviously, the Puritans were not the first, nor the last, to believe that they had a direct line to God. Their inspiration, of course, was Hebraic, it was to be found in the Old Testament where they read that the nation Israel had had a covenant with Yahweh. The fact that Israel was not notably successful in living up to its part of the bargain did not discourage the Puritans from believing that they could do so. From the beginning, then, the group that was to predominate in the whole northeast section of what became the United States believed that it was the chosen people of God. This fact was to have a profound influence on the development of the American mentality. Long after Winthrop was in his grave Puritan influence was felt, for it was his descendants who dominated American literature and who consequently spread Puritan attitudes where they might otherwise not have taken root.

The Puritan covenant with the Deity was conceived as a

The Development of America's Sense of Mission 67

corporate one. It was important, of course, for individuals to live the good life, not in the hope of individual reward only but because the very existence of the community was at stake. The covenant with God was a community contract and the community had to uphold its part of the bargain or suffer punishment as the Israelites of old had suffered when they had gone astray. The Bible was filled with examples of the consequences of non-performance. The outbreak of smallpox and other diseases, Indian wars, natural disasters such as earthquakes, even fires raging through Boston, were seen as signs of God's displeasure with the community. The soul searching we associate with Puritanism was not confined to the individual. There was community soul searching as well. Church councils analyzed the lapses in community life and suggested corrective measures. The Reforming Synod of 1679 is a prime example. The church leaders produced a catalogue of the failings of the society which pictured Boston and environs as a variety of Sodom and Gomorrah. Among the many sins catalogued were apostasy, spiritual pride, pride in fancy clothing, neglect of worship, sleeping during prayer, oaths and swearing, tale bearing, back-biting, intemperance, lawsuits, the "Idolatrous practice of health-drinking," gaming, over-charging in business, naked necks and arms, "naked Breasts, and mixed dancing...."[6] Our prurient interest feeds on such historical documentation. How much stock a historian should put in such an analysis, of course, is another matter. I suspect this condemnation was weighted with homiletic hyperbole. But for the Puritan leaders communal perfection was the goal: if the society did not live up to expectation, serious punishment and the wrecking of their holy community would result.

The struggle was not only against the garden variety of sin. From the earliest days the leaders sought to protect the covenant by imposing strict ideological purity on the community: an internal threat to the corporate covenant was posed when fellow saints within the community raised unsettling challenges to the presuppositions of the leadership. This is why the objections to Puritan practice by Roger Williams and Anne Hutchinson—just to name the more famous non-conformists—loomed so large in the infant community. Williams' insistence that the Puritan colony should openly separate from the Church of England and its episcopal government, and Mistress Hutchinson's insistence that the colony's leaders were following a covenant of works rather than a covenant of faith, and that she experienced direct revelations from

God, promised to disrupt the order which the leaders were struggling valiantly to establish. Although, initially at least, the leadership considered both to be saintly persons, they saw no alternative but to banish them as a threat to the corporate covenant.[7]

The flight of Williams and Hutchinson and their followers to the south to what evolved into the contentious colony of Rhode Island confirmed the leadership's worse fears. Rhode Island was a theological cesspool that the Puritans had to put up with, for, with his winning ways, Roger Williams talked the British government into granting him a charter. Changeable in theological views, in politics and business he displayed much acumen. Permission was granted in 1644 to join surrounding communities with Providence in a union which created Rhode Island under a "democratical" charter.

Williams and Hutchinson were internal threats to Puritan order, in the sense that they were dissenters among their fellow Puritans. An "external" threat was posed by the coming from the outside of members of groups that had an antipathy to the Puritan persuasion: such left-wing groups of the Reformation as Baptists and Quakers. We shall limit ourselves to the latter as an example of what the people of Massachusetts Bay had to contend with. To understand why the Puritans were upset by the incursion of the Friends, we must remember that the quietism we associate with the present-day Quakers was not characteristic of them in the seventeenth century. Their very nickname apparently was given them by those who scoffed that they quaked under the alleged spirit of the Lord. Such an emotional, noisy lot—aside from questions of ideology—were unlikely to be received kindly by the much more restrained Puritans. They did not appreciate the tendency of the Quakers to rise in the middle of a church service to challenge the preachments of the minister, or their wearing sackcloth and ashes as a commentary on the state of the Puritan commonwealth. The running of Quaker ladies nude through the streets of Massachusetts Bay towns—an interesting, not to say provocative, form of protest in any age—they did not think conducive to public order.[8] They showed their disapproval by banishing them from the colony. When they insisted on returning time and again, the Puritan leaders thought they had no recourse but to hang the offenders on Boston Common.

Some of the saints sought to depart from Massachusetts in peace. Almost from the beginning, pressure on the leaders to allow

The Development of America's Sense of Mission 69

the migration was intense. After the cramped quarters of the Old World, the New seemed to offer unlimited possibilities for expansion. This can be no better illustrated than in the petition of early settlers of Newtowne (Cambridge) to the Great and General Court of Massachusetts to be allowed to move on, since they felt crowded. They felt crowded, significantly, in both acreage and ideology. Having secured permission to move down the Connecticut Valley, where they founded Hartford in 1636, they gained not only more land to spread out on but the ability to establish a colony that reflected their own particular ideas. What the founders of Connecticut did was to be replicated time and again. The constant movement of the frontier was to become a feature of American life and the promise that it offered to Europeans as individuals, or as groups which were feeling the pressure of religious or economic deprivation, was great. The hope held out by the New World was a new experience for Europe as well.

A later generation of Bay Staters erected a statue of Anne Hutchinson—with eyes raised to heaven, holding a child by the hand, with a Bible in the other—in front of the Massachusetts State House in Boston, a symbol it may be supposed of recompense by a more liberal age for the intolerance of the fathers. What later generations tended to forget, however, was that the Puritans of New England were intolerant on principle. Intolerance was part of their contract with God. They had moved across the ocean to erect in New England the English church in purified form. To maintain that purity in the face of both internal and external threats, intolerance became state policy.

Only those who had gone through a conversion experience, and convinced the members of the church that it was genuine, were allowed to "own the covenant" and join that select group of believers. All the residents in a community, however, were expected to attend worship. This was an attempt to maintain and improve the tone of the community and to keep its members in line. Also designed to promote stability was the provision made early on that only church members would be allowed to exercise the franchise. The state would then be in the hands of the ideologically pure.

The Simple Cobler of Aggawam, by the sometime American Puritan clergyman and lawyer Nathaniel Ward, among other matters of concern to the Puritans, dealt with dissent. He made it clear that the Puritans had set up their colony for themselves and felt no obligation to welcome elements disruptive of their plan, for tolerance of error in belief is plainly a design of the devil. "I dare take upon me, to be the Herauld of *New-England* so farre, as to proclaime to the world, in the name of our Colony, that all Familists, Antinomians, Anabaptists, and other Enthusiasts, shall have free Liberty to keep away from us, and such as will come to be gone as fast as they can, the sooner the better."[9]

However it was guarded against, as we have seen, dissent did arise, both from internal and external sources. The attempts to stem it were to come increasingly under criticism from England, especially after the Civil War and its aftermath, when the English themselves learned to live with dissent. In the end, however, it was not the challenge posed by dissenters that led to change in Puritan ways, nor criticism from abroad, but rather a strain felt within the system itself. It grew from the experience of many in the second and third generations who did not feel as strong a compunction to conversion as had their parents. In Puritan theory, of course, conversion was the free gift of God, without any initiation on the part of the subject. Indeed, the decision had been made before the individual was born (predestination) and—in the strictest interpretation—even before the creation of the world. That was the theory. A present-day social psychological perspective might suggest a reason why the number of conversions fell off. The younger generation, not having experienced as their parents had persecution in the mother country, and enjoying the relative security of America, felt less pressure for the change of heart that conversion would bring. Fewer, therefore, had the experience, even among those who were living upright lives and, from every other perspective, should have been reckoned among the Elect.

The consequences for the state and society were potentially devastating. Membership in the church was, after all, highly prized by the first generation. A slackening off of church membership, serious for that institution, of course, would have dire consequences for the state as well, since suffrage was tied to church membership. A means had to be found to counter this trend. The Half-Way Covenant was the controversial solution suggested. While not meeting all the needs of the society, it would at least keep the churches going. A person leading a good life, but who had not yet had the conversion experience, would be allowed to "own the covenant" and present his children for baptism, thus perpetuating the church. He could not, however, sit at the "Lord's table" (participate in the communion) or vote in church affairs. It was

The Development of America's Sense of Mission

fervently hoped, of course, that he would be converted sooner or later (in God's good time), but for now at least it was thought the future of the church was assured.

This solution was not appealing to all. It certainly spelled the watering down of earlier standards—a declension it was called—and the issue was bitterly fought, dividing churches and the community. In 1662, however, a gathering of church leaders formally approved it, though in some places the dispute continued. A declension it may have been in their eyes, but from our perspective it was a sign of liberalization. Whether this departure would have spelled ultimate doom of the City upon a Hill we shall never know, for other events were to intervene.

In the first generation the Puritans struggled with the enormous task of establishing a new society in a hostile environment. The difficult soil of New England insured that they would not emulate the plantation life of Virginia. The much more rigorous climate of the northeast also insured that their farming would never go beyond the subsistence level and that they would have to turn to other ventures as well. It was shipping, shipbuilding and fishing that primarily brought economic success. This generation did an impressive job of hewing out of the wilderness a setting for a new civilization. Although their creed demanded that their thoughts always be on God, given their circumstances, it was inevitable that they give much thought to worldly matters. A city on a hill, like all cities, required much building and maintenance of physical facilities, and much attention to political arrangements. The second and third generations were at greater ease in Zion, however, and subject to the temptations that come with wealth. As we have seen, such meetings as the Reforming Synod of 1679 made a wholesale condemnation of the wickedness that had developed in society. The emergence of the jeremiad—a ritualistic discourse which lamented the declining morals of the Puritan society—tells us much about the mood of the second and third generations: the leaders of the churches believed that the children were falling away from the high ideals and performance of the fathers. The most talented of them all at lamentation, Cotton Mather, makes this a major theme of his famous ecclesiastical history of New England, the *Magnalia christi americana*.

It is probably no accident that apocalyptic and eschatological ideas come to the fore in this period. The increasing conviction of declension, of the inability to perform like Winthrop and the first generation, had prompted the hope of divine intervention to put things right. God, after all, had intervened time and again when the Israelites had failed to observe the conditions of the covenant. Cotton Mather and his equally famous father, Increase, were probably the prime exponents of this approach. There is an anomaly in Cotton Mather, a Fellow of the Royal Society, eagerly promoting inoculation against smallpox and seeking to make other contributions to eighteenth-century science, yet looking to extraterrestrial forces for the salvation of society. As Perry Miller has so brilliantly put it, the Mathers marched into the Age of Reason loudly proclaiming the end of the world.[10]

That apocalyptic tendencies became widespread, however, is attested by the remarkable popularity of Michael Wigglesworth's *Day of Doom*, a best seller from its publication in 1662. Apparently it was read and recited vividly by all age groups. Its colorful, dread imagery, of course, contributed much to its success. Wigglesworth painted a picture of vile wretches in their cups, and unwise virgins who let their lamps run low on fuel, and a degenerate society that was generally not prepared for the coming of the Lord:

(5)
For at midnight brake forth a Light, which turn'd the night to day,
And speedily an hideous cry did all the world dismay.
Sinners awake, their hearts do ake, trembling their loynes surprizeth;
Amaz'd with fear, by what they hear, each one of them ariseth.

(6)
They rush from Beds with giddy heads, and to their windows run,
Viewing this light, which shines more bright then doth the Noon-day Sun.
Straightway appears (they see't with tears) the Son of God most dread;
Who with his Train comes on amain to Judge both Quick and Dead.[11]

The temptation to quote all 224 stanzas must be resisted. Of the same quality as Dante's *Divine Comedy* this verse is not. But it conveys the full power of Puritan conviction. The separation of the sheep and goats and "the unsufferable torments of the damned"[12] are vividly pictured, as are the glowing rewards of those who had remained pure: "...God above in arms of love doth dearly them embrace." Lest it be suspected that such an embrace might pale in comparison with the pleasures of sin on earth, Wigglesworth assures his readers that such bliss will not "grow stale through frequency of use...."[13]

Apocalyptic thought, of course, predates Christianity, having arisen among the Jews, as seen in the Book of Daniel and, especially, in the literature of the Intertestamental period, which is to be found in the Apocrypha and Pseudepigrapha. St. Paul's letters in the New Testament—the earliest writings in that collection—make it clear that he expected the return of Christ on the clouds of heaven and the end of the world in his own lifetime. Paul died in approximately A.D. 60. Toward the close of the century, however, the eschaton having failed to occur, Christians began to adapt the faith to this new reality. The Gospel of John, considered by scholars to be from this period, makes it clear that belief in Jesus Christ assures eternal life. Although the author gives lip service to the eschaton, it is clearly not his prime concern. The revised message takes its place: believe and immediately you will be saved. Under such circumstances, the date of the eschaton becomes less important to believers. There have been notable flourishes of expectation of the end from time to time over the centuries since, with predictions of precise dates, all of which had to be explained away or reinterpreted after the failure of the eschaton to come as announced. This phenomenon recurred in the United States, especially in the nineteenth century, and has its adherents in our own time. Examples of this approach to religion are given in Professor Lippy's essay in this collection.

It should be pointed out that the Puritans—indeed, Europeans generally—had not coped with extensive woodlands such as those found in America. It was but a short leap to the conclusion that the dark, threatening woods were a favorable environment for the nefarious deeds of the age-old enemy of mankind. The devil's lure was powerful, as attested to them by the witchcraft that broke out in Salem in 1692 (just to name the most familiar example). The hanging of witches was an attempt to rid society of the demon's minions.

How convenient it was, as well, to see in the aborigines another servant of the archfiend. The ambivalent attitude of the Puritans toward the Indians was demonstrated time and again. The efforts of the saintly John Eliot to convert them to Christianity and thus strike a blow against Lucifer and for the kingdom of light had strong support in the community. On the other hand, belief that the red man was the tool of the devil was bound to ease consciences when the Puritans thought it necessary to engage in slaughter. The Indians, indeed, posed an enigma to Puritan theologians. How could the red man have failed to be informed of the soteriological act of Christ? Why was he left out of the Christian dispensation? On this, as on most other things, Cotton Mather engaged in speculation. The devil, he wrote in the *Magnalia*, was responsible for "seducing" the Indians in America. His purpose was to get them "and their posterity out of the sound of the *silver trumpets* of the *Gospel*, then to be heard through the Roman Empire...."[14]

The uncertainty generated by the loss of the Massachusetts Bay charter in 1684 probably contributed to apocalyptic speculation. If the children had lost the nerve and conviction of Winthrop and the fathers, if the effort to erect the "city upon a hill" to which they aspired had been aborted by the incorrigible waywardness to which man was subject, it is understandable that the Mathers and others might fall back on old Christian modes of thinking and would hope for divine intervention to make possible what human hands had so obviously failed in accomplishing. It would be too much to expect that the restored Stuart monarchy would look kindly on their old Puritan enemies in their haven in New England and not try to punish Massachusetts Bay, a colony which was notably lacking in the spirit of cooperation with royal authorities. The alienation between England and Massachusetts went much deeper, however. The English experience of the Civil War and the Protectorate of Cromwell had wrought a profound change in attitudes in the mother country. Cromwell had been particularly tolerant of religious diversity and had allowed even the most noisy groups their head. The growing spirit of tolerance infected the English Puritans and a gulf developed between them and their intolerant brothers in New England. The actions of the New Englanders in mistreating dissenters gave Puritanism a bad name, complained their brothers back home.

The new charter of 1691—from the government of William and Mary, following the Glorious Revolution which drove the last Stuart, James II, from the throne—deprived Massachusetts leaders of the power to control events. The most notable feature of that instrument was a prohibition against making church membership a prerequisite for voting. From here on in, those who met a property qualification were to have a say in the government regardless of the quality of their spiritual lives. With all kinds and conditions of men allowed to participate, gone was the opportunity to achieve the ideal Winthrop had stated on the *Arbella* sixty years before.[15]

In our day, when many Americans are tolerant or indifferent to matters of religion, we tend to judge our Puritan forebears harshly, disappointed that they were men of their time and not twentieth-century liberals. They are judged too harshly. There was a nobility in their voyage across a wide, dangerous ocean and their mighty struggle in a "howling wilderness" to erect, in effect, a city of God on earth. There is poignancy in the fact that, like all attempts before and since, they were not allowed to succeed, largely because of the encroachments of a hostile world around them.

This necessarily brief and selective survey of American beginnings has revealed certain themes that play a continuing role in American thought. The American Puritans' presumption that they were to serve as a model to others was one of their great bequests to future generations. The attitude long outlived the loss of their "audience" in England and is stamped indelibly on the American character. Of course, it would not have survived were it not that later developments sustained the belief and even strengthened it. We shall consider these below.

A concomitant of this was the idea of America as a haven. It served as an asylum for those who considered themselves oppressed. This was certainly true of the Plymouth Colony and of Massachusetts Bay. As much as the latter group may have objected, America served as a haven for other dissenters as well. When they did not get their way in Massachusetts, they created havens of their own. Rhode Island is the earliest example. Later, however, she is joined by Pennsylvania. William Penn consciously set out to create a haven for his fellow English Quakers. Good businessman that he was, however, he knew that Friends were too few adequately to populate his extensive land grant. Therefore he turned his efforts to attracting religious dissenters on the Continent, groups that were being persecuted by the Catholics on the one hand and by Protestants (Lutherans and Calvinists) on the other. German pietistic groups from such areas as the Palatinate responded enthusiastically to the offer of freedom of belief and cheap land. (In Revolutionary times that most prominent of Pennsylvanians, Benjamin Franklin, estimated that one-third of the colony was German-speaking.)

The American colonies, generally, became the object of migration by dissenting groups. Welcomed or not by the established Anglican churches of the South, Presbyterians came there in large numbers as they did to the North. French Huguenots, escaping Louis XIV's revocation of the Edict of Nantes in 1685, joined in the migration. Other dissenting groups, such as Baptists, Methodists, Unitarians, and Universalists, migrated from abroad, but also arose indigenously.

At the same time that the established Calvinistic churches of the New England colonies (excluding Rhode Island, of course) and the established Anglican churches in some of the Middle Colonies and the South sought to control thought, the proliferation of dissent made it impossible. The dissenters, up and down the coast, were quite insistent on their right to worship as they chose, no matter how vigorously the colonial governments and established churches attempted to impose uniformity. This insistence became stronger in the eighteenth century, especially in Revolutionary times. The favoritism in law and custom enjoyed by the established churches and their clergy was bitterly resented by the dissenters. In several of the states they won important concessions from the standing order but did not cease their clamor until they achieved full equality. Their struggle was a strong impetus to separation of church and state following the Revolution.

On one point, however, established and dissenting groups agreed: the behavior in the community should be subject to a strict moral code. We tend to associate this notion with our Puritan heritage, but in this regard the Puritans were merely men of their time. Anglicans and Puritans might disagree on some social matters—on whether games could be played on Sunday, for instance—but in most matters of morality they and dissenting groups were of one mind.

Between the founding of the colonies and the Revolution of 1776 there stood less than two hundred years. The difference between the world view of the first colonists and that of the founders of the nation, however, is immense. In this period the scientific revolution was profoundly secularizing the outlook of educated Americans. Obviously one sees the continuities in Christian culture from one age to the next, but one is tempted to remark that the differences between the world views held by, say, John Winthrop and Thomas Jefferson would have to be measured in light-years. The influence of the modern scientific revolution was so profound that the very nature of God was transformed. The God of the Puritans who gave man's life on earth His personal attention, who was intervening in human history, rewarding and punishing the actions of men and nations as He so pleased, is reformed—in the minds of men—to a Creator who has, after the analogy of the watchmaker, created the world and set it working according to a natural law. His creation's

The Development of America's Sense of Mission

workings are regular, predictable. While earlier Christian centuries found their revelation between the covers of the Scriptures, the men of Enlightenment found theirs in the regular workings of this universe, the operations of which were obvious to them, they believed, because of the instrumentality of God-given reason, that is, reason working on the raw material of empirical observation. It is this latter characteristic that spells the real difference between the old and the new science. Galileo Galilei, to take a good example, set about the task of verifying the theories of Copernicus empirically by observing the workings of the heavens through the recently-developed telescope. The interplay of empirical observation and the application of reason explains—as best a thing so remarkable can be explained—the accomplishment of Isaac Newton. Sir Isaac was to put his imprint on the Age of Reason, during which he, in effect, became a household god.

If man could observe and figure out natural workings of the universe with reason unaided by Scripture, so, it was believed, he could observe and figure out what God required in the moral sphere as well. The writings of the deists affirm their faith that man learns ethical behavior in the same manner as he learns about nature: by observation, by trial and error. The God who observes such stumbling about by men obviously is quite different in His nature from His predecessor. Gone is the impatient, wrathful deity of earlier times. Indeed, this new deity is infinitely benevolent. He loves His children and seeks to happify them.

This was the intellectual world in which the men of the Enlightenment lived.[16] Remaining constant however, throughout, was the belief that America was a very special place. The Winthropian City upon a Hill was freed from its Calvinist coloring but it survived. The Puritans had hoped for the divine establishment of heaven on earth in America; by the late eighteenth century, God's direct intervention no longer seemed necessary for the establishment of heaven on earth in America. Of course Christian doctrine has never encouraged the view that this world is a good place in which enduring happiness can be expected, and the Puritans, with their Calvinist belief in God's arbitrary election of those to be saved at the Last Judgment, were pessimistic indeed about the improvement of this world by mere human means. But for the American revolutionaries—our "founding fathers"—this world was not a vale of tears in which to await the initiation by God of His kingdom on earth, but rather a place where material and physical reality held great future promise. The idea of progress began to supplant God's revealed schedule of events as the ethical principle motivating history's movement: human intellect and effort and the approbation of a distant prime mover seemed quite enough to guarantee a secular heaven on earth to future generations of Americans. Nevertheless, the American dream as framed by Thomas Jefferson in the Declaration of Independence is a direct, secular extension of the Puritans' biblical teleology. Thus America became in the minds of the oppressed and disadvantaged of Europe a symbol of hope, a land of economic and political, as well as spiritual opportunity, a chance to break with the past and start a new life.

This vision of America is evidenced in much of the literature of the Revolutionary period. Possibly its strongest expression is to be found in the writings of Thomas Paine, who was himself a recent immigrant and who rose from obscurity in England to a role of great importance as an advocate of revolution shortly after his transfer to the New World. It was his personal experience, no doubt, as well as the developing ideology of the Revolution, which led him to proclaim America as a haven for the oppressed of all the world.

The immediate purpose of his tract *Common Sense* (1776) was to persuade those Americans who were still on the fence to come down on the side of revolution. We have the word of prominent contemporaries that it was quite effective. Dr. Benjamin Rush, the Philadelphia physician whose home served as a center for some of the more notable revolutionaries (the cousins John and Samuel Adams, Thomas Jefferson, among others) urged Paine to write the tract, since Paine presumably had little to lose and he much.[17] Washington, who was already in the environs of Boston as leader of the American forces, was sure that the combination of bombardment of American coastal towns by the British and Paine's pamphlet would have the effect of convincing the hesitant that there was no choice. He himself had been accustomed to toasting the king's health at his officers' table, a custom which, after reading *Common Sense* he gave up.[18]

Paine had the exquisite gift of being able to take a complex idea and translate it into memorable prose which appealed to both the elite and the common man. His treatment of the subject of monarchy is a good example. He held up to scorn the very notion of monarchy itself, picking as examples some of its most absurd characteristics. As for the monarchy of England, it stemmed from that "French bastard" William of Normandy, who crossed the Channel with his "banditti" and seized the British throne in 1066. Paine asked if, in truth, the Conqueror was not "in plain terms a very paltry rascally original" for the present occupant of the British throne whom he represented as a "royal brute."[19] Poor George! When Paine was finished with him, it was difficult for Americans again to take seriously his royal pretensions. Paine also appealed to latent American nationalism. America had come of age, he said. There was something basically ludicrous about the tiny island of Britain telling expansive America how to run its affairs, something absurd in the image Paine projected of three million Americans trooping down to the shore each time a British ship docked to hear what measure of liberty they were to be allowed! What is most striking for our purposes is that Paine did not confine himself to the self-interest of Americans, but, rather, pictured the new United States—as he christened them—to be a haven, "an asylum" for the oppressed of all nations. Liberty had been stamped out on every continent but America:

O ye that love mankind! Ye that dare oppose, not only tyranny, but the tyrant, stand forth! Every spot of the old world is over-run with oppression. Freedom hath been hunted round the globe. Asia, and Africa, have long expelled her, Europe regards her like a stranger, and England hath given her warning to depart. O! receive the fugitive, and prepare in time an asylum for mankind.[20]

Not only was America a refuge for those who sought liberty, but, according to Paine, America had the opportunity, because of her favored position, to do something never before possible in human history. America could "begin the world over again."

Jefferson's Declaration of Independence claimed that that was exactly America's intention. The idea of a social contract was an abstraction for European intellectuals. Among Americans, however, it was taken for granted, for it was part of their own experience: with them the idea had become flesh. They could point to the compact adopted on the *Mayflower* in 1620 when it became clear that it was to land well to the north of the patent held by the Virginia Company. Their compact pledged that they would not go off on their own—as some had threatened—but together create a community. In a sense the Puritans to the north of them in Massachusetts Bay a decade later formed a compact as well: a covenant which they conceived they had made with their God. In that case it was a decision by the leadership to transform the charter of a stock company granted them by the crown into a frame of government for Massachusetts Bay, a clear act of rebellion against the Stuarts. Connecticut is another case in point. When Thomas Hooker and his associates received permission of the Massachusetts Bay Great and General Court in 1636 to move to the Connecticut River, Hartford became the main town of the new settlement. The *Fundamental Orders* (1639) was the first written constitution to serve as a basis for a government in this country.

The Americans, then, could claim some experience with the social contract. If their experience was not exactly what the theorists had in mind, it was close enough. When confronted with the tyranny of the British government in the 1770s, therefore, they knew how to respond. They would break the bonds that tied them to England because the monarch had abused his power and mistreated his loyal subjects. Where in the debate over taxation the Americans had claimed their rights as Englishmen, Jefferson now proclaimed their natural rights as human beings. The argument no longer had the petty implication that the colonists were too cheap to pay through taxation their share of the cost of the French and Indian War, but had been lifted to cosmic proportions: "When in the course of human events, it becomes necessary for one people to dissolve the political bands which have connected them with another, and to assume among the powers of the earth, the separate and equal station to which the Laws of Nature and of Nature's God entitle them, a decent respect to the opinions of mankind requires that they should declare the causes which impel them to the separation."

The rights which the Americans were claiming for themselves were declared to be God-given and unalienable—could not be taken from them. They had the right to dissolve an oppressive political contract and to form a new one among themselves. Jefferson held out more than a new form of government. Free men, in a free country, were to be guaranteed not only life and liberty, but conditions which would allow them to pursue happiness. This was indeed a revolutionary proposition. Never before in history had a government conceived its function in such terms. For that matter, never in all of Christian history had such a radical idea been entertained. Christianity had fostered the notion that life was spent in a vale of tears, in a trial of virtue, and only in the afterlife, it was conceived, would such an unearthly state as happiness be possible.

The God of the Enlightenment apparently saw things differently than the God of earlier centuries. Although deists scoffed

The Development of America's Sense of Mission

at the notion of revelation through the Scriptures (which they rejected as the product of superstition of an unenlightened age), they were firm in their conviction that the world was the creation of a benevolent God who wished them well here and hereafter. Nature and Nature's God, to whom Jefferson referred, were benevolent and smiled on that part of Nature called man. There was no room in their worldview for a covenantal relationship between an elect group and God, there was no room for apocalyptic and eschatological expectations which were so foreign to cool reason and part and parcel of the superstitions of Christianity which they rejected out of hand. It must be noted that the Enlightenment was restricted to relatively few men and women of intellect (although historians have christened the age in their name). Enlightenment attitudes, however, crept into various other levels of society and undermined old beliefs, religious and secular. The result was that apocalyptic and eschatological expectations became the province of religious fringe groups in American society.[21] Characteristics of apocalyptic thinking in secularized form, however, continued as part of the mindset of some Americans (as emerges in other essays in this collection). The majority of Americans accepted the idea of progress which stemmed from the Enlightenment and the promise of modern science and technology. This blended nicely with the natural optimism of Americans who looked forward to the taming of a new and rich continent. The tendency to look on the bright side of things became a strong component in the American makeup. Exuberance over America and its potential is a theme common in the writings of Americans of the time. This optimism was not often shared, or even understood, by Europeans whose history gave them little to look forward to.

The American attitude toward Europe, on the other hand, was ambivalent. Two examples of this ambivalence are seen in the careers of Franklin and Jefferson. Benjamin Franklin, who spent many years in England as an agent (lobbyist) for several American colonies and who enjoyed the congenial company of fellow "natural philosophers" (scientists) of the Royal Society and other pleasures of English society, could contemplate spending the rest of his days there. Mrs. Franklin refused to cross the ocean, however, and ultimately the worsening relations between Britain and the colonies forced on him the hard choice of coming down on the side of independence and necessarily returning home. During much of the war, however, he enjoyed the pleasures of French society while serving as a diplomat for the American states.

Jefferson, with his omnivorous appetite for learning, could also enjoy the cultural circles of France as an American minister at the conclusion of the Revolution, but he was not enthusiastic at the prospect of Americans receiving an education in Europe. Not only were their morals in danger, but there was the threat that they would be dissatisfied with their own country upon their return to it. His response to the question of an American as to the best place to study, written from Paris in 1785, expresses his view in a cogent manner:

> Let us view the disadvantages of sending a youth to Europe. To enumerate them all would require a volume. I will select a few. If he goes to England he learns drinking, horse-racing and boxing. These are the peculiarities of English education. The following circumstances are common to education in that and the other countries of Europe. He acquires a fondness for European luxury and dissipation and a contempt for the simplicity of his own country; he is fascinated with the privileges of the European aristocrats, and sees with abhorrence the lovely equality which the poor enjoys with the rich in his own country: he contracts a partiality for aristocracy or monarchy; he forms foreign friendships which will never be useful to him, and loses the season of life for forming in his own country those friendships which of all others are the most faithful and permanent: he is led by the strongest of all the human passions into a spirit for female intrigue destructive of his own and others happiness, or a passion for whores destructive of his health, and in both cases learns to consider fidelity to the marriage bed as an ungentlemanly practice and inconsistent with happiness: he recollects the voluptuary dress and arts of the European women and pities and despises the chaste affections and simplicity of those of his own country; he retains thro' life a fond recollection and a hankering after those places which were the scenes of his first pleasures and of his first connections; he returns to his own country, a foreigner, unacquainted with the practices of domestic economy necessary to preserve him from ruin; speaking and writing his native tongue as a foreigner, and therefore unqualified to obtain those distinctions which eloquence of the pen and tongue ensures in a free country; for I would observe to you that what is called style in writing or speaking is formed very early in life while the imagination is warm, and impressions are permanent.[22]

Jefferson's letter to his old law teacher and political collaborator, George Wythe, written from Paris in August, 1786, is a perfect example of his negative attitude toward the Old World and his great hope for the New:

> The European papers have announced that the assembly of Virginia were occupied on the revisal of their Code of laws. This, with some other similar intelligence, has contributed much to convince the people of Europe, that what the English papers are constantly publishing of our anarchy, is false; as they are sensible that such a work is that of a people only who are in perfect tranquility. Our act of freedom of religion is extremely applauded. The Ambassadors and ministers of the several nations of Europe resident at this court have asked of me copies of it to send to their sovereigns,

The Development of America's Sense of Mission 83

and it is inserted at full length in several books now in press; among others, in the new Encyclopedie. I think it will produce considerable good even in these countries where ignorance, superstition, poverty and oppression of body and mind in every form, are so firmly settled on the mass of the people, that their redemption from them can never be hoped. If the almighty had begotten a thousand sons, instead of one, they would not have sufficed for this task. If all the sovereigns of Europe were to set themselves to work to emancipate the minds of their subjects from their present ignorance and prejudices, and that as zealously as they now endeavor the contrary, a thousand years would not place them on that high ground on which our common people are now setting out. Ours could not have been so fairly put into the hands of their own common sense, had they not been separated from their parent stock and been kept from contamination, either from them, or the other people of the old world, by the intervention of so wide an ocean. To know the worth of this, one must see the want of it here. I think by far the most important bill in our whole code is that for the diffusion of knowledge among the people. No other sure foundation can be devised for the preservation of freedom, and happiness. If any body thinks that kings, nobles, or priests are good conservators of the public happiness, send them here. It is the best school in the universe to cure them of that folly. They will see here with their own eyes that these descriptions of men are an abandoned confederacy against the happiness of the mass of people. The omnipotence of their effect cannot be better proved than in this country particularly, where notwithstanding the finest soil upon earth, the finest climate under heaven, and a people of the most benevolent, the most gay, and amiable character of which the human form is susceptible, where such a people I say, surrounded by so many blessings from nature, are yet loaded with misery by kings, nobles and priests, and by them alone. Preach, my dear Sir, a crusade against ignorance; establish and improve the law for educating the common people. Let our Countrymen know that the people alone can protect us against these evils, and that the tax which will be paid for this purpose is not more than the thousandth part of what will be paid to kings, priests and nobles who will rise up among us if we leave the people in ignorance...."[23]

Jefferson's negative attitude toward Europe was probably shared by most Americans and has continued down to the twentieth century. It is much too soon to say that it has been eliminated as a result of the intimate involvement of the United States in European affairs, especially since World War II.

It is well known that John Adams, looking back in 1818 on the events that led to independence, concluded that the real Revolution had transpired in the hearts and minds of the Americans even before the war broke out, and when the colonists realized that England did not have their interests at heart, the bonds which held the two people together were broken.[24] His close friend, Dr. Benjamin Rush, also thought the Revolution and the war were distinct events. He believed that the Revolution had a social impact that went much beyond the war, an impact that was continuing on after the war. He saw Americans as in a plastic state, due to the heat generated by the Revolution. It was crucial that advantage be taken of the situation before the heat was dissipated and the opportunity for molding plastic Americans into true republicans was lost.[25] This explains the urgency that he, Jefferson, Noah Webster and others felt for the creation of an educational system which would prepare the Americans for self-government.

The word "system" is misleading, however, since, from the beginning, American education has been a local affair. Jefferson's plan of education, for instance, which he urged Wythe to promote (in the letter quoted above), was designed for Virginia. It was based on the idea that, if American liberty was to survive, the people must be educated to protect it. A strong component of historical study was included, therefore, Jefferson believing that that would prepare the people to recognize threats to liberty when they appeared. Jefferson's plan provided for universal education at the elementary level, with a provision for advancing the most able students, regardless of family wealth, on to higher levels, with the choice few reaching the university at the pinnacle of the structure. The cream of the crop he assumed would be prepared to emerge as leaders of this democratic society.[26] The system was to be supported by tax money at the county level, which best explains why it was not implemented. The conservatives who dominated the county governments felt no imperative to educate the children of the poor. They took care of their own—if they bothered at all—using tutors or plantation schools.

Rush's plan for universal education for Pennsylvania was similar in several respects to Jefferson's. Although it was not to be implemented in every detail, it did lead to universal education up to a certain age. The pattern of settlement in compact towns in the Northern and Middle States, compared to the extensive plantation settlement of Virginia and the South, goes far toward explaining the relative success of universal education there. It was also a matter of attitude. Here, too, we see the strong influence of Puritanism living on in its insistence that each person be capable of reading the Scriptures for himself. The practical effect of this position was a government-mandated and -supported school system.

It was in the post-Revolutionary years that Noah Webster began his career as "school master to America." Despite the fact that control of education was to be maintained at the local level, his influence was national, indeed was a nationalizing force. His *Dictionary*, first published in 1806, was to have a profound influence in creating an American version of the language. At a different level, his "blue-backed" spellers and his grammars molded the way young Americans learned their tongue.

Webster believed that the common man would insist on participating in government and, therefore, should be prepared by the schools for this task. American history and government, therefore, were to be a central part of the curriculum. Webster advocated that the child learn to "lisp" the names of Washington and other heroes of the Revolution at the same time that he recited his ABCs.[27] The Webster schoolbooks, thus, instilled in young Americans the faith that America was a very special place in the scheme of things. The message was reinforced by the long line of readers produced later in the nineteenth century by William Holmes McGuffey which included a fair number of patriotic pieces.[28]

For the American adult of the nineteenth century, the ten volumes of the *History of the United States* published by the politician-diplomat-historian George Bancroft (1800-1891) provided cosmic assurance of America's mission in the world. In this romantic version of the Whig view of history, the seed of democracy which originated in the forests of Saxony and was planted in England during the Anglo-Saxon migrations was transplanted by the colonists on the shores of America where it came to full flower, a plant tended by the divine hand. Bancroft left no doubt that Jacksonian democracy was the ultimate expression of God's plan for mankind.

The heritage of the eighteenth-century Englightenment and its doctrine of progress, the success of the American Revolution, the stability achieved by the republic under the Constitution of 1787, the seemingly endless land and resources of the West—these were responsible for the overcoming of the dour outlook of the predominant Calvinism. American character was stamped with an optimism and an orientation toward the future which have been leading features of American society and which, as pointed out above, have puzzled other less fortunate peoples. Even the bloody Civil War did not succeed in overcoming the belief in progress and American optimism. Since that war was ultimately interpreted as a struggle to rid the nation of the evil of slavery, as well as a fight to preserve the Union, it acted instead as a positive reinforcement.

The belief that America occupied a unique place in the scheme of things and that it was a haven for the oppressed was reinforced in the nineteenth century by the thousands of Europeans who opted for a new beginning in the New World. Many came for the most basic of reasons: they wanted to eat. Their Old World homes were abandoned when their national economies could not meet this most basic of expectations. To take one notable example: when continuous attacks of potato blight resulted in widespread famine in Ireland, increasing numbers scraped meager resources together and ventured across the ocean to America. Many thousands who had known nothing but rural life became inhabitants of the United States coastal cities, simply because they had no money to move inland. The same was true of other national groups, of course. On the other hand, several of the groups—the Germans, for instance— had resources sufficient to allow them to push inland to the rich soil of the middle section of the nation and attempt to duplicate there the better aspects of their lives in their fatherlands.

Although we tend to associate the migration motivated by economic troubles with the nineteenth century, J. Hector St. John de Crevecoeur had already noted it in the late eighteenth century:

> In this great American asylum, the poor of Europe have by some means met together, and in consequence of various causes; to what purpose should they ask one another what countrymen they are? Alas, two thirds of them had no country. Can a wretch who wanders about, who works and starves, whose life is a continual scene of sore affliction or pinching penury—can that man call England or any other kingdom his country? A country that had no bread for him, whose fields procured him no harvest, who met with nothing but the frowns of the rich, the severity of the laws, with jails and punishments, who owned not a single foot of the extensive surface of the planet? No! Urged by a variety of motives, here they came. Everything has tended to regenerate them: new laws, a new mode of living, a new social system; here they are become men: in Europe they were as so many useless plants, wanting vegetative mould and refreshing showers; they withered, and were mowed down by want, hunger, and war; but now, by the power of transplantation, like all other plants they have taken root and flourished! Formerly they were not numbered in any civil lists of their country, except in those of the poor; here they rank as citizens.[29]

Crevecoeur, in his *Letters from an American Farmer*, may have been the first to hold up the ideal of America as a melting pot:

> What... is the American, this new man? He is neither an European, nor the descendant of an European, hence that strange mixture of blood, which you will find in no other country. I could point out to you a family whose grandfather was an Englishman, whose wife was Dutch, whose son married a French woman, and whose present four sons have now four wives of different nations. *He* is an American, who, leaving behind him all his ancient prejudices and manners, receives new ones from the new mode of life he has embraced, the new government he obeys, and the new rank he holds. He becomes an American by being received in the broad lap of our great Alma Mater. Here individuals of all nations are melted into a new race of men, whose labours and posterity will one day cause great changes in the world.[30]

Economic necessity, however, was not the only impetus to migration. Hatred of politically oppressive regimes was responsible for attracting to America individuals whose great talent was to be responsible for molding important aspects of American life. The failure of the liberal revolutions of 1848 was particularly significant in this regard. In these years Germans made up a particularly large percentage of the immigrants. For example, Carl Schurz was to leave the Rhineland and emerge in the American Midwest as a significant politician who went on to serve as a diplomat, a Union general, a senator and a cabinet officer. Isaac Mayer Wise, to take another example, after his migration from Bohemia was a shaper of Reform Judaism in America. His long career was most closely associated with Cincinnati where, among many other accomplishments, he founded the Hebrew Union College.[31]

Those who came to the United States because of both economic and political reasons had to accommodate to the fact that America was not perfect, that the streets were not paved with gold—as apparently was believed by some peasant types (who, being peasants, should have known better). But, on balance, conditions were so much better than in the fatherlands that they made their peace with the reality of the situation. It was much easier to accomplish because the United States offered one thing that was lacking in the Old World: promise. There was the promise that with hard work—and, in many cases, luck—they could enjoy a much higher standard of living than theretofore. That, at least. The greater hope, of course, was the possibility of true wealth. A national myth developed that millionaires were being made every day, that one could go from rags to riches. The migrations of so many nationalities to America were conceivably the greatest in history. The resulting mix of people could have dire consequences, but the idea of America as a place of opportunity for all, although it did not overcome all ethnic frictions, was by then part of the national ideology.

The skepticism, not to say cynicism, of the middle twentieth century has made light of the nineteenth-century ideal of the melting pot. The claim has been made that ethnic ties were as strong as ever and melding of the population did not really take place to any appreciable extent. This proposition is doubtful. It may be true that third and fourth generation Americans are seeking their "roots" in the Old World and are sentimentally making much of their origins. But a fondness for macaroni does not an Italian make.

Nor a fondness for Munchner beer a German. Whatever the nostalgia for the past, no notable number has chosen reverse migration to live in the relatively crude surroundings of, say, a Sicilian village. Blacks, with the rise of African nations to world attention, understandably are expressing a desire to trace their origins, but that they are Africans or would be comfortable with a "return" to that continent is highly unlikely. With any of the national or so-called ethnic groups, one has only to challenge their "Americanism" to discover their real allegiance. One need only point to the extensive intermarriage among national groups in the second and successive generations to see how wrongheaded such assertions of continued isolation are.

The idea of America as an asylum continued strong in the nineteenth century. It had its most notable expression in "The New Colossus" of Emma Lazarus, the last lines of which are inscribed on the pedestal of the Statue of Liberty:

> Give me your tired, your poor,
> Your huddled masses yearning to breathe free,
> The wretched refuse of your teaming shore,
> Send these, the homeless, tempest-tost to me,
> I lift up my lamp beside the golden door![32]

The sonnet, which has perpetuated the author's fame, still holds a firm place in the sentiment of the American population, despite the fact that, from 1924 to the present, legislation has severely restricted the flow of the oppressed to the famous haven.

The great influx of immigrants to the northern cities coincided with the quickening pace of industrialization following the Civil War. It was in these years that the United States began its transformation from a predominantly rural and agricultural to a predominantly urban and industrial nation. The immigrants, the "older" Americans moving from the farms, provided the manpower needed for the transformation, and American intellectuals, most notably William Graham Sumner, provided intellectual justification for the harsh realities of a raw industrial society. The strain of laissez-faire, free enterprise, which is found in American thinking was greatly magnified in these years. So much so that some Americans mindlessly asserted that free enterprise and

The Development of America's Sense of Mission

America were one. The necessity for collectivistic action by government in the depression of the 1930s thus met much resistance from those who insisted that the New Deal amounted to a betrayal of the nation.

At the same time that the United States was welcoming thousands of newcomers to her shores, she was resolutely expanding west. The notion of "Manifest Destiny" fit very well with the conviction that the United States had a special mission in the world. There is no reason to believe that the country could not have lived a prosperous and comfortable life east of the Mississippi River, the border settled in the very generous terms yielded by Britain at the close of the Revolution. She would have had two extensive coasts and an excellent river system. However, the Americans in the old Northwest (present Middle West) feared control of the Mississippi by another nation would work to their disadvantage, since whoever controlled the river and its mouth could control American shipping from the West. Furthermore, the Americans had developed a voracious hunger for land, a luxury denied to crowded Europeans. The Louisiana Purchase, arranged between President Jefferson and Napoleon at the beginning of the nineteenth century—one of the great land deals of history—inevitably drew the population to the trans-Mississippi West.

When Mexico stood in the way of the national aspiration to extend from ocean to ocean, it proved relatively easy to pick a quarrel and to deprive her of more than two-fifths of her national domain. This included what became the states of Arizona, Nevada, California and Utah, and parts of New Mexico, Colorado and Wyoming. Of course the question of the accession to the United States of "independent" Texas (formerly Mexican territory) was one of the issues that led to the Mexican War (1846-1848). There were vigorous protests by some Americans at this outrageous treatment of a weaker neighbor, but if one's destiny were claimed to be manifest, critics stood little chance of rousing many consciences to action. The dispute between the United States and Britain over the Oregon question was settled amicably, the British realizing that American hunger for real estate being what it was, she would be at a distinct disadvantage in competing at such a distance.

The purchase of "Seward's Icebox" in 1867, if not exactly demanded by Manifest Destiny, was accomplished relatively easily. Although some asked what in heaven's name Americans needed with such a presumed barren waste as Alaska, the hunger for land was insatiable—and the purchase would accomplish the subsidiary goal of getting the Russians out of North America.

When Americans ran out of continent to conquer, some looked elsewhere. There were those in the United States who advocated expansion in the Caribbean area. Although filibustering expeditions to Cuba, Mexico and Nicaragua in the 1850s got nowhere, the Spanish-American War at the close of the century proved a boon to advocates of imperialism. Conveniently, such national expansion could be justified on the ground that "little brown brothers" of Cuba, the Philippines, etc., would benefit from American eleemosynary efforts. Since these brethren were under the rule of the Spanish, Americans could not quite claim to be Christianizing them—no matter what the predominant Protestant may have thought of the papal version of the faith—but they could nevertheless pretend to save them by teaching them the ways of democracy.

It can be objected that in its imperialistic efforts in Cuba and the Philippines, the United States was merely reflecting an international trend. The nations of Europe were busily engaged in gobbling up large expanses of land and populations in Africa and the Far East. Although this was the case, the nations of Europe were more hard-headed about the economic justification of their expansionist efforts.

The most persuasive proof that can be offered that the immigrants of the nineteenth century were truly absorbed into the American ideology is to be seen in the national unity Americans maintained when their government involved them in wars against the homelands from which they came. Although there was opposition to the world wars, it came more from those who were convinced that the United States was being sucked into arguments not of its own making. Reasserted in this particular opposition were the old suspicions of Europe as degenerate and beyond redemption. It was not reasonable for Americans to become involved in warfare which was just another expression of ancient quarrels.

The American desire to teach the world its superior way of life certainly played a strong part in its involvement in the first and second world wars. The cry that America was "to make the world safe for democracy" reflected the conviction that this nation was unique. Woodrow Wilson's promulgation of the Fourteen Points (1918) was squarely in the American tradition in its insistence on

The Development of America's Sense of Mission   91

self-determination for the national groups which were parts of the Austro-Hungarian Empire.[33] This was a reassertion of the American belief in the social contract. Wilson, in his herculean effort to persuade the nation to join the League of Nations, was a true representative of American attitudes. He has been severely criticized by some scholars for his so-called "messianic" notions, but, if he had them as charged, he was merely reflecting the American conviction that the United States was superior to the rest of the world. Those who effectively blocked Wilson's efforts to persuade America to join the League of Nations can be seen as representing another strain of American thought that held Europe in thorough suspicion.

It is a short ideological step from America's crusade to make the world safe for democracy to its struggle against fascism in World War II. If anything, the disillusionments of the inter-war period, and its conviction that Europe had made a shambles of things yet again, resulted in a greater assurance of American purity. When involvement did come, therefore, it was again with the conviction that the Americans had a "job to do" in smashing an evil Hitler and his cohorts in the Axis.

America's sense of its moral imperative was not allowed to subside with the conclusion of the war and the establishment of the United Nations. The falling out of wartime comrades led to the competition of two economic and ideological systems. Suspicion of each other's goals was reflected in the Cold War. The Soviet Union accused the United States of being the arch exemplar of a corrupt capitalist colonialism which sought to accomplish by economic means the enslavement of the less powerful nations of the world. The United States, in turn, saw the Soviet Union as seeking to promote the goal of a world communism by subversion of weaker neighbors. The economic competition of the two powers dominated the world scene and the nuclear arms race between them naturally was seen as a threat to the survival of mankind. Certain nations which chose to call themselves the "third world" have successfully played the two superpowers off against each other, seeking aid from the one more anxious to please at any given point.

With the Russian Revolution and the exposition by Marxism-Leninism of an ultimate establishment of a communist system world-wide, the American Revolution for the first time had an ideological competitor. This competition has led to the American government's swing to the right. The ideals of the American

Revolution, if not abandoned, were advocated with less conviction, and violent overthrow of governments, even the most repressive regimes, was frowned upon by successive American administrations. The Central Intelligence Agency, which grew out of a predecessor organized during World War II, indulged in political subversion and assassination in support of right-wing regimes, and severely damaged the reputation of America as a promoter of justice and self-determination. This allowed the Soviets to pose as the friend of the underprivileged, despite the fact that their own government allowed no freedom of expression and ruled its own society oppressively.

America's dedication to the "containment" of communism led to its involvement in Korea and Vietnam. Although the former was officially blessed by the United Nations (at a point in 1950 when the Soviet Union had absented itself from the Security Council because of another dispute), it was a case of the United States seeking to restrain the northern communist government from taking over the southern non-communist regime. In the latter case, although begrudging recognition was made by some that the Vietnamese were seeking to throw off the colonialism of the French, several United States administrations interpreted the struggle as an attempt of a monolithic world communist movement to establish itself in Southeast Asia. Thus, millions of lives and untold wealth were spent in what was, ultimately, an unsucessful effort. The American soul-searching that resulted from that defeat is still in process at this writing and no one can foresee the outcome.[34] There are definite indications, however, that the divisions within the population over the war and the ultimate defeat have dampened American enthusiasm to continue in the role of a world policeman.

Dampened—but did not quite eliminate it. Although the emotional scars of involvement in what came to be considered an unjust war in Vietnam kept the nation from easily committing troops to trouble spots such as Angola, the assumption of American foreign policy continues to be that the United States knows better what is good for nations than their own people and governments.[34] This is seen time and again, but no more so than in the case of Latin America (from the proclamation of the Monroe Doctrine in 1823 to the present). This paternalistic attitude emerged recently, for example, in the Senate debates over the Panama Canal Treaty in early 1978. Inevitably, some expressed fear of the spread of communist influence, but—more striking—it became clear that

The Development of America's Sense of Mission

some opponents of the treaty looked on Latin Americans as "little brown brothers" still, when they raised objections to the pact on the grounds that the Panama government was unstable and, furthermore, that the Panamanians lacked the American "know-how" to operate the canal.

I have attempted to trace the development of what I have called an American ideology from its origins in the Puritan experience through the American Revolutionary era, through the great expansion of the American population in the nineteenth century, to our own time. There are obvious lacunae in the presentation, as is inevitable under limitations of space. But I believe the continuities are obvious and that the character of American actions in the twentieth century can be traced to the attitudes formed in an earlier age.

Of course this American ideology is not cast in iron and is subject to change. The searing national experiences of the twentieth century are bound to have their effect. For instance we can speculate as to whether the optimism of Americans and their belief in progress will survive the buffeting they have received from two world wars, a desperate economic depression, the Korean and Vietnam Wars, the assassinations of President John F. Kennedy, Senator Robert Kennedy, and Dr. Martin Luther King, Jr., and the subsequent riots, the Watergate Scandal and near-impeachment of Nixon, etc.

We can speculate—but only a historian of a future generation will be able to answer with any assurance.

Notes

[1] Clinton Rossiter, *Seventeen Eight-Seven: The Grand Convention* (New York: Macmillan, 1966), p. 23.

[2] As he sailed along the coast of what is now Venezuela on his third voyage, Columbus speculated that the incredible amount of fresh water pouring into the sea from the Orinoco River must have its source in paradise. This brief flight of fancy past, he returned to his original, if equally mistaken, notion that he was in the Orient. After the admiral's death, when it became clear that Europe had to deal with a vast new continent it had never suspected was there, a posthumous claim of discovery was made in his behalf by his son, a claim which has been repeated ever since. Professor Edmundo O'Gorman has asked, however, whether a man can be credited with discovery of something which to his dying day he never suspected. He discusses this question and Old World notions concerning the New World in *The Invention of America* (Bloomington: Indiana University Press, 1961). An instructive discussion of the conflicting notions of America held by Europeans during the Renaissance is found in Howard Mumford Jones, *O Strange New World* (New York: Viking Press,

1964).

³This is to be found in various editions, such as that of William T. Davis (1908; New York: Barnes & Noble, 1959), which, to a great extent preserves the original spelling. Readers who are not willing to invest the small sum of patience required to master seventeenth-century spelling and abbreviations can turn to the edition with modernized spelling, edited by Samuel Eliot Morison (New York: Knopf, 1952).

⁴This can be consulted most conveniently in the anthology of Perry Miller and Thomas H. Johnson, eds., *The Puritans* (1938); reprinted in 2 volumes (New York: Harper & Row, 1963).

⁵"You are the light of the world. A city set on a hill cannot be hid. Nor do men light a lamp and put it under a bushel, but on a stand, and it gives light to all in the house. Let your light so shine before men, that they may see your good works and give glory to your Father who is in heaven." Matthew 5:14-16 (Revised Standard Version).

⁶The report of the synod is found in Peter George Mode, *Source Book and Bibliographical Guide for American Church History* (Menasha, Wisc.: George Banta Publishing Co., 1921).

⁷The most instructive recent treatment of Williams, one that sets his views into the context of his biblical typology rather than twentieth-century liberalism, is in Perry Miller, *Roger Williams,* which reprints Williams' major works, with a running commentary by Miller (New York: Antheneum, 1962). Edmund S. Morgan, *Roger Williams: The Church and the State* (New York: Harcourt, Brace & World, 1967), deals with the aspects of Williams' thought that got him into the most trouble. The "antinomian" controversy which developed around Hutchinson is dealt with in Emery J. Battis, *Saints and Sectaries* (Chapel Hill: Univ. of North Carolina Press, 1962). See also David D. Hall, ed., *The Antinomian Controversy, 1636-1638* (Middletown, Conn.: Wesleyan University Press, 1968) for a collection of original documents. The "orthodox" position on these matters is covered in Larzer Ziff, *The Career of John Cotton* (Princeton: Princeton Univ. Press, 1962).

The view of Williams, expressed by Governor Bradford of Plymouth, where Williams had also spent some time, was probably the prevalent one: "... a man godly and zealous, having many precious parts, but very unsettled in judgment...." *History of Plymouth Plantation,* ed. Davis, p. 299.

⁸"...Where the truth could not be published quietly and unopposed, as came to pass in New England, then there it was to be published dramatically by going into the streets in sackcloth and ashes to act out the lamentable condition of people, or naked to symbolize the falsity of the pretenses of the opposing society." Larzer Ziff, *Puritanism in America: New Culture in a New World* (New York: Viking, 1973), p. 140.

⁹Miller and Johnson, eds., *The Puritans,* I, 227.

¹⁰Perry Miller, *The New England Mind: from Colony to Province* (1953; Boston: Beacon Press, 1961), p. 185.

¹¹Miller and Johnson, II, 588.

¹²Miller and Johnson, Stanza 212, p. 604.

¹³Miller and Johnson, Stanza 223, p. 606. Those who would like to suffer the full *Day of Doom* may do so in the edition of Kenneth B. Murdock (New York: Spiral Press, 1929), which includes some of Wigglesworth's other poetic effusions.

¹⁴*Magnalia christi americana; or, the Ecclesiastical History of New England,* ed. Thomas Robbins, et al., 2 vols. (1852; New York: Russell & Russell, 1967), I, 42. A new edition, by Kenneth B. Murdock and published by Harvard, is currently in process and reproduces the original typography as closely as possible. The first volume appeared in 1977. For a discussion of the relationship of the Puritans and Indians, see Alden Vaughan, *New England Frontier* (Boston: Little, Brown, 1965).

¹⁵The new charter also united Plymouth and Massachusetts Bay, thus ending the independent history of the former.

The Development of America's Sense of Mission   95

¹⁶For a discussion of the various facets of the movement, see Ernest Cassara, *The Enlightenment in America* (Boston: Twayne, 1975).

¹⁷Cassara, p. 74.

¹⁸Samuel Eliot Morison, *The Oxford History of the American People* (New York: Oxford Univ. Press, 1965), p. 220.

¹⁹Thomas Paine, *Common Sense*, in *The Life and Works of Thomas Paine*, ed. William M. Van der Wyde, 10 vols. (New Rochelle, N.Y.: Thomas Paine Memorial Historical Association, 1925), II, 117.

²⁰Paine, II, 150.

²¹The terminology of apocalypse and eschatology proved serviceable to preachers of the Great Awakening in the 1730s and 1740s. The same was true in the so-called Second Awakening which is often dated from the revival at Cane Ridge on the Kentucky frontier in 1801. Revivalism, with its concomitant camp meetings, became a permanent fixture of American religion, especially in the West, and drew heavily on apocalyptic imagery provided by the letters of St. Paul, the Gospels, and the Book of Revelation. In the late nineteenth century the terminology also proved useful to Fundamentalism. The Fundamentalist Movement arose in reaction against Modernism, which had embraced Darwinian evolution, the Social Gospel, and the Higher Criticism of the Bible.

²²Thomas Jefferson to John Banister Jr., Paris, 15 October 1785, in *The Papers of Thomas Jefferson*, ed. Julian P. Boyd, 19 vols. to date (Princeton: Princeton Univ. Press, 1950-) VIII, 636-37.

²³Thomas Jefferson to George Wythe, Paris, 12 August 1786, in *The Papers of Thomas Jefferson*, X, 244-45.

²⁴"...What do we mean by the American Revolution? Do we mean the American war? The Revolution was effected before the war commenced. The Revolution was in the minds and hearts of the people.... The people of America had been educated in a habitual affection for England, as their mother country; and while they thought her a kind and tender parent, (erroneously enough, however, for she never was such a mother) no affection could be more sincere. But when they found her a cruel beldam, willing like Lady Macbeth, to 'dash their brains out,' it is no wonder if their filial affections ceased, and were changed into indignation and horror.

"*This radical change in the principles, opinions, sentiments, and affections of the people, was the real American Revolution.*" John Adams to Hezekiah Niles, Quincy, 13 February 1818. *The Works of John Adams*, ed. Charles Francis Adams, 10 vols. (1850-56; New York: AMS Press, 1971), X, 282-3.

²⁵Benjamin Rush to Charles Nisbet, 1783, quoted by Lyman H. Butterfield, Introduction, *Plan of Education, 1785, as Drafted by Benjamin Rush for the Trustees of Dickinson College* (Carlisle, Pa.: Dickinson College, 1973), p. 7. Dr. Rush's plans for public schools and education of women are found in Frederick Rudolph, ed., *Essays on Education in the Early Republic* (Cambridge, Mass.: Belknap Press of Harvard University Press, 1965), pp. 1-40.

²⁶Jefferson's plan for education in Virginia is reviewed in Cassara, *The Enlightenment in America*, pp. 154ff.

²⁷See Noah Webster, "On the Education of Youth in America," in Rudolph, *Essays on Education in the Early Republic*, pp. 43-77.

²⁸*McGuffey's Sixth Eclectic Reader*, 1879 edition, has been republished with a Foreword by Henry Steele Commager (New York: New American Library, 1963).

²⁹*Letters from an American Farmer and Sketches of Eighteenth-Century America*, with a Foreword by Albert E. Stone, Jr. (New York: New American Library, 1963), pp. 62-63.

³⁰*Letters from an American Farmer*, pp. 63-64.

³¹Both Schurz and Wise wrote volumes of *Reminiscences* which related their

intellectual development, as well as their peregrinations, in a colorful manner. Wise's appeared in 1901, Schurz's in 1907-08.

[32]*The Poems of Emma Lazarus,* 2 vols. (Boston: Houghton, Mifflin, 1888), I, 203.

[33]The Fourteen Points and related documents may be most conveniently consulted in Henry Steele Commager, ed., *Documents of American History,* 7th ed., 2 vols. in 1 (New York: Appleton, Century, Crofts, 1963), II, 137-44.

[34]No matter how great the disillusionment suffered as a result of set-backs to United States overseas ventures, and despite the challenge posed to America's traditional self-image by intellectual skeptics, there is reason to believe that a large proportion of the American population continues to assume that their nation is a providential development in history, that God has given it a special mission to perform. Thus, one of the pronounced elements in sermonizing in the mainline churches is a combination of biblical covenantal terminology and nationalistic sentiment. Among Fundamentalist groups the biblical imagery takes on a pronounced apocalyptic and eschatological hue. Politicians, furthermore, possibly out of conviction but certainly in an effort to please, often lace their rhetorical efforts with what Franklin D. Roosevelt referred to as "that God stuff." Americans are accustomed to political addresses with strong religious overtones, often appeals for greater defense spending—coupled, of course, with appeals for lower taxes—based on the notion that America, because it is God's country, can be "second to none."

IV.
The Myth of Apocalypse and The American Literary Imagination

Lois Parkinson Zamora

"And now," observes Adam, "we must again try to discover what sort of a world this is, and why we have been sent hither."
"The New Adam and Eve," Nathaniel Hawthorne

American literature has often taken into account one of our country's most persistent myths about itself, its unique and indispensable role in creating the future. Our national sense of drive into the future and our belief that such movement holds the promise of essential change is founded in the history of our earliest Puritan settlers and in their Christian world view. Christianity teaches that the ends of both the universe and the individual will be very different from their beginnings, that time does not repeat itself but moves in irreversible fashion toward salvation. Historical movement is understood to be evolutionary rather than cyclical, the present a product of past actions and attitudes as surely as the future will be a product of our present actions and attitudes: time is neither aimless nor endless but moves toward a predetermined and transcendent end. Our best writers have constantly questioned the nature of that end, and they have often framed their questions in the terms of the myth of apocalypse.[1]

The myth of apocalypse has been given philosophical, social and historical definition in the preceding essays of this collection; in literature, the use of the word "apocalyptic" as a critical term implies a basic concern with the nature of temporal reality. The myth of apocalypse describes the beginning and the end of time and places human history in the context of the history of the universe. Like the myth, "apocalyptic" literature may be said to confront the full implications of man's "fall into time," to use Mircea Eliade's phrase: it considers mortal man's relationship to a time-bound world and to its end.[2] Furthermore, apocalyptic literature is concerned with this relationship of man to temporal reality not only as it *is* but as it *should be*. Apocalypse is, after all, a myth of radical

97

transformation, a myth of transcendence. Old worlds can be supplanted by new ones, and if man has "fallen into time" from his original timeless Eden, there is yet hope for a future paradise: time is impelled forward by a moral dialectic, the present always future-tending. Apocalyptic literature is thus inherently revolutionary, proposing the radical discontinuity of history in the work of art and in the external world. Apocalyptic literature can be called religious literature if we remember that the root sense of the word "religious" is "bond": it concerns itself with the bond which, according to the writer, connects man to the changing forms of temporal reality. From Puritan times onward, much of America's best literature has been apocalyptic, questioning our individual and collective bonds to the world's time and to the world's end.

The myth of apocalypse, and thus apocalyptic literature, contains both a positive and a negative side.[3] In the myth, millennium is opposed to cataclysm, reward to retribution, salvation to damnation, order to chaos, and in St. John's Revelation (perhaps the most complete version of the myth and the one to which I will be referring in this essay), these opposites find symbolic expression in the metaphoric contraries of Babylon and the New Jerusalem, the Whore and the Bride, the Christ and the Antichrist. It is the *tension* between these symbolic opposites that creates the compelling ironies in apocalyptic literature and carries forward the literary dialogue. (Apocalypse is not *simply* a synonym for cataclysm, as Professor Bergoffen has made clear in her initial essay of philosophical definition. When the dialectic between cataclysm and millennium disappears, when the vision is merely optimistic *or* pessimistic, we do not have apocalyptic literature but fairytale. This has been too frequently the case in our recent "doomsday" literature.) Thus Puritan literature is apocalyptic in its description of the great melodrama between the absolute antitheses of good *and* evil, light *and* darkness. And the symbolic nature of a good portion of American fiction, with its rich interplays of lights and darks and its penchant for abstract characters, allegorical plots and idealized locations owes much to the forms of apocalypse. Indeed, the general dialectical tendency of the American mind to see life as a collision of radically opposed forces and values has its source and its perfect expression in the myth of apocalypse.

While I am aware of this binocular quality of America's literary vision, I want nevertheless to trace in this essay a long-term shift in emphasis from the millennial to the cataclysmic side of the myth of

The Myth of Apocalypse 99

apocalypse and the short-term fluctuations between those extremes. It seems to me that one might almost chart American literature as a series of alternations between optimism and pessimism about our future, a kind of sistole and diastole of millennial expectations and cataclysmic ones, with the latter variety becoming more and more predominant in our own time. Although our best literature has always been a mixture, in varying proportions, of the two sides of the myth, there are nevertheless periods when the tension slackens: if, in our own century, the negative extreme seems in ascendance, it is quite the opposite in much of our earlier literature. Of course this is mere speculation which I can only hope to make specific and significant in the discussion of literary works that follows. I am aware of the hazardous business of abstracting a plot from something so complex as American literature, or of reducing complex works of art to mere re-tellings of the same myth. Nevertheless, by relating several works of American literature to the dualistic mythology of apocalypse, I hope to suggest their characteristic modes, their peculiar vision of human experience, their understanding of what it means to be a mortal individual on what is likely to prove a mortal planet. Furthermore, I hope by tracing this branch of our mythic ancestry to outline an essential characteristic of America's literary culture.[4]

I

I have already mentioned in the introduction to this collection the magnificient expectations which Europe directed toward America, beginning with Christopher Columbus himself, who entertained the idea, upon reaching unknown lands, that he had found the terrestrial paradise promised by Scripture. Grandiose expectations continued when it became clear that this was indeed a new world to the west and not just the east coast of Asia. After all, from the time of classical antiquity there had been myths of a paradise to the west: with the advent of America, it seemed at last that fantasy and reality must surely coincide.[5] Romantic fantasies of travel and adventure, based on travel reports of the explorers, were very popular, particularly in England and Spain, the two countries most involved in the exploration and settlement of North and South America. In Spain, the most popular romance of all was the *Amadís de Gaula*, by Garci-Rodríguez de Montalvo, written after 1492 and published in 1508, a series of adventures in faraway lands full of strange flora and fauna. (It is the *Amadis* that undoes Don Quixote de la Mancha one hundred years later: clearly Cervantes understood the irrational attraction of such exotic utopian visions. A sequel to the *Amadis, Las Sergas de la Esplandián*, describes a tribe of Amazon women and their queen Calafa from the "island of California": that Cortés was searching for that exotic island as he traveled north after his conquest of Mexico is attested to by the name he gave the coastal land.[6]) Sir Walter Raleigh's descriptions of the world, almost as fantastical as the Spanish romances in parts, and the travel literature of Richard Hakluyt were incredibly popular in late sixteenth-century in England. Thus Europeans immediately enveloped the new world with what one scholar describes as "a sort of potential reality that was ever on the brink of being fulfilled."[7] Utopian literature was inspired by the exploration of America, and in turn inspired its exploration.

English and Spanish Renaissance poets—Michael Drayton and Garcilaso de la Vega in particular—found the realization of their pastoral visions in the newly discovered land, and John Donne preached the "great uses" of America in God's plan for the redemption of the world in a sermon to the Honorable Company of the Virginia Plantation on November 13, 1622. America was to serve as an arena for mass conversions, a bulwark against Catholicism, an asylum for the outcasts of English society, a spur to trade. Bishop George Berkeley reflected similar sentiments in "Verses on the Prospect of Planting Arts and Learning in America"; the poem was much quoted and depicted visually, through the middle of the nineteenth-century, as Professor Glanz shows in her essay on Emanuel Leutze's heroic mural in the nation's capital:

> Muse, disgusted at an age and clime
>   Barren of every glorious theme,
> In distant lands now waits a better time,
>   Producing subjects worth fame.
>
> In happy climes, the seat of innocence,
>   Where nature guides and virtue rules;
> Where men shall not impose for truth and sense
>   The pedantry of courts and schools,
>
> There shall be sung another golden age.
>   The rise of empires and of arts,
> The good and great, inspiring epic rage,
>   The wisest heads and noblest hearts.
>
> Not such as Europe breeds in her decay,

Such as she bred when fresh and young,
When heavenly flame did animate her clay,
By future poets shall be sung.

Westward the course of empire takes its way;
The first four acts already past,
The fifth shall close the drama with the day—
Time's noblest offspring is the last.

America was the land of the future, luminously and variously imagined.

These magnificent expectations directed toward America were linked conceptually with the exhaustion and corruption of Europe, as is immediately apparent in Donne's sermon and Berkeley's poem. The Puritans' vision of America as an example for the Old World, a "city on a hill," as Governor Winthrop put it in his sermon to the Massachusetts Bay colonists aboard ship bound for America, has already been mentioned in preceding essays. The Puritans felt that they sailed for a land where they might establish a theocracy, in essence God's kingdom on earth. With this belief that America was to be God's particular historical instrument for the redemption of the Old World, it is not surprising that the most persistent theme in our early literature (and indeed in much of our subsequent literature) is America's historical identity, and that along with sermons, history was its chief literary mode. Because history was a divine pattern governed by God Himself, even the slightest event had significance. Despite their theory of election, the Puritans religiously studied the historical evidence of God's will: although one's ultimate fate was considered to be already determined, one should not in the meantime ignore God's action in and reaction to human affairs. The historian was therefore bound to record everything and interpret everything in terms of God's design. (For this reason, Puritan histories are often odd mixtures of literal pettiness and allegorical grandeur.) Almost every Puritan kept a diary to determine his individual role in God's plot, and community leaders were by definition the community's historians as well as its theologians.[8] Like God's history, The Book of Revelation, to which they frequently refer, the Puritan histories depict the great struggle on earth between the forces of good and evil which will be truncated by the commencement of God's kingdom on earth. This dialectic worked in the microcosm as it did in the macrocosm: the individual could only be raised up by God after the sinful self had been laid low, just as the community felt that it must leave the Old World in order to initiate the millennial kingdom in America.

William Bradford's history, *Of Plymouth Plantation*, begun in 1630 and completed in 1650, may be considered the beginning point of American literature.[9] It describes the exodus of the small band of Puritan separatists from the corrupt Old World to build a New Jerusalem in "those vast and unpeopled countries of America, which are fruitful and fit for habitation...."[9] Always beneath the surface of Bradford's history flicker apocalyptic tensions: the group has left Europe because of "wars of opposition [which]... Satan hath raised, maintained and continued against the Saints, from time to time, in one sort or another"; and they arrive at Cape Cod "by God's good providence" despite "dangerous shoals and roaring breakers" and the "dangers of the night." Bradford's symbolic vision of the Pilgrim's voyage to America does not blind him to its actualities. He can describe, in the same sentence, America as "fruitful and fit for habitation" and yet as "devoid of all civil inhabitants, where there are only savage and brutish men which range up and down, little otherwise then the wild beasts of the same." As the voyagers arrive at the promised land, "What could they see but a hideous and desolate wilderness full of wild beasts and wild men? .... Neither could they, as it were, go up to the top of Pisgah [the mountain from which Moses viewed the promised land] to view from this wilderness a more goodly country to feed their hopes.... If they looked behind them, there was a mighty ocean which they had passed and was now as a main bar and gulf to separate them from all the civil parts of the world." (The early settlers' ideals were obviously urban rather than pastoral: the New Jerusalem, not the wilderness, is what they envisioned. It is only with the Romantic Movement in Europe that the wilderness *per se* came to portend promise rather than menace.) The course of human history is full of wishful thinking, but there is no more poignant scene in American literature than when Bradford recognizes that the gulf separating Europe's wishful thinking about America from the reality of the American wilderness is as great as the "mighty ocean" they have just crossed.

Like Bradford, Cotton Mather in his *Magnalia Christi Americana: or, The Ecclesiastical History of New-England: from Its First Planting in the Year 1620, Unto the Year of Our Lord 1698* sees the settling of the New World as the symbolic and actual culmination of God's historical plan. He begins his General Introduction, "I write the wonders of the Christian religion, flying from the depravations of Europe, to the American strand,"[10] and speaks of "another and better world" which Christ is preparing for His people in America. Like Bradford, Mather is always aware of the cosmic conflict between good and evil operating in history, but the power of darkness that opposes God's will seems, ironically, to be embodied less in an invisible Satanic actor than in the very land where the Puritans have come to seek God's kingdom. Mather suggests that it is the very "terrible wilderness" of the "dark regions of America" that poses the chief threat to God's community. Using an image from Revelation, he represents the "Regiones Exterae" of America as the "outer darkness" which God's light has had to overcome: "But behold, ye European Churches, there are golden candlesticks (more than twice seven time seven!) in the midst of this outer darkness." Bradford's quiet disillusionment in the American wilderness becomes in Mather's history a vacillation between the apocalyptic visions of America as paradise on earth and hell on earth, exhibiting the tormented ambivalence toward the natural world which was to become a characteristic feature of American literature.

It is in a work by Cotton Mather's father that we have the best example in our literature of the union of apocalyptic theology and American history. Increase Mather's "New Jerusalem," written in 1687, is an interpretation of St. John's account of the last days of the world in terms of New England's contemporary history.[11] Mather believed that God revealed Himself in historical cycles of prefiguration and fulfillment: by studying Old Testament types, one might see prefigured the events of the New Testament, and by extension, the events of New England's future. In this kind of typological commentary, it was possible to make a symbolic association between the Israel of the Old Testament and New England. Mather based his suggestion that New England was to be the site of the fulfillment of God's promise to Israel in part on St. John's description in Revelation 22:10, where the New Jerusalem is described as *descending* from God out of heaven. If the city was to descend, it was clearly to be an earthly rather than a heavenly location, and the Puritans could continue to expect the end of time when that descent would take palce. Mather never dated the coming end, for that would have been presumptuous, and he hastened to assure his readers that Christ's direct intervention in human history would be necessary to rectify contemporary corruptions in New England before He could initiate the "new heaven and new earth," but rectify them He surely would. Mather was not always this positive about America's eschatological promise, and even this show of optimism was all but lost in the increasingly loud laments that it was not the kingdom of Christ but the day of doom that New England should expect at any moment.[12]

The second and third generation of American settlers could hardly fail to notice that the New Jerusalem so confidently expected by the founders had not in fact descended onto American soil. Indeed, the settlements seemed farther than ever from this glorious end of time. It is Jonathan Edwards who is best known for his doomsday sermons, although it is safe to say that every preacher in New England between 1660 and the Revolution preached a good portion of hellfire and brimstone. The conventional apocalyptic imagery of the Day of Judgment, the seven vials of wrath, the last assize, the devouring flames, the catalogue of pestilences, the chaos of pandemonium were all exploited to the ample extent of their terror: thus Thomas Shepard, as early as 1646, warned his listeners: "Thou art condemned, and the muffler is before thine eyes. God knows how soon the ladder may be turned. Thou hangest but by one rotten twined thread of thy life over the flames of hell every hour," and Edwards, in one of the most famous passages of American literature, writes in his sermon "Sinners in the Hands of an Angry God," "The God that holds you over the pit of hell, much as one holds a spider, or some loathsome insect, over the fire, abhors you, and is dreadfully provoked .... You hang by a slender thread, with the flames of divine wrath flashing about it, and ready every moment to singe it, and burn it asunder...."[13] The individual's need to reform was always balanced against the suggestion that human nature was incapable of reform. Indeed, the general rhetorical strategy of these sermons was to balance the terror of doom against the hope of millennium, to create a palpable tension between anxiety and assurance, between God's wrath and His mercy.[14] The Puritan community as a whole, so the argument went, had been unable or unwilling to maintain its sanctity under the terms of the new covenant and would not be changed into the New Jerusalem as had been originally thought, but certain individuals might still escape perdition. Oddly enough, these denunciations did not seem to be depressing: Shepard and Edwards and the rest found inspiration in man's dependence on God, and from the continued popularity of their sermons, one imagines that their listeners did too. The end of time was still eagerly anticipated as the moment when God's justice would prevail, when the sinful would be punished and the virtuous rewarded.[15] The Puritans' belief in God's retributive justice made the destruction of the world a positive act.

In *A History of the Work of Redemption*, a series of sermons by Edwards first published in America in 1786, twenty-eight years after his death and forty-seven years after they were first delivered, the theologian proposed his theory of history and, inevitably, his theory of history's end. Casting theology in the form of history, as had his predecessors, Edwards finds that history is unified by a grand conception, a design, a causal chain of events. History is orderly, with the determination of that order lying outside of it presiding over it. Perry Miller, in his classic study of Jonathan Edwards, writes of Edwards' divinely directed historical order: "The order is an instantaneous concept; translated into time, it becomes the historical record, and in this temporalized fragmentation of the eternal, men may read through their senses, for they can learn by no other means, the idea of the perfect beginning and end."[16] There is, on the whole, a steady progress toward this perfect end, but there are nevertheless periods of "declension," when mankind slips into great sinfulness and must be redeemed by revivalists. The Old Testament prophets, the early Christians, the leaders of the Reformation had gone about God's "work of redemption," and now, Edwards implied, he himself, in Northampton, Massachusetts, during the religious revival known as the Great Awakening, might be the next of God's official workers of redemption. Edwards felt that the evangelical outpouring of the Awakening might just herald a really great work, perhaps even the millennium, as Professor Lippy has already noted in a preceding essay in this collection.[17] Edwards wrote in his journal, "I think if we consider the circumstances of the settlement of New England, it must needs appear the most likely of all American colonies, to be the place where this work shall principally take its rise."[18]

Just as we are ready to call Jonathan Edwards' history as much a product of a medieval mind as the preceding Puritan histories or indeed as the sculpted visions of the Last Judgment on the west fronts of Gothic cathedrals, we come to the last paragraph of his history. We read that the flames which will ultimately envelope the earth will represent the moment when God's justice is accomplished, but, says Edwards, *that time will never come.* The same man who suggested that history might culminate in Northampton here insists that history will in fact never culminate: the Last Judgment cannot be fixed in time, the end of the world transcends mere finite dates in historical chronologies. This is a remarkable assertion, for it suggests a very modern understanding of apocalypse. The chronological reality of the world's end is of less significance for most contemporary Americans than is its psychological and spiritual reality: Edwards' private journals reflect upon this very idea, one that he knew was too conoclastic to explore publically and which reached print only posthumously in his *History of the Work of Redemption*. The process of secularization of the myth had begun. Edwards realized that an end which gives meaning to history is as much a psychological necessity as it is a doctrinal one.

Although the apocalyptic literature of the seventeenth and eighteenth centuries is primarily in histories and sermons, the Reverend Michael Wigglesworth chose to supplement his sermons with poetic expressions of the impending cosmic disaster. In his poems "The Day of Doom" and "God's Controversy with New England," Wigglesworth sought to popularize the subject that he felt to be of the most urgent importance, God's impending judgment of sinful mankind.[19] First printed in 1662 and reprinted numerous times thereafter because of its great popularity, "The Day of Doom" is a lilting piece of doggerel with two hundred and twenty-four stanzas, written in colloquial diction to be easily memorized. Following the literary conventions of apocalypse, the poem catalogues the lurid details of the last days but ends with the "wond'rous happiness" of Christ's eternal reign. Although it is the cataclysmic side of apocalypse that engages his poetic imagination, Wigglesworth's vision of the end, like Edwards', is never merely cataclysmic: as with Edwards, the day of doom is a positive event, heralding Christ's eternal kingdom.

Wigglesworth's poem, "God's Controversy with New England," specifically locates the day of doom in New England and ties God's historical plan to American history in good Puritan fashion. Again we see the conventional trappings of apocalypse as Wigglesworth traces the degeneration of New England from its initial purity through its current apostasy. God speaks in thunder to contemporary New England, denouncing its wickedness. This poem ends, however, on a curious and unfamiliar note: in four brief stanzas which depart from the stanzaic structure of the rest of the poem, Wigglesworth states his love for New England, "dearest land to me," sounding one of the first notes of native patriotism in our literature. How unlike Bradford's "hideous and desolate wilderness" and Cotton Mather's "outer darkness" is

Wigglesworth's final line: "Still in New England shall be my delight." This patriotism comes to full flower a little more than a century later, with the American Revolution and the emergence of the American republic, when once again, as at the time of its discovery, America's destiny was to be described in the most optimistic of terms.

II

After the Revolution and during the first decades of the nineteenth century, America seemed more than ever before a place of immense promise. (One thinks of John Winthrop's great optimism about the "city on the hill," but that optimism was expressed before ever setting foot on American ground, and we have already discussed the ambivalence that the early Puritans felt toward the American wilderness once they actually arrived.) Just as the European Reformation had needed America as the site for its urban ideal of the New Jerusalem in the seventeenth century, so European Romantics in the late eighteenth and early nineteenth centuries needed the idea of the American wilderness to reinforce their theories of the natural goodness of man when in a pristine natural setting, away from the corruption of artificial civilization. In fact, the success of Rousseau's doctrine of the intrinsic goodness of man (against centuries of belief in original sin) was surely due in part to the existence of a mythical American land where Nature was undefiled. And if the European Romantics' doctrines depended upon the American wilderness, the American wilderness in turn depended upon the Romantics for mythic definition: the Romantic Movement was the major formative influence in the myth of the American pioneer and his retreat into the essential being of nature in the New World. In "America, a Prophecy," Blake used the American Revolution to symbolize the break with the past that preceded the apocalypse, portraying that Revolution as a search, beyond "struggling afflictions," for "another portion of the infinite," and Chateaubriand portrayed the "Red Indian" as the timeless product of nature, noble and wise. If, as Wordsworth had said, nature was a world of ready wealth, where could one find such riches as in America?

America thus continued to represent to Europe, as it had for two centuries, an unparalleled freedom from the encumbrances of the past, an opportunity to discontinue history and begin again. The encumbrances now were not so much religious and ecclesiastical, as they had been for the Puritans, as social and political; nevertheless, the basic apocalyptic sense of the Puritans—that history was renewable in America—is imaginatively associated with the optimism of the new republic. The apocalyptic images used by the Puritans to describe their experiences in America were secularized in the nineteenth century, just as the purposes for settlement had become secular. The image of the New Jerusalem is supplanted by the natural images of wilderness, the forest, the more classical natural image of Arcadia, or a secular Eden. The New Jerusalem was, after all, a *city*, no matter how divine its architect, and America was now above all a symbol of the rejection of the *urban* past. Instead of the apocalyptic contraries of God and Satan, light and darkness, history came to be seen as a dialectic between innocence and experience, and Eden became the symbolic setting like that dialectic, for wasn't Eden a pristine natural setting for America? And wasn't the American pioneer a New Adam, experiencing unfallen nature once again?[20] (If Eden seems somehow unlike the New Jerusalem—a reversion into the past, rather than a projection into the future—the two are nevertheless cognates in their visions of timeless perfection. America's innocence was geographical and moral but, above all, it was temporal.)

Thus Winthrop's image of a glorious city to describe his hopes for America and Bradford's terrifying image of its uncivilized wilderness must be exactly reversed to express America's sense of its future in the last quarter of the eighteenth and most of the nineteenth century: in our literature, as in reality, the future lay westward, away from the city and into the woods. Bishop Berkeley's lines, "Westward the course of empire takes its way," written a century and a half earlier, had never seemed more apt.

If, as I have said, Bradford's history of Plymouth Plantation is the first piece of American literature chronologically, Benjamin Franklin's autobiography must be the first literary product of a thoroughly American sensibility. At the age of seventeen, Franklin ran away from the colonial capital of Boston to New York and then west to the capital of the frontier state of Pennsylvania. Through the American virtues (American because Franklin said so) of industry, sobriety, thrift, honesty and the sheer force of his own personality, he became the leading citizen of Philadelphia—and indeed of Paris as well. It is no wonder that Ben Franklin, "self-made" man, author of his own world, believer in the social perfectability of humanity, should become Europe's darling, for he conformed to Europe's long-held view of America as having no useable past, only the present and a luminous future. (In his *Autobiography*, Franklin discusses the nature of time, which he felt to be completely manipulable, completely subject to the order he himself should decide to impose: one can hardly imagine a greater departure from the Puritans' belief in God's rigid scheme for the future of the world.) He dismisses almost casually the doctrines of election, the final judgment of sinners, the holocaust, which the Americans of preceding generations had found so compelling, a dismissal the Unitarians later made orthodox. The concept of inherited guilt, of original sin, was as far from the reality of Emerson, Thoreau and Whitman as it was from the reality of Franklin, who was much more interested in science than he was in theology.

Much of our nineteenth-century literature is set in the mythic territory of the virgin forest, or at least at its edge; thus the characters—and their creators—consciously shed what historical memory and social convention they might have possessed, participating in what is by now a literary tradition: the portrayal of America as the site of apocalypse, of transformation from Old World to New. Franklin in the *Autobiography* is only the first of a long line: Crevecouer's "new man," Cooper's Natty Bumppo and Eve Effingham, Thoreau's archetypal American "experiment" at Walden Pond, Whitman's songs of Adamic innocence on the open road, Mark Twain's Huck Finn. (Melville moves his characters to the south seas, but the search for a New World remains constant.) All of Hawthorne's characters vacillate back and forth between civilization and the wilderness, a spatial movement with symbolic implications as we will see in *The Blithedale Romance*. A major theme in Cooper, Mark Twain and Melville is the forming of male companionships outside the constraints of social rank, family ties, female demands.[21] And when the woods no longer offer an escape from time, when the western expanse proves itself limited after all, there continues a palpable nostalgia for that mythical land. Whitman, in "Facing West From California's Shores," asks in an uncharactistically subdued voice, "But where is what I started for so long ago?/And why is it yet unfound?" (We begin to understand why some of our most pessimistic contemporary fiction is set in California, the dead end of the westward movement, where American possibilities seem to have run out: notable examples are Joan Didion's *Play it as it Lays*, Thomas Pynchon's *The Crying of*

Lot 49, Sam Shepherd's play *Angel City* and Nathanael West's *The Day of The Locust,* to which I will return. Didion's masterful essays on the subject are collected under the title, *Slouching towards Bethlehem,* a phrase based on W.B. Yeats' poetic vision of apocalypse, "The Second Coming.") When F. Scott Fitzgerald, in the famous last paragraphs of *The Great Gatsby*, places America's original promise in the context of its twentieth-century reality—Gatsby's "incomparable milk of wonder" and the "foul dust that trails his dreams"—he sounds a note almost as poignant as governor Bradford's three hundred years earlier. Apocalyptic visions of an ecstatic future do not fade easily in American literature.

Thus, in our literature from the Revolution to the mid-nineteenth century, there are only occasional glances toward the negative side of the apocalyptic myth, few symbolic equivalents to the seven trumpet woes, the seven vials of God's wrath, the Day of Judgment. The major exception is Edgar Allan Poe, who wrote several stories and a cosmological treatise about the catastrophic end of the world;[22] in general, however, the fact of the world's end was almost forgotten in the rush to begin anew. And if there were ever portents of cataclysm, one simply walked half a day to the west and began again: as Huck Finn puts it, "I reckon I got to light out for the territory ahead of the rest, because Aunt Sally she's going to adopt and civilize me, and I can't stand it. I been there before." In "Life without Principle," Thoreau wrote with characteristic hyperbole that he would not go around the corner to see the world blow up. Of course he had done something like that when he had left Concord for Walden Pond, but his interest was never in the *end* of the Old World but in the *beginning* of the New. Such was the emphasis of American literature on the regenerative vision inherent in the myth of apocalypse during the first half of our republic's history.[23]

III

To note that America in the first decades of the Republic was not the pristine and innocent place that our writers at times chose to portray it is as irrelevant as to note that Winthrop's vision of a city on a hill and Mather's vision of the New Jerusalem were also fantasies: the point is that the idea of America continually kindled imaginative fire. And of course we know that even those writers most enchanted by millennial visions *did* recognize, in varying degrees, the disparity between their visions and reality. Crèvecoeur, in his *Letters from an American Farmer* (1782), exalts in the first eight of his twelve letters the "great American asylum" from the ancient prejudices and manners of Europe, but even he must interrupt his description of "the most perfect society now existing in the world" to acknowledge the horrors of the American institution of slavery. After a trip to Charleston where he saw Negroes cruelly abused, his prose begins to reflect an apocalyptic interplay of light and darkness, as much to embody the racial composition of the new nation as to express the struggle between the abstract forces of good and evil. In his ninth letter, he attempts to comprehend the presence of slavery in a new world whose very essence, it had seemed to him, was freedom, concluding his lament with a remarkably contemporary question: "Such is the perverseness of human nature; who can describe it in all its latitude?"[24] (Crevecoeur in this letter anticipates the abolitionists' apocalyptic visions before and during the Civil War, when it was generally held that racial injustices were among the portents of the coming end: one need only to re-read the words to "The Battle Hymn of the Republic" to understand that the Civil War was conceived in terms of the Battle of Armageddon, and *Uncle Tom's Cabin* to sense the urgent expectations of cosmic retribution against slaveholders.[25] In more recent times, the racial opposition between black and white has been rendered in the explicitly apocalyptic prose of Richard Wright, Ralph Ellison and James Baldwin, whose essay *The Fire Next Time* describes —as its title suggests—the volatile racial situation and its predictable end in America.[26]) The French immigrant Crèvecoeur, who begins by expounding Romantic ideas of the essential goodness of man in nature, declares in his final letter that he intends to escape the vices and abuses he has perceived in civilization by seeking refuge in the simple life of an Indian tribe. Although Crèvecoeur doesn't tell us, we imagine that the refuge he envisions lies to the west.

The American promised land had been invaded not only by racial exploitation but also by the technological exploitation of nature. The pioneer, with his ax and his rifle, was capable of great destruction. Cooper's account, in *The Pioneers* (1829), of the gratuitous massacre of wild pigeons suggests the war that the pioneers carried on with nature. It was precisely when the pioneer realized that the wilderness was not timeless or inexhaustible and that provisions had better be made for the future that he called upon technology more advanced than his ax and rifle to help him subdue nature. Inland waterways, roads, aid in exterminating the Indians were needed, and as the machines that accomplished these feats were provided, the pioneer could create a comfortable future.[27] This opposition of man to nature prepared the way for our own century's technological view of nature as something to be manipulated and "developed" for human use.

The explosive industrial expansion in the nineteenth century was seen by all our imaginative writers as a threat to the special purity of the American landscape. Washington Irving's very popular story, "Rip Van Winkle" (1820), described what must have been the typical experience of the age: if one weren't careful, one might doze off like Rip and wake to find the landscape utterly transformed around one (an experience not unlike that of the inhabitants of Los Angeles in the 1950s or of Houston in the late 1970s, one might add, except that Americans during the nineteenth century were not yet inured to incessant change). The agent of upheaval seemed to be that diabolical machine, the locomotive; as such, it was often described in hostile terms, a disruption of the idyllic calm of the countryside.[28] Hawthorne and Emerson both suggest the chaos that the railroad brought by referring in particular to the noise of the locomotive; Hawthorne uses the railroad in his story "The Celestial Railroad" to dramatize his contemporaries' misguided sense of progress. Thoreau, our greatest celebrator of unspoiled nature, feels both attraction to and repulsion from the "iron horse": "When I hear the iron horse make the hills echo with his snort like thunder, shaking the earth with his feet, and breathing fire and smoke from his nostrils (what kind of winged horse or fiery dragon they will put into the new Mythology I don't know,) it seems as if the earth had got a race worthy to inhabit it." But, sighs Thoreau, the social critic, "If all were as it seems, and men made the elements their servants for noble ends!"[29] Forever reminding his contemporaries to simplify their lives in accordance with nature, Thoreau uses as his examples of primal simplicity Adam and Eve, and children, of whom he says, "Every child begins the world again." The opposite of this natural innocence for Thoreau was mechanical materialism, and he can think of no worse indictment of the materialistic man, tied to his work, than to say: "He has no time to be anything but a machine": he is "the tool of his tools."

To slavery and industrialism was added yet another problem to

The Myth of Apocalypse 113

undermine the millennial visions of our mid-nineteenth-century literature. The individual freedom which seemed so attractive to America had as its terrifying consequence the destruction of cohesive community and meaningful traditions. Alexis de Tocqueville observed in his analysis of American democracy, published in America in 1840: "Not only does democracy make every man forget his ancestors, but it hides his descendants and separates his contemporaries from him; it throws him back forever upon himself alone and threatens in the end to confine him entirely within the solitude of his own heart."[30] And Emerson, the great proponent of self-reliant individualism, nevertheless explores its disadvantages as well as its advantages in several essays and longer works. In "Society and Solitude," he wrote, "But how insular and pathetically solitary are all the people we know!" And in "Man the Reformer," he worries that "the general system of our trade (apart from the blacker trades, which, I hope, are exceptions denounced and unshared by all reputable men), is a system of selfishness; is not dictated by the high sentiments of human nature ... but is a system of distrust, of concealment, of superior keenness, not of giving but of taking advantage."[31] Tocqueville and Emerson made explicit in these comments what Hawthorne and Melville were beginning to express in their fiction and Whitman in his poetry.

It was Whitman who was most exhilarated by the individual's opportunity in America to create and re-create himself, and it was also he who saw most clearly the elemental loneliness of the enterprise.[32] For all his expansive optimism and his confidence in the sanctity of his innocence, the apocalyptic visionary is at times overwhelmed by the solitude of his self-created world. The very first lines of *Leaves of Grass* suggest the dichotomy between the self and a meaningful community: "One's-self I sing, a simple separate person,/Yet utter the word Democratic, the word En-Masse." The conjunction is "yet," not "and": Whitman understood the contradiction he proposed. In poem after poem, he describes the "vacant, vast surroundings" of the self-created American, but the loneliness was little enough price to pay for such freedom, or so it seemed until the Civil War. The war deeply affected Whitman's sense of America's promise for the "simple, separate person": how could innocence survive such national hatred, devastation, fratricide? In "A Sight in Camp in the Daybreak Gray and Dim," a war poem from the "Drum Taps" section of *Leaves of Grass*,

Whitman describes America's loss of innocence in terms of Christ, whom St. Paul had first called the new Adam. Uncovering the bodies of the dead on the southern battlefield, the speaker says, "Young man I think I know you—I think this face is the face of the Christ himself,/Dead and divine and brother of all, and here again he lies." Again, indeed. After the war, the "yet" that separated Whitman's opening lines ("One's-self I sing, a simple separate person,/yet utter the word Democratic, the word En-Masse.") comes to represent a great gulf between individual and national aspirations. In another poem from the "Drum Taps" section, "Long, Too Long America," Whitman writes:

Long, too long America
Traveling roads all even and peaceful you learn'd from joys and prosperity only,
But now, ah now, to learn from crises of anguish, advancing, grappling with direst fate and recoiling not,
And now to conceive and show to the world what your children en-masse really are,
(For who except myself has yet conceiv'd what your children en-masse really are?)

Whitman's bombast seems tinged with ironic self-knowledge, gained from the "crises of anguish" of the war. For Whitman, the Civil War was, as Melville had said, "a sad arch between contrasted eras."

The fiction of Hawthorne and Melville, like the poetry of Whitman, suggests that the decade preceding the Civil War and the war years themselves are the fulcrum of American literature. While Hawthorne and Melville locate a part of their fiction in sites of pristine innocence, they locate another part in that dark, unsearchable region—the human heart: the expansive movement outward in space is counterbalanced by a movement inward and downward into the psyche, where renewal is *not* a matter of a half day's walk westward. Millennial visions are more and more often opposed to visions of doom: pessimism about America's eschatological destiny begins to outweigh optimism; by our own century it is a brooding vision of the cataclysmic end of time that prevails.

IV

In the work of Nathaniel Hawthorne, we sense the end of American innocence. A descendant of the Puritans who had settled Massachusetts in the seventeenth century, he knew with a kind of

The Myth of Apocalypse 115

sure intuition what Bradford and Cotton Mather had had to learn by painful experience in America: that the virgin wilderness can be the site of evil as well as innocence and that the lack of a past does not assure a New Jerusalem in the future.[33] Like his Puritan ancestors, Hawthorne constantly considers the nature of history, the relationship of the past to the present and to the future. He cannot accept the idea that American history is moving constantly toward a glorious consummation, as Puritan millennialism would have had it, but neither does he express unqualified visions of doom. His best novels are products of his own divided sympathies on the matter: R.W.B. Lewis describes his characteristic fiction as "that of the Emersonian figure, the man of hope, who by some frightful mischance has stumbled into the time-burdened world of Jonathan Edwards...."[34] In *The Scarlet Letter,* Hawthorne sets this strongly felt dialectic between millennial and cataclysmic visions in early Puritan times. Hester Prynne's optimism is set in opposition to the severity of the Puritan belief in divine retribution in history. Transported to the woods, she can imagine a new life for herself and Dimmesdale where their past mistakes would be completely effaced: "Begin all anew! Hast thou exhausted possibility in the failure of this one trial? Not so! The future is yet full of trial and success. There is happiness to be enjoyed!"[35] The novel ends only a few pages after this scene. Hester returns to Boston and voluntarily resumes the burden of the scarlet A, suggesting the ambiguity of the promise of a liberated future: the narrator's comment that "an evil deed invests itself with the character of doom" concludes the novel.

The Blithedale Romance (1852) also tests America's promise, this time in the contemporary setting of a utopian community patterned after Brook Farm in Roxbury, Massachusetts, where Hawthorne had spent several months as a young man. The Blithedale community initially represents for its participants what America had represented for the Puritans, a place removed from the past and from urban corruption where they might begin again. (Hawthorne understood that the religious socialism of his Puritan ancestors had evolved directly into the secular socialism of the nineteenth century: many utopian communities were founded on the same faith in the possibility of historical renewal as were the early Puritan communities in America.[36]) Of course Miles Coverdale, the narrator, is never totally naive about removing himself to a timeless paradise: he describes the wintry Blithedale as a "cold Arcadia," and suggests that the group was united by a negative rather than an affirmative bond: "We had individually found one thing or another to quarrel with in our past life, and were pretty well agreed as to the inexpediency of lumbering along with the old system any further. As to what should be substituted, there was much less unanimity. We did not greatly care—at least, I never did—for the written constitution under which our millennium had commenced. My hope was, that, between theory and practice, a true and available mode of life should be struck out...."[37] But even this relatively moderate aspiration meets with failure: evil irrupts into the community in the form of one of Hawthorne's dark personages, Westervelt, who is repeatedly associated with the Antichrist, and is, in his mysterious way, the agent of chaos and destruction in Blithedale. A less insidious evil force is Hollingsworth, the social reformer, whose facile faith in progress is cast into doubt by his willingness to exploit innocence in its service. When Zenobia, an artificial beauty in the midst of nature (who reminds the narrator of Eve), commits suicide, death and thus time ostentatiously enter Blithedale where, despite initial optimism, they were never really absent anyway. Blithedale becomes no more than an "Arcadian affectation": the experiment, which reiterates the archetypal American hope of withdrawal from a limited present reality in order to create a new world in the future, fails.[38] Our subsequent literature has only reinforced Hawthorne's sense of that failure.

Like Hawthorne, Melville understood too well man's contradictory impulses toward both good and evil to suggest, as had Cooper, Franklin, Crèvecoeur, that seeking an innocent new world and finding it in America were almost the same thing. Melville's fiction always represents the violently opposed visions of paradise and hell typical of apocalypse. In his early novels, Melville removed the search for a timeless paradise from the American wilderness to the South Seas. D.H. Lawrence, an author who felt the tensions that work in human history as acutely as Melville did, wrote of *Typee* (1846), "Poor Melville! He was determined Paradise existed. So he was always in Purgatory.... Melville had to fight, fight against the existing world, against his own very self. Only he would never quite put the knife in the heart of his paradisal ideal."[39] The mood of historical catastrophe that hangs over the *Pequod* in *Moby Dick* (1851) is always counterpointed against the hope of transcending history and the finite, temporal world. Ahab rages against God's limited creation and his own human limitations: had not man been tricked by God with expansive, timeless visions of infinite consciousness? Thus Ahab rages against time itself, against process without finality, without revelation: the white whale becomes, for the tortured spirit of Ahab, the uttermost limit, the end where time will cease and the finite self will be overcome. Ahab is both victim and diabolical agent, Christ and Antichrist, and in both roles it is the great white abstraction of Moby Dick that provides his Armageddon.

The shift from millennial to cataclysmic expectations in American literature is nowhere better measured than at the end of *Moby Dick*, when Ahab and the entire ship, save the coffin in which a sole survivor floats, are destroyed. Lawrence writes:

> Doom! Doom! Doom! Something seems to whisper it in the dark trees of America. Doom!
> Doom of what?
> Doom of our white day. We are doomed, doomed. And the doom is in America. The doom of our white day....
> Melville knew. He knew his race was doomed. His white soul doomed. His great white epoch, doomed. Himself, doomed. The idealist, doomed. The spirit, doomed....
> The *Pequod* went down. And the *Pequod* was the ship of the American soul. She sank, taking with her negro and Indian and Polynesian, Asiatic and Quaker and good, businesslike Yankees and Ishmael....
> But *Moby Dick* was first published in 1851. If the Great White Whale sank the ship of the Great White Soul in 1851, what's been happening ever since?
> Post-mortem effects, presumably.[40]

Lawrence expresses his sure sense of the apocalyptic tension in *Moby Dick* with his litany of contraries: white transcendent consciousness is opposed by the blackness of doom—and is subsumed by it. For all its hyperbole, Lawrence's conclusion, "post-mortem effects," suggests quite correctly the shift toward the negative side of the myth of apocalypse which characterizes the literature of our own century. In much of our serious literature, the tension between opposing forces has all but collapsed: as in the early years of the American republic, the extremes of hope and despair have conflated, but instead of the largely unalloyed optimism of our nation's early writers, we are much more likely to find a sense of hopelessness about our history and our history's end. Racial injustice, technological and industrial expansion, individual isolation from communal values—imperfections in the American paradise which our nineteenth-century writers sensed uneasily—seem to have overwhelmed our contemporary writers, causing increasingly frequent visions of cataclysm in the literature of our time.

V

"He knew his race was doomed. His white soul doomed. His great white epoch doomed...": Lawrence's description of Melville could as well apply to William Faulkner, for Faulkner's fiction explicitly embodies the "doom of our white day." In recent times, it is Faulkner who has inherited the mantle not only of Melville, with his brooding intensity of purpose, but also of Hawthorne, with his Puritan sense of the moral burden of history. If, as I have argued, apocalyptic literature is primarily concerned with the nature of time itself and with the moral imperatives which impel time forward, surely Faulkner's novels are among the most apocalyptic of our century. His apocalyptic vision is cataclysmic: whatever gleam of American millennialism that might remain is largely extinguished: the South becomes a prime example of the decline and decay of America's sense of its destiny.[41] Faulkner's fiction unfolds, layer after layer, the surface of the present to reveal the racial and economic corruption of the past, a corruption so pervasive that the present degeneration and ultimate destruction of the South are foreordained. Injustice to blacks and the destruction of the wilderness through personal greed are the sins of the fathers now visited upon the sons: the South in Faulkner's novels is a world defeated by its excesses, doomed by its pride and pretensions, and most of all by its terrible moral heritage of slavery. Faulkner's fiction is mythic and symbolic, concerned with the destinies of a race and a civilization in a region where the soil had been "manured with black blood," where the bones of men are planted along with the crops: "the yet intact bones and brains in which the old unsleeping blood that had vanished into the earth ... still cried out for vengeance."[42] Crevecoeur's question about the perversity of human nature after seeing slaves in Charleston—"Who can describe it in all its latitude?"—is surely answered with the name of William Faulkner.

The Sound and the Fury (1929), *As I Lay Dying* (1930), *Light in August (1932), The Hamlet* (1940) are all part of Faulkner's tightly knit chronicle of decay: degeneration and death are the subjects of each of these novels, and in each the tragic past of the South renders men's struggles futile, dooming their present and their future. In each, one might almost say that Faulkner *celebrates* the dark grandeur of destruction, the violence, perversion, murder, racial hatred of a rotting civilization. Still, as I have insisted before, such cataclysmic visions become dramatic only when portrayed against more optimistic visions, however vestigial, of human possibilities. Faulkner's cosmic pessimism transcends mere doomsaying because at his best he embodies his dark visions as terrible divergences from America's original potential as a regenerate world.

This dramatic tension between America's early promise and its present reality is always palpable in the collection of stories *Go Down Moses* (1942), Faulkner's most extensive historical vision. The ages of Yoknapatawpha county, from the pristine wilderness inhabited by the Chickasaw Indians, through the invasion of the Anglo-Saxon usurpers and Reconstruction, up to the impoverished present, are envisioned with the comprehensiveness of the apocalyptist who stands beyond the end of time, presenting history in its entirety. In "The Bear," Ike McCaslin comes to understand this universal design. He sets out with the illusion of the purity of the New World but learns that this divinely offered second chance has been tainted by the sins of slavery and spiritual pride.[43] Ike rejects his tainted heritage, both material and cultural, but his memory of lost innocence causes him to spend his life symbolically atoning for that loss. Ultimately Ike's escape from the curse of familial guilt is undermined by the fact that he has no children: the curse will be perpetuated by another branch of the family.

Absalom, Absalom! (1936), like *Go Down, Moses*, allows us to behold an awesome vision of the beginnings and the ends of all human enterprise. Faulkner's perspective and the perspectives of the various narrators in the novel are relentlessly apocalyptic: like St. John in Revelation, they project the patterns of creation, growth, decay, renewal, and final catastrophe onto history. When Thomas Sutpen rides into Yoknapatawpha County, Mississippi, in the shape of "man-horse-demon," there is no doubt that a new world is about to be created: "Immobile, bearded and hand palm-lifted the horseman sat...," determined to "drag house and formal gardens violently out of the soundless Nothing and clap them down like cards upon a table beneath the up-palm immobile and pontific, creating the Sutpen's Hundred, the *Be Sutpen's Hundred* like the oldentime *Be Light*" (pp. 8-9). Sutpen brings both brute force ("his band of wild niggers like beasts half-tamed to walk upright like men") and a representative, however effete, of European civilization ("the French architect with his air grim, haggard, and tatter-ran,") with which to reenact the archetypal American experience of creating a new world out of the wilderness. The novel's title links ironically the creation of Sutpen's

Hundred to the establishment of the house of King David, to whom God had promised to build a house and preserve his posterity forever.[44] Whereas the establishment of David's house was proof of his right relation to God's plan of history, Sutpen's house is built according to his own design, a design based on slavery and economic exploitation of the land. The house reeks, we are told, of "slow protracted violence with a smell of desolation and decay as if the wood of which it were built was flesh" (p. 366). When the house burns, with two of his children inside, we understand that the holocaust testifies to the end of Sutpen's world, with its false conception of civilization and history. When the destruction of Sutpen's house is linked to the destruction of the South, we are not surprised, for the promised land has been irrevocably cursed.[45]

It is Miss Rosa, sister-in-law of Sutpen, embittered and aged spinster, who initiates the narration, and it is her cataclysmic vision that dominates the novel. It is she who draws Quentin into his consideration of Sutpen's history, and she who causes Mr. Compson to expand on her version to his son. Miss Rosa's account ranges forward and backward in time, giving a dark and fatalistic cast to Sutpen's world by presenting its history whole, its firey end evident even as its beginning is related. Miss Rosa, like St. John in his Revelation, obeys the urgent imperative to "write the things which thou hast seen, the things which are, and the things which shall be hereafter" (Rev. 1:19). Relating Sutpen to the curse laid upon the land she tells Sutpen's story to Quentin in order to explain God's historical plan, so that people "who have never heard her name nor seen her face will read it and know at last why God let us lose the War..." (p. 11). And just as St. John stands beyond the end of time and narrates the history of the world from his atemporal point of view, so Miss Rosa narrates from a point beyond the end of history—or at least from a point beyond the end of Sutpen's history: for her, the two histories are coterminous. Thus, in "the dim coffin-smelling gloom of her house," she tells Quentin that her life "was destined to end on an afternoon in April forty-three years ago," when she understood that Sutpen had created "two children not only to destroy one another and his own line, but my line as well" (p. 18). And again, like St. John, Miss Rosa is always visible in the history that is being revealed: St. John frequently begins his sentences with "And behold, I John saw...", Miss Rosa often beginning hers in a slightly more subdued but equally obtrusive phrase, "I saw," initiating sentence after sentence in incantatory fashion, or

The Myth of Apocalypse 121

concluding a descriptive passage, "That's what I found." (The medieval apocalypse tapestries often place the figure of St. John at the side of the scene which he is describing, an expression of distress upon his face as he watches the terrors of his revelation unfold; so our peripheral vision constantly registers Miss Rosa's disapproving presence.) For Miss Rosa, as for the traditional apocalyptists, time is a vehicle of divine purpose, but there is no reward—only retribution—at the end of time.

True to her Puritan heritage, Miss Rosa views history as morally dualistic, as a prolonged Armageddon in which the forces of God and Satan engage in terrible warfare.[46] Her language of hellfire and brimstone is appropriate to one reared "in dim halls filled with that presbyterian effluvium of lugubrious and vindictive anticipation..." (p. 60). Miss Rosa casts Sutpen in the role of Satan, insisting upon his demonic character with such appellations as "ogre" and "the evil's source and head." The cosmic battle between God and Sutpen is made explicit when Miss Rosa explains why "God let us lose the War": she says that "only through the blood of our men and the tears of our women could He stay this demon and efface his name and lineage from the earth" (p. 11). But Sutpen is not effaced from her memory: long after his death, his memory returns to obsess her, a dark god galloping across the land on a black stallion. During her penultimate visit to his house, accompanied by Quentin, she senses Sutpen's presence in the darkness. Up until this moment, Miss Rosa has been an observer of the history she recounts, but as she whispers to Quentin, "I'm going inside. Give me the hatchet," she makes her assault upon that history. It is at this moment that Quentin understands that there is "something fierce and implacable and dynamic driving down the thin rigid arms" (p. 367) and he understands that it is hatred rather than fear that moves her: perhaps, as Mr. Compson suggests, Miss Rosa sees herself as an instrument of retribution in the cosmic conflict.

If Miss Rosa's apocalyptic narrative is almost entirely cataclysmic, it contains nevertheless a vestigial memory of the promise that was once inherent in the land. She tells Quentin that at age nineteen she sensed the potentiality of time, knowing then that "living is one constant and perpetual instant when the arras-veil before what-is-to-be hangs docile and even glad to the lightest naked thrust," and knowing too that the prisoner soul, for all its "sickness somewhere as the prime foundation," nevertheless "wroils ever upward sunward, tugs its tenuous prisoner arteries and veins and prisoning in its turn that spark, that dream which ... repeats...all of space and time and massy earth..." (pp. 142-143). But the dream has, with the exception of this vague memory, vanished: "the dreamer, waking, says not 'Did I dream?' but rather says, indicts high heaven's very self with: 'Why did I wake since waking I shall never sleep again?' " (p. 143). Thus Miss Rosa, herself the awakened dreamer, lays to rest forever the American dream of a new and innocent world.

Miss Rosa's view of history is reflected by the other narrators and by Sutpen as well. They all share her fatalism and her sense of the exhaustion of human possibilities, feeling the terrible weight of time as they attempt to understand the temporal design of which they are, willy nilly, a part. Mr. Compson's narration is filled with allusions to Greek tragedy which suggest his historical fatalism as surely as Miss Rosa's apocalyptic references to sin and damnation reflect hers; Sutpen goes to Grandfather Compson to tell his story only when he understands that it is time itself that will undo him; Quentin asks his father why Miss Rosa should be so obsessed with Sutpen's destruction, for Quentin himself knows with a sure instinct that they will all be destroyed in any case. Even Shreve understands that the historical truth that he and Quentin have sought somehow leads to holocaust: he says that their account "clears the whole ledger, you can tear all the pages out and burn them..." (p. 378). Thus *Absalom, Absalom!* presents various narrative versions of the betrayal of the New World's promise by the sins of racism and greed, and suggests the ways in which we attempt to know the past and to deduce from it the movement of time toward its end.

Unlike Faulkner, several of our modern writers have envisioned an apocalypse which will be neither a racial nor a theological event, but a technological one: Henry Adams was the earliest of our century's writers to foresee such an end. If the millennial optimism of Cooper, Thoreau and Hawthorne was at times threatened by the irruption of machines into their pastoral realms, Adams' vision of the future is absolutely overwhelmed by the technological innovations of his time. He can see nothing but ultimate annihilation as a result of our enslavement to our own scientific discoveries.

Like all the writers whose work I have termed apocalyptic, Adams is constantly seeking historical design behind the concretions of reality. He writes that the task of the historian is to discover the energy that motivates a given society.[47] In a brilliant study of medieval Europe, *Mont-Saint-Michel and Chartres* (1904), subtitled "A Study of Thirteenth-Century Unity," Adams analyses the power of Christianity and more specifically the mystical energy exuded by the Virgin, as the force behind the otherwise inexplicable cultural achievements of that century. Searching for a comparable source of energy to explain the events of his own century and ours, Adams finds a metaphor at an exposition of modern technology, the Paris Exposition of 1900. Here he witnesses the dynamo. In *The Education of Henry Adams* (1907), subtitled "A Study of Twentieth-Century Multiplicity," Adams expresses his sense of the conflicting forces at work in history: he feels the antithesis between the Virgin's mystical spirituality and the scientific materialism of thermodynamic power in his world as acutely as the Puritan historians had felt the antithetical forces of the Christ and the Antichrist in theirs. But the Virgin's energy seems to Adams to be all spent, and even thermodynamic energy is exhausting itself: the second law of thermodynamics, the law of entropy, had been, by the turn of the twentieth century, established as a scientific fact.[48] Expressing this relatively new concept in his later works, Adams describes the gradual leveling of energy in the universe and the molecular equilibrium called heat-death at the end of the process. The world he envisions is moving toward its extinction inexorably and irreversibly; the end is not to be orchestrated with the great crescendo of apocalyptic cataclysm but rather with the descrescendo of entropic chaos.[49]

Among recent writers who have used the law of entropy as a metaphor for the inevitable end of our culture are Joan Didion, Norman Mailer, William Burroughs, James Purdy, and Thomas Pynchon and Nathanael West.[50] Their eschatology, based on this law, is far more pessimistic than is conventional apocalyptic eschatology: the end is not caused by man's action and God's reaction, but is produced by decomposition, disintegration, and gradual loss of energy and differentiation. The anthropomorphism of the traditional apocalypse, with its implicit sense of purposeful history responding to human as well as to divine actions, yields to the bleak mechanism of a purely physical world which is irreversibly running out of energy. Whereas the apocalyptic vision sees a causal relationship between past, present and future, the law of entropy, when applied to human affairs, negates such rational temporal continuity: history does have a direction as it moves toward heat death, but it admits no human influence, no logical relationship between cause and effect. The world drifts, as Pynchon puts it in his short story called "Entropy," "into the graceful decadence of an enervated fatalism."[51]

In his two short masterpieces, *Miss Lonelyhearts* (1933) and *The Day of the Locust* (1937), the metaphor of entropy, along with the cataclysmic imagery of perverted nature from Revelations, become Nathanael West's primary narrative means of creating fictional worlds where order has given way to chaos and the future holds nothing but sure annihilation. In *Miss Lonelyhearts*, the physical world is decaying despite the season: "Although spring was well advanced, in the deep shade there was nothing but death—rotten leaves, gray and white fungi, and over everything a funereal hush."[52] And the human beings who inhabit this wasteland are themselves physically disfigured and decaying even as they twitch and shudder in violent death throes. Miss Lonelyhearts contemplates the world of those with "broken hands and torn mouths" who write to him for help, a world which he recognizes as his own: "A desert, he was thinking, not of sand, but of rust and body dirt, surrounded by a backyard fence on which are posters describing the events of the day. Mother slays five with ax, slays seven, slays nine.... Inside the fence Desperate, Broken-hearted, Disillusioned-with-tubercular-husband and the rest were gravely forming the letters MISS LONELYHEARTS out of white-washed clam shells..." (p. 25). The advice-to-the-lovelorn columnist, trying like the ancient apocalyptists to explain the suffering in this world in terms of a transcendent plan, can hardly expect divinely revealed truth in a world where language is prey to entropy. The only word which he perceives is his own name, with its implications of solitude and alienation, its implications that Miss Lonelyhearts has supplanted God as receptor of cries for help. Although he longs implicitly for the "sharp two-edged sword," as Christ's message is described in Revelation, so that he might bring an end to human suffering, Miss Lonelyhearts' advice is hardly enough to oppose the moral, emotional and physical death of his society. Despite his demonic editor's suggestion that priests have been replaced by newspaper columnists, Miss Lonelyhearts' words are not the alpha and omega of anything, least of all suffering. The bleached and inert pattern of letters, traced by clam shells on parched ground, are the only revelation that can be distinguished.

The metaphor of entropy becomes explicit as Miss Lonelyhearts, wandering the streets in a fevered delirium, finds himself looking into the window of a pawnshop. Surrounded by the detritus of the pawnshop—fur coats, diamond rings, watches, shotguns, fishing tackle, mandolins—each item a mute and inert symbol of lost hopes and unfulfilled dreams, Miss Lonelyhearts contemplates this physical evidence of entropic decline: "Man has a tropism for order. Keys in one pocket, change in another. Mandolins are tuned G D A E . The physical world has a tropism for disorder, entropy. Man against Nature...the battle of the centuries.... Every order has within it the germ of destruction. All order is doomed, yet the battle is worthwhile" (pp. 30-31). In his delirium, Miss Lonelyhearts imagines order among the rubbish: "a phallus of old watches and rubber boots, then a heart of umbrellas and trout flies, then a diamond of musical instruments and derby hats, after these a circle, triangle, square, swastika." Inevitably he attempts to make a cross. His vision shifts to a beach, cluttered like the pawnshop with random and undifferentiated piles of junk—bottles, shells, chunks of cork, fish heads, pieces of net—which increase with every incoming wave. Despite his "enormous labors," he cannot define a cross in the flotsom and jetsom of his world of increasing entropy. Miss Lonelyhearts' assertion that the battle for order is worthwhile is undermined and subverted by the predetermined nature of its outcome: whereas apocalyptic eschatology envisions a future which depends upon man's faith and will and not upon the mechanical laws of the physical universe, the entropic vision of the future is necessarily a foregone conclusion. The apocalyptist foresees the future because he believes that God has revealed it to him, not because the laws of statistical probability have made it inevitable.

In *The Day of the Locust*, West uses the demonic imagery of apocalypse to give metaphoric definition to the social disintegration which he portrays, although the metaphor of entropy is present too, implicit rather than explicit as it is in *Miss Lonelyhearts*. The title of the novel is taken from Revelations 9:3-9, where the end has been revealed and the violent disruption of natural processes serves as prelude to that end. "Out of the smoke there came forth locusts upon the earth."[53] But unlike St. John's vision, West's does not contain a promised new world to counterbalance the destructive upheaval of the old: there is no potential divine order to replace actual secular chaos.

West's demonic vision may perhaps best be understood in the terms of Northrup Frye's archetypal criticism. Frye begins his study of archetypes with a discussion of apocalyptic imagery and demonic imagery, opposing these categories. For Frye, apocalyptic imagery embodies the "forms of human desire," whereas demonic imagery is the "presentation of the world that desire totally rejects: the world of the nightmare and the scapegoat, of bondage and pain and confusion.... And just as apocalyptic imagery in poetry is closely associated with a religious heaven, so its dialectic opposite is closely linked with an existential hell."[54] Frye catalogues the inversions, "the demonic parodies," of apocalyptic imagery frequently associated with the "world that desire rejects": The Eucharist symbolism becomes the symbolism of cannibalism; the beloved becomes a harlot, witch, siren; the marriage of two souls in one flesh may take the form of hermaphroditism, incest, or homosexuality. In nature, the animal world is populated with monsters and vicious beasts of prey, the vegetable world is comprised of foreboding forests, the mineral world of deserts and labyrinthine mazes without exit: "Cities of destruction and dreadful night belong here, and the great ruins of pride....Images of perverted work belong here too: engines of torture, weapons of war, armor, and images of a dead mechanism which, because it does not humanize nature, is unnatural as well as inhuman" (p. 150). I do not intend to suggest that all these demonic images are present in West's novel, or that the novel may be completely understood by categorizing images and then multiplying examples within the categories. However, the extent of West's brutally pessimistic vision can be fully appreciated only when we place it (as has West) in the apocalyptic tradition and then observe his distortion of the conventions of that tradition by conflating the metaphoric dualities of millennium and cataclysm into a singular fixation on the latter.

West's sense of the betrayal of America's promise is apparent in the setting of *The Day of the Locust*. If, as I have suggested, Faulkner presents vestigial and veiled memories of the unspoiled past of the virgin land, implicitly casting present degeneration in terms of what might have been, so West also invokes what might have been, but his presentation of lost dreams and missed opportunities is neither vestigial nor veiled. Los Angeles, the City of Angels, Hollywood, heart of the glamor and wealth of the movies, and California, named by Cortés after an imaginary utopian island, are ironically inverted by West into a 1930s wasteland of despair and ultimately of holocaust. Natural phenomena are described by lurid analogies to the inorganic and the mechanical:

> The edges of the trees burned with a pale violet light and their centers gradually

turned from deep purple to black. The same violet piping, like a Neon tube, outlined the tops of the ugly, hump-backed hills... (p. 61).

They stopped to watch a hummingbird chase a bluejay. The jay flashed by squawking with its tiny enemy on its tail like a ruby bullet. The gaudy birds burst the colored air into a thousand glittering particles like metal confetti (p. 113).

Death seems to coat the "bare ground and jagged rocks" of the country surrounding the city and the poppies which manage to sprout between them: "Their petals were wrinkled like crepe and their leaves were heavy with talcumlike dust" (p. 113). And human beings are constantly compared to the non-human and placed in organic contexts: Homer Simpson is a "poorly made automaton," like "one of Picasso's great sterile athletes, who brood hopelessly on pink sand, staring at veined marble waves" (p. 83); Harry Greener is "like a mechanical toy that had been overwound" (p. 92).

The protagonist of the novel, Tod (spelled with one d, as is the German word for death), is a kind of inverted Gatsby, a young artist recently arrived from the East, who constantly characterizes the inhabitants of Los Angeles as moribund, as having come to Los Angeles to die. Far from viewing them as latter day pioneers who have courageously headed westward toward a promising frontier, leaving their pasts behind in the dustbowls of North Dakota or Oklahoma (as John Steinbeck portrays them in his novel of apocalyptic title, *The Grapes of Wrath,*) West describes only the boredom and disappointment of their lives, and their manic search in the false worlds of the movies for an antidote to their failure. However, the tawdry illusions of the movies will never suffice, the narrator tells us, "to make taut their slack minds and bodies." On one movie set, in chaotic disarray are large celluloid swans, a Greek temple dedicated to Eros in which the god lies face down on a pile of old newspapers and bottles; Tod struggles and only barely manages to find his way out of the baffling labyrinth of junk which closes around him on the set: the skeleton of a Zeppelin, a bamboo stockade, an adobe fort, the wooden horse of Troy, the bones of a dinosaur, the upper half of an ersatz Merrimac. There is nothing, the narrator assures the reader, that won't turn up sooner or later, "having first been made photographic by plaster, canvas, lath and paint" (p. 132). The artificiality of Hollywood productions and of the people who aspire to populate those cinematic microcosms only reflects the greater sham of the macrocosm. The movies are continuous with Los Angeles itself: "the Mexican ranch houses,

Samoan huts, Mediterranean villas, Egyptian and Japanese temples, Swiss chalets, Tudor cottages, and every possible combination of these styles" (p. 61) are also made of plaster, lath and paper. The superficiality of aesthetic conception is reiterated in the mode of construction.

This is a world to be rendered, the narrator notes, not by Winslow Homer or Thomas Ryder, great painters of healthy American landscapes and people of the past, but by Goya and Daumier, masters of distortion and caricature, of irrational and bizarre worlds of pain and destruction. By means of allusion, but more directly by means of his narrative use of demonic imagery, Nathanael West allies his fiction to the tradition of the grotesque in Goya and Daumier, as well as in Salvator Rosa, Francesco Guardi, Monsu Desiderio, Alessandro Magnasca, "painters of Decay and Mystery" whose art conveys their rage at human injustice and stupidity.[55] However, in these artists' paintings, as in West's fiction, rage gives over to a vision of hopeless absurdity, of cosmic pointlessness: behind their specific criticism is an overwhelming sense of despair at the very possibility of any belief, of any future. To return to Northrup Frye's terms, theirs are portrayals of worlds that desire rejects, realms of "perverted or wasted work, ruins and catacombs, instruments of torture and monuments of folly" (p. 150).

In the final scene of the novel, a frenzied mob enacts Tod's artistic rendering of mass violence in his painting, "The Burning of Los Angeles." The scene is specifically related by West to Biblical visions of apocalypse. Tod thinks of himself in the role of Jeremiah, predicting civil war not only in Los Angeles but in all America, wondering why he should feel such satisfaction at the thought: "Were all prophets of doom and destruction such happy men" (p. 118)? He spends his nights in Hollywood churches, sketching the worshipers. In the "Tabernacle of the Third Coming," (the name an ironic parody of the apocalyptic expectation of Christ's Second Coming), Tod fully understands the latent violence of the people for whom the typically American pursuit of a new world in the west has ended in betrayal and futility. He listens to the messianic rage of a man who stands up to speak: "The message he had brought to the city was one that an illiterate anchorite might have given decadent Rome." The City of the Angels is inverted into the City of the Beast: "He claimed to have seen the Tiger of Wrath stalking the walls of the citadel and the Jackal of Lust skulking in the shrubbery..." (p. 142). The references to the myth of apocalypse, with its dual vision of

The Myth of Apocalypse 129

cataclysm and millennium, makes the firey finale of the novel the more horrendous, for the constructive countervision of apocalypse is starkly and irrevocably absent from the novel. After all, even Jeremiah predicted doom so that his listeners might reform before it was too late, so that Israel might yet be accomplished. However, the novel's bloody culmination is presented as the inevitable fulfullment of the prophecies of doom, the only end possible.

The riot is sparked by a Hollywood premiere where Tod's Californians, disillusioned with their own lives, have thronged to see the movie stars who fuel their fantasies: "At the sight of their heroes and heroines, the crowd would turn demoniac.... Individually the purpose of its members might simply be to get a souvenir, but collectively it would grab and rend" (p. 176). West, like St. John in his Revelation, sees human destiny in collective terms, the fate of the individual and the community at last coinciding, the damned described as hordes, swarms, undifferentiated masses. Thus, the crowd moves blindly, ponderously, tolerating the police "as a bull elephant does when he allows a small boy to drive him with a light stick" (p. 177). West suggests that the mindless violence of the masses is due in large part to what have come to be called, appropriately, the mass media. The mob is well acquainted with, even seeks violence, because: "Every day of their lives they read the newspapers and went to the movies. Both fed them on lynchings, murder, sex crimes, explosions, wrecks, love nests, fires, miracles, revolutions, wars. This daily diet made sophisticates of them" (p. 178). In *Miss Lonelyhearts,* West specifically states that the cause of the Californians' despair lies precisely where they search for its cure: "Men have always fought their misery with dreams. Although dreams were once powerful, they have been made puerile by the movies, radio, and the newspapers. Among many betrayals, this one is the worst" (p. 39). If Henry Adams found in the technology of the dynamo the source and symbol of the entropic decline and ultimate annihilation, Nathanael West locates it in the technology of the mass media, for those media have perverted language itself, turning man's most important tool for social order into a source of chaos and destruction.[56] And had West written only a decade later, he would surely have added television to his list.

The climactic scene in Robert Coover's novel *The Origin of the Brunists* (1966) resembles the mob scene in *The Day of the Locusts* in its depiction of the uncontrolled fury of the disaffected. The novels are also related in their criticism of the ways in which the mass media manipulate the hopes of the disaffected to escape from their dismal world without changing that world at all, thus creating confusion, frustration and, ultimately, destruction.

In the apocalyptic cult called the Brunists, Coover creates in the apocalyptic cult called the Brunists, a fictional analogue to the numerous religious cults such as those discussed by Professor Lippy in his essay in this volume, cults which during the course of American history have appeared frequently, narboring urgent expectations of the end of the world. As the economic and social situation degenerates in the coal mining town where the novel is set, the characters attempt with increasing desperation, even frenzy, to "read" history and interpret its signs about the time and even the place of the end of the world. (According to one of the novel's apocalyptists, the end of the world may not occur everywhere: perhaps only the residents of West Condon may be privileged to behold the wonder!) Coover is a master at evoking the paradoxes of American fundamentalist apocalypticism: the longing for future disaster as a solution to present disaster, the strengthening of belief in an imminent end precisely because the end repeatedly fails to occur, the attribution of symbolic significance to the least historical detail in order to create mythological systems which depreciate historical reality, and so on.[57] (Even the appellation "Brunists" has ironic resonances: the name of the pathetic "apocalyptist" and supposed "founder" of the group, Giovanni Bruno, recalls that of Giordano Bruno, the Italian philosopher who was burned at the stake in 1600 for imagining the possibility of innumerable worlds in an infinite universe.) Only one character seems to recognize the self-delusions of the Brunists, the error inherent in putting everything into simplistic categories which deny "the thick tangle of endless ambiguities that were the one true thing of this world."[58] But this wisdom on his part merely emphasizes the lack of it everywhere else. Coover's subsequent novel makes even fuller use of the myth of apocalypse with its potential for escapist fantasy.

In *The Universal Baseball Association, Inc., J. Henry Waugh, Prop.* (1968), Coover combines baseball-as-American-myth with the myth of apocalypse, also a particularly American myth, as I have perhaps amply demonstrated by now. J. Henry Waugh lives in the fantasy world of the Universal Baseball Association, a league which he has invented and whose games he plays without board or counters, with only three dice and a ledger to enter the standings and statistics produced by the rolls of the dice. While the rules and patterns of baseball are the conscious determinants of Henry's game, the patterns of apocalypse are also present, although Henry seems to be unconscious of them. The numerology of Revelations is invoked: triple ones and sixes—symbolic of the Trinity and the Beast, Christ and Antichrist—trigger the most spectacular events of the game (and the novel), events which are construed in terms of the ethical dualism of apocalypse, the Armageddon of the UBA. (The effective end of the UBA occurs when Henry *places*, rather than rolls, triple sixes on his kitchen table.) As in *The Origin of the Brunists*, Coover brilliantly portrays the need of the lonely and persecuted to convert history into schematic myth, to remove themselves from the present by creating fictions about the future. In the final chapter of the novel, that process is especially sharply conceived: the events of the UBA are re-enacted ritually in Henry's dislocated mind, alleviating his alienation and finally subsuming altogether his actual world of boring job and tyrannical boss. The myth of apocalypse serves the fortunes of Henry's fantastical baseball world, providing him with a means of escaping temporal reality rather than confronting it and incorporating it into his vision.

I began by tracing an "apocalyptic tradition" in American literature and I have concluded by looking at two contemporary writers whose work concerns itself with endings but which nevertheless departs from that tradition. Too much of our contemporary literature, it seems to me, is characterized by an antagonism toward nature such as that portrayed by West or by a distrust of experience such as that inherent in the escapist fantasies portrayed by Coover. While admirable works of fiction in many respects, these novels reflect the tendency of our recent fiction to be more visions of doom than visions of apocalypse. In our age of nuclear capability, ecological pollution and dietary contaminants, population bombs and energy crises, we find too rarely in our fiction complex visions of a temporal world which still contains both good and evil, hope and despair, where time may still be a vehicle for human fulfillment.

There are of course important exceptions to the cataclysmic construction of apocalypse in contemporary fiction: Saul Bellow's *Mr. Sammler's Planet,* Norman Mailer's *An American Dream,* Walker Percy's *The Second Coming.* Another exception is represented in a passage toward the end of *The Heart is a Lonely Hunter* (1940), by Carson McCullers, and it will serve to conclude my own discussion. Biff Brannon, cafe owner in a small southern town, experiences an apocalyptic moment, a moment of revelation, as he stands in the pre-dawn gloom. He sees the past, present and future from the comprehensive perspective of the apocalyptist, and sees too the "radiance and darkness" of hope and despair which necessarily attend human experience. Biff's apocalyptic vision is particularly modern, however, for he does not designate a specific terminus of history:

For in a swift radiance of illumination, he saw a glimpse of human struggle and of valor. Of the endless fluid passage of humanity through endless time. And of those who labor and of those who—one word—love. His soul expanded. But for a moment only. For in him he felt a warning, a shaft of terror. Between the two worlds he was suspended. He saw that he was looking at his own face in the counter glass before him. Sweat glistened on his temples and his face was contorted. One eye was opened wider than the other. The left eye delved narrowly into the past while the right gazed wide and affrighted into the future of blackness, error, and ruin. And he was suspended between radiance and darkness. Between bitter irony and faith. Sharply he turned away.[59]

Despite the "endless fluid passage of humanity through endless time," Biff does envision an end which is not made explicit in this passage but is clear nonetheless: that end is his own. In our own time, with the lengthening scale of history where beginning and end recede from our own position in the midst of time, as Frank Kermode has put it, the end becomes an individual predicament. Biff understands, as the Brunists and Tod Hackett don't, that his own end and the collective end will *not* coincide, that he cannot hope to escape the terrors of his own unknown future by means of the imminent imitation of a brave new world—or the imminent destruction of the old world, for that matter. Nonetheless he, and we, gain understanding our mortal condition from the mythic struction of apocalypse, which imposes shape upon human time and suggests a cosmic context for our individual ends. Andre Malraux once suggested that the function of art is to define man's mortality; the myth of apocalypse, when not distorted by undue emphasis on its cataclysmic element, has often provided in American literature the temporal perspective necessary for such definition.

Notes

[1]See Walter J. Ong, S.J., "Evolution, Myth, and Poetic Vision," in *Comparative Literature: Matter and Method*, ed. A. Owen Aldridge (Urbana: Univ. of Illinois Press, 1968), pp. 308-328, for an interesting discussion of both cyclical and linear

The Myth of Apocalypse   133

temporal patterns in American poetry.

[2] Mircea Eliade, *Myths, Dreams, and Mysteries* (New York: Harper & Row, 1968), p. 154.

[3] See Thomas J.J. Altizer, "Imagination and Apocalypse," *Soundings*, 43 (1970), 398-412.

[4] For a discussion of myth and its uses in this regard, see Kenneth Burke, "Ideology and Myth," *Accent*, 7 (1947), 195-205.

[5] See Leslie Fiedler, *The Return of the Vanishing Americans* (New York: Stein and Day, 1968), pp. 29-42, "The World without a West." Fiedler discusses the various ancient myths of a paradise to the west, beginning with Homer and Hesiod, then Celtic and Icelandic and Irish myths: "All that is necessary to make Celtic and Christian fantasy one is to realize that the earth is mythologically as well as geographically round; that the paradise lost in the East can be regained by sailing west" (p. 32).

[6] Walker Chapman, *The Golden Dream: Seekers of El Dorado* (New York: Bobbs-Merrill Co., Inc., 1967), pp. 123-125. See also Chapter 8, "Raleigh and the Gold of Manoa" (pp. 307-351).

[7] Chapman, p. 124. Raleigh wrote that in Guiana, where he had gone in 1595, there was "a nation of people whose heads appear not above their shoulders.... They are reported to have their eyes in their shoulders, and their mouths in the middle of their breasts, and that a long train of hair groweth backward between their shoulders." Raleigh did not claim to have seen the headless men with his own eyes, "yet for mine own part I am resolved it is true." See Raleigh's *The Discoverie of the Larger, Rich, and Beautiful Empire of Guiana, with a relation of the Great and Golden City of Manoa (which the Spaniards call El Dorado)*, trans. V.T. Harlow (London: The Argonaut Press, 1928), p. 56. See also Chapman, p. 329.

That Europeans have continued to invest in the idea of America their fondest dreams has been made newly clear by Peter Conrad in *Imagining America* (New York: Oxford Univ. Press, 1980).

[8] See, for example, the autobiography and journal of Thomas Shepard, edited by Michael McGiffert under the title *God's Plot: The Paradoxes of Puritan Piety* (Amherst, Mass.: Univ. of Mass. Press, 1972). Shepard and other Puritans wrote diaries for their children's spiritual edification as well as to understand God's plan for their own individual histories.

[9] William Bradford, *Of Plymouth Plantation 1620-1647*, ed. Samuel Eliot Morison (New York: Knopf, 1959), for this and further quoted material from Bradford.

[10] Cotton Mather, *Magnalia Christi Americana*, 2 vols. (Hartford: S. Andrus & Sons, 1855); cited passages are from Mather's "A General Introduction," reprinted in *The American Puritans: Their Prose and Poetry*, ed. Perry Miller (Garden City, N.Y.: Doubleday, 1956), pp. 60-72.

[11] Mason I. Lowance, Jr., "Increase Mather's New Jerusalem Manuscript and Millennialism in Late Seventeenth-Century New England," *Proceedings of the American Antiquarian Society*, vol. 88, 1977. See also Sacvan Bercovitch, *The American Jeremiad* (Madison: Univ. of Wisconsin Press, 1978).

[12] Mather led the synod of Boston church that drew up a formal report, entitled "The Necessity of Reformation," that listed the moral afflictions of the time, and in a tract entitled "A Brief History of the War with the Indians," he interpreted the New Englanders' defeat by Philip as God's punishment for their sins. His sermon titles include such cataclysmic overtones as "The Day of Trouble is Near."

[13] Thomas Shepard, *The Sincere Convert: Discovering the small number of true Beleevers, And the great difficulty of saving conversion*, 4th ed. (London: 1646), p. 72; Jonathan Edwards, "Sinners in the Hands of an Angry God," in *American Poetry and Prose* (Boston: Houghton Mifflin, 1970), p. 68. The list of Puritan apocalyptists

includes John Cotton and Thomas Goodwin, who both wrote commentaries on Revelations in 1639, and Samuel Sewell, who wrote *Phaenomena Quaedam Apocalyptica*, or in its English title, *The New Heaven Upon the New Earth*, in 1697.

[14]See McGiffert, pp. 3-32.

[15]See the final chapter, "The End of the World," in Perry Miller, *Errand into the Wilderness*. (Cambridge, Massachusetts: Harvard University Press. 1956).

[16]Perry Miller, *Jonathan Edwards* (Toronto: William Sloane Associates, 1949), p. 314. I am indebted throughout this discussion to Miller's exposition of Edwards' thought.

[17]Jonathan Edwards, "History of the Work of Redemption," in *The Works of President Edwards* (New York: Burt Franklin, Publisher, 1968), V, 11-282. See also *Apocalyptic Writings*, Vol. V of *The Works of Jonathan Edwards*, ed. Stephen J. Stein (New Haven: Yale Univ. Press, 1977).

[18]Miller, *Jonathan Edwards*, pp. 326; 318.

[19]Miller, ed., *The American Puritans*, pp. 289-300.

[20]R.W.B. Lewis, *The American Adam: Innocence, Tragedy, and Tradition in the Nineteenth Century* (Chicago: Univ. of Chicago Press, 1955), has been very useful to me throughout my discussion of nineteenth-century authors.

[21]D.H. Lawrence, in his study of nineteenth-century American literature, finds the common theme uniting all the writers to be this urge to escape from civilization, especially from European civilization: "Somewhere deep in every American heart lies a rebellion against the old parenthood of Europe... A vast republic of escaped slaves.... The masterless. Whatever else you are, be masterless. 'Ca Ca Caliban/Get a new master, be a new man'." *Studies in Classic American Literature* (1924; rpt. New York: Viking, 1964), pp. 4-5. See also Fiedler, *The Return of the Vanishing Americans*.

[22]Poe wrote "Eureka," a treatise in which he explains as scientifically as he is able the annihilation of the world; apocalypse is also thematic in several of his short stories such as "Al Aaraaf" and "The Masque of the Red Death," and in poetical metaphysical pieces such as "The Conversation of Eiros and Charmion," "The Colloquy of Monos and Una," and "The Power of Words." H. Bruce Franklin states that there is no major nineteenth-century American writer who did not write some science fiction or at least one utopian romance. Leslie Fiedler in turn links science fiction to the myth of apocalypse: the dream of apocalypse is the myth of science fiction, "the myth of the end of man, of the transcendence or transformation of the human—a vision quite different from the extinction of our species by the Bomb, which seems stereotype rather than archetype." See H. Bruce Franklin, *Future Perfect* (New York: Oxford, 1970); Leslie Fiedler, "The New Mutants," *Partisan Review*, XXXII (Fall, 1965), 508; David Ketterer, *New Worlds for Old: The Apocalyptic Imagination, Science Fiction and American Literature* (Garden City, N.Y.: Anchor Press/Doubleday, 1974) for a general discussion of apocalypse and science fiction.

[23]One can, perhaps, ascribe too much importance to the wilderness in explaining the sense of endless possibility of this period. The lack of any sense of an ending is also at the heart of the nineteenth-century theoretical history. The charting of universal history became by the mid-nineteenth century a means of explaining America's secular destiny as it had been for the Puritans a means of explaining their divine destiny. George Bancroft, like Cotton Mather, concluded that America was the culmination of a universal historical process, but unlike Mather, he saw it not as a process soon to be truncated by divine justice or by anything else, for that matter: the end of the process simply didn't exist. Bancroft, before the New York Historical Society in 1854, stated, "Everything is in motion, and for the better. The last system of philosophy is always the best.... The last political state of the world likewise is ever more excellent than the old." George Bancroft, "The Progress of Mankind," in

Literary and Historical Miscellanies (New York: Harper and Brothers, 1855), p. 517. The doctrine of progress was of course the property of English historians as well as American: Herbert Spencer wrote in *Social Statics* in 1851: "always toward perfection is the mighty movement—toward a complete development and a more unmixed good, subordinating in its universality all petty irregularities and falling back, as the curvature of the earth subordinates mountains and valleys." (New York: Robert Schalkenbach Foundation, 1954), p. 263.

[24]Hector St. John de Crèvecoeur, *Letters from an American Farmer* (New York: Dutton, Everyman's Library, 1951), pp. 167-168.

[25]Garry Wills, *Inventing America: Jefferson's Declaration of Independence* (Garden City, N.Y.: Doubleday, 1978). Wills, in his prologue, analyzes the Gettysburg Address, especially the rhetorical uses of Biblical phrases and images in the Gettysburg Address. He suggests that President Lincoln's speeches so deeply touched—and still touch—our national imagination because he understood the hold of the English Bible on the American Protestant mind: Biblical patterns and phrases became more and more evident as Lincoln grew into a messianic vision of his office and an apocalyptic vision of the Civil War. See also Ernest L. Tuveson, *Redeemer Nation* (Chicago: Univ. of Chicago Press, 1968), chs. 1 and 2.

[26]It is interesting to read the comments of James Baldwin on the apocalyptic mentality of Mrs. Stowe. He says, "The virtuous rage of Mrs. Stowe is motivated by nothing so temporal as a concern for the relationship of men to one another—or even, as she would have claimed, by a concern for their relationship to God—but merely by a panic of being hurled into the flames, of being caught in traffic with the devil.... Here, black equates with evil and white with grace; if, being mindful of good works, she could not cast out the blacks—a wretched, huddled mass, apparently claiming, like an obsession, her inner eye—she could not embrace them either.... *Uncle Tom's Cabin*, then, is activated by what might be called a theological terror, the terror of damnation....." And speaking of St. Claire and Miss Ophelia, characters in Stowe's novel, Baldwin says, "Neither of them questions the medieval morality from which their dialogue springs: black, white, the devil, the next world—posing its alternatives between heaven and the flames—were realities for them as, of course, they were for their creator." *Notes of a Native Son* (New York: Bantam, 1964), pp. 12, 9.

[27]Lewis Mumford, *The Golden Day: A Study in American Experience and Culture* (New York: Boni and Liveright, 1926), especially Chapter II, "The Romanticism of the Pioneer." See also Cecilia Tichi, *New World, New Earth* (New Haven: Yale Univ. Press, 1979).

[28]See Leo Marx, *The Machine in the Garden: Technology and the Pastoral Ideal in America* (New York: Oxford Univ. Press, 1964).

[29]H.D. Thoreau, *Thoreau: Walden and Other Writings*, ed. Joseph Wood Krutch (New York: Bantam, 1965), pp. 191, 125, 109.

[30]Alexis de Toqueville, *Democracy in America*, ed. Phillips Bradley (New York: Knopf, 1956), II, 99.

[31]Ralph Waldo Emerson, *Emerson's Complete Works*, 12 vols. (Boston: Houghton Mifflin, Riverside Edition, 1904), VII, 9; I, 232. See also "New England Reformers," III, 249-285.

[32]See Georges Poulet, *Studies in Human Time*, trans. Elliott Coleman (Baltimore: Johns Hopkins Press, 1956), for a discussion of the temporal nature of Whitman's poetic vision. Poulet argues that Whitman was acutely aware of the one-directional process of history and felt it a necessary condition for poetic activity: the poet necessarily participates in the ongoing work of the universe. A different view of Whitman's historicity is expressed by Walter J. Ong, S.J., "Evolution, Myth and Poetic Vision," in *Comparative Literature: Matter and Method,* ed. A. Owen Aldridge (Urbana: Univ. of Illinois Press, 1969), pp. 308-328. The shift in Whitman's attitude

toward America's individual and collective destinies can also be seen in such poems as "To a Stranger," "This Moment Yearning and Thoughtful," "I saw in Louisiana a Live-Oak Growing," "When I Peruse the Conquer'd Fame," "The Noiseless Patient Spider." See *Leaves of Grass* (New York: New American Library, 1955).

[33]In three early short stories, Hawthorne exposes what he conceives to be the simplistic optimism of the idea that American history is moving constantly onward and upward. "The Celestial Railroad" portrays an American "Christian," sure that he is on the direct road to heaven in his wonderful machine, who discovers that in fact he is headed for hell. "The New Adam and Eve" is set on the day after a "terrible catastrophe," when "the universal bankruptcy was announced by peal of trumpet." And in "Earth's Holocaust," America's repeated efforts to discontinue history and begin again are treated with particularly trenchant irony. Nathaniel Hawthorne, *Mosses from an Old Manse* in *The Complete Writings of Nathaniel Hawthorne* 13 vols.(Boston: Houghton Mifflin, 1900), IV, 259-288; V, 1-31, 195-229.

[34]Lewis, *The American Adam*, p. 113.

[35]Hawthorne, *The Scarlet Letter*, in *The Complete Writings*, VI, 286-306.

[36]See Arthur Eugene Bestor, Jr., *Backwoods Utopias: The Sectarian Origins and the Owenite Phases of Communitarian Socialism in America, 1663-1829*, 2nd ed. (Philadelphia: Univ. of Pennsylvania Press, 1970).

[37]Hawthorne, *The Blithedale Romance*, in *The Complete Writings*, VIII, 50, 86-86.

[38]A.N. Kaul, *The American Vision: Actual and Ideal Society in Nineteenth-Century Fiction* (New Haven: Yale, University Press, 1964), especially the chapter on Hawthorne, pp. 139-212. Kaul notes the specific analoges made by Hawthorne between Blithedale and the Puritan experiment: "In *The Blithedale Romance* [Hawthorne] presents the utopian experiment at Brook Farm as an extension of the Puritan tradition. The backward glance of comparison runs like a rich thread through the pattern of [*Blithedale*], making explicit the significance which the American romancer saw in this otherwise quixotic enterprise" (p. 196).

[39]Lawrence, *Studies in Classic American Literature*, pp. 138-139.

[40]Lawrence, pp. 159-160.

[41]Flannery O'Connor, Katherine Anne Porter, and Walker Percy must be included among those Southern writers whose vision is termed apocalyptic. Ihab Hassan alludes to this Southern penchant: "The South, of course, is a place where the dialectic of innocence and guilt, communion and estrangement, primitivism and ceremony, can be clearly observed; it is a place where the Protestant mind and the folk spirit have not succumbed entirely to business ethics or urban impersonality." *Radical Innocence: The Contemporary American Novel* (Princeton: Princeton Univ. Press, 1961), p. 79. See also the chapter on O'Connor in John R. May, *Toward a New Earth: Apocalypse in the American Novel* (Notre Dame: Univ. of Notre Dame Press, 1972).

[42]William Faulkner, *Absalom! Absalom!* (New York: Random House, 1936), p. 231. (Subsequent references to this work are cited parenthetically in the text.) The reference is specifically to Haiti, but the parallel to Mississippi is explicit, for it is in Haiti that Sutpen learns how to exploit the Negro and the land, lessons which he ruthlessly applies in Mississippi.

[43]See R.W.B. Lewis, "The Hero in the New World," in *The Picaresque Saint* (New York: Lippincott, 1956, pp. 179-219). The similarities between Ike and Huck Finn are suggested in their identification of slavery as a kind of original sin and in their reversal of the conventional morality that legitimizes social injustice.

[44]See Viola Sachs, *The Myth of America: Essays in the Structures of Literary Imagination* (The Hague: Mouton, 1973), p. 103. The chapter on *Absalom, Absalom!* is useful in its discussion of the archetypal material in the novel.

The Myth of Apocalypse 137

⁴⁵Several critics have dwelt on Sutpen's history as a paradigm for the history of the South. See Donald M. Kartiganer, "Faulkner's *Absalom, Absalom!*: The Discovery of Values," *American Literature*, 37, 3 (November 1965), p. 291; Walter Sullivan, "The Tragic Vision of *Absalom, Absalom!*," *South Atlantic Quarterly*, 50 (October 1951), 552-566; F. Garvin Davenport, Jr., *The Myth of Southern History: Historical Consciousness in Twentieth Century Literature* (Nashville: Vanderbilt Univ. Press, 1970).

⁴⁶Peter Swiggart, *The Art of Faulkner's Novels* (Austin: Univ. of Texas Press, 1962), especially the chapter entitled "A Puritan Tragedy: *Absalom, Absalom!*."

⁴⁷Henry Adams, *The Education of Henry Adams* (New York: Modern Library, 1931), pp. 389, 382.

⁴⁸Norbert Wiener, *The Human Use of Human Beings: Cybernetics and Society*, 1st ed. (Boston: Houghton Mifflin, 1950), p. 31. This and the second edition, published by Doubleday in 1954, provide useful explanations of the theory of entropy.

⁴⁹Henry Adams, *The Degradation of the Democratic Dogma* (New York: Capricorn Books, 1958). This collection of essays, published as a group after Adams' death, documents the historian's interest in applying the second law of thermodynamics to historical phenomena. In one essay, "A Letter to American Teachers of History" (1010), Adams outlines the development and implications of the idea of entropy, starting with the publication of William Thompson's article "On a Universal Tendency in Nature to the Dissipation of Mechanical Energy," in October, 1852, in which "this young man of twenty-eight...tossed the universe into the ash-heap..." (pp. 137-138). Adams explains that physicists soon gave their support to Thompson's theory, "but to the vulgar and ignorant historian it meant only that the ash-heap was constantly increasing in size; while the public understood little and cared less about Entropy, and the literary class knew only that the Newtonian universe, in which they had been cradled, admitted no loss of energy in the solar system, where the planets, at the end of their planetary years, returned exactly to their positions at the beginning" (p. 138).

In another essay of this collection, "The Rule of Phase Applied to History" (1909), Adams takes his title from Willard Gibbs' formulation of the "Rule of Phases" in his tract, "Equilibrium of Heterogenous Substances." Adams says that Gibbs' "Rule of Phases" defied translation into literary language, but as his chapter title indicates, he nevertheless translates it, as do many contemporary novelists, into a metaphor for their perceptions of the degenerative tendencies of modern society.

⁵⁰Tony Tanner, "The American Novelist as Entropologist," *The London Magazine*, October 1970, pp. 5-18.

⁵¹Thomas Pynchon, "Entropy," *Kenyon Review* 23 (Winter, 1960), 281. For a more specific discussion of Pynchon's fiction, see my articles, "The Entropic End: Science and Eschatology in the Works of Thomas Pynchon," *Science/Technology and the Humanities*, III, (Winter, 1980).

⁵²Nathanael West, *Miss Lonelyhearts* and *The Day of the Locust* (New York: New Directions, 1962), p. 38.

⁵³The passage in Revelations is based on a passage from Exodus 10:3-6, 13-15, describing God's punishment of Egypt: "At dawn the east wind brought the locusts. They swarmed over the whole land of Egypt and settled down on every part of it. Never before had there been such a fierce swarm of locusts, nor will there ever be. They covered the surface of the whole land till it was black with them.... Nothing green was left on any tree or plant throughout the land of Egypt."

⁵⁴Northrup Frye, *Anatomy of Criticism: Four Essays* (Princeton: Princeton Univ. Press, 1957), p. 147. Subsequent references are cited in the text. Frye's complete definition of apocalyptic imagery is useful in understanding Revelation:

The apocalyptic world, the heaven of religion, presents, in the first place, the categories of reality in the forms of human desire, as indicated by the forms they assume under the work of human civilization. The form imposed by human work and desire on the *vegetable* world, for instance, is that of the garden, the farm, the grove, or the park. The human form of the *animal* world is a world of domesticated animals, of which the sheep has a traditional priority in both Classical and Christian metaphor. The human form of the *mineral* world, the form into which human work transforms stone, is the city. The city, the garden, and the sheepfold are the organizing metaphors of the Bible and of most Christian symbolism, and they are brought into complete metaphorical identification in the book explicitly called the Apocalypse or Revelation, which has been carefully designed to form an undisplaced mythical conclusion for the Bible as a whole. From our point of view this means that the Biblical Apocalypse is our grammar of apocalyptic imagery (p. 141, emphasis Frye's)

[55]West:, *The Day of the Locust*, pp. 60, 131-132, 142.

[56]Thermodynamic entropy is closely related to the realm of communications. Just as molecular organizations are prey to increasing disorganization, so is the information carried in any given message; if entropy is a measure of disorganization, the information contained in a message is a measure of organization. See Jagjit Singh, *Great Ideas in Information Theory, Language, and Cybernetics* (New York: Dover, 1966), p.76.

[57]Sociological treatment of these phenomena upon which Coover's novel is based is by Leon Festinger, Henry W. Riecken and Stanley Schachter, *When Prophecy Fails: A Social and Psychological Study of a Modern Group that Predicted the Destruction of the World* (Minneapolis: University of Minnesota Press, 1956).

[58]Robert Coover, *The Origin of the Brunists* (New York: Bantam Books, 1966), p. 462.

[59]Carson McCullers, *The Heart is a Lonely Hunter* (1940; rpt. New York: Bantam, 1953), p. 306.

V.
The American West as Millennial Kingdom

Dawn Glanz

LIVING in an age threatened by potential nuclear holocaust, we readily identify apocalypse with ultimate destruction; but the term more correctly refers to a class of writings in the Judeo-Christian tradition which purport to reveal not only the end of the present order, with all its wickedness and suffering, but also the glorious rewards God has in store for His faithful. St. John's canonical Book of Revelations, the apocalypse most familiar to Christians, does indeed contain dramatic accounts of cataclysmic occurrences—plagues, persecutions, famines and wars; but St. John also foresaw beyond these grim events a bright future awaiting the righteous in the millennium, an era of one thousand years of human perfection ruled over by Christ.

John's colorful language and vivid descriptions have inspired in the visual arts fascinating images which not only illustrate his apocalypse, but also reflect how a particular society has adopted apocalyptic and millennial thinking to help itself explain the past and the present, and to reasure itself about the future. For example, Mozarabic Spain (the Christian population of the Iberian peninsula living under the Moslem occupation) produced between the eighth and twelfth centuries a number of remarkable illuminated manuscripts of commentaries on the apocalypse by Beatus of Liebana. Executed in a primitive and coloristic style, the images have a directness and intensity matching St. John's powerful vision. It has been suggested that the popularity of these apocalypse manuscripts was directly related to the religious situation in medieval Spain, where the Church was fraught with internal heresies and overshadowed by the spectre of Mohammedanism.[1] The message of the apocalypse, especially as interpreted by Beatus, enabled the faithful to understand this disturbing state of affairs.

The Beatus manuscripts illustrate all aspects of John's apocalypse—visions of demons and devils as well as the glorious revelation of the Lamb and the New Jerusalem; but in many respects these illuminations lie outside the mainstream of the apocalyptic tradition in western art, which resides instead primarily in the numerous images of the Last Judgment to be found in painting and monumental sculpture.[2] The millennial vision of the heavenly city did not fire the imaginations of Romanesque sculptors or Renaissance painters to the same degree that the mere idea of damnation could. By far the most interesting parts of Last Judgment images are the descriptions of the damned. On the sculpted tympanum of the Church of St. Foy at Conques (12th century), the orderly array of the Blessed in Heaven on the left is bland and dull in comparison to the animated contortions of the wicked and their demon-tormentors in Hell on the right. Centuries later, when Luca Signorelli painted his fresco of The Damned Cast Into Hell in the Cathedral of Orvieto (1499-1503), he filled the foreground with an entire catalogue of tortures, including the image of a woman whose toenails are being extracted by a man-like fiend. We can better appreciate the vividness of Signorelli's imagery, and the imagery of Albrecht Durer's magnificent series of woodcuts illustrating the apocalypse executed at about the same time, if we recall that each artist began his project in the closing years of the fifteenth century, at a time when most of Christendom was anticipating the fulfillment of St. John's Revelation with the Second Coming of Christ in the year 1500.

In contrast to the rich tradition of apocalyptic Last Judgment imagery, there are few if any images of the millennial kingdom that could serve as a visual tradition for an artist imbued with millennial expectations. This is definitely the case in the American art of the nineteenth century. When the Quaker painter Edward Hicks envisioned the millennial state in his many paintings of *The Peaceable Kingdom*, he actually relied on the vision of Isaiah rather than St. John: The lion shall lie down with the lamb, and a little child shall lead them. Furthermore, he embellished his image with a motif derived from America's still meagre artistic tradition: the central group from Benjamin West's well-known painting of William Penn's Treaty with the Indians. In adding this image to the background of his composition, Hicks gave his millennial kingdom a peculiarly Quaker and American stamp.

While the visual traditions of millennial imagery are scant, the literary tradition of millennialism in American is quite strong. America has had a tradition of such thinking since the days of the Puritan divines in seventeenth-century New England.[3] Cotton Mather, and later in the eighteenth century Jonathan Edwards and

The American West as Millennial Kingdom

Timothy Dwight, among others, gave devout attention to the study of biblical prophecy and apocalyptic, especially to St. John's Apocalypse. Their studies led them to interpret contemporary history as a fulfillment of apocalyptic predictions. They began to suspect that God was indeed working His purpose out, just as the Revelator had prophesied—and He was doing so in America, at that! Edwards, as Professor Lippy has stated in his essay in this collection, perceived the Great Awakening of the 1740s as a sign that the coming of Christ's kingdom on earth was imminent.[4] His grandson Timothy Dwight in like manner viewed the American Revolution as a part of the grand scheme of redemption, although he believed the American victory was to be just a prelude to other events which, he predicted, would culminate in the year 2000 with the actual commencement of the millennium. Dwight also spoke repeatedly of the American nation as a people whom God had chosen as His agents in the accomplishment of His plan. America, according to Dwight, was to become a paradigm of peace, righteousness and freedom, and her virtues would go forth to redeem the rest of the world.[5] His contemporaries echoed his sentiments by proclaiming the citizens of the New Republic "a people peculiarly favored of Heaven," and "God's American Israel," drawing what was to become an often-used analogy between the American nation and the Chosen People of the Old Testament.[6] Thus was born the concept of America's special place in world history, forwarding God's plan for world redemption and thereby fulfilling biblical prophecies.

Millennial thinking, and particularly the concept of America's messianic role, persisted well into the nineteenth century and was especially evident in the way Americans regarded their nation's remarkable expansion into the West during the 1840s and 50s.[7] When they described and advocated western expansion, their diction was distinctly biblical, derived from Old Testament history and prophecy. Pioneers were likened to Abraham, Moses and Joshua, and western territories were referred to as the new Promised Land.[8] As one congressional orator put it, emigration was a "glorious, divine impulse. Let it exert its sway until the world shall become a common republic and mankind a united brotherhood."[9]

Images of westward expansion in the visual arts of the period give tangible form to the messianic self-concept implicit in expansionist rhetoric. Artists, for example, drew visual analogies between western pioneers and the Holy Family. Two paintings of emigrant families dated from mid-century are cases in point. William S. Jewett's *The Promised Land* (1850; Evanston, Ill., Terra Museum of American Art) undoubtedly drew its inspiration from the long tradition of depictions of the Holy Family resting on the Flight into Egypt. A pioneer mother and her child are seated on the ground under a tree in a landscape setting, while the father (Joseph's counterpart, dressed in western garb) stands nearby gazing on the wilderness landscape stretched before him. The child is curiously dressed in an ermine-trimmed coat, probably an allusion to the divinely royal ancestry of the Christ Child. With the title of the painting, however, Jewett introduces another analogy, in which he likens the pioneer family to Moses and the Israelites viewing the Promised Land of Canaan from the top of Mount Pisgah. Jewett's family looks out from a promontory onto the prospect of their own promised land, in this case probably California, where Jewett was residing in 1850.[10] This amalgam of allusions to Old and New Testaments implies a continuity between the two, which the painting extends to America's present and future prospects. Just as the Exodus prefigured the Flight into Egypt, so the Promised Land prefigured the millennial kingdom to be inaugurated by Christ at His Second Coming. The prophecies of both Old and New Testaments will be fulfilled, Jewett implied, in America's Far West.

George Caleb Bingham's painting of 1851, *The Emigration of Daniel Boone into Kentucky* (St. Louis, Washington University Gallery), celebrates Boone and his family as archetypal pioneers, the forerunners of the western emigrants whose overland treks to California and Oregon had attracted national attention in the 1840s.[11] This painting also derives from the imagery of the flight into Egypt; but here Bingham focusses on the figure of Rebecca Boone, seated Madonnna-like on her white horse at the apex of the composition. There can be little doubt that the artist wished his audience to recognize Rebecca as a modern-day Madonna, for he dressed her in a Marianic headpiece altogether inappropriate to pioneer dress, a fact made even more conspicuous by the contrast of this drapery with the more conventional bonnet worn by Boone's daughter riding nearby. Bingham was evidently paying tribute to the entire class of pioneer women who played such an important role in the settling of the frontier, for a lithograph of his painting done sometime during the 1850s bears the dedication, "To the Mothers and Daughters of the American West." But we must not overlook the

The American West as Millennial Kingdom   143

possibility that Bingham had yet another analogy in mind. Christians familiar with biblical exegesis are aware that the Virgin Mary has a counterpart in St. John's apocalypse, where, in Chapter 12, he describes a woman "who brought forth a man child, who was to rule all nations with a rod of iron.... And the woman fled into the wilderness, where she hath a place prepared of God." It is not impossible that Bingham and perhaps some of his audience, read the figure of Rebecca Boone as a Madonna-cum-Woman-of-the-Apocalypse, bringing to the wilderness the redemptive influence of Christian civilization.

The paintings by Jewett and Bingham originated at a crucial point in the history of expansion, at a time when the optimism of the 1840s was giving way to mounting sectional tensions in national politics. The era of expansion had brought with it a growing fear on the part of Northerners that slavery would spread into the western territories and would thus upset the balance between slave states and free. Eventually sectional strife and the slavery issue overshadowed all else in national politics, and the Republic edged its way toward civil conflict.

As the crisis mounted, so too in Northern states did the anticipation of an apocalyptic drama. As Ernest Tuveson and George Fredrickson have pointed out in separate studies, the mood of America in the years immediately preceding the Civil War was one of anticipation—both optimistic and apprehensive.[12] There was indeed an expectation of the coming millennium, but it was also becoming increasingly clear that the nation was plagued by the evil of slavery and that reform or purgation would be necessary before Americans as the Chosen People could enjoy the millennium. When civil war finally broke out, therefore, Americans in the Northern states with millennial expectations could view it as the battle of Armageddon in which the forces of good (Union and liberty) would destroy once and for all the apocalyptic beast (secession and slavery). For southern Americans, the terms were of course reversed, but their sense of the cosmic nature of the conflict coincided with that of their northern adversaries. Tuveson, quoting literature published in the first years of the war, demonstrates most convincingly that for many Americans the parallel between the apocalyptic war and their present crisis was more than just an analogy; it was the actual fulfillment of the visions revealed to St. John on the isle of Patmos.[13]

It is in this context that we must consider Emanuel Leutze's mural commemorating westward expansion, painted in the Capitol Building in Washington, D.C. in 1863, during the troubled years of the war.[14] Of all the American images of Westward expansion, this one most fully describes the West as the locus of the millennial kingdom. The mural shares with apocalyptic millennialism four important traits: a sense of optimism occasioned by the revealed prospect of a bright future for those chosen by God; a reading of contemporary events as the fulfillment of the historical plan revealed by St. John; the concept of a messianic mission for a chosen group of people as a part of the redemptive scheme of history; and an acceptance of tribulations as a necessary prelude to the victory promised by God to His chosen.

We are fortunate that Leutze left a set of notes describing the mural, outlining its intent, and identifying its various elements.[15] These notes are invaluable to any analysis of the work, and I will refer to them frequently in the following discussion. They tell us first that the mural was to be one of a projected series of four paintings in the Capitol representing the "four great causes of prosperity of the country."[16] The intent of the painting, whose subject is specified as "Emigration to the west," was "to represent as near and truthfully as the artist was able the grand peaceful conquest of the great west.... Without a wish to date or localize, or to represent a particular event, it is intended to give in a condensed form a picture of western emigration, the conquest of the Pacific slope." Leutze thus presents the winning of the west as the strenuous and peaceful achievement of America's population, and not as the result of military victory (as in the Mexican War) or diplomacy (as in the Oregon Treaty).

The form of Leutze's project encourages an interpretation in the context of religious imagery. Its layout, consisting of a large central image bordered by an elaborate margin at the top and sides, and below by a long narrow painting which functions as a kind of predella, suggests a huge altarpiece with a sacred theme. The ornamental side margins, which are actually painted on the walls flanking the mural, consist of a vine motif forming arabesques and rondels containing small scenes and, in the the center to either side, portraits of Daniel Boone and George Rogers Clark. These scenes provide (in the artist's own words) "a playfull [sic] introduction from earlier history as a prelude to the subject of the large picture." The episodes depicted are a mixture of Christian and mythological scenes which can be considered types of prefigurations of westward migration. They include a child watching a flight of herons

The American West as Millennial Kingdom 145

(signifying, according to the artist, "migratory emotions"); Moses leading the Israelites through the desert; the Israelite spies with the grapes of Eschol (a motif which symbolizes the abundance of the Promised Land); Hercules dividing the pillars of Gibraltar and opening the way west to the Atlantic Ocean; the Argonauts in search of the golden fleece (the "first search for gold"); and the Magi following the star to the west. As in the case of religious paintings, the presence in the margins of typological scenes and prefigurations implies that the subject of the mural is to be considered the fulfillment of events prophesied by the past.

The upper margin contains, in addition to the banner, an eagle shielding under its wings personifications of "union and liberty" which the artist describes as "influences of superior intelligence." There are also figures identified as an axeman, hunter, agriculturalist and missionary. As counterpoints to these symbols and representatives of American civilization on the frontier, Leutze also presents an Indian "creeping, discharging an arrow at the hunter," and another "covering himself with his robe sneeking [sic] away from the light of knowledge." Thus, as one contemporary description stated, the border illustrates the "advance of pioneer and civilized, over savage life," in which the opposition of the benighted Indian will prove no match for the superior forces of civilization."[17]

The predella beneath the mural depicts a coastal scene, identified in the artist's notes as the "Golden Gate, entrance to [the] harbour of San Francisco." In describing this part of the painting, Leutze quotes from the last verse of Bishop George Berkeley's poem, "On the Prospect of Planting Arts and Learning in America," a popular work among American patriots, and one from which the artist also borrowed the title of his painting:

> Westward the course of Empire takes its way
> The first four acts already past.
> A fifth shall close the drama with the day.

Leutze concludes, "The drama of the Pacific ocean closes our Emigration to the west."

Leutze's choice of the Golden Gate to represent the ultimate goal of emigration is particularly significant in view of its associations with El Dorado—suggesting not only a land of gold, but a "golden land" for a golden—i.e., millennial—age. Also significant is his view of history as a drama (a view which also characterizes apocalyptic thought) in which arrival at the Pacific Coast is the denouement of the preceding action.

The imagery of the borders and "predella" thus outlines the history of emigration from its earliest manifestations to its ultimate goal, and, moreover, it identifies emigration with the advance of civilization. We have, in other words, a synopsis of the progress of history, which, as the image of the retreating Indian suggests, is to be viewed as irresistible. The mural itself depicts the high point of this progress: a wagon train of American pioneers reaching the top of a mountain range, the last barrier separating them from their goal. As Leutze presents it, all events from earlier history lead up to this climactic moment. In his notes the artist describes the central action of the composition in diction that suggests the familiar analogy between the pioneers and the Israelites of the Exodus:

A party of Emigrants have arrived near sunset on the divide (watershed) from whence they have the first view of the Pacific slope, their "promised land" "El Dorado," having passed the troubles of the plains, "The Valley of darkness," & c.— The first are pressing eagerly forward—the dim line of the Western ocean can be traced on the horizon to the left—on the right rise rocky mountains—

Discovery of the distant ocean is made simultaneously by three groups of emigrants: a trapper to the left, pointing out the path ahead; a pioneer family resting on the rocky ground; and in the middle distance, climbing to the top of an outcropping which forms the peak of the composition, two figures, one waving his hat and another bearing an American flag. These groups, arranged on an ascending diagonal, create a dynamic movement upward which culminates in the exuberant waving of hat and flag.

The mood of the painting is thus predominantly hopeful and triumphant, recalling apocalyptic promises of the eventual rewards God has in store for His people. In the nineteenth century, St. John's urban image of the millennial reign, the New Jerusalem, had been supplanted in the popular artistic imagination by more pastoral images, as Professor Zamora also notes in her study of the literature of the period. It is the image of the Promised Land and the Chosen people, taken from Old Testament prophecy, which seems to be conscious and deliberate in Leutze's mural. We must remember that millennialists invoked the story of the Israelites in order to describe their own sense of America's God-ordained mission. For them, Old Testament history was itself a prefiguration of apocalyptic revelations, which were in turn to be equated with America. Thus

The American West as Millennial Kingdom   147

the lessons of both Old and New Testament pointed to the bright destiny of the United States. The words of Isaiah, for example, could provide a text for the painting:

> And it shall come to pass in the last days, that the mountain of the Lord's house shall be established in the top of the mountains, and shall be exalted above the hills; and all nations shall flow unto it.
> And many people shall go and say, Come ye, and let us go up to the mountain of the Lord, to the house of the God of Jacob....
>
> And in that day there shall be a root of Jesse, which shall stand for an ensign of the people; to it shall the Gentiles seek: and his rest shall be glorious.
> And it shall come to pass in that day, that the Lord shall set his hand again the second time to recover the remnant of his people, which shall be left....
> And he shall set up an ensign for their nations, and shall assemble the outcasts of Israel, and gather together the dispersed of Judah from the four corners of the earth.
> *Isaiah* 2:2,3: 11: 10-12

One wonders how many Bible-reading Americans in the nineteenth century (or indeed in the twentieth), reading these passages from the Old Testament, might have visualized the ensign as the American flag!

Attention focuses on the family group in the foreground, which Leutze identifies as a "frontiere [sic] farmer (Tennesseeian)" and "his suffering wife with her infant in her arms." The husband, supporting the reclining figure of his wife with one arm, gestures with the other to the left, pointing out "the glories of the promised land." The daughter is "cheering her mother with expressions of delight and surprize," while the "mother has folded her hands thanking for escape from dangers past (religious feeling indicated)." Next to them stands their son, described as a "type of young American" who "looks thoughtfully into the future,"— significantly toward the western horizon. We may read this family group, the keystone of the composition, as representing all pioneer families and their expectations. Having suffered hardships and persevered, they are now to be rewarded with entry into the Promised Land.

A comparison between this group and a motif from the tradition of apocalypse illustrations is instructive at this point. Perhaps the best-known series of illustrations of the Book of Revelations are Albrecht Durer's woodcuts, published in 1498.[18] The last print in the narrative order of this series of fifteen images illustrates two passages from the last chapters of the St. John's vision, one telling of the binding of Satan for a thousand years (i.e., the millennium) and the other describing the Angel showing John the New Jerusalem. Dominating the foreground of Durer's image is the figure of an angel with a key forcing a chained beast (the dragon Satan) into a hole (the bottomless pit). Behind this group rises a steep hill, toward the top of which stand another angel and the Revelator. The angel gestures with his right arm toward a city situated in the background and to the left, while he looks back at John, who stands at his side to the right, holding his hands together as in prayer. This motif of the angel pointing out to his companions the entrance to the New Jerusalem can also be found in images of the Last Judgment in Italian and Flemish paintings of the fifteenth century, where it forms part of the scene from the Elect being ushered into Heaven.[19] Although the motif in Durer's print and the pioneer couple in Leutze's mural are not identical, the general design of the two groups is the same: figures set on a raised ground, one pointing out to the left a vista, the other clasping hands together in reverent response. More important, however, is the fact that the visual similarities are paralleled by analogous content, for in both images the figures are looking out toward a long-awaited and blessed realm.

There is in Leutze's composition ample evidence that arrival at the threshold of the west has been achieved at the expense of hardships and struggles. The pioneers' ascent is arduous, and an occasional animal skeleton and broken wheel are reminders of disappointments and failures. We find also among them "a lad who has been wounded, probably in a fight with the Indians," and a young woman "in doubt whether there be not more troubles ahead." In a smaller painting made in preparation for the mural, Leutze even included in the background a group of pioneers burying one of their companions in a grave marked by a large cross—perhaps a hint of martyrdom.[20] Although the artist eliminated this episode from the actual mural, he evidently believed that an essential factor in the drama of emigration was the pioneers' endurance of hardship and tribulation. The theme of trials endured and opposition overcome is entirely consonant with the spirit of apocalypse, and also with Old Testament history and prophecy, which stressed that the faith of the Chosen People must be tried and purified in order to earn them their reward.

We must remember also that Leutze began his mural at a time of national crisis; and we should therefore consider its optimism in this

The American West as Millennial Kingdom   149

context. Although the artist had been contemplating the possibility of a government commission in the Capitol since the early 1850s and had originally proposed the subject of emigration as early as 1857, he submitted preliminary oil sketches of the mural and received the contract for the work only in 1861, as the nation was mobilizing for war.[21] It is likely then that as he developed his theme, he was fully aware of its potential significance to the impending conflict. Indeed there is evidence that as the war intensified, he altered his first ideas somewhat, for the final painting displays some significant changes from the earlier sketches. One of these changes, mentioned above, was the elimination of the burial scene, perhaps because it sounded too tragic a note for the time, already saturated with reports of Civil War casualties. Even more telling, however, is the addition in the final mural of a negro boy, placed almost in the exact center of the foreground, and accompanying a mother and child who are not so prominent in the compositions of the preliminary sketches. According to Anne Brewster, writing in 1868 of an interview she had once had with the artist, these figures were intended "to teach a new gospel to the continent, a new truth which this part of the world is to accept—that the Emigrant and the Freedman are the two great elements which are to be reconciled and worked with." "The young, beautiful Irish woman" was also to be seen as a "new Madonna."[22] The essence of Brewster's interpretation, which she claims was approved by Leutze himself, was that western emigration promised salvation and reconciliation for the country by offering freedom and social justice to the nation's and the world's oppressed. True to millennialist expectation, still pervasive among Americans after the conclusion of the Civil War, Brewster saw in Leutze's painting the promise of a new era, in which America, a messianic nation now purified of evil by the trials of the War, would preach to the rest of the world the gospel of reconciliation between races and nationalities. To be sure, her interpretation strongly reflects the urgent need of the post-war era for the unifying of diverse national and racial elements; but her perception of the painting's moral message, as well as its hope for a bright future, apparently gets to the core of Leutze's intent.

The very act of commissioning and executing a painting of national history at a time of crisis could be considered a symbolic act of faith, and indeed there is evidence that it was so interpreted. In a memorandum dated June 20, 1861, Captain Montgomery Meigs, Superintendent of the Capitol Extension, wrote to the Secretary of

War concerning final approval for the mural commission. His words are revealing and are worth quoting at length:

> The design of Mr. Leutze for the western staircase of the Capitol typical of emigration to the Pacific, was submitted to the Secretary of War at a time when the Capitol itself was hardly out of danger.
>
> The Government was exerting itself to create and move an army to its defence [sic] and putting a stop to all expenditures not absolutely necessary for that defence [sic].
>
> The Secretary did not permit the work to be then commenced.
>
> The people of the country have so responded to the call of their Government that danger to the Capitol has now passed away, and it is a question worthy of consideration whether the Government by pursuing in some degree the project of completing its Capitol would not give to the people a welcome assurance of its confidence in its own strength and in its patriotism of its people.
>
> The people... probably would hail with joy such evidence of the determination and confidence of the Government.[23]

The painting did indeed have the desired effect. A year after the contract for the commission was signed, Nathaniel Hawthorne, writing "Chiefly About War Matters" in the *Atlantic Monthly* of July 1862, described a recent visit to the nation's Capitol, during which he had seen Leutze at work on the mural. About the painting and its effects on his morale, Hawthorne wrote:

> [The painting] looked full of energy, hope, progress, irrepressible movement onward, all represented in a momentary pause of triumph; and it was most cheering to feel its good augury at this dismal time, when our country might seem to have arrived at such a deadly stand-still.
>
> It was an absolute comfort, indeed, to find Leutze so quietly busy at this great national work, which is destined to glow for centuries on the walls of the Capitol, if that edifice shall stand, or must share its fate, if treason shall succeed in subverting it with the Union which it represents. It was delightful to see him so calmly elaborating his design, while other men doubted and feared, or hoped treacherously, and whispered to one another that the nation should exist only a little longer, or that, if a remnant still held together, its center and seat of government would be far northward and westward of Washington. But the artist keeps right on, firm of heart and hand, drawing his outline with an unwavering pencil, beautifying and idealizing our rude material life, and thus manifesting that we have an indefeasible claim to a more enduring national existence. In honest truth, what with the hope-inspiring influence of the design, and what with Leutze's undisturbed evolvement of it, I was exceedingly encouraged.[24]

Hawthorne's article was on the whole a pessimistic commentary on the War, but he was able to see and describe in Leutze's mural the vision of a better world to come, a vision offered by a prophetic artist to a troubled nation as a hopeful alternative to the grim reports arriving at the capital from Fort Sumpter, Bull Run, Richmond and

The American West as Millennial Kingdom   151

Antietam.

The appeal of Leutze's mural to its contemporary audience lay in its ability to present an immediate and concrete image of America's millennial expectations. In the 1840s, the progress of American civilization—deemed inevitable and irreversible—was identified with the physical advance of the American population westward across the continent. By 1860 when slavery and sectionalism had become the over-riding issues of the day, many Americans had begun to view their nation's progress in terms of moral regeneration directed toward expunging slavery from the Union. Even in these changed circumstances, however, westward expansion could serve the concept of progress. First, as an historical phenomenon, it provided a message of encouragement to the supporters of the Union; for, just as Providence had enabled Americans to conquer a continent, so would it assure their victory in a moral struggle to purify and strengthen their Union. Next, the westward movement could function as a metaphor for moral regeneration, with emigration symbolizing a kind of national Pilgrims' Progress, as it were, in which democracy could leave behind the old, the outworn, and the corrupt, and move west toward perfection. Finally, the West itself, that virgin land, could be seen as an agent in the regenerative process, working its beneficial effects on the American population. "The land is the appointed remedy for whatever is false and fantastic in our culture," wrote Emerson in 1844, and he continued:

> The great continent we inhabit is to be physic and food for our mind, as well as our body. The land, with its tranquillizing, sanative influences, is to repair the errors of a scholastic and traditional education, and bring us into just relations with men and things.[25]

Thus it is not difficult to see how the West could have come to symbolize the millennial realm. Although St. John had described this realm as a "heavenly city," Americans found it possible to envision it also as a new Eden, a pristine land such as that which actually existed in the West beyond the Rocky Mountains.

Although the shock of civil war may have shaken Americans' faith in their national destiny, the optimism generated by the promise of the millennium sustained them at least in the early stages of the ordeal, as it must have sustained the early Christians for whom St. John wrote his apocalypse. In Leutze's mural, Americans found evidence that the Promised Land, Paradise

Regained, the Millennial Kingdom, was indeed at hand.

Notes

[1]C.H. Dodwell, *Painting in Europe, 800-1200* (Pelican History of Art; Baltimore: Penguin Books, 1971), pp. 96-103.

[2]For a concise yet insightful discussion of Last Judgment imagery, see Albert E. Elsen, *Purposes of Art: An Introduction to the History and Appreciation of Art*, 3rd ed. (New York: Holt, Rinehart & Winston, 1972), pp. 50-52.

[3]For full-length studies of this tradition, see Ernest Tuveson, *Redeemer Nation; (Chicago: University of Chicago Press, 1968)*; also James West Davidson, *The Logic of Millennial Thought: Eighteenth-Century New England* (New Haven: Yale Univ. Press, 1977).

[4]Davidson, pp. 16-17.

[5]Tuveson, pp. 103ff.

[6]Sermon preached by Thomas Barnard in 1795, quoted in Tuveson, *Redeemer Nation*, p. 31; Ezra Stiles, "The United States Elevated, to Glory and Honor: Sermon preached... May 8, 1783," in John W. Thornton, ed., *The Pulpit of the American Revolution: Political Sermons of the Period of 1776* (1860; rpt. New York: Da Capo Press, 1970), p. 403.

[7]Tuveson offers a detailed discussion of millennial thought in relation to Manifest Destiny in Chapter 4 of *Redeemer Nation: See also* Albert K. Weinberg's seminal study, *Manifest Destiny: A Study of Nationalist Expansionism in American History* (1935; rpt. Chicago: Quadrangle Books, 1963), esp. Chapter 6.

[8]One example from Congressional debate over the Oregon Treaty will serve as a typical example:

...Nothing could be more interesting than the narrative given of the travels... of the thousands who are marching... to Oregon.

These accounts constantly remind us of the travels of the patriarchs of old; and looking back through the dim vista of time... we see Abraham and Lot pitching their tents in the land of Canaan and the plains of Jordan...; when Moses and Aaron... conducted the children of Israel in the pilgrimage through the wilderness....
Remarks of Representative Ficklin, in *Congressional Globe*, 29th Cong., 1st Sess., 1846, Appendix, p. 175.

[9]Remarks of Representative McClernand, *Congressional Globe*, p. 277.

[10]For the few published facts about Jewett's life, see Helen C. Nelson, "The Jewetts: William and William S.," *International Studio*, 83 (Jan.-April 1926), 39-43; Elliot Evans, ed., "Some Letters of William S. Jewett, California Artist," *California Historical Society Quarterly*, 23 (1944), 149-77; idem., "William S. and William D. Jewett," *California Historical Society Quarterly*, 33 (1954), 309-22. The family in Jewett's painting has been identified by George R. Stewart as Captain Andrew Jackson Grayson, his wife, and son: ("The Prairie Schoner Got Them There," *American Heritage*, vol. 13, no. 2, (Feb. 1962), p. 16.

[11]To date the most comprehensive study of Bingham is Maurice E. Bloch's two-volume work, *George Caleb Gingham*, Vol. I: *The Evolution of an Artist*; Vol II: *A Catalogue Raisonne* (Berkeley: Univ. of California Press, 1967).

[12]Tuveson, *Redeemer Nation*, p. 187; George Fredrickson, *The Inner Civil War: Northern Intellectuals and the Crisis of the Union* (New York: Harper & Row, 1965).

[13]Tuveson, Chapter 6. Tuveson cites in particular Hollis Read, *The Coming Crisis of the World; or, The Great Battle and the Golden Age* (1861), and, most tellingly,

The American West as Millennial Kingdom 153

Julia Ward Howe's poem, "The Battle Hymn of the Republic" (1862).

[14]Previous discussions of the mural include Raymond L. Stehle, " 'Westward Ho!': The History of Leutze's Fresco in the Capitol," *Records of the Columbia Historical Society of Washington, D.C., 1960-62,* ed. F.C. Rosenberg (Washington: Columbia Historical Society, 1963), pp. 306-22; Justin G. Turner, "Emanuel Leutze's Mural *Westward the Course of Empire Takes Its Way,*" *Manuscripts,* 18, no. 2 (Spring 1966), pp. 4-16; and Barbara Groseclose, *Emanuel Leutze, 1816-1868: Freedom Is the Only King* (Exhibition Catalogue; Washington: Smithsonian Institution Press, 1975), pp. 60-62, and Catalogue entry No. 101, pp. 96-97. Stehle and Turner present a history of the project, while Groseclose offers in addition a comprehensive interpretation of its meaning. She sees the painting as "not simply the celebration of the emigrant settling of the West but a far deeper (if somewhat historically fuzzy) characterization of the New World Eden." She also believes it reflects Leutze's conviction that America must be built "upon the hopes of the politically and economically oppressed masses of the Old World." Her discussion is certainly the most penetrating to date, and I fully concur with her interpretation. My own analysis, I believe, does not contradict hers, but adds to it by providing another perspective from which to view the meaning of the painting.

[15]The notes are transcribed in full in Turner, "Emanuel Leutze's Mural," pp. 14-16.

[16]The other three murals were not executed, nor are their intended subjects specified in Leutze's notes. His entire program even for the one completed mural was never carried out as he had planned, for he had hoped to supplement it with murals on the side walls representing "the earlier history of Western Emigration, in illustrations from Boone's adventures, the discovery of the valleys of the Ohio, Mississippi—."

[17]Samuel Douglass Wyeth, *Diagrams of the Floor of the Senate and House of Representatives.... Also, Descriptions of Leutze's Picture, "Westward the Course of Empire Takes Its Way...."* (Washington: 1865), n.p.

[18]Erwin Panofsky, in *The Life and Art of Albrecht Durer,* 4th ed. (Princeton, N.J.: Princeton Univ. Press, 1971), describes Durer's Apocalypse woodcuts as "among what may be called the inescapable works of art... which no later artist could or can ignore" (p. 59). Leutze, a German-born artist who returned to his homeland for several years to study and practice art, could scarcely have been ignorant of Durer's work.

[19]See, for example, Rogier van der Weyden's large altarpiece in Beaune, or Fra Angelico's panel in the San Marco Museum, Florence. These images derive from sculptural representations found on church tympana, most of which date from the twelfth century.

[20]The painting belongs to the National Collection of Fine Arts, Washington. In another, less finished preliminary sketch in the Gilcrease Institute of American History and Art in Tulsa, Oklahoma, the cross, but not the burial scene, is visible. See Groseclose, *Emanuel Leutze,* p. 60, and Catalogue entries Nos. 99 and 100, pp. 96-96.

[21]Anne Brewster, "Emmanuel [sic] Leutze, The Artist," *Lippincott's Magazine,* 2 (July-Dec. 1968), 536.

[23]Quoted in Charles E. Fairman, *Art and Artists of the Capitol of the United States of America,* 69th Cong., 1st Sess., Senate Document No. 95 (Washington: U.S. Gov. Printing Office, 1927), p. 202.

[24]Nathaniel Hawthorne, "Chiefly About War-Matters," *Atlantic Monthly,* 10 (July—Dec. 1862), 46.

[25]Ralph W. Emerson, "The Young American," *The Dial,* 4 (April 1844); quoted in *Manifest Destiny,* ed. Norman A. Graebner (New York: Bobbs-Merrill Co., 1968), p. 7.

VI.
The Apocalyptic Vision in American Popular Culture

John Wiley Nelson

VISIONS of an abrupt end to the promise that was "America" haunt the popular consciousness of Americans and increasingly dominate the symbolism of popular drama and popular religion. To paraphrase Aristotle, humanity by nature desires to know the meaning of the end of things.[1] Is there *telos* (a meaning in the end which redeems the present) in the *finis* (the final breaking off) of life? Is there ultimate destiny in the final destruction of our hopes and dreams? I intend here to trace the contours of these visions as they appear in the popularly acclaimed ruminations of Hal Lindsey, found initially and pre-eminently in *The Late Great Planet Earth*, and then in the humanistic and naturalistic portrayals of the same vision in popular films, television and science fiction. In order to do this I need first to define my method of inquiry and then the nature of apocalyptic eschatology.

I. Methodological Considerations and Assumptions

The method employed here combines the insights of the sociology of knowledge with the intuitions and assumptions of philosophical theology into a stance on the nature of popular culture. My view of popular culture, however, falls within the mainstream of scholarly opinion in that area, developing out of ideas presented in John Cawelti's *The Six-Gun Mystique*, and following the basic assumptions of such scholars as Ray Browne, Marshall Fishwick, Russel Nye, and, of course, Robert Warshow.[2] My position is spelled out in detail elsewhere[3], but I want to set its parameters briefly before we begin our primary study of apocalyptic eschatology.

Popular culture is the symbolic reflection of what people already believe. Whether the transcendent symbolism of *Casablanca* or the omnipresent iconic arches of McDonald's, popular culture is a people's self-understanding writ large. Distinguishing my view of popular culture within the mainstream of opinion, however, is the thesis that the relation of those who participate in popular culture experiences to the icons and symbols of popular culture is a religious one, and in a sense, highly liturgical. In a nutshell: popular culture is to what Americans believe as worship services are to what members of institutional religions believe. John Cawelti started my mind in this direction in *The Six-Gun Mystique*:

In earlier, more homogeneous cultures, religious rituals performed the important function of articulating and reaffirming the primary cultural values. Today, with cultures composed of a multiplicity of differing religious groups, the synthesis of values and their reaffirmation has become an increasingly important function of the mass media and the popular arts.[4]

More significant for present purposes than how my view of popular culture is different from other popular culture scholars is what distinguishes the general opinion of popular culture scholars from three other positions. First, the elitist view holds that art is good (for you?), and that popular culture, not being art, is therefore junk. Ray Browne writes:

Elitist critics of our culture—notably such persons as Dwight Macdonald and Edmund Wilson—have always insisted that whatever was widespread was artistically and esthetically deficient, therefore unworthy of study. They have taught that "culture" to be worthwhile must necessarily be limited to the elite, aristocratic, and the minority.... William Gass, for example, takes the extreme position that "the products of popular culture, by and large, have no more esthetic quality than a brick in the street."[5]

I agree that popular culture does not normally qualify as art, but some popular entertainers (e.g., Bob Dylan, Paul Simon, George C. Scott, Cicely Tyson, et al.) and some popular works (*South Pacific, The Ox Bow Incident, One Flew Over the Cuckoo's Nest, The Shootist, Sargeant Pepper's Lonely Hearts' Club Band,*et al.), present a substantially artistic experience in a popular format. Furthermore, the separation of cultural icons and symbols into two categories, valuable (art) and junk (popular culture) simplistically misrepresents the issue of significance. For anyone interested in the self-understanding of a people, popular culture is by far a better barometer than art. The elitist view is myopic and foolish.

Second, sociologist Herbert Gans has argued that popular culture is for the masses what art is for the elite.[6] On the contrary, art stimulates, provokes, challenges, even undermines existing values by examining the superfically agreeable way we express existing beliefs. Popular culture, on the other hand, reaffirms existing beliefs, ritualistically reassuring us that everything is, after all, going to turn out to our satisfaction. As Cawelti says, using the word "formulaic" to emphasize the stereotyping routinization of popular culture:

Much of the artistry of formulaic literature involves the creator's ability to plunge us into a believable kind of excitement while, at the same time, confirming our confidence that in the formulaic world things always work out as we want them to.[7]

Third, the reflective, liturgically satisfying quality of the popular culture experience means that only those people, products and artifacts of the culture which do provide that experience will be popular. This means that popular culture scholarship rejects the Marxist and/or paranoiac contention that the ruling classes use popular culture to mesmerize and manipulate the working classes, directing their thoughts away from social revolution in the former case, or making millions off their hard-earned wages in the latter. Conspicuous consumption of popular culture tends to entrench existing beliefs and to provide provocative symbols for inchoate values, just as the repeating of ritual prayers transfers the force and meaning of prayer from substance to form. But popular culture most effectively communicates values when it meets expectations and reaffirms values and opinions already held by its participants. As Russel Nye says:

Popular art confirms the experience of the majority, in contrast to elite art, which tends to explore the new. For this reason, popular art has been an unusually sensitive and accurate reflector of the attitudes and concerns of the society for which it is produced.... The popular artist corroborates (occasionally with great skill and intensity) values and attitudes already familiar to his audience; his aim is less to provide a new experience than to validate an older one. Predictability is important to the effectiveness of popular art; the fulfillment of expectation, the pleasant shock of recognition of the known, verification of an experience already familiar....[8]

Consigning some methodological considerations concerning philosophical assumptions to a reference note[9] leads us more to define our terms with the following caveat. The theological traditions of Judaism and especially Christianity provide the background for the definitions of eschaton and apocalyptic which occupy us next. The American popular vision of "apocalypse" seems to outstrip not only biblical tradition but the latest revisions of the dictionary as well: few five syllable adjectives are so loosely applied as "apocalyptic." Almost all senses of the word today defy the unqualified simplicity of the synonym "revelation" and cling necessarily to the meaning of the word it has traditionally modified, "eschaton," the final days of the world.

II. Definitions of Apocalyptic and Prophetic Eschatology

A. Apocalyptic Eschatology

Apocalyptic literally means "pertaining to revelation or disclosure," and is rooted in the Greek word, Αποκαλυψις; in the title of the last book of the Bible, it is translated "Revelation." The type of revelation intended by that title is not intra-worldly, historical or progressive, dawning upon one's mind in the midst of human activities, but is rather a radical, supernatural in-breaking of eminently Divine activity. Furthermore, the word "apocalyptic" refers to a type of "eschatology." Eschatology means the study of (-logy) the "last days" (eschaton), and includes such biblical-theological images and symbols as The Last Judgment, The Second Coming of Christ, the New Heaven and the New Earth, a messianic banquet, the Antichrist, Armageddon, the "Four Horsemen of the Apocalypse", and just about any and everything in the biblical Book of the Revelation to John (RSV). Apocalyptic eschatology is the tradition which expects the Last Days (of the world, history, the present time) to be ushered in by a radical, supernatural break in history.

The tradition of apocalyptic eschatology begins long before the New Testament book of Revelation. Developing from the exilic experience of the Jews, as evidenced in *Ezekiel* and *Deutero-Isaiah*, it grew full blown in post-exilic Judaism, and dominated the book of Daniel (in the Protestant Canon) and the intra-testamental books of the Roman Catholic Canon.[10] These fascinating documents chronicle the growing apocalypticism of the Judaic faith, which became more and more shaped by a fierce tenacity in the face of almost overwhelming deprivation.[11] Israel's hopes had been so high; and now, while claiming to be the chosen people of the only true God, they suffered defeat, exile, servitude and a dependent vassal relationship to distant ruling powers. In the midst of this deprivation, their faith and its promises only increased.[12] Tension between faith's promise and the reality of life is not uncommon in the history of faith. But, as biblical scholar Ulrich Mauser says:

> ...for the apocalypticists, the perennial tension was intensified to the breaking point. What had always been a contrast between the actual reality of life and the claim on reality imposed by faith became to the apocalypticists a deadly clash between irreconcilable hostile powers. They could no longer think of change, they had to visualize radical transformation; deeply frustrated by slowly advancing evolution, they could not help but expect catastrophic upheaval; incapable of being at home in their world and unable to find fulfillment in the time that set the limit to their years, they perceived the dawn of another world and of another time. Therefore, their language became full of oppositions of unmitigated conflict between that which is now and that which is yet to come, and their visions built up a grammar of hope in which the coming of God as the world's royal sovereign spelled the end of the world as they knew it.[13]

The Gospels made little use of this climate, with the exception of certain well-known passages like Mark 13 (Luke 10) and Matthew 24-25. The Gospel of John divests eschatological expectation of any future reference, concentrating totally on the present appearance of the Kingdom in Jesus. The early letters of Paul fully expect an imminent eschaton, but without reliance on apocalyptic images. Only in Revelation does apocalyptic eschatology return in the earlier post-exilic, Old Testament style. Thus, the tradition of apocalyptic eschatology dates back to 586 BC, when Jerusalem was destroyed and the Hebrews exiled, and continues through the New Testament period.

B. Prophetic Eschatology

Apocalyptic eschatology is not the only form of eschatological expectation found in the Scriptures. Contrasting sharply with it is what we call, following Martin Buber's designation, "prophetic eschatology."[14] Although we are not concerned here with prophetic eschatology in itself, distinguishing its meaning from that of apocalyptic will help us to understand better the nature of apocalyptic eschatology.

Initially prophetic and apocalyptic eschatology have two common characteristics. First, they are both purposeful eschatologies: both intend their visions of the future to provide the present with meaning. The end must somehow justify or redeem the present, at least the present self-understanding of the belief-holder. Even a last day in which practically no one escapes alive to *any* future can be meaningful if it is perceived as a judgment upon evil trends in the present. Some meaning or purpose adheres when dire predictions of catastrophe prove true and those who paid no heed suffer their just deserts. Second, prophetic and apocalyptic eschatologies agree that the "last day" brings to an end the world as presently understood. An eschatology, whether apocalyptic or prophetic, describes the end of one way of life, and, almost always, the beginning of another. The manner in which the new world emerges, and its resemblance to the previous world, remain debatable issues normally distinguishing apocalyptic from prophetic eschatologies—as we shall see. Whatever the differences, both eschatologies portray the "last days" of the oppressive suffering or frustrating underdevelopment of the "good," and the "last days" of the unjust triumph or troublesome interference of "evil."

More relevant to our discussion are the *differences* between apocalyptic and prophetic eschatologies, several of which have been noted in detail by Professor Bergoffen in the initial essay of this collection. First, prophetic eschatologies envision the end-time as a transitional fulfillment of tendencies that are essentially a part of the present historical, socio-political process. On the contrary, apocalyptic eschatologies look for an end-time characterized by an abrupt disruption of the present order, the judgment and destruction of the tendencies of that order, and the suppression of the old order by a "new heaven and new earth." Apocalyptic eschatologies tend, therefore, to portray the end-time as a chaotic period in which powerful forces violently confront the evil nature of a world whose last days have come. On the contrary, for prophetic eschatologies, in which the last days crown the possibilities of past and present, only those who resist the coming fulfillment find the end-time chaotic or disruptive. Second, whereas apocalyptic eschatologies distinguish simplistically between good and evil, envisioning salvation for the former and damnation for the latter, prophetic eschatologies optimistically trust that evil will be won over and even used purposefully, to serve and enrich the good, just as a discordant note can set off even higher harmonies in musical compositions. Third, prophetic eschatologies experience the end-time as a delightfully surprising revelation of the inevitable fulfillment. The element of inevitability springs from a strong confidence in the forces producing the joyous fulfillment; the element of surprise arises from prophetic eschatology's lack of precise time-tables or preoccupation with "signs of the times" that might herald the final moment of transition to the new age. The mood evokes patient progress. The apocalyptic vision, on the other hand, augers an inevitable confrontation of good and evil presaged by signs, omens and predicting handwriting on the wall. The mood combines a dark, anxious foreboding with pretentious moral posturing.

Most important among their differences is that prophetic eschatology views the present world situation with confident optimism while apocalyptic eschatology feels only despair for this world.[15] This difference explains the essentially different tone of the prophetic and apocalyptic visions in American popular culture, the former basically optimistic, the latter pessimistic. Although the end envisioned in apocalyptic eschatology is not properly a vision of doom, as has already been stated in several of the preceding essays, it is undeniably the doomsday side of apocalyptic exchatology that has captured our popular imagination and has manifested itself in our popular forms. Thus, in apocalyptic eschatology, evil seems everywhere victorious; that which is good and decent no longer holds its own. What can reverse the situation? Nothing offered by the possibilities of the present order. Radical surgery is required.

Having distinguished traditional apocalyptic from traditional prophetic eschatology, I want now to distinguish contemporary prophetic and apocalyptic eschatologies dependent on a supernatural Being from contemporary prophetic and apocalyptic eschatologies built on humanistic or naturalistic assumptions. The contemporary forms of prophetic eschatology will be only briefly described, since the focus of our inquiry is the contemporary forms of apocalyptic eschatology. Still, the inclusion of the former will help to illustrate that our sense of our own efficacy in the world affects directly the choice of either prophetic or apocalyptic eschatology: the more pervasive the feeling of loss of control over one's life, the more prophetic eschatology gives way to apocalyptic. The presence of strong apocalyptic motifs in American popular culture may well indicate an increasing sense that the human experiment in its present form in America is slowly but surely failing.

III. Contemporary Prophetic and Apocalyptic Eschatologies

A. Eschatologies Dependent on a Supernatural Being and/or Evidencing a Divine Purpose.

The Apocalyptic Vision in Popular Culture 161

1. Prophetic Eschatology. The Judaism of Buber and Abraham Heschel, among others, and the Christianity of Protestant Liberalism and of Thomistic paleontologist Teilhard de Chardin represent this view.[16] The possibilities for good in the original Creation win out; evil is converted, redeemed by the suffering of those who bore it bravely in the darkest hours before the dawn. One meets grace in this world and through it.

2. Apocalyptic Eschatology. This tradition did not end with The Revelation of St. John. The extreme form of fanatical righteousness it engenders finds adherents in our time: it is flourishing on Planet Earth in the incredible best seller by Hal Lindsey, *The Late Great Planet Earth*.[17] If we look at an example of popular apocalyptic of the sort assuming personal and Divine purpose, we could do no better than a book which at this writing had sold nine million copies since 1970. In addition, Lindsey's *Satan is Alive and Well on Planet Earth,* published in 1972, is in its tenth printing as of this writing; and his *The Terminal Generation* is now in its sixth printing after publication in 1976.

Lindsey's opening argument sets the tone for the book: he is concerned with credibility. And he should be: he must convince us that we should believe him on two counts: that a revelation written in 90AD was actually describing events that will occur in the 1980s, and that we have better reason to believe Hal Lindsey than countless of his predecessors who attempted and failed at precisely what he is about—interpreting the symbols of the Book of Revelation in terms of the events of their own times. His approach to the former issue involves demonstrating that it was not uncommon for the Old Testament prophets to make predictions of events occurring from one hundred to eight hundred years in the future, and that every single one of the conditions of the life and death of Jesus Christ had been previously foretold by the prophets and that every one of the prophesies concerning the life and death of Jesus came true. If one accepts the unquestioned (by Lindsey) assumption that the significance of the prophets is their ability to foretell the future, and the corresponding assumption that the significance (Lindsey uses the word "credentials") of the life and death of Jesus Christ rests upon their occurrence as fulfilled prophesy, then Lindsey's argument may sound convincing. Unfortunately most modern scholarship finds these assumptions naive and simplistic at best, since the value of the prophetic materials for the Christian faith has virtually nothing to do with the so-called ability of the prophets to predict future events.[18]

Where Lindsey scores most effectively, however, is in his attempt to establish his personal credibility in the face of the embarrassing failure of past apocalyptic prognosticators. Why should we believe him, when all his predecessors were wrong? Lindsey explains in *The Late Great Planet Earth* that the one important event overlooked by these people has now occurred:

> The one event which many Bible students in the past overlooked was this paramount prophetic sign: Israel had to be a nation again in the land of its forefathers.... With the Jewish nation reborn in the land of Palestine, ancient Jerusalem once again under total Jewish control for the first time in 2600 years, and talk of rebuilding the great Temple, the most important prophetic sign of Jesus Christ's second coming is before us. This had now set the stage for the other predicted signs to develop in history. It is likely the key piece of a jigsaw puzzle being found and then having the many adjacent pieces rapidly fall into place.[19]

The evidence for this claim he finds in *Zechariah* and in the words of Jesus recorded in Matthew 24, particularly verses 32-34. Interpreting Jesus's parable of the fig tree to refer to the restoration of Israel, and Jesus's statement about "this generation" not passing away until He returns to mean "the generation that would see the signs—chief among them the rebirth of Israel," Lindsey concludes through simple addition that Jesus will return in the 1980s, since a "generation" in the Bible is "something like forty years," and Israel reclaimed its land in 1948 (pp. 53-54).

Lindsey's books endlessly recount the "signs" of these times which, he says, prove that we are truly the "terminal generation." Satan is actively granting power to his or her forces to create "inventions which will come from the spirit world and fantastic displays of miracles and wonders that the ancient Scriptures predicted would occur in the days just before this present civilization would end."[20] Other signs, which Lindsey calls "birth pangs" of the new age, quoting Matthew 24, are world famine, earthquakes, unusual weather changes, an increasing crime rate, and the appearance of false prophets. This last he identifies particularly as Maharishi Mahesh Yogi of Transcendental Meditation, Werner Erhard of est, and Sun Myung Moon of the Unification Church.[21] In *Satan is Alive and Well on Planet Earth,* Lindsey attempts to attribute practically the entire intellectual foundation of contemporary thought to Satanic influence: "You and I and our children have been ingeniously conditioned to think in terms that are contrary to biblical principles and truths in all of these areas—

and without even realizing it.... There is only one person who had anything to gain by so radically conditioning the thinking of mankind, and that person is Satan. He was the real genius and impetus behind each of these men and their ideas which we are going to discuss."[22]

He then lists the work of the following as "thought bombs" whose shock waves and fallout have "contaminated" the thinking of the twentieth century: Immanuel Kant, G.F. Hegel, Kierkegaard, Marx, Darwin and Freud. Contemporary art, music (though he admits knowing nothing about contemporary music), education, the press, film, television, *ad nauseum*, all reflect the despair inflicted upon the world by these Satanic influences that presume to deprive us of sure answers. As Lindsey says, "anxiety minus an answer equals despair," as surely as iron rusts when exposed to rain and wind and glass breaks when it is dropped.[23]

Enough of signs. What does the predicted future look like? Relying almost entirely upon *Ezekiel, Daniel* and *Revelation*, Lindsey interprets the apocalyptic symbols found therein to produce the following script for the middle 1980s. He explains that Ezekiel meant the "God, of the land of Magog" to refer to modern Russia, which, with its Arab and African ("one of the most active areas of evangelism for the Communist 'gospel' is in Africa") allies, will sweep down from the north, invade Israel and take Jerusalem.[24] During the period immediately preceding this takeover, the "Roman Empire" will be revived through unification of ten European common market states, because the power and influence of the United States of America will begin to fade. This new "United States of Europe" will ultimately be ruled by a great charismatic man, who will unite the "Christian" West against this Russian threat in the Middle East. This "Antichrist" will be worshipped by a "one-world religion" (the great Babylonian Harlot of *Revelation*) comprised of a faithless Christianity, led astray by secularism and the ecumenical movement, and the recently revived "religions" of astrology, witchcraft and drug-induced mind expansion, all luridly described in chapter ten of *The Late Great Planet Earth*.

The European alliance under the Antichrist will totally destroy the Russian forces. In the meantime, an army of two million Red Chinese will cross the Euphrates and will attack the forces of the Antichrist at Har-mageddon, which is identified as the Mount of Megiddo and the plain of Jezreel: this will be the great, predicted Battle of Armageddon (pp. 162ff). In the resulting exchange of nuclear weapons fire, one-third of the world's population will be destroyed, just as St. John, in chapter VIII of *Revelation,* describes the destruction of "the third part" of the world. Then Christ will return again, just as the battle reaches its peak, not this time to save the world, but "as a lion to judge those who rejected the free gift of salvation from sin," and to protect the believers from the total destruction promised at Armageddon (p. 174). He will establish an earthly Kingdom which will last one thousand years in which "even the animals and reptiles will lose their ferocity and no longer be carnivorous. All men will have plenty and be secure. There will be chicken in every pot and no one will steal it" (p. 177)! The end of the thousand-year reign of Christ will produce a brief rebellion of some of the chidren of believers, just as Satan rose out of the pit of hellfire and brimstone for a short while before being permanently vanquished, but Christ will triumph swiftly, and then, all the faithful followers will go to heaven. Lindsey describes it:

Heaven is a real and breath-taking place. We will not wander about as disembodied spirits, playing harps throughout an ethereal expanse. We shall live forever in the presence of God, fellow heirs with Christ, as kings and priests forever, with no more sorrow or tears. We shall know an ecstatic, endless joy surrounded by an earth and heaven of indescribable beauty. If you think of the most beautiful place you have ever been, then amplify its beauty beyond your comprehension and imagine what it would be like without death, disease, or any curse upon it, you may have an inkling of heaven (p. 178).

Lindsey's approach to Scripture resembles that of most contemporary apocalyptic authors. Generally speaking, they tend to be conservative in their stated methodology, eschewing contemporary methods such as form criticism and historico-textual analysis.[25] They normally appeal to what is "clear" or "plainly true" in the Scriptual text, condemning modern scholars who "interpret away" the simple truth of God's Word in Scripture. Unfortunately, Lindsey rarely follows his own advice. Instead, he claims special powers of interpretation for himself and other contemporary apocalyptists, powers which would be superfluous if Scripture were actually full of "plain," "ordinary," "literal" meanings. He says:

Today Christians who have diligently studied prophesy, trusting the Spirit of God for illumination, have a greater insight into its meaning than ever before. The prophetic word definitely has been "unsealed" in our generation as God predicted it would be....

The writer doesn't believe that we have prophets today who are getting direct revelation from God, but we do have prophets today who are being given special insight into the prophetic word....

We are not attempting to read into today's happenings any events to prove some vague thesis. This is not necessary. All we need to do is know the Scriptures in their proper context (pp. 181, 89, 77).

The proper context is, of course, *Lindsey's interpretation* of the "plain," "ordinary," "literal" meanings of Scriptural words.[26] The many examples of his interpretations of *Daniel* and *Revelation* that are preceded by statements like "it is sometimes difficult for the Bible reader to grasp this symbolism" belie any claim that the biblical material is in any sense clear or plainly evident. On the one hand, Lindsey says, we shouldn't believe scholars who try to explain away the clear and evident meaning of the text; on the other hand, Lindsey uses his own "special insight" to mold biblical material into his own interpretive scheme, constantly telling us not to worry because he will clear up the mystery or explain the strange symbol.

Those who bring to Lindsey a paranoia and despair sufficient to forge the camaraderie of the apocalyptic vision may find his logic inescapable, for he provides his own Catch-22. Like the faith-healer whose failure falls on the insufficient faith of the sick and crippled, Lindsey suggests that any doubts on the reader's part just serve the presence of Satan: "Where do you stand in this conflict? Perhaps you're having trouble accepting these things. If you are, guess who is helping you think that way."[27]

B. Humanisitic and Naturalistic Eschatologies.

In humanistic eschatologies, the Human Race, as an on-going species, takes the place of a Divine Being: the purpose fulfilled in the eschaton is the triumphant survival of that Race. In naturalistic eschatologies, Mother Nature smashes an impertinent offspring's attempts to usurp Her Throne. This normally takes the form of an anti-technology polemic, though more diffused comments sometimes appear, such as the movie based on James Dickey's novel *Deliverance*. However, naturalistic eschatologies, which are always apocalyptic, should not be confused with humanistic eschatologies, which may be pro- or anti-technology or neither, and either prophetic or apocalyptic or combinations of both. Thus, a considerable amount of overlapping and fusing of prophetic and apocalyptic elements appears in humanistic and naturalistic eschatologies: for instance, *Battlestar Galactica* more resembles *Star Wars* in mood than *Star Trek*, although all three utilize elements of the classic Western form, and all three employ some degree of anti-technological criticism. Yet *Star Trek* is decidedly a prophetic eschatology in its sense of the continuity of the present and the future, whereas *Star Wars* and *Battlestar Galactica* emphatically represent apocalyptic eschatology, with its sense of the discontinuity of history and of the need for a radical break between this degenerate age and a better future.

The high mass of American popular cultural drama, the Western, is in both form and substance essentially eschatological; that is, it portrays a deliverer-hero (incarnating divine goodness and power) in eschatological battle with villains (incarnating all that dehumanizes and impedes social progress) over the future fulfillment of a good (but impotent) community of women, domesticated husbands, children, schools, churches and the other fruits of civilized and happy family life.[28] At stake is the future of civilization itself, of all that is good and decent and, of course, American. Although the Western may be more or less a horse opera (such as *Shane* 1953) or more recently *Billy Jack* (1971) and *Walking Tall* (1973), form counts most, so that one might argue (as I have) that *Casablanca* (1943) was the greatest American Western ever made.[29] The eschatology of the Western is basically apocalyptic: good and evil are simplistically defined and radically distinguished; evil is judged irredeemable and thus justifiably and violently destroyed; the final battle in which good is victorious is chaotic and disruptive rather than transitional. However, the Western makes one point that is inherent in the prophetic, rather than the apocalyptic tradition: the new age continues and fulfills the possibilities of the old age, rather than inaugurating a totally different world: the way of life of the good community had been fully established and recognized as good *before* the final battle ever began. So the Western form adapts both prophetic and apocalyptic ingredients as one or other of its elements receives stress and attention. When a popular genre combines a general scenario with episodes, the broad outlines of the plot may be apocalyptic while the episodes, being more Western in style, may resemble prophetic eschatologies.

1. Contemporary Prophetic Eschatologies. Two types of prophetic visions appear prominently in popular humanistic and

naturalistic eschatologies. The first type, a humanistic pro-science type, emphasizes the significant contribution of science to the production and development of the new world. An early film of H.G. Wells' classic science fiction novel, *The Shape of Things to Come* (1934), depicts a thirty-year world war that has reduced the world to barbarism. The future is restored by an altruistic band of scientists calling themselves "Wings Over the World." By 2036, as the film ends, the hero has just launched his daughter and son-in-law on the first space flight, confounding attempts by a political demagogue who has aroused the rabble with anti-science harangues; the scientist brags aloud to a frightened compatriot of the great future of man: "First this little planet... and then all the laws of mind and matter that restrain him... then the planets about him...."[30]

Another example of this humanistic pro-science eschatology is the most famous science fiction trilogy ever written, Isaac Asimov's *The Foundation Trilogy*—still found easily in bookstores after thirty years. The trilogy details the disintegration of the Galactic Empire, and the way in which a group of shrewd, mind-reading psychologists called the Second Foundation reduce the projected thirty thousand years of resultant barbarism to a mere thousand years. These psycho-historians battle superstition, religion, mercantilism and a mutant demagogue with power over the human mind and defeat them all with scientific know-how and the right intentions.

Television has contributed *The Six Million Dollar Man* and *The Bionic Woman* to this type. In *The Six Million Dollar Man*, scientific knowledge gives Steve Austin what he needs to redeem the present. Both of the "bionic" shows are episodic, following Western formats, though with a James Bond—international spy flavor. The mood and setting are prophetic, the new age growing out of and fulfilling the old age, with the great help of science.

The second major type of prophetic eschatology in popular culture might be called an evolutionary humanism. *Homo sapiens* has reached the end of its time: the species is evolving into a new form of existence, as superior to what we have known as we humans are to the rest of the animal world. The transition may be resisted by some, but such resistance will be as vain as the resistance that non-thinking life might have posed to the development of thinking life. This form of eschatology is chiefly represented by a trio of famous science fiction novels, all prize winners, and all still in print: *Slan*, by A.E. VanVogt, first published in 1940 and reissued in 1968;

Childhood's End, Arthur Clarke's masterpiece of the genre from the early fifties; and *More Than Human*, by Theodore Sturgeon, from the same period. Clarke co-authored (with Stanley Kubrick) one of the few science fiction films to tell this story, however tentatively, *2001: A Space Odyssey* (1969). Briefly re-telling the myth of the transition to human life from pre-human life in an introductory prologue, *2001* skips the rest of human history to focus intently on the final days (eschaton) of the present species, with no more than a surrealistic glimpse into the awesome possibilities ahead. Amidst incredible special effects, Kubrick manages to convey the message of the transition past and to come through the use of a smooth and shiny black obelisk.

So much has been written on *Star Trek* that I will confine my comments to an expansion of the thesis that the series is a prophetic rather than apocalyptic eschatology.[31] The Enterprise is a starship of the United Federation, whose mission (supposedly of five years duration) is to spread the word of the Federation to the stars: that the new world of peace and justice, etc., etc., has already been established; that the old world of war and strife, of chaos and the possibility of the fiery end of the human species, has come to an end. Episodes of the program feature villains (Klingons and Romulans, especially) and misguided, menacing mosters of varous sorts. But none of these seriously challenges the already established mood. Very few are violently dispatched, and the sweet satisfaction of revenge against the wicked which accompanies apocalyptic eschatologies is missing entirely. Mostly, the crew of the Enterprise—and especially Captain Kirk—spread truth, individualism and the Federation Way wherever they go, pausing occasionally to deliver sermonic monologues for creative freedom and against the dominance of computer technology. Mainly, like the Americans of the same decade, the Federation starships roam the universe, meddling in other people's social systems.

These were the sixties. The seventies shift the scene radically from the prophetic toward apocalyptic.

2. Contemporary Apocalyptic Eschatologies. Although the possible variations on the apocalyptic themes are manifold, four rubrics gather a fair number of examples into workable categories. We shall discuss them in the following order: a. the anti-Western; b. humanity versus the natural world; c. humanity versus technology; and d. political conspiracy paranoia.

a. The anti-Western.[32] I said above in discussing the standard

Western form that its eschatology, while employing apocalyptic themes, bears one unmistakeable mark of the prophetic type: the resolution by which fulfillment occurs lacks any critical attitude toward the "old order," so that the "new world" merely continues the already established and certified goodness inherent in the "old world." The sound of the Western is optimistic and hopeful: we are basically "O.K." and will continue to do just fine, once the villainous forces external to our community are annihilated. The anti-Western savagely reverses the situation, denouncing what the Western has so nobly celebrated, revealing in its place a decaying civilization which is evil to the core. Judgment hovers in the air like an executioner's blade; signs of the end-time abound in self-righteous caricature of moral turpitude; and no hope whatsoever for the old order mitigates the pervasive sense of inevitable doom. The mood of apocalypse supersedes that of prophecy.

The anti-Western appeared in nascent form in the early fifties, undoubtedly as a result of the double blow to the American Dream caused by the Korean War and the McCarthy hearings. Basically "good" citizens turned out to be responsible for the villainous "angry mob" murder of a Japanese-American farmer in John Sturgis's *Bad Day at Black Rock* (1955); and in *High Noon* (1952), Sheriff Gary Cooper threw his badge in the dirt out of disgust for the cowardice of the townspeople. Outlaw and sheriff switched moral positions in *One-Eyed Jacks* (1960), so that the "respectable" sheriff proved vicious and untrustworthy. In David Miller's *Lonely are the Brave* (1965), only laconic Sheriff Walter Matthau escaped scathing broadsides that were leveled against America's most cherished institutions. *Hombre* (1967) and *The Professionals* (1966) ridiculed the naiveté of previous film paeans to the nobility and goodness inherent in the American soul—*Stagecoach* (1939) and *The Searchers* (1956), respectively.[33] Suddenly outlaws were heroic and posses were villainous scavengers or ominous, faceless mobs as in *The Wild Bunch* (1969) and *Butch Cassidy and the Sundance Kid* (1969).

Only in the Seventies did the anti-Western reach full apocalyptic proportions, and that in three quite different films: *High Plains Drifter* (1973), *McCabe and Mrs. Miller* (1971) and *Taxi Driver* (1977). *High Plains Drifter*, starring and directed by Clint Eastwood, tells with stunning visual images a complex, multi-level story of a town called Lagos, a community bounded symbolically by water (a lake), desert and mountains. A bearded Eastwood, dressed in the wide-brimmed hat and long coat he made famous in the "spaghetti westerns" of the late sixties, drifts in from the hills and shortly is recruited by local officials to defend the town from three desperadoes expected to return from the territorial prison (where the town put them) to wreak havoc on the community.[34] Eastwood's "price" is a *carte blanche* in the town. We see through a series of flash-backs that the three desperadoes had previously been hired by the town to kill their own marshall, who had discovered that the town mine was largely on government property and had planned to inform the government. The flashbacks present scenes from the actual murder of the marshall, at night, in the open street with bull-whips while the townspeople watch from the shadows. The marshall is played by an unbearded Clint Eastwood. Since the murder was a certified success, we have in the returning Eastwood not the traditional deliverer-hero Christ figure, but rather the Apocalyptic Christ of the Last Judgment, come to settle accounts. From every significant local citizen, he takes a prized possession as part of the price of "defending" the town. Blankets from a general store go to an old Indian; one WASP's barn is torn down by Mexican carpenters and the wood used to build tables for a welcoming picnic for the returning outlaws. Eastwood takes the mayor's sign of office (his hat) and the sheriff's badge and gives them to a midget, formerly the butt of the town's jokes. A foul-mouthed female opportunist is raped; the wife of another town leader is taken to bed. All the guests of the hotel are forced out into the street to make room for the Drifter, and the hotel is subsequently totally destroyed in an unsuccessful attempt to dynamite Eastwood to bits. He has the whole town (and "especially the church") painted red, and changes its name to "Hell." As the desperadoes ride in, Eastwood rides out, leaving the cowardly townspeople to their own devices. The outlaws burn and pillage the town, only to be singly dispatched by a shadowy Eastwood, returning amidst the flames of "Hell" to wreak vengeance on the murderers. Staring across the dark street at the tall spectre outlined against the flames, the leader of the desperadoes screams "Who are you?"—and then dies, still wondering.

Robert Altman's *McCabe and Mrs. Miller* judges the community and the deliverer-hero figure. Into the mountain mining town of Presbyterian Church rides a mysterious stranger, John McCabe (played by Warren Beatty). Though actually a rather bumbling con-artist, he is mistaken for a famous gun-fighter and never denies the honor. He brings the town its first social institution (beyond a scurvy bar called Sheehan's), in the persons of three disgusting-looking prostitutes. The arrival of Julie Christie as Mrs. Miller, a prostitute of intelligence and good business sense, develops into the construction of a high class house of ill-repute, with mandatory showerhouse and lavish interior furnishings. Christmas that year is celebrated by John McCabe (JC) and Mrs. Miller (MM) and most of the townsmen at a birthday celebration for one of the prostitutes in the whore house, with Christmas carols playing in the background, while the church stands empty.

The town becomes prosperous. A mining company offers a fair price for the mine. McCabe, believing himself a shrewd businessman, ridicules the proposal, and waits for a higher price. Three gunmen come instead. In kneedeep falling snow, they battle, McCabe fleeing for his life. With luck, he kills them all, but lies mortally wounded himself, snow piling up around him. During his "brave" gunbattle, Mrs. Miller lies virtually comatose in an opium den and the townspeople fight to save the local Presbyterian Church from burning to the ground. The Church, merely an outer shell whose cross was affixed the day the first prostitutes arrived, is filled with twisted, rusted metal and trash from the community. Before the fire, no one in the community had ever been inside. No one witnesses the unnecessary gunfight or sees the foolish McCabe dying at the other end of the town: the town is left as bereft of spiritual and moral quality as it began.

Taxi Driver competes the cycle. *High Plains Drifter* judged the community. *McCabe and Mrs. Miller* judged both the hypocrisy of civilization and the foolish bravado of the deliverer-hero. *Taxi Driver* presents its community with little comment, focusing all its attention on the "deliverer-hero" and the "justice" he violently brings to the community. A Vietnam veteran (played by Robert DeNiro) drives a taxi in New York City. Filled with disgust for the moral squalor of the city, a disgust honed by psychotic anger developed in the war, DeNiro encounters and pursues relationships with a stereotypical WASP "good woman" (played by Cybil Sheppard) and "a woman of dubious virtue" (a child prostitute, played by Jody Foster). Both relationships fail for different reasons. He buys a suitcase full of guns, straps them to his body, shaves his head, and tries unsuccessfully to assassinate Cybil Sheppard's boss, a political figure running for election. Frustrated by this, he "rescues" the child-prostitute, shooting his way past her pimp, the brothel owners and bodyguards in the bloodiest ten minutes in movie history. He is nearly killed himself, but survives.

He is clearly a volatile and dangerous maniac—the film has competently documented this. Is he arrested, put away, locked up, strapped to a couch? The camera pans away from the flashing lights of the cop cars that reported to the shootout scene, and suddenly we see the wall of an apartment. The camera pauses at several newspaper clippings, describing how this brave and daring taxi driver had single-handedly taken on the mob, shot several of the vermin himself, and rescued a teen-age victim of their vice ring, restoring her safely to her parents in Iowa. DeNiro is again on the street, casually driving his cab, chatting and joking with other drivers. Even Cybil Sheppard, by accident a passenger in his cab, looks at him with a new, reverent awe, the Hero of an apocalyptic nightmare.

b. Humanity versus the Natural World. Apocalyptic films and science fiction novels of this type claim that human exploitation of the natural world provokes inevitable, catastrophic consequences. Nature will not be mocked or misused. A good example of this type is the so-called "disaster film," particularly *The Poseidon Adventure* (1972), *Earthquake* (1975), *The Towering Inferno* (1974) and the several *Airport* films. Howard Schechter and Charles Molesworth have delineated some of the characterstics of the disaster film:

First, we define disaster movie as a film whose *raison d'etre* is the portrayal of a catastrophe involving the spectacular destruction of some colossal human creation (skyscraper, jumbo jet, ocean liner, city) and the mass of humanity inhabiting it.... In disaster films... people do not die at the hands of their fellow men but as a result of being trapped in a place (or thing) that is either sinking, crumbling, burning or exploding.[35]

In short, the common denominator among all these films—the central situation or fantasy which they depict—is the devastation of some supreme technological achievement (an unsinkable ship, a fire-proof building, a mammoth airplane, a metropolis) by the natural world (p. 46).

The cast in these films reflects the *Stagecoach* technique: stereotyped or representative characters are thrown together by circumstances and forced to react to the catastrophic situation. They represent a microcosm of humanity and are normally led by a "figure of outstanding strength or virtue," whose moral vision is vindicated, becoming the film's "lesson" (p. 47). The group, without moral direction against the vaguely understood agent of destruction, looks to this leader, who must not only orchestrate their escape but also make the disaster comprehensible. Schechter and Molesworth write: "The 'crime' for which the [leader's] atonement is demanded is more an act committed by the species than by any particular criminal or criminal type" (p. 48). What they call "atonement" we would call the satisfying judgment of an apocalyptic eschaton: the end envisioned by apocalypse implies the overthrow of evil and the triumph of good. And as to the experience engendered by the film: "These movies reflect a dimly realized sense of *technological guilt* in the minds of Americans—guilt over the depredations of an unbridled technology—and an unconscious need to see Nature strike back, assert its dominance, wreak vengeance on the mechanical world and the being who engendered it" (p. 46).

A similar and familiar apocalyptic scenario occurs not by nature's striking back but by human technological—particularly nuclear—mistakes. Fear of the end of the world precipitated by nuclear disaster motivated several films in the late fifties and early sixties. *On the Beach* (1959) portrays the dismal last days of human life on an earth decimated by nuclear war. *Dr. Strangelove* (1963), directed by Stanley Kubrick, satirically depicts the nonsensical way in which the devasting final War actually begins. *The Day the Earth Caught Fire* (1962) tells the story of accidental, simultaneous detonations by the United States and the Soviet Union that knocks the Earth into an increasingly lower orbit around the sun. More recent films of the same type are *Planet of the Apes* (1967), and especially *Beneath the Planet of the Apes* (1969). In the former, action takes place on a future earth where nuclear war has wiped out human civilization, reducing the remaining humans to primitive existence while Apes build a new world. *Beneath the Planet of the Apes* extends the story to the total destruction of the Earth by a superbomb, assembled and worshipped by the last remaining cadre of mutant scientist-intellectuals. These films, almost entirely pessimistic in mood, hold out little hope for survival. Occasionally a human remnant does survive the holocaust, as in the science fiction classic by Walter Miller, *A Canticle for Liebowitz*, escaping in rocketships to other planets just as the final catastrophe occurs.

Another form of the nuclear mistake terrorizes humanity with small insects or animals enlarged to monster proportions by atomic radiation. Examples are *Them* (1954; ants), *Night of the Lepus* (1976; rabbits) and *Food of the Gods* (1977; rats, wasps).

c. Humanity versus Technology. The evil effects of a rampant technology afflict humanity in scores of science fiction novels, television episodes and films. Here humanity must contend not with the revolt of the natural world, with its imminent destruction, or with its monstrous perversion, but rather with technology itself, the demonic machine or its demonic inventor. Of the many forms which such confrontation takes, let's examine three.

When Isaac Asimov published his collection of short stories entitled *I, Robot* (1950), popular culture knew virtually nothing of the computer. Asimov's series of stories described the birth, growth, development and perfecting of the robot computer between 1996 and 2064 AD. All does not proceed smoothly, by any means, but Asimov, as usual, promotes a prophetic eschaton, a world where robots eventually take over the welfare of humanity—to the great benefit of the grand new world ushered in by their perfection. What a blessing! However, computers had, by 1967, become a proverbial household word, and anxiety about their presence had greatly increased. *Star Trek* began to preach caution in episodes like "The Ultimate Computer," "Return of the Archon," "The Immunity Syndrome" and "The Doomsday Machine." In 1969 Stanley Kubrick's visual groundbreaker *2001: A Space Odyssey* appeared. A computer named HAL (IBM), programmed to operate a Jupiter probe, falls prey to a human anxiety—self-preservation—and revolts, killing all the astronauts save one, Bowman (Keir Dullea). Bowman manages to stop HAL before HAL stops him, and in one of the most startlingly moving scenes in the film, the computer regresses to childhood nursery rhymes as Bowman slowly disconnects its ability for creative thinking. From that point on, the public knew to beware of the large computer. In *The Forbin Project* (1970), a massive United States computer links up on its own with a Russian counterpart data bank, and the merged machines take over the world. In *Demon Seed* (1977), a computer rapes (seriously!) Julie Christie and brings forth its own offspring. And in *Westworld* 1973, computer robots, programmed to entertain humans in exciting movie scenarios, such as the western gunfight, start shooting back.

Behind every computer sits a scientific megolomaniac. Mary Shelley started it all in the popular consciousness with *Frankenstein*, though in her novel the monster is arguably at fault. The film mold for this variation on the apocalypse theme was *Forbidden Planet*, a 1956 rip-off of Shakespeare's *The Tempest*.

The Apocalyptic Vision in Popular Culture 175

Commander Adams (played by Leslie Nielsen) and his crew land on a planet previously visited by another space team. They find only Dr. Morbius (Walter Pidgeon) and his daughter (Ann Francis) left alive, the rest of the previous party having been wiped out horribly by some strange monster. Morbius shows Adams the "inside" of the planet, Altair IV: the entire underground contains a gigantic self-repairing computer, fueled indefinitely by nuclear power. The computer is the work of a master race, the Krel, who formerly inhabited the planet but have since mysteriously disappeared without a trace. The monster, who, it is discovered, wiped out the Krel millions of years ago, rises again to attack the new search party. The monster is invisible and appears in the film only in one incredible scene (especially for 1956) when it passes through an electronic power field. Even then, it's shape—a huge, raging outline of a lion-like figure—is barely discernible. Why were Dr. Morbius and his daughter spared? Why has the monster again appeared, when a space ship from Earth arrives and orders the doctor home, away from his research on Krel? Edward Edelson, in his study of science fiction films, describes it:

> The ship's doctor, knowing that he is sacrificing himself, exposes himself to one of the Krel's mind-boosting machines and learns the truth. The monster is the creation of the mind of Dr. Morbius, who has mastered the secrets of the Krel and who has fallen victim to the same dark powers of the subconscious....
> The Krel mastered a method of transferring matter by thought alone, and this new ability released the dark and hidden powers of their subconscious minds—"the monster from the id." It was this monster who wiped out the Krel.... In the final scene, the monster relentlessly burns its way through thick shielding to attack Morbius and his daughter. Shouting "My evil self is at that door," Morbius is killed by the monster. With a last effort, Morbius throws a switch which will destroy the planet in an hour. The spacecraft escapes in time... letting them watch Altair IV and the secrets of the Krel destroy themselves in a burst of flame that consumes the planet.[36]

In a variation on the same theme, Ursula LeGuin describes an apocalypse brought on by a liberal do-gooder in her book *The Lathe of Heaven*. George Orr (Well?) dreams and his dreams come true. Unfortunately he comes under the care of William Haber, a psychiatrist with a machine for studying dream patterns. Haber discovers that the world actually changes to fit George's dreams. By programming the dream study machine, Haber is able to control the direction of George's dreams, and so proceeds to change the world, freeing it from war, disease and over-population. But each change brings drastic unforeseen side-effects. More changes are necessary to counter these, until finally near chaos, the fabric of reality itself begins to tear away, and the world that was is gone forever.

The latest examples of the human war with technology are *Star Wars* and *Battlestar Galactica*. In both films, the forces of good are in the minority and on the run. The rebels of *Star Wars* clearly present no real threat to the overwhelming power and numbers of the dictatorial Empire, and the human members of the *Galactica* "wagon train" are the very last remnant of the human race itself. In both, the forces of evil manifest the anonymous precision of a cold, cruel, heartless machine.

Battlestar Galactica, although containing prophetic elements, is essentially apocalyptic in outlook. A television series, it appeared episodically, each individual show adopting more or less the form of the traditional western, continuing the prophetic theme of the transition of the good community intact into the new world of the future. But the setting of the show itself, the background that gives individual episodes their contextual meaning, rings decidedly apocalyptic. A "race" of robots—called Cylons—all but destroyed the human race in the penultimate "armageddon" with which the series opened. Commander Adams and the crew of the Battlestar Galactica escaped. Returning to their home planet, the only one not totally destroyed by the Cylons, the Galactica crew pick up the few thousand last surviving humans, herd them into various sorts of interplanetary flying machines, and head out across the Galaxy with their "wagon train." Their goal is the original planet of humanity—called Earth--which they seek hither and yon across the universe. All the while they are doggedly pursued by a flotilla of Cylon ships led by a Judas Iscariot human named Baltar. The humans constantly demonstrate their superiority as "warriors" to the red-eyed Cylon robots, but the former are so outnumbered that every victory has that "by the skin of your teeth" character. Though the episodic victories taste not unexpectedly like the familiar American western, flavored perhaps with hope for the underdog, the setting significantly differs from the dominant sense of security about future possibilities characteristic of the traditional western or *Star Trek*. It reflects the difference between prophetic and apocalyptic eschatologies and suggests a developing suspicion in the American gut that our own technology may be tipping the scales of control against its creator.

Star Wars, though a feature film, is no less an episode. The film self-consciously resembles the Saturday afternoon serial of the forties and fifties, and opens in that style. We are told the story—which looks futuristic—takes place "a long, long time ago." Several paragraphs describing what happened in the first five or six episodes of the "serial" flow away from us on the screen in the old movie serial style. And we jump in right in the middle of the action. Even at the end, though temporary victory is secured, we realize that the villain (Darth Vader) has escaped (to return in the next episode?) and we know that the Empire still rules most of the Galaxy. So, even though the victory of the forces of good seems "western" and thus prophetic in its eschatology, the context of the film is episodic.

The conflict between humanity and technology most effectively communicates the apocalyptic mood in *Star Wars*. Though more subtle than *Battlestar Galactica*, the conflict itself is no less pervasive. The ruling group is called the "empire," the rebel's group the "republic." The moving "planet" of the Empire is a moon-sized machine called the Death Star, cold, grey and metallic through and through. The moon home of the rebel base flowers with rich-hued green forests. The troops of the Empire wear anonymous white armor, and are individually indistinguishable; we never learn whether they are human or merely androids. The fighting men of the rebel home base sprout recognizably distinct accents, as they answer to a roll call; these are individualized real human beings from distinguishably different places. Their faces more resemble drafted human beings than movie-style warriors (unlike the handsome young turks of *Battlestar Galactica*). The rebel robots (C3P0 and R2D2) display the normally human characteristics of freedom of choice and loyalty and love for one another; the most visible Empire robot, a menacing-looking black spheroid, moves to assault the heroine with a long, terrifying hypodermic needle. The rebel heroes, Luke Skywalker and Hans Solo, idealist youth and cynical individualist, sport stylishly casual clothes and male adolescent goof-off manners; the Death Star commander and his men wear grey uniforms that fit tightly at the neck, accentuating their pinched, somber faces. Luke spurns technological aids and delivers his bombs relying solely on the Force, a divine harmonic Power unifying all beings. The Death Star leaders spurn the superstitious religiosity of belief in the Force for the technological mastery they maintain and expect to render absolute with the Death Star Ray. Among the villains, only Darth Vader (Dark Invader) believes in the Force. And, in the final confrontation, when the pluck and courage and chance-taking of the rebel wins out, the Death Star ultimately destroys itself. Even the most efficient technological masterpiece has a vulnerable spot we learn. Maybe this will save us all.

    d. Political Conspiracy Paranoia. Our last type of popular apocalyptic vision fears a silent invasion and take-over by the enemy which is complete before we have sufficiently become aware of its presence to defend ourselves. Here the world ends with a whimper, but no less radically, and with no less despair than if it had ended with a bang. In *Village of the Damned* (1962), and its sequel, *Children of the Damned* (1963), alien invaders impregnate the female population of an entire English town and sire a blond, blue-eyed super-race. In Robert Silverberg's novel *Nightwings*, a world supposedly prepared to prevent such invasions tires after centuries of uneventful watching and waiting, only to be surprised and totally defeated when the invasion actually comes. Eternal vigilance is the price of liberty. In the film *Futureworld* (1977), the sequel to *Westworld* (see above), important, international visitors to a futuristic amusement park are copied, murdered and replaced with robots answerable only to their creators. But for all this, these stories end hopefully, with the defeat of the conspiratory invaders or with signs of a coming redemption.

    The Parallax View and *Invasion of the Body Snatchers* are much more representative of the paranoia of the populace: should such an invasion occur, we shall not escape. There is no hope. *The Parallax View* panders to the still-lingering suspicion that all our assassinated leaders fell victim to a common plot against which—if people will not listen, and they won't—we are virtually powerless. *Invasion of the Body Snatchers* (1978) scraps the upbeat ending attached to the first film version (1956) and presents us with the inevitable victory of a conformist society of "pod" people over the individualist world we so cherish today. Organic seeds from deep space fall to earth, blossom into orange flowers, and reproduce robotic replicas from their large green pods. These replicas are singularly without humor, imagination, creativity or anxiety. They are completely at peace with themselves. What is left of us crumbles into dust, is swept up into waste pans, and dumped in omnipresent garbage trucks. The film ends with clear proof that all is lost. Shudder.

IV. Postscript

    The values of the old world turn out to mask hypocrisy and

The Apocalyptic Vision in Popular Culture

deception. Mother Nature lashes back, shaking and baking our preening towers of technological Babel. Our own computers take over the world; our robots run amok and shoot us in the back. Scientists meddle with the natural order and make a mess; nuclear mistakes transform reality into a monstrous judgment on our own technological megalomania. The communists may have settled for detente, but alien beings of another sort conspire to kill our leaders and turn us into pod-people. We fight a running, fleeing battle with an empire of machines to which we ourselves have given life. No wonder Hal Lindsey can sell nine million people the hope that Jesus is coming in the 1980s to rescue the good guys from an "Armageddon" between 200,000,000 Chinese and the forces of the United States of Europe and their Antichrist leader, to be fought in Israel!

How can we explain this onslaught of fear, anxiety, paranoia and technological guilt? Well, first, apocalyptic is as American as the hot dog, a fact which the other essays in this collection should amply demonstrate. Second, after the civil rights movement, the burning of the cities, the assassinations, the birth of the drug culture, the Vietnam War and Watergate, who wouldn't feel anxious, paranoid and guilty? The Sixties ate the sour grapes, and the teeth of the Seventies are set on edge. Third, there is a growing sense that only radical, in-breaking action can successfully resolve problems today. Troubles may wax and wane, but they never seem to get resolved: they linger on, without clear-cut solutions. And, fourth, we have become understandably afraid of our technology. We pollute our air, poison our water, wipe out our wild, free animals, defoliate our land. Television is cheap entertainment, but we find that we get what we pay for. The hours spent before the tube seem wasted, without productivity, lost. As children we ran and played; our children sit and watch. Computers get more helpful, but also more complicated. Who understands them? Who can fix them if they break down? Our future seems to be taken out of our hands as we inherit it. We have lost control of our own destiny, and we fear that this may be The End. And it may.

Notes

[1] *Aristotle*, ed. Philip Wheelwright (New York: Odyssey, 1951), p. 67.
[2] Browne, Fishwick, Nye, David Madden, and others, as well as younger scholars such as Jack Nachbar, Mike Marsden, and Ralph Brauer have contributed

immeasurably to my thinking through their writings, through the *Journal of Popular Culture*, and especially through the annual meetings of the Popular Culture Association.

[3] A more complete explication of this method can be found in my book, *Your God is Alive and Well and Appearing in Popular Culture* (Philadelphia: Westminster Press, 1976).

[4] John G. Cawelti, *The Six-Gun Mystique* (Bowling Green, Oh.: Popular Press, 1970), p. 31.

[5] Ray B. Browne, "Popular Culture: Notes Toward a Definition," in Ray B. Browne and David Madden, *The Popular Culture Explosion* (1972), p. 205.

[6] See Herbert Gans, *Popular Culture and High Culture* (New York: Basic Books, 1974).

[7] John G. Cawelti, *Adventure, Mystery, and Romance* (Chicago: Univ. of Chicago Press, 1976), p. 16.

[8] Russel Nye, *The Unembarrassed Muse: The Popular Arts in America* (New York: Dial, 1970), p. 4.

[9] The opinions concerning popular culture that I assert here assume the following to be true of the nature of reality: that the "world" is not a natural place which thinking beings inhabit but rather is the construct of the intention of thinking beings. Here "intention" refers not as much to psychological projections unique to individuals as to the way in which humans supply the aspects of "reality" missing from perception. For example, to see the front of a barn means to see a barn, a whole barn with sides and insides, not merely the front of a barn—unless such perception takes place on a movie lot where we know the "front" to be a false front. That which is perceived always comes with a context, a context which we supply—and this is true as well of the values we hold in reference to the world. Although some values are transcultural, most are culturally determined, and bound to the culture which they describe. To be an American is not as much to live within the bounds of the U.S. as it is to hold certain fundamental beliefs about life in common with other Americans. Our "world" is not merely organized according to beliefs and values, but it is itself a valued way of seeing reality.

The assumptions and insights of philosophical theology shape my approach in the following way: philosophical theologians maintain that culturally induced beliefs and values reveal a transcendental structure, an organizational form that is universally true, and that the values in the human world are systematically organized and soteriologically directed.

The founder of this "movement" was, of course, Edmund Husserl. I come to his view of reality by way of Alfred Schutz, *The Phenomenology of the Social World*, with Thomas Luckmann (Evanston: Northwestern Univ. Press, 1973). Other projects developed by Husserl's followers which have influenced my thought are Paul Ricoeur, *The Symbolism of Evil* (New York: Harper & Row, 1967), and Maurice Merleau-Ponty, *Phenomenology of Perception* (New York: Humanities Press, 1962). The best survey of the movement is Herbert Spiegelberg, *The Phenomenological Movement*, 2 vols. (Hague: Nijhoff,1965). The best introductory exposition of Husserl is, in my opinion, found in Edward Farley, *ecclesial man* (Philadelphia: Fortress Press, 1975). For an introduction to the phenomenological world view with a minimum of technical language, see Peter Bergman and Thomas Luckmann, *The Social Construction of Reality* (New York: Irvington, 1966).

[10] See I and II Esdras; Baruch; I and II Maccabees, Enoch, IV Ezra, et al.

[11] This material is taken from a series of four lectures delivered in the Pitcaern-Crabb Summer Seminar at Pittsburgh Theological Seminary in June, 1977, by New Testament Scholar Ulrich Mauser, under the general topic of New Testament eschatology.

The Apocalyptic Vision in Popular Culture

[12]Ulrich Mauser, "Heavenly Geography or Parable of Hope? The Nature of Apocalyptic Images," unpublished, pages 8-9 of the lecture manuscript cited above. (Used by permission of Professor Mauser.)

[13]Mauser, pages 9-11.

[14]This distinction is found in Martin Buber, "Two Foci of the Jewish Soul," *The Writings of Martin Buber*, ed. Will Herberg (New York: Meridian, 1956). Buber writes that "the prophetic belief promises a consummation of creation, the apocalyptic, its abrogation and supersession by another world, completely different in nature; the prophetic allows the "evil" to find the direction that leads toward God, and to enter into the good, the apocalyptic see good and evil severed forever at the end of days, the good redeemed, the evil unredeemable for all eternity; the prophetic believes that the earth shall be hallowed, the apocalyptic despairs of an earth which it considers hopelessly doomed; the prophetic allows God's creative original will to be fulfilled completely, the apocalyptic allows the unfaithful creature power over the Creator, in that the creature's actions force God to abandon nature.... The apocalypticists wished to predict an unalterable immovable future event which can be predetermined with mathematical accuracy. Not so the prophets of Israel. They prophesy for the sake of those who turn... that is, they do not warn of something which will happen in any case, but of that which will happen if those who are called upon to turn do not turn from their evil ways. The Book of Jonah is a clear example of what is meant by prophesy (p. 273).

[15]See Martin Rist, "Apocalypticism," *The Interpreter's Dictionary of the Bible*, Vol. I (New York: Abingdon Press, 1962), pp. 157-161.

[16]Within Judaism the best spokesmen are Martin Buber, *Between Man and Man* (New York: Macmillan, 1965), *I and Thou* (New York: Scribner, 1970) and *Good and Evil* (New York: Scribner, 1953); and Abraham Heschel, *Between God and Man*, ed. Fritz Rothchild (New York: Harper Bros., 1959), and *God in Search of Man* (New York: Meridian Books, 1959).

[17]Lindsey is represented in the following: *The Late Great Planet Earth*, with C.C. Carlson (Grand Rapids: Zondervan, 1970), *Satan is Alive and Well on Planet Earth*, with C.C. Carlson (New York: Bantam, 1974), *The Liberation of Planet Earth* (Grand Rapids, MI.: Zondervan, 1976), and *There's A New World Coming* (New York: Bantam, 1975).

[18]Contemporary scholarship understands the prophets not as foretellers of the future by some special prescience but rather as astute observers of the contemporary scene. Knowing the God they served and keenly observing the hypocrisy and injustice of their times, they merely promised inevitable confrontation with the divine wrath by elaborating what they knew of this God from tradition and personal experience. See Abraham Heschel, *The Prophets* (New York: Harper & Row, 1962), pp. xvii ff., 23-26, and Chapter nine; Martin Buber, *The Prophetic Faith* (New York: Harper Torchbook, 1960), pp. 2-3, 103 ff; Bruce Vawter, C.M., *The Conscience of Israel* (New York: Sheed and Ward, 1961), pp. 52-58; Gerhard Von Rad, *The Theology of Israel's Prophetic Tradition*, Vol. II of *Old Testament Theology* (New York: Harper & Row, 1965), pp. 99-125; Edmund Jacob, *The Theology of the Old Testament* (New York: Harper & Row, 1965), pp. 99-125. For an interesting argument asserting that our God cannot know the future, see Arthur Danto, *Analytical Philosophy of History* (Cambridge: University Press, 1965).

[19]Hal Lindsey, *The Late Great Planet Earth* (Grand Rapids: Zonervan, 1970), pp. 43, 57-58. Subsequent references to this work are cited parenthetically in the text.

[20]Lindsey, *Satan is Alive and Well on Planet Earth*, p. 25.

[21]Lindsey, *The Terminal Generation,* pp. 59-65, 75-82.

[22]Lindsey, *Satan*, p. 71.

[23]Lindsey, *Terminal Generation*, p. 25.

182   The Apocalyptic Vision in America

[24] Lindsey, *The Late Great Planet Earth,* chapter six.
[25] Lindsey, *Satan,* pp. 27-28.
[26] Lindsey, *Satan,* p. 2.
[27] Lindsey, *Satan,* p. 51.
[28] A more complete explication of the Western form as the "high mass of popular culture" can be found in my book *Your God is Alive and Well and Appearing in Popular Culture,* pp. 30-55.
[29] Nelson, pp. 46-55.
[30] The *Things to Come* of the Seventies is *Close Encounters of the Third Kind.*
[31] Among the various manuals and books of blueprints and paperback versions of the television episodes, all of which complement and extend the detailed knowledge that trekkies crave of the series and its stars, are two books which tell the story of *Star Trek* fairly well: David Gerrold, *The World of Star Trek* (New York: Ballantine, 1973), and Stephen Whitfield and Gene Roddenberry, *The Making of Star Trek* (New York: Ballantine, 1968).
[32] See Nelson, pp. 56-86.
[33] The symbol of movieland "America," John Wayne, starred in both these films, and they were both directed by the greatest myth-maker in the history of American film, John Ford. *The Searchers* was Wayne's favorite film.
[34] Shot by Italians on location in Spain, and dubbed into English, the "Spaghetti" westerns catapulted Clint Eastwood to fame during the late sixties. The first, *A Fistful of Dollars,* was an Italian remake of a Japanese Samurai film called *Yojimbo.* The other two Eastwood films were *For a Few Dollars More* and *The Good, the Bad, and the Ugly.* The only "spaghetti" western to win critical acclaim was Sergio Leone's tribute to the American Western, *Once Upon a Time in the West.*
[35] Harold Schechter and Charles Molesworth, " 'It's not nice to fool Mother Nature'; The Disaster Movie and Technological Guilt," *Journal of American Culture,* I, 1 (Spring, 1978), 45-50. Subsequent references to this article are cited parenthetically in the text.
[36] Edward Edelson, *Great Science Fiction from the Movies* (New York: Archway, 1976), pp. 106-107. See also Andrew J. Greeley, "Varieties of Apocalypse in Science Fiction," *Journal of American Culture,* 2, 2 (1979), 279-287.

VII.
The Evolution and Imminent Extinction of an Avaricious Species

Michael Emsley

To its inhabitants, every age seems the best of times and the worse of times. It is then quite natural, we reassure ourselves, that we should imagine our present age of nuclear warheads, ecological perturbations, energy crises, population bombs and dietary contaminants to be more fraught with anxiety, to be closer to annihilation, than ever before. After all, we continue in consolatory tones, the end of the world has been expected for at least two thousand years and it has not happened yet. The early followers of Christ awaited at any moment his second coming and the abrupt truncation of history that would result; the approach of the year 1000 sent much of Christendom into a frenzy.[1] In the sixteenth and seventeenth centuries, the approach of the day of doom was so real that there were countless predictions of the exact time of its occurrence: Martin Luther, in a preface to The Book of Revelation in 1545, saw the world teetering on the brink of the final holocaust, and the Swiss theologian Henry Bullinger, drawing upon the numerology of Revelation, concluded that in 1666 the world would surely end.[2] The many apocalyptic dates predicted by members of American religious groups have been discussed by Professor Lippy in a preceding essay. Of course the world has had the disconcerting habit of not cooperating with these carefully calculated dates for its termination, and the very fact of its continued existence would seem to discourage further predictions of its demise. Despite all of these endings that have failed to occur (it can, after all, happen only once), I believe with great conviction that our own age *is* in fact different from previous ages, and that because of the acceleration of technological change, predictions of imminent catastrophe are far more justified now than they have ever been before. Such predictions are now based on scientific observation rather than on religious inspiration.

Like the ancient apocalyptists, I am concerned here with the history of the world from its beginning to its end, not as it has been revealed by God (indeed, I do not credit such revelations), but as it has been revealed by the empirical investigations of scientists. I want to begin my world history at the beginning, with the creation of our universe, because in order to understand our own time, with its incredible acceleration of change, we must understand how slowly our world and our species evolved. Most of us are so used to the idea of progress that we do not realize that only in a tiny fraction of recorded history have the lives of men been subject to repeated and revolutionary changes.[3] Not until the Renaissance and the age of the voyages of exploration to the New World does real environmental and social change occur rapidly enough to be noticeable during the span of an individual lifetime. The pace of man's ability to use tools to change his world during the last four and one-half centuries, and especially during the last hundred years, is unprecedented, as is the nature of those changes: the steam engine, the modern smelting of metals, telecommunications systems based not only on telegraph and transoceanic cables but on space satellites, atomic energy, are technological advances unparalleled in earlier history. Thus, just as the apocalyptist insists that the theological significance of the end of history can be understood only in the context of the whole divine plan for history, so I insist that the scientific significance of the impending apocalypse makes sense only if we understand man's relation to his environment and his use of technology from the very beginning. By resuming the whole history of man and his planet, I hope to achieve a perspective in which our own era of technological progress will be placed in its proper perspective.

When the Puritans came to the New World in the early seventeenth century, they expected God's hand to work on earth for their betterment: had not St. John predicted that Christ would return to establish his New Jerusalem on earth? That expectation of heaven on earth became secularized during the enlightenment, when the hand of God was supplanted by the idea of progress as the agent of human betterment. For most contemporary Americans, progress is still considered to be an ethical principle, an unlimited and quasi-spontaneous process which will guarantee a secular heaven on earth as surely as God's hand was thought by the Puritans to guarantee a divine heaven on earth. It is this unbridled faith in technological progress that is fast converting the American dream into a nightmare and has brought us, in my opinion, to the brink of disaster. Whether it is possible to revise the expectations

Evolution and Imminent Extinction 185

which the idea of progress has instilled, and hence to revise the uses of our technology, is the most important, and perhaps the final question that our civilization faces.

Astronomers debate the age of the universe, and as new data come to hand, the best estimates are extended beyond the twelve billion years, the consensus of a decade ago, to between eighteen and twenty billion years.[4] Data on stellar emissions, which are now gathered by sophisticated instruments on satellites, show to the satisfaction of most astronomers that not only are all the surrounding galaxies receding from us, but the farther they are away the faster is their speed of recession. The consistency of these observations suggests that the universe is expanding away from an explosive primeval "big bang."

An intriguing question is whether the universe will continue to expand, or whether the rate of expansion will diminish until the universe rests poised, ready to contract into the ultimate black hole.[5] It may be that we are now examining the universe during an unique expansion or during an alternating cycle of expansion and contraction: the accuracy of the calculation depends upon the total mass of the universe which is at best a somewhat speculative estimation!

The most popular view of the origin of the earth is that it was formed by the aggregation of cold interstellar dust, and indeed, we are still regularly accumulating this meteoric material. The accuracy of modern radioactive dating enables us to be reasonably precise in the estimation of age. Data from rocks in many parts of the earth's crust, and from the moon and meteorites, place their greatest age at just over four and a half billion years. Yet it was only 350 years ago that an Irish archbishop, John Ussher, calculated from a genealogical study of the Bible that the world was created in the year 4004 B.C. Dr. Lightfoot, Chancellor of the University of Cambridge in England, who also took the Bible to be the revealed truth of God, added that the event took place at 9 o'clock in the morning on Tuesday the twenty-third of October! As man has increased his scientific knowledge, so has he increased his estimates of the age of the earth.

Although the ingredients of the earth's primeval atmosphere are not known with certainty, there is little doubt that they were substantially different from those which we find today. In contrast to the contemporary atmosphere, of which about twenty per cent is oxygen and eighty per cent is nitrogen, there was no oxygen at all. The popular view is that the most abundant primordial gases were methane (marsh gas), ammonia, hydrogen, and water vapor. Using various mixtures of these gases and such sources of energy as ultraviolet light, heat and electric discharges, laboratory biochemists have synthesized a wide array of the complex organic compounds which occur in living material.[6]

Judging by the increased oxidation of ancient rocks, the earth's early atmosphere began to contain more and more oxygen about two million years ago. The geological banded ironstone formations indicate a widely fluctuating oxygen level before the concentration stabilized and began to approach that which we know today. Is it coincidence that we find fossils of the earliest photosynthetic algae at about the same time? Although not every biologist is satisfied with the evidence, many accept as plausible the idea that it was the photosynthesis of the earliest marine plants that was responsible for the appearance of oxygen in our atmosphere.[7] The oxygen, though at first poisonous to organisms which were not accustomed to it, later was put to work as a chemical tool for the extraction of additional energy from sugars. Today almost all forms of life are dependent upon the regular supply of oxygen for the release of energy to drive their cellular machinery. The bumper-sticker slogan, "Have you thanked a green plant today?" is quite to the point.

Although the circumstances surrounding the emergence of man are no longer shrouded in romantic mystery, they will, perhaps, never be known in fine detail because of the paucity of informative relics.[8] The vast majority of our known animal fossils are of shelled organisms living in shallow water, where the animals themselves were abundant and the conditions for preservation were optimal. Man and his recent ancestors were never numerous, and the ancestral habitats of tropical forests or savannahs were most inhospitable to the processes of fossilization. The acid soils dissolved the calcium salts in bone, and the high temperatures favored rapid microbial decomposition. There was also an abundance of scavengers. For effective fossilization there has to be very quick incarceration, in such sediment as flood silt or volcanic ash, or perhaps by a roof-fall in a cave. Only then is the skeleton protected and permitted to become gradually fossilized by mineral substitution from ground water.

However, even without fossils we can draw inferences concerning our ancestry by comparing our own physical condition with that of other species. Our extreme dependence upon binocular vision at the expense of our sense of smell, our phenomenal manual dexterity and superb muscular coordination are characteristics that we find elsewhere only in arboreal primates. It is interesting that nearly all modern primates give birth to their young singly. Canopy life is hazardous without the added burden of carrying young, so a single infant is the practical limit. Even though we no longer live in trees, we still bear a mark of our ancestry in the size of our litters. Current opinion favors the separation of the common ancestor of man and ape from that of monkeys about twenty to twenty-five million years ago. Our early ancestors, which were widely distributed throughout the Old World tropics, are known as dryopithicines. In Africa, the more ape-like representatives were typified by the discovery of *Proconsul* by Louis Leakey in the early 1930s.[9] Data drawn from the comparative biochemistry of man, gorilla and chimpanzee suggest that the human species separated from that of the gorilla and chimpanzee about five million years ago.

We have little evidence of the culture of man prior to about two million years ago, at which time we find crude Oldewan stone hand-axes chipped only on one edge in East Africa. At a concurrent horizon Louis and Mary Leakey interpreted circular stone walls as wind-breaks surrounding temporary occupation sites. Associated with some of these sites were the bones of a single very large animal, such as an elephant. It would seem to have been impossible for these animals to have been carried to the camp sites, so the camps were probably built around the fallen carcass. The disproportionate number of leg bones of smaller animals suggests that the limbs had been cut off in the field and carried back to camp. At some sites there were piles of tiny fragments of bones of mice and other small animals, which had possibly been passed out in human feces.

Although the evidence is incomplete, it seems that during the early occupation of the plains of Africa, man was an opportunistic, nomadic, small-game hunter and gatherer who moved with the seasons and shared food among the band members, a way of life not remarkably dissimilar from that of the modern tribes which inhabit the arid areas of southwestern Africa.[10] We can only speculate on the social organization of these early societies, for there is no hard evidence upon which to base conclusions. However, successful hunting techniques would have placed a premium on cooperative skills, which may well have been important in the development of group activity, family organization and, ultimately, of language. The upper limits of population size of these early hunter-gatherers have been estimated from ecological principles by calculating the carrying capacity of the inhabited land. A generally agreed number for two million years ago is about 100,000 individuals.

The line leading to modern man, and the development of technology, can be traced without interruption from the early *Homo erectus*, who occupied southern Europe, central, eastern and southern Africa, southeastern and southwestern Asia, China and Java between 1,250,000 and 300,000 years ago. We find their remains associated with Acheulian stone tools chipped on all surfaces, and in southern Europe and China we find evidence of the human use of fire. The exact date of the earliest use of fire is uncertain, but it was undoubtedly over 300,000 years ago in southern France and Hungary and was perhaps even earlier in the Choukoutian caves near Pekin. The application of fire to cooking offers a number of advantages to humans. For example, proteins are denatured, vegetable cell walls are ruptured and the toxins of many poisonous plants are rendered innocuous: these processes enabled the existing hunting and gathering techniques to support a larger population of humans. Furthermore, the fire-light would have extended the effective length of the day for those employed in tool-making and other crafts. The camp fire itself may have become a social center where ideas about past and future hunts were exchanged. The improved food supply of successful hunting would have conferred a strong selective advantage on those skilled in the cooperative use of communication; however, just as importantly, the control of fire would have enabled man to displace large animals from caves and enabled him to colonize northern latitudes, where the low night temperatures would have previously made habitation impossible.

During the last three million years, there have been a series of climatic oscillations which have influenced the size of the polar caps. The ability to withstand cold, either by the use of fire or the manufacture of clothing, would have enabled man to increase his range up to the frontiers of the glaciers. The oldest evidence for the use of processed animal skins is about eighty thousand years ago in the Crimea, where tents were made by stretching animal skins over a wooden frame and anchoring them to the ground with the bones of mammoths. However, neither wood nor skins preserve well, so the use of these materials may well have been much more extensive and ancient than we know.

The development of man's culture by the use of fire, hunting techniques, and tool-making began to advance in many parts of the Old World. The size of the human brain enlarged to nearly three times that of man's three million year old ancestors: by 200,000 years ago, man had acquired a cranial capacity of about 1250 milliliters, well within the lower range of modern humans, whose average is about 1400 milliliters. Man's tool-making skills had become more refined and the size of his game increased accordingly. It is at this point in time that *Homo erectus* is deemed arbitrarily to have become *Homo sapiens*. Of course the evolutionary progression of man was a continuum, but for convenience sake, we discriminate between ancient and modern man with separate specific names.

The most significant cultural advance appears about sixty thousand years ago: it is then that we find for the first time the fossil bones of deceased humans not randomly scattered but ritualistically buried. We discover family groups all aligned in a single direction, and the bodies of some individuals accompanied by hand-axes and cave-bear skulls. It is tempting to surmise that this was the birth of religion. Perhaps man was beginning to ask the question "Who am I?" "Where did I come from?" Or more significantly "Where am I heading?" Were the favorite hand-axes buried with their owners for use in the next life? Were the bear skulls trophies of which the deceased could later boast? Other human remains have been found in caves with dense halos of pollen around their heads, evidence of having been buried with garlands of flowers. Is it coincidence that the pollen was mostly of flowers that are well known today for their medicinal properties? This period seems to have seen the birth of thoughts beyond the day to day practicalities of staying alive. Man was acquiring a quality possessed, as far as we know, by no other species—an understanding of death. Man, in the eyes of man, became special, much too valuable just to be born, live, die and be thrown away.

Concurrently with these intellectual developments, we find communities specializing in tool-making. One group would make hand-axes, another would make fleshing blades. The sophistication of the tool-making techniques demanded much conceptualizing and an intimate knowledge of materials. Presumably, the products would have been exchanged by barter, so there would have been the initiation of trade and the beginnings of craftsmen's guilds.

About thirty thousand years ago we find the experience of

visual art in the form of carved figurines, which, by virtue of their resemblance to pregnant women, are presumed to have been involved in fertility rites. The obscure places where animals were depicted on cave walls suggests that this art form was also ritualistic rather than decorative or instructional.

Thus far, our focus has been exclusively on the Old World continents of Europe, Africa and Asia. *Homo sapiens* is not known to have occurred in Australia before about thirty thousand years ago, and the date of arrival in America is controversial, but probably not before seventy thousand years ago. The evidence for the entry of man into America is tantalizingly vague. Although there are substantial relics of human activity in North America dating back about thirteen thousand years, the trail peters out except at two California sites, one at Yuha, reliably dated at 22,000 years of age by radio-active carbon dating, and the other the 48,000 year-old remains of San Diego man, dated by the relatively untested and now seriously challenged techniques involving amino acid racemization.[11]

The traditional view of the colonization of America has been that a small band of humans from northeastern Asia entered Alaska across the Bering Straits during a period of extreme glacial activity, at which time the floor of the Straits would have been exposed by the depression of the sea level. It has been estimated that during the crest of the last ice age twenty thousand years ago, the level of the oceans was depressed by about sixty fathoms (360 feet), the absent water being locked up in the polar caps as unmelted snow and ice. The fact that the native South and Central American tribes, which are supposed to have been descended from this early invasion, are blood group OM invites the supposition that the first immigrants were all of that blood type and therefore somewhat small in number. However, if the evidence of man in America 48,000 years ago is valid, then we have to look back to one of the previous ice-ages, 55,000 or even 135,000 years ago, for the most likely time of entry. If either of these earlier dates is correct, then man seems to have dispersed rather slowly, for it was not until 9,000 years ago that man had reached Tierra del Fuego, and the evidence of man's presence in South America is restricted to the last fourteen thousand years. It is frustrating that we have no opportunity of looking for evidence in the Bering Straits, but the pathway that many may have taken is now covered by the sea.

Man has been held responsible for the extermination of all the

Evolution and Imminent Extinction

very large animals in North America, the largest animals becoming extinct immediately after the invention of the detachable clovis spear and arrow head. Over a period of one thousand years, from about 11,500 to 10,500 years ago, the ground sloths, straight-horn bison, mammoths and mastodons all disappeared. Alternative views involving disease, rapid climatic change and over-population have been offered, but none is as tenable as man's predation.[12] This explanation for the disappearance of these species, that twelve thousand years ago man was a novel predator who was not recognized as dangerous by the game animals until it was too late, seems to be undercut by the presence of the earlier human fossils.[9] Nevertheless, the explanation can be rescued: the abundance of blood group A among North American Indians whose ancestral lands are north of latitude thirty-two degrees North suggests that there was a second invasion of humans carrying this different blood type. Perhaps the earlier colonists were in harmony with the larger animals and did not molest them, whereas the later arrivals, about 12,000 years ago, were more hostile and used refined hunting techniques learned elsewhere to decimate their naive prey.

About eleven thousand years ago in southwestern and southeastern Asia, man began to develop an entirely new life style. The traditional hunter-gatherer activities were forsaken for sedentary agriculture. Exactly how the transition was accomplished is uncertain and controversial, and there may be no single explanation applicable to all areas.[13] The paradox of the problem is that it would presumably take adverse population or ecological pressure to stimulate the development of a new mode of existence, yet how can stressed people have the time and strength to wait for the maturation of a crop and be able to protect it from praedial larceny? Carl Sauer favors the initial development of a sedentary life along the banks of large rivers such as the Tigris, Euphrates, Indus, Ganges and Mekong.[14] Sauer considers the river bank a relaxed environment which would have provided a rich renewable source of water, fish and fuel floated from upstream woodlands. It is difficult to imagine experimental agriculture being carried out under other than hospitable conditions. The absence of maritime plants from our agricultural heritage would seem to preclude an ocean shore-line as a viable alternative hypothesis. In southwest Asia, the harvests were principally grass seeds such as the progenitors of modern wheat, rye and barley, whereas in southeast Asia, husbandry skills were concentrated on root crops and other plants which can be vegetatively propagated.

The domestication of animals soon followed, although it is not known whether by hand-raising young, or by the herding of the more docile wild adults. Each geographical region has made its own contribution to our domesticated stock, and the natural behavior and ecological requirements of the early domesticates separated the early agriculturalists into two disparate types of people, the pastoralists and cultivators. The pastoralists who herd goats, sheep, or cattle, depend totally upon their animals and seasonally herd them to favorable grazing grounds. These continuously nomadic tribes are exemplified by the modern Masai of East Africa and are in sharp contrast to the sedentary cultivators such as the Kikuyu. Traditionally, these two types of life styles, the nomadic and the agricultural, have been irreconcilable, for they are competing for the same natural resource—fertile land. Ancestral rivalry based on this separation is responsible for many contemporary tribal feuds.[15]

The enhanced opportunities for reproductive out-crossing by the pastoralist nomads contrasts markedly with the inbreeding that is characteristic of village life. Extensive inbreeding allows disadvantageous genes to be expressed more frequently, producing various genetic disabilities. Villagers living under primitive conditions also suffer from higher levels of hook-, tape- and roundworm parasites, because poor sanitation leads to constant reinfection. So, in spite of richer food supplies, the life expectancy of the early agriculturalists was probably not longer than that of the pastoralists. However, it is likely that birth rates were substantially higher.

Studies of the !Kung bushmen of the Kalahari desert region of southern Africa show that those few remaining individuals among the !Kung who retain their ancestral hunting and gathering lifestyles breast feed their children for about four years, during which time they do not ovulate and therefore cannot become pregnant again.[16] The wide age-spacing of the children in bands of twenty to thirty individuals ensures that there are few, if any, children of the same age in a band. This diverse age structure leads to close parental control and domestic harmony. The children are constantly in the company of their mothers until the age of five or six, during which time they are continuously exposed to adult conversation and behavior. This developmental situation is very like that recently discovered in chimpanzees by Jane Goodall and

Evolution and Imminent Extinction

may in fact illustrate the social structure of early man.[17] In contrast, those !Kung individuals who have settled as cultivators in neighboring Botswana have lives and life-styles similar to the Western model in that the women become pregnant within a year or so after the birth of each child. The mechanism of ovulation regulation in the !Kung, and presumably in other humans too, is thought to be dependent upon nutritional level. The average hunter-gatherer has only just enough daily calorie intake to maintain a lean and spare body. The added burden of breast-feeding reduces blood-sugar levels to the point that ovulation is inhibited. The cultivator has a much higher carbohydrate intake and does not therefore experience this inhibition of ovulation. Similar results have been found in Western humans under medical treatment for nutritional disorders and among women athletes and joggers.[18]

It is probably this increase in fecundity among agriculturalists that was responsible for the human population explosion that took place after the agricultural revolution some eleven thousand years ago. Demographers have estimated that the total population of the world when agriculture had its beginnings was between five and ten million people. If that estimate is correct the world's human population had multiplied only a hundred-fold, from 100,000 to 10,000,000 during the preceding two million years!

The invention of agriculture brought with it a social revolution, for in a static society there is the opportunity for accumulating wealth in the form of tangible property and land. With release from nomadic life, not only can family size increase, but the need for a large labor force requires that it should. The weak response of modern Third World countries to the West's appeal for birth-control is not because they are ignorant, but because they cannot afford birth-control—not the birth-control devices *per se*, but the risk of being short of labor to work their land. An unmechanized farmer's livelihood depends on the productivity of his children, and the family elders depend upon their progeny for sustenance in their old age. Hence the traditional premium placed on the birth of male children. In the rural tropics, the only use for daughters is as traders in the market place or to be sold off as wives. Many Western societies still cling tenaciously to this premium on the birth of a son, although in our modern society the original purpose has vanished and has been transformed into an index of virility for the father.

The agriculture that developed at the eastern end of the Mediterranean remained in a state of quiescent experimentation for several thousand years, the so-called "silent millennia." During this period, the first cities of Catel Huyuk and Jericho were established as centers of trade and religion. Slowly the new culture diffused throughout Europe and Asia. The pastoralists dispersed along with the expansion of knowledge and contributed to a genetically very diverse population in western Europe. Six thousand years ago, Mediterranean wheat had spread to China, Chinese rice had reached Europe, and the Sumerians had invented the wheel and the art of writing. This was the birth of modern civilization, along with the bureaucracy and elitist groups that characterize all modern societies.

Meanwhile in Central America a similar revolution was under way, but utilizing different plants as a basis for agriculture. In the central Mexican mouuntains, about seven thousand years ago, an agricultural society developed a staple diet of beans, squash and corn. These three crops are very well integrated, for the corn grows up and provides support for the beans, while the squash provides a good ground cover against erosion. Nutritionally, these crops also reinforce one another, for the protein-rich beans complement the starch of the corn, and the dried squash fruits can be fashioned into eating and cooking utensils. Although the culture of agriculture spread rather slowly across the lowlands of North America, there seems to have been considerable early exchange along the Andes as far as Peru. Lowland South American agriculture has provided only pineapple and cassava (better known to Westerners as tapioca). The only animals domesticated in the Americas were the guinea-pig and llama in the Peruvian Andes, and the North American dog and turkey.

It is important to notice that agriculture has been, since prehistoric times, a temperate and upland tropical activity. The agricultural systems of the lowland tropics are notable for their poor durability. The ruins at Angkor Wat and Chichen Itza lie buried in the jungles of Cambodia and Mexican Yucatan as monuments to civilizations that failed. In the case of the Mayans of Yucatan, agricultural failure seems the most plausible reason for their sudden collapse. The successful tropical societies were confined to high altitudes with temperate climates, such as those of the Incas and Aztecs. Lowland tropical soils are notoriously infertile, for the uptake of nutrients from the soil by the roots of the plants is so fast that almost all the nutrients are in the standing crop of vegetation. Furthermore, the year-round high temperatures enable such a rapid

Evolution and Imminent Extinction   195

build-up of pests and diseases that agriculture, as practiced in temperate climates, is doomed to failure.[19] At northern latitudes and at higher elevations, the seasonal cold periods reduce pest populations so that each new growing season is essentially a new start. The lowered temperatures retard the decay of fallen vegetation so that there are always a few inches of decaying organic matter on the surface of the soil, slowly releasing nutrients during the course of the year: if the natural vegetation is cleared, the soil still has a substantial reserve of nutrients in its organic matter for the good growth of a cultivator's crop. In contrast, when tropical lowland land is cleared, the erosion caused by exposing the soil to the full force of tropical rains and the chemical changes brought about by the heat from the direct rays of the sun render the soil unmanageable. When the very common tropical lateritic soils are so exposed, they bake into a brick-hard material good only for road making. The two thousand-year old temples at Angkor Wat are made of such sun-hardened laterite.

The only long-term successes in peasant farming in the lowland tropics have been with the traditional slash-and-burn technique. A half-acre plot of forest is cleared of underbrush and small trees and the cuttings burned. The ashes are scattered over the ground and a crop of guinea-corn, cassava or some other fairly quick-growing crop is planted. The isolation of the plot prevents the immediate germination of weed seeds and invasion by pests, and an economic harvest can be gathered with a minimum of additional effort. However, after two plantings, the nutrient levels will have declined to the point that a third crop is not practicable, so the farmer clears a new patch and starts over again. The first patch is allowed to return to natural vegetation for seven or more years, by which time wind- and water-borne nutrients will have restored the soil fertility to a viable level and it can be planted once again. When a harvest is taken from the land, particularly when of grain, a significant amount of nitrogen and other scarce elements is removed from the soil, and these can only be recovered by the biological activity of micro-organisms and by immigration from nearby areas. If the period in which the land lies fallow is insufficient, then the declining fertility of the soil will place the viability of the whole agrosystem in jeopardy, a situation which through increasing population pressure is widespread throughout the tropics.

As we have seen, the cooking of food is an ancient custom, yet prior to the discovery of the concentrated power of coal, the only fuels available to man were wood and animal dung. More wood has been hand-carried by man than all the coal ever mined, and wood is still the only fuel available to over three-quarters of the population of the world.[20] The rate at which the world's tropical forests are disappearing is overwhelming: perhaps as much as half of the world's woodland have vanished since 1950, with the annual losses running between one and two per cent—twenty-five to fifty million acres. Two-thirds of Latin America's original forest is gone or seriously depleted, half of Africa's woodlands has disappeared, one-quarter of Thailand's forests have been consumed in the last ten years, one-seventh of the Philippines' woodlands in the last five. The United Nations estimates that eighty million Asians, practicing slash-and-burn agriculture, cut some forty-eight million acres of woodland per year, with only a part of that woodland regrowing when the farmers move on. Extensive logging has also been a major cause of the depletion of lowland forests in Asia and elsewhere, the Amazon region being a partial exception due to sheer immensity. Tropical forests cover ten per cent of the earth's surface but host nearly half of the earth's plant and animal species: continued cutting at the present rate could eliminate up to twenty per cent of the species by the end of this century. While there has been encouraging development of fast-growing species of Leguminous trees, the impoverishment of fuels and soil fertility that has retarded the development of the tropics in the past will do so in greater measure in the future.

From whatever form of oppression the founders of the United States were escaping, they were people of initiative and courage, for they wrenched themselves away from their European homelands and took an eminently foolhardy risk in sailing into the unknown. The country in which they settled had been relatively undisturbed by the million and a quarter native American Indians, who apart from setting fires and cutting trails through the forest had made little impact on the natural vegetation. The Amerindian culture was primitive, without writing, metallurgy or the wheel. Although horses evolved in North America, they dispersed into Asia at some time in the past, perhaps as man came from the other direction, and then became extinct in North America. So, when the early Europeans landed there were no horses in America, and without draught animals, agricultural development was impossible. It was not long before European horses and other domesticates joined their immigrant masters. Initially, there was an acute shortage of labor

Evolution and Imminent Extinction   197

in the United States, for without mechanization every job had to be carried out by hand. Tragically for the Amerindians, the immigrants brought diseases to which they had no resistance, and thousands died of ailments which would have caused a European little more than temporary discomfort. Having alienated or infected the relatively small number of Indians, the new Americans turned to the well-established practice of importing slaves and indentured laborers. It has been estimated that eleven million slaves were shipped from Africa, of whom nine and a half million survived. An additional seventeen million indentured laborers came from India and the Orient, four and a half million of whom stayed on in America after their contractual term of service was complete. Thus, the genetic diversity of man in the United States of America was as rich as anywhere in the world, a fine foundation for a new nation.

The discovery of Appalachian coal quickly industrialized the northern east coast cities and much of the need for slave labor was reduced. Industrialization encouraged the movement of people from rural to urban areas; a process of urbanization that is still taking place. As societies change from agricultural to industrial economies, the reduced need for a large labor force is reflected in birth rates. The reduction in the birth rate which accompanies industrialization is termed the "demographic transition," and has been manifest in the growth of all the presently developing nations. Data from England show that the annual number of live births per thousand of the population fell from 37 in 1800 to 15.5 in 1950.

However, while two centuries of industrialization have substantially reduced the birth rates of the developed nations, the advances in modern medicine over the last sixth of that time has had a dramatic effect on death rates over the whole world. The chief cause of death in Middle Age Europe was disease: around 1350, bubonic plague, transmitted by the rat flea (*Xenopsylla choepsis*) killed a quarter of the population of Europe and almost half the people in England. Black death reappeared in 1665 and was nearly as catastropic. In 1550, only thirty percent of European children survived at age twenty, and less than eight per cent reached fifty! Royalty were no exception to the ravages of disease, for Queen Anne (1665-1714) gave birth to 17 children yet none of them lived past the age of eleven.

The expectation of life at birth in England in 1450 was less than thirty-five years, only a little better than the estimated twenty-nine years for the Neanderthals who lived some forty thousand years earlier. Through disease control, the life expectancy in the United States had risen to forty years by 1900 and to over seventy for both sexes by 1975. In 1940, the death rates in Mexico were comparable to those in England in 1840, but by 1950 they were similar to those of England in 1900, a 60 year improvement in only 10 years. Again, Algerian moslems in 1964-67 had mortalities that matched those of Sweden in 1771-80, yet by 1954 mortality had been reduced to that of Sweden in 1880; a one hundred year improvement in just eight years! This great advance in life expectancy, wrought by improved medical and sanitary facilities, has its concomitant problem: global population explosion.

Between the Agricultural Revolution of eleven or twelve thousand years ago and the end of the European Age of Exploration in about 1650, the population of the world increased from about ten million to 500 million, a fifty-fold increase in a little over ten thousand years, or, put another way, the population doubled every 1500 years. As the world population grew at an exponential rate, the doubling time became progressively foreshortened. By 1850, only two hundred years later, the population had doubled again to one billion, and the next doubling, to two billion, had occurred by 1930. The last doubling, to four billion, took place in 1975, a mere forty-five years later. At present growth rates the population of the world can expect to double to eight billion in thirty years, that is, just beyond the turn of the century—unless catastrophe intervenes.[21]

Doubling a population leads not only to doubling the demand for food and other resources but also to doubled demand for social services such as schools, roads, police and other community needs. Of course doubling time varies in different parts of the world.[21] England has a stable population without growth, Eastern Germany is actually declining, while Iran and Saudi Arabia have doubling times of twenty-three years. But, because of the large initial populations, the principal regions of growth are southern Asia, Africa and Latin America, with doubling times of about twenty-five years. The sheer volume of world humanity and its rapid rate of growth has frightening implications for North Americans, for there are simply not enough resources for everyone and it is doubtful that the United States will be allowed to continue to enjoy indefinitely the disproportionately large amount of resources she now enjoys.

The turning point in American development was the discovery of oil and natural gas in 1859, even though seventy years of development passed before oil supplied more than ten per cent of

Evolution and Imminent Extinction

America's energy needs. The American oil industry was initially based upon domestic deposits, but it was not long before the corporations began purchasing drilling rights overseas. The legislated, artificially cheap source of power fueled an economy that was the most productive in the world. America became the world's technological leader, especially in the development and industrial application of ideas generated by foreign research. After World War II, high levels of automation, expanding markets, a 3½ per cent annual growth in productivity, provided a standard of living for Americans that was unequalled anywhere else in the world. The farmlands, heavily fertilized with synthetic fertilizer manufactured by an energy-expensive but cheap process utilizing natural gas, became the most productive crop lands in the world. In concert with domestic agriculture, the pesticide industry flourished and supplied more than half the world's needs. The automobile and highway industries drafted a blueprint for personalized transportation that sparked a love affair with the automobile that is still aflame. This was the nation that was to put a man on the moon.

Taking advantage of its economic superiority, America has been devouring sixty per cent of the energy and material resources of the world while representing only six per cent of the population. Oil, minerals and hardwoods have been shipped from foreign soil with little consideration for the long-term future of the indigenous population. Until recently, the inhabitants of these countries were too ignorant, too poor or too weak, to prevent the sale of their birthright so cheaply. But during the last decade the world has undergone an educational revolution and the underdeveloped countries now feel that they have been robbed in their sleep. It would be an injustice to the many honorable Americans who have dedicated their working lives to overseas assignments to accuse them of complicity in what many would label dishonest business practices. The relationship is more that of an elder brother who looks after a younger sister and takes from her those toys which she is considered to be, as yet, too young to enjoy or value. However we attempt to justify the United States' programs of aid and development, there is little doubt that the recipients now regard the United States as a country of brash, affluent pirates. We can expect little generosity from them in the hard times ahead.

This attitude of our earthly companions would matter little if we were self-sufficient, but we have developed an appetite for energy that cannot be satisfied from our own resources.[22] We are now competing directly not only with the developed countries but also with the developing countries who are just realizing the standard of living they have been missing for centuries. Their efforts to catch up with the industrial West are directed not only at improving the living conditions of their citizenry but also at enabling them to benefit from the reduction in birth rates which accompany industrialization. But it is too late. The world's resources have been diminished to a critical level by profligate consumption in the already developed countries, and the prices are now so high that only the rich nations can afford to buy. Herein lies the basic cause of world discontent: the United States is viewed as an insatiable giant who must be controlled.

This crisis, serious though it is, could be ameliorated to some extent if United States citizens would believe that the problem really exists. Perhaps because of years of inept public relations by both industry and government, the present attitude in the United States is one of disbelief and skepticism. There has been little response to appeals for conservation beyond those that affect the pocket-book, and even those have produced very limited results. Fuel shortages are met with anger and impatience, and inflation is blamed on the government, gougers and middle-men. There is no lack of understanding—indeed, perhaps there is intentional ignorance—of the facts of contemporary economic life: it is this refusal to admit that there is a problem that is the most serious problem of all. Of course America was settled by people who believed that the New World had a special historical role to play, one dictated by God himself; this "American ideology" has been discussed by Dr. Cassara in his essay on the apocalyptic attitudes in American history. With four hundred years of belief in our unique national mission, it has been quite impossible to convince Americans that this privileged status might at last be tenuous or even terminating.

Our current energy problems have been compounded by serious errors in the publicized estimates of our energy reserves.[23] Most of the data published give the longevity of our reserves at present levels of consumption. Levels of consumption, however, will not remain constant but will rise sharply, partly because of the increase in the United States population (which, excluding undocumented immigrants, will exceed 250 million by the end of the century) and partly because the consumption per person is also rising.[24] The older citizens who still adhere to frugal habits learned fifty years ago are being replaced by a generation which was brought up during the "buy now, pay later" period of demand for instant gratification. One only has to watch the suburban teen-agers cruising the fast-food outlets in their four-barrel, 440 cubic-inch gas-guzzlers to realize that they, and their parents, are quite unaware of the gravity of our situation. (One feels certain that there are at least a few who are aware of the energy crisis, but have decided that, if sailing on the Titanic, they might as well go first-class.)

To the critics who counter that we will be able to buy all the energy we need with our grain production, one must first appreciate that our climate has been very kind to us in the past decade and cannot be necessarily expected to continue so favorably. Even more crucial to an understanding of the situation is the fact that American agriculture was built on the premise of cheap energy. More energy is invested in a bushel of grain, in the form of fertilizer, pesticides and implement fuel, than is extracted in the form of food.[25] As energy costs go up, the prices of pesticides and fertilizers (one of the most energy-expensive manufacturing processes) will push the price of food almost out of reach of the public. There is no possibility of returning to large-scale peasant-style "organic gardening," for there is, as yet, no complete substitute for pesticides.[26] Furthermore, the plant breeders have given us high-yielding but genetically uniform strains of planting material, so that if a disease becomes established, it will spread through the crops as an epidemic. We saw a shadow of this with the corn season in 1972. World fisheries have declined since 1971, so we can not expect to compensate for declining yields with products from the sea.

The frightening fact is that there is no solution to the American problem. Even if the opposition to nuclear sources of energy were overcome and satisfactory dumping sites for radio-active wastes could be found, America does not have sufficient domestic reserves of uranium to fuel her planned conventional reactors past the turn of the century. For developing nations that are without their own reserves of coal or oil, such as Brazil and India, nuclear power is the only option, so we can expect the price of uranium to continue its dramatic rise. Over most of America, solar power is insufficiently predictable to be suitable for much more than heating hot water in residential buildings. Coal, America's "ace-in-the-hole," is the only hope, but it will require a massive injection of capital if coal is to be utilized efficiently and cleanly.[27] The environmentalists will have to compromise if we are to harness this resource in time, for although the technology is available, the industrial processes for gasifying or liquifying coal are far from fully developed on a national scale. The efficient extraction of oil from tar sands and oil shale requires vast quantities of water, yet the deposits are in the western states where water is already in short supply.

The energy crisis on its own would be ample cause for concern, but there are two other problems which are going to become increasingly serious in the United States and elsewhere. First, since the baby boom of the fifties and sixties, the declining birth-rate and the extension of life afforded by modern medicine has changed the age structure of the United States. The proportion of people over sixty years of age is increasing each year and, unless there is a massive return to motherhood by career women who have delayed having children and are now approaching the end of their reproductive life, this trend will continue until the end of the century. With a proportionally smaller work force, the income from taxation will be unable to support the aging population's demand for services. If the economy could continue to grow at historic rates there would be hope, but with the inevitable depression caused by a mere one per cent yearly increase in energy production, the taxes generated by the employed will be quite inadequate to support those too old or infirm to work. What will be the attitude of the workers toward the non-workers? Judging by the popularity of recent Proposition 13s, it will not be merely mute indifference.

The second hazard concerns our diet. If we look back over human evolution, we see that man has spent several million years evolving a digestive and excretory system that could deal with all the chemicals normally encountered in a hunting and gathering diet. Just eleven thousand years ago, through the development of agriculture, our diet was changed in terms of the relative proportions of various foodstuffs, but not in the variety of chemicals ingested. During the last twenty five years, the Food and Drug Administration has registered over two thousand chemical additives to our food. None of these synthetic chemicals is known in nature and there has been no previous exposure of our metabolism to them. During man's evolution, adaptation to his diet was achieved by differential survival. Those individuals who could metabolise the food materials survived, while those that were unable died.

Our bodies are now being asked to allow selection to act immediately with regard to these food additives. Those of us who are affected by these chemicals will suffer some impairment and

Evolution and Imminent Extinction 203

perhaps die prematurely, and those who are fortunate in being unaffected will leave more children and *Homo sapiens* will advance his tolerance to these substances. However, in the process of selection there will inevitably be mortality and ill-health. Through additional disability from the effects of water and air pollution, and other exposures such as radiation, the demand for health services during the next two decades will far outstrip our ability to provide them.

During the last decade, astronomy has become the fastest growing science, the public curiosity being kindled by the specter of UFOs and the mounting prospects of discovering life elsewhere in the universe.[28] This interest is manifest in the success of such motion pictures as *Star Wars, Close Encounters of the Third Kind*, and television's *Battlestar Galactica*, an interest discussed in more detail by Professor Nelson in his essay. However, the popularity of extra-terrestrial phenomena may be a greater measure of dissatisfaction with life on earth than of fascination with the unknown. The possibility that the settlement of other planets might alleviate the increasing scarcity of space and resources on this planet is a slight one, for such settlement will necessarily be dependent on the earth's own limited resources.

We have got to face the fact that we have modified our environment so radically that we must now modify our own behavior and expectations in order to continue to live in it. We must become aware that our American faith in technological progress is not the virtue that it may have been when our continent was still relatively unexploited. Official recognition of the apocalyptic situation which our technology has created has recently come in the form of an eight-hundred page report released to the public in July, 1980, by the State Department and the President's Council on Environmental Quality. The report, entitled "The Global Report to the President—Entering the Twenty-First Century," predicts shortages of just about everything except people, pollution and famine. Among specific prognoses: two million plant and animal species to be annihilated, deserts to claim one-fifth more pasture and cropland, the population of Mexico City to reach thirty million, further division of rich and poor with the result of increasing social and political disruption, and so on. It remains to be seen whether the grim future projected in this report will arouse increased interest in measures which might forestall the waste, starvation, pollution described as more than likely to occur by the beginning of the next century. Americans have not, as I have already noted, proved very willing to adjust their ever-increasing material desires for the sake of the environment, although legislated controls have proved at least partially effective in limiting industrial pollution, dietary contaminants, and inordinate consumption of resources in some areas. Although classical economists may want to assure us that the technological changes of the modern era are merely quantitative, I think that the far-reaching results of those changes indicate their qualitative nature. Our increased mastery over nature has proved instead to be an increased slavery: the more we have extracted from nature, the less remains, and we will surely have to pay our debts in the near future. These debts will threaten the survival of our nation and our species.

Notes

[1] Frank Kermode, *The Sense of an Ending: Studies in the Theory of Fiction* (London: Oxford Univ. Press, 1966), pp. 9-14.

[2] R.W.B. Lewis, "Days of Wrath and Laughter," in *Trials of the Word: Essays in American Literature and the Humanistic Tradition* (New Haven: Yale Univ. Press, 1965), pp. 198-199.

[3] See Carl Sagan, *The Dragons of Eden: Speculations on the Evolution of Human Intelligence* (New York: Ballatine Books, 1977), especially the first chapter, "The Cosmic Calendar"; see also Norbert Wiener, *The Human Use of Human Beings: Cybernetics and Society* (Boston: Houghton Mifflin, 1954), pp. 40-47.

[4] F. Hoyle, *Ten Faces of the Universe* (San Francisco: W.H. Freeman and Co., 1977).

[5] B.M. Tinsley, "From Big Bang to Eternity?" *Natural History Magazine*, 84, 8(October 1975), 102-104.

[6] C.E. Folsome, *The Origin of Life: A Warm Little Pond* (San Francisco: W.H. Freeman & Co., 1979).

[7] P. Cloud and A. Gibor, "The Oxygen Cycle," *Scientific American*, 223, 3(September 1970), 110-123.

[8] G.B. Campbell, *Human Kind Emerging*, 2nd ed. (Boston: Little, Brown, 1979).

[9] D.C. Johanson and T.D. White, "A Systematic Assessment of Early African Hominids," *Science*, 203, 4378 (1979), 321-330.

[10] G. Issac, "The Food Sharing Behavior of Protohominoids," *Scientific American* 238, 4 (April 1978), 90-108.

[11] B.A. Wood, *Human Evolution* (London: Chapman and Hall, 1978).

[12] P.S. Martin and A. Long, "Death of American Ground Sloths," *Science*, 186, 4164 (1974), 638-640. Replies from M.S. Boyce and J.J. Boyce and by P.S. Martin and A. Long, *Science*, 4222 (1976), 102. See also P.S. Martin, "Sloth Droppings," *Natural History Magazine*, 84, 7 (August/September 1975), 74-81.

[13] C.A. Reed, ed., *Origins of Agriculture* (The Hague: Mouton, 1978).

[14] C.O. Sauer, *Agricultural Origins and Dispersals*, 2nd ed., (Cambridge: M.I.T. Press, 1962).

[15] J. Reader, "Microcosm of a Continental Force: Tribalism in Kenya," *Smithsonian* 10, 3 (June 1979), 40-51.

[16] R.B. Lee and I. Devore, eds., *Kalahari Hunter-Gatherers: Studies of the !Kung San and their Neighbors* (Cambridge: Harvard Univ. Press, 1976).

[17] J. Goodall, Lecture to Washington Audubon Society, May 14, 1979, U.S. National Museum of Natural History, Washington, D.C.

[18] R.E. Frisch, and J.W. McArthur, "Menstrual Cycles: Fatness as a Determinant of Minimum Weight for Height Necessary for their Maintenance and Onset," *Science*, 185, 4155 (1974), 949-951.

[19] R.H. Janzen, "Tropical Agroecosystems," *Science*, 182, 4118 (1973), 1212-1219.

[20] E.P. Eckholm, "The Firewood Crisis," *Natural History Magazine*, 84, 8 (October 1975), 6-22. See also "Vanishing Forests," *Newsweek*, 24 Nov. 1978, pp. 117, 120, 122. For a general treatment of tropical forests, see my book, *Rain Forests and Cloud Forests* (New York: Harry N. Abrams, 1979).

[21] World Population Data Sheet of the Population Reference Bureau, Inc., 1337 Connecticut Avenue, N.W. Washington, D.C. 20036.

[22] E.T. Hayes, "Energy Resources Available in the United States, 1985-2000," *Science* 203, 4377 (1979), 233-239.

[23] A.R. Flower, "World Oil Production," *Scientific American*, 238, 3 (March 1978), 42-49.

[24] B. Commoner, *The Closing Circle: Nature, Man and Technology* (New York: Bantam Books, 1971).

[25] D. Pimental, L.E. Hurd, A.C. Bellotti, M.J. Forster, I.N. Oka, O.D. Sholes and R.J. Whitman, "Food Production and the Energy Crisis," in *Food: Politics, Economics, Nutrition and Research*, ed. P.H. Abelson (Washington: American Association for the Advancement of Science, 1978), pp. 121-127.

[26] T.R.E. Southwood, "Entomology and Mankind," *American Scientist*, 65, 1 (1977), 30-39.

[27] E.D. Griffith and A.W. Clarke, "World Coal Production," *Scientific American* 240, 1 (January 1979), 38-47.

[28] See C. Sagan and F. Drake, "The Search for Extraterrestrial Intelligence," *Scientific American*, 232, 5 (May 1975), 80-89. For a more pessimistic view of the possibilities of other civilizations within our universe, see R.G. Wesson, "Wrong Number?" *Natural History Magazine*, 88, 3 (March 1979), 9-22.

VIII.
Apocalypse Yesterday
Thomas R. DeGregori

"There is a question in the air, more sensed than seen, like the invisible approach of a distant storm, a question that I would hesitate to ask aloud did I not believe it existed unvoiced in the minds of many: 'Is there hope for man?' "[1] Thus, Robert Heilbroner, one of the most intelligent, sensitive, and perceptive economists in America today, begins his book, *An Inquiry Into The Human Prospect*. Paul Ehrlich, probably the best known prophet of doom in the 1960s and 1970s, is more emphatic than Heilbroner. He opens his book *The Population Bomb*, with the assertion: "The battle to feed all of humanity is over. In the 1970s and 1980s hundreds of millions of people will starve to death in spite of any crash programs embarked upon now."[2] Ehrlich and many of his illustrious contemporaries use the image of the Four Horsemen of the Apocalypse: War, Famine, Pestilence, and Death.[3] The very use of the apocalyptic metaphor by some authors for their prophecies implies that they have some concept of the long history of similar prophecies. These current prophecies differ, however, in that they are being made by scientists, using scientific evidence.[4] It is reasonable, then, to use the scientific method of empirical testing on some of these authors' projections to give us at least a partial basis for assessing their recent pronouncements. As Garrett Hardin states, "To have any science at all we must generate falsifiable statements and have nothing to do with statements that are not falsifiable. Science is inherently vulnerable. It is proudly so."[5] Hardin further argues that "science does not admit invincible assertions into its sanctuary."[6] Thus, I will use the methods of scientists to test the validity of their apocalyptic dicta.

Fortunately for our inquiry, some of the 1960s and early 1970s prophets of doom were highly specific as to the nature and time of the forthcoming disasters. Occasionally they hedged their bets by phrasing their forecasts as scenarios. Ehrlich, in one of his "scenarios" printed in 1969, specifies a series of catastrophes that were to be the lot of mankind during the 1970s. "The end of the oceans came late in the summer of 1979 and it came even more rapidly than the biologists had expected."[7] "By September 1979, all important animal life in the ocean was extinct."[8] "Earlier in the year, the bird population was 'decimated'."[9] Along the way, fifty million a year were dying of malnutrition, famine gripped many countries, the green revolution was a failure as yields were falling, 200,000 a year were dying of pollution, the midwest part of the United States was turning into a desert, diseases of all kinds were on the increase, and chaos was spreading. Amidst all these crises was a baby boom in the United States.[10] Ehrlich concedes that it is "a pretty grim scenario," but, "unfortunately, we are a long way into it."[11] In his succeeding works, it is difficult to find any indications of policy or other changes that were made to ward off this catastrophe.

Ehrlich published his prophecies widely and in some surprising places like the *Wall Street Journal* and *Reader's Digest*.[12] He also called attention to other works of similar orientation such as *Famine 1975! America's Decision: Who Will Survive*, by William and Paul Paddock.[13] The Paddocks were as certain of the coming catastrophe as Ehrlich. "Nothing can stop the locomotive in time. Collision is inevitable. Catastrophe is foredoomed.... Now it is too late."[14] There is little potential for agricultural increase; hybrid wheats are little used outside the U.S. (and presumably won't be); food production is static.[15] Famine—1975; catastrophe—1982.[16] The four horsemen are in their saddles and ready to ride.[17] Though world famine cannot be avoided, it can be "ameliorated."[18] Amelioration consists of saving ourselves and some others but not everyone. They state boldly, "Herewith is a Proposal for the Use of American Food: Triage."[19] Triage is based upon the French wartime medical practice of separating the wounded into three categories: 1) those who would survive without immediate medical assistance, 2) those who could survive but only with immediate medical attention, and 3) those who could not survive no matter what was done for them. Obviously, scarce medical personnel turned their attention to the second group, then to the first, leaving the third group to die. Triage as an international aid policy argues that certain nations or peoples are doomed and that food assistance merely delays and thereby worsens the inevitable catastrophe. Further, trying to save the many could imperil the future of the few. This view is essentially a variant of the famed Lifeboat Ethic, i.e., if too many are allowed on board, it sinks! There are, as Hardin says in another but similar context, limits to altruism.[20]

Nineteen seventy-five has come and gone, and 1982 is here. It is difficult to find evidence for the Paddocks' predictions. Yet in their 1976 reprint (as *Time of Famines*), they confidently assert that "this volume demonstrates that it is possible to predict the course of at least some human events."[21] They made no changes whatsoever in their text to prevent any perceptions that the data were "massaged."[22] In their postscript they accuse their critics of being blindly optimistic, guilty of "boosterism worthy of Babbitt," and simply not knowing "what they are talking about."[23] They also found the world's population to be "growing at an accelerating rate," which it was not then and is not now.[24] Unequivocally, they maintain that "the Time of Famines is here."[25]

Scientists such as Ehrlich and Hardin or applied scientists with field experience such as the Paddocks (an economist and an agronomist) gave respectability to doomsday prophecies. Even more prestige was added when the Club of Rome asked a group of M.I.T. researchers led by Donella and Dennis Meadows to do a study of the human predicament using computers and the world dynamics approach of an M.I.T. engineer, Jay Forrester. Among the results was the widely publicized book, *The Limits to Growth*.[26] The tone of this volume is certainly not shrill, and their forecast for the apocalypse is on the order of 100 years, give or take a few decades, depending upon assumptions. Their general conclusion is that:

If the present growth trends in world population, industrialization, pollution, food production, and resource depletion continue unchanged, the limits to growth on this planet will be reached sometime within the next one hundred years. The most probable result will be a rather sudden and uncontrollable decline in both population and industrial capacity.[27]

The Limits to Growth study believes, however, that ecologically sound growth is sustainable far into the future provided that we change our ways. And, of course, the sooner we change, the "greater will be ... [the] chances of success."[28]

Ehrlich, in defending the Paddocks' advocacy of triage, makes reference to Pascal's Wager.[29] Simply stated, Pascal, a French philosopher and mathematician, probability theorist and gambler, reasoned that belief in the Christian God entitled one to an afterlife of eternal bliss and that non-belief meant damnation. If there was no God, both the believer and the non-believer were dead. The non-believer gained no benefit for being right but suffered a loss for being wrong, while the believer benefited from being right but suffered no loss as a consequence of being wrong. Consequently, there was everything to gain and nothing to lose by believing in God. Pascal also looked at the odds of eternal life against the short period of one's terrestrial life, so even if a price had to be paid, it was small in comparison to the gains. Similarly, Ehrlich argues that if the Paddocks (and Ehrlich himself) are right, we can expect disaster, and if we accept their rightness, then through triage and other actions we can ameliorate the forthcoming catastrophe. Presumably, if they are wrong, there won't be a doomsday even if we practice triage.

There is a series of obvious fallacies in Ehrlich's reasoning. Practicing triage is not costless, particularly if the doomsday forecasts are wrong. If advocacy is successful in changing policy (and, after all, that is the object of advocacy), a very large number of people would suffer privation and possibly death who might otherwise be helped. And what about those who create the practice of triage? Keeping others out of the lifeboat isn't a pleasant thought and is fraught with moral and ethical implications even when the lifeboat is full to capacity. And, if it is far from capacity, keeping others out is downright immoral. Certainly, triage is not consistent with Ehrlich's statement elsewhere that we "must all learn to identify with the plight of our less fortunate fellows on Spaceship Earth if we are to help both them and ourselves to survive."[30] The Pascal's Wager argument is equally applicable (or inapplicable) to any doomsday scenario and to the implied policies for its prevention.

Basically, Ehrlich favors foreign aid by countries like the U.S. with special emphasis on the "technology of birth control."[31] He has spoken against "the export of death control," which one author, John R. Maddox, termed "paternalistically offensive."[32] Yet Ehrlich does find that Hardin in his book *The Limits to Altruism*, arguing for inequality and privilege, "makes his case straightforwardly and in some ways persuasively."[33] Hardin is basically an opponent of aid to poor countries and makes a strong appeal for privilege both within poor countries and within the world community.[34] Jay Forrester's work also has its political and ideological implications. Forrester developed the systems dynamics approach that was the basis for the famed Meadows report commissioned by the Club of Rome on the limits to growth. He admits that his work might "give the appearance of favoring upper income groups and industry at the expense of the underemployed."[35]

Harvey Simmons finds Forrester to be impatient with democratic processes and in favor of policies that reduce health care and food supplies in order to save the World System from collapse.[36]

One of the ironies of the basic criticisms of doomsday forecasting is that the very politics criticized, the export of death control and food assistance, may be critical factors contributing to the solution or at least the amelioration of the population problem. It is generally recognized that falling infant mortality rates will eventually lead to falling birth rates. Since a fall in birth rates begins later and initially falls more slowly, the first impact of decreased infant mortality and extended longevity is to increase the net reproduction rate (birth rates minus death rates), i.e., increase population. In time the falling birth rates overtakes the death rate (or at least the rate of decline of birth rates is greater than the rate of decline of death rates), and what is called the demographic transition takes place as it has in the industrialized world. In the 1960s it may have been naive optimism to believe it would take place in the third world countries. But from the mid 1970s on, there is increasing evidence that precisely this transition has been taking place. Even the Ehrlichs now recognize that "equity" seems to be an "essential factor" in "reducing birthrates." "When people are given access to the basics of life—adequate food, shelter, clothing, health care, education (particularly for women), and an opportunity to improve their well-being—they seem to be more willing to limit the size of their families."[37]

The general world population picture is spotty, giving considerable grounds for hope and also for serious concern. A number of formerly poor countries have emerged as middle income countries with life expectancies approaching those of industrial countries and with birth rates that have fallen dramatically in recent years. There is strong and increasing evidence of falling birth rates in most countries, even the poorest ones. Nevertheless, there is cause for concern because the evidence is weakest for the Indian subcontinent, where population control is needed badly, and for Africa, where in many areas there is no evidence of population slowdown. Recent World Fertility Surveys indicate that in most parts of the world women desire fewer children. Further, age at marriage is rising, reinforcing other trends for lowering birth rates. Family planning programs are succeeding.[38] Still, even if our most optimistic interpretations of the population data are correct, there still will remain a population problem. As every demographer (doomsday prophet or other) recognizes, even when fertility falls to net reproduction, the young age structure of a previously growing population can mean population growth for decades before it levels off. And the current optimism about population growth is based upon declines in the rate of population increase.

The question is not whether we have problems of food supply and population but what kind of problems and how bad they are. Many contend that the problem is not aggregate food production but rather income distribution. D.S. Miller, in *Nutrition and the World Food Crisis*, states: "Food requirements are about 2,000 kilocalories per day per man, woman, and child, and global agriculture produces something in excess of 4,500 kilocalories per head per day of crops suitable for human consumption. Much of this food is used inefficiently for feeding livestock to provide animal products for the rich, but even so there is about 2,500 kilocalories per head per day available for human consumption. So, please let us not hear about the 'World Food Crisis'."[39] And the author further argues that "all the evidence suggests that farmers can cope with the supply problem providing it is made worth their while."[40]

There is in fact considerable evidence to support this last assertion. There was another study commissioned by the Club of Rome about the time of the Meadows report. This one was on the theoretical maximum food production possible in the world.[41] They find that "taking into account the possibilities of irrigation and the limitations in crop production caused by local soils and climatic conditions, the absolute maximum production ... is almost forty times the present cereal crop production."[42] Calculating on the basis of sixty-five percent of the total of available land (sixty-five percent being the percentage of the current land in production that is in cereal crops), the potential output is thirty times the present production. The authors make a number of assumptions, such as use of the latest technologies, fertilizers, seeds and multiple cropping during all the growing days of the year. They recognize that in each specific area there are reasons why the absolute maximum cannot be reached. Even so, it does indicate a potential for agricultural development that is considerably beyond current production.[43] Further, they assume no change in technology. Some of the research efforts and possibilities recommended by the National Research Council of the U.S. National Academy of Sciences are simply astounding in their potentials. Among others are further possibilities for genetic manipulations of plants, development of nitrogen fixing bacteria for cereal crops, improvement in photosynthesis, and production from currently unusable acidic soils.[44] These are not pie-in-the-sky recommendations. Much of the research that the NRC called for has been under way for some time and shows signs of success.[45]

On mineral resources, the same story prevails. Robert Solow, in combating some of the fears of imminent resource exhaustion, gives the following U.S. government estimates for years of availability and the crustal abundance of some of our minerals.[46]

	Known Reserves	Ultimately Recoverable Reserves*	Crustal Abundance
Coal	2736 yrs.	5119 yrs.	----
Copper	45	340	242×10^6 yrs.
Iron	117	2657	1815×10^6
Phosporus	481	1601	870×10^6
Molybdenum	65	630	422×10^6
Lead	10	162	82×10^6
Zinc	21	618	409×10^6
Sulphur	30	6897	----
Uranium	50	8455	1855×0^6
Aluminum	23	68,066	38500×10^6

*with current technology

Solow defines "known reserves" as those recoverable using current technology. Technology is continually creating new resources. Resources do not exist apart from technology. The raw materials of the universe become useful to humans and therefore resources as a result of technological change. Further, science and technology are, through processes of alloying, creating new materials. This allows for resource substitution in case of scarcity. As many writers have noted, long before one runs out of a resource, there are myriad possibilities for recycling and reprocessing waste.

One wonders, if we are being overwhelmed by population and are at the same time running out of resources, as the doomsayers insist, what has been the aggregate impact upon the world's people? Despite all this travail, economic development has been unprecedented and has exceeded all forecasts.

In average per capita income the developing countries grew more rapidly between 1950 and 1975—3.4 percent a year—than either they or the developed countries had done in any comparable period in the past. They thereby exceeded both official goals and private expectations. That this growth was real and not simply statistical artifact may be seen in the progress that occurred simultaneously in various indexes of basic needs. Increases in life expectancy that required a century of economic development in the industrialized countries have been achieved in the developing world in two or three decades. Progress has been made in the world in the eradication of communicable diseases. And the proportion of adults in developing countries who are literate has increased substantially.[47]

Preliminary data from World Bank and other sources indicate that, though development has been slowed, it has continued through the latter part of the 1970s.[48] In the United States economic growth slowed during the 1970s, but it was not vastly lower than that of the 1960s. Despite the carcinogens in our food and the pollutants in the air, we added 2.3 years to our life expectancy at birth bringing it to 73.2.[49] This brings to a total of over thirty years that we have gained in life expectancy this century. With all the ways that we abuse modern technology, just think of the gains we can make (and have made) with its proper use.

Of all the resource questions, energy is the most complex and controversial. Energy shortages experienced in the United States in the 1970s were the result of political and pricing decisions and not of any resource shortage. Currently, research is going on toward improved ways of using fossil fuels, such as coal, toward nuclear fusion, and toward solar, wind, ocean current, and geothermal sources of power. In the last few years with increased prices for oil and periodic uncertainty of availability, the oil importing industrial countries have made significant improvements in energy conservation, particularly conservation in the form of increased efficiency in the use of energy. There is no lack of energy sources, merely a lack of the technologies to exploit them cheaply. The availability of cheap gas and oil has undoubtedly delayed work in all this area, but there is no reason not to believe that eventually we will succeed in this area as we have done in other areas in the past. The canard that there is insufficient uranium for nuclear power in the United States or in the world just will not stand up to scrutiny.[50]

Many of the doomsday deadlines noted earlier in this article have long passed, but this has not slowed the tempo of such prophecies. *The Limits to Growth* book has the twenty-ninth day riddle. A "lily plant doubles in size each day. If the lily were allowed to grow unchecked, it would completely cover the pond in 30 days, choking off other forms of life in the water." On what day will the lily cover half the pond? The twenty-ninth.[51] The twenty-ninth day riddle has become commonplace among those who are fearful of the future implications of current economic trends.[52] Past prophecies may not have been precisely right, but we are warned that the pond is half full.

People in the United States and elsewhere are living longer at higher material standards of living and with more education than any previous generations have ever known. The question arises as to why the gloom about the human predicament and why the prophecies of catastrophe in the name of science? Though I do not pretend to have a complete answer, I will offer some comments that might contribute to a partial understanding. That we have a long history of apocalyptic predictions means that in some way this vision is part of our culture, an assumption aptly demonstrated by other essays in this volume. Recently, this apocalyptic vision has tended to be clearer and stronger on the coming catastrophe than on the new world that will arise from it. Religious visionaries in our society have both condemned modern science and tried to use it to buttress their beliefs. It is understandable, then, that some segments of the public will respond to predictions of calamity by scientists. It is less understandable that scientists would make their sensational terms that are alien to the ethics and mores of modern science.

In the predominantly Protestant Christian culture of the United States and the Christian culture of the European industrial countries, the work ethic has played an important ideological role in explaining and justifying inequality of wealth within a country and among nations. It has become obvious that we have to work less to acquire our daily bread and that this may cause guilt pangs in terms of traditional beliefs. If we are drawing our usufruct too easily, something must be wrong. The party is over. The price we paid is insufficient and so we will have to pay the full price some day soon. To use Ehrlich's baseball metaphor, "Nature Bats Last."[53]

T.C. Sinclair argues that there has long been a strain of religious thought in Western culture that opposed economic progress, particularly industrialization. Quoting R.W. Tawney, he notes that advancing wealth was viewed as bringing with it avarice, cupidity, and a weakening of traditional relationships. "Much of the moral idealism which in earlier times found expression in various movements of social reform appears now, particularly in the USA, to seek an outlet in the environmentalist movement."[54] Pollution has become a symbol of our moral degradation. We have sold our soul for affluence and judgment day will soon be upon us.

In this author's judgment, there is considerable confusion on the issues of development and resource limitation, owing to a lack of understanding of the nature of technology and technological change. What the critics of modern technology fail to realize is that the main difference between current and earlier technological change and diffusion is one of scale. Modern technology is truly global in its impact. Modern technology is a problem solving process, and problem solving generally creates other problems to be solved. Five centuries or more ago, before the development of flues, Europeans heated their homes (i.e., solved the problem of cold) and created massive amounts of pollution indoors. People throughout the world have (and many continue to do so) drawn their water from local sources that are used for animals and the repository for various waste materials. They are using and drinking polluted water. Those lucky enough to have access to modern technology heat or cool their homes efficiently and drink (relatively) clean water. Few would argue that these problems are not solved better than they were previously, but in the process of solving them, we, the creators and users of the technology, have succeeded in creating air and water pollution that transcends the home and village and encompasses regions, continents, and is of near global proportions. To argue that modern technology creates pollution while earlier ones didn't is to deny the facts of real life experiences of most of the world's population.[55] The difference is that our problems now transcend the home and village and must be solved at the global level and can only be solved with modern technology. Twentieth-century populations with their problems and aspirations will not find solutions in nineteenth-century technologies.

The scale of modern technology is also a factor in technology transfer and the change it engenders. The rapidity and magnitude of the potential cultural changes involved in using modern technology are enough to overwhelm many cultures. But it also offers unparalleled opportunities not only for material improvement but also for cultural advancement. In sum, industrial technology dwarfs our previous technologies in its power to do good or evil. Those who would have us reject it are, to say the least, confused. The real choice lies in the opportunity to understand the nature of technological change and to use it intelligently to serve human purposes.

The economics model (meaning the basic body of theory and method used by most economists) argues that we have little to worry about from resource exhaustion. As a mineral or some other resource becomes more scarce, the price system acts as a mechanism for transmitting this information. As the price of a resource rises, we find ways of conserving it and we work to develop technology to use it more efficiently. One author has noted that as we move to greater resource scarcity, pollution becomes less of a problem because there will be less waste of resources (pollution) when the resources are scarce and their expense relative to the price of labor and capital.[56] Rising prices of one resource cause substitution of less scarce resources. It appears that in the biologist, ecologist, and Club of Rome models, feedback mechanisms tend to worsen problems. From Malthus onward, forecasts of doom almost invariably are based on a form of exponential growth that brings the end upon us suddenly and without warning. However, those who accept such forecasts will not be surprised by the end, in the way that those who accepted the faith wouldn't be surprised at either the apocalypse or the golden age that followed. In the economist model of the price system, most (if not all) of the feedback mechanisms are positive in the sense that they provide the signals for correction and redemption.

Possibly a position between these two models is appropriate, or at least that is mine. Clearly, technology has solved many problems, but in doing so has created others. Possibilities of serious general resource exhaustion are considered remote and virtually unlikely by most economists. However, there are other threats to human life that are not signalled to us through price. Groups convened by the U.S. National Academy of Sciences have concluded that the increasing CO_2 in the atmosphere is likely to lead to a warming of the climate and that chloroflurocarbons (from aerosol sprays) are adversely affecting the ozone in the stratosphere and are thereby likely to increase skin cancer.[57] Oddly, these are phenomena with a very large potential for damage, yet they receive far less publicity than other less founded prophecies. One presumably would be cheap to cure (there are alternate propellants for aerosols), while reducing pollution further (which we are doing) will be costly but necessary on a variety of grounds. Chlorofluorocarbons are outlawed in the United States but unfortunately they continue to be used elsewhere. One author, Professor Sylvan Wittwer, presenting a paper at the meetings of the American Association for the Advancement of

Science (the publishers of *Science* magazine) argued that a warming of the globe *might* be beneficial to agriculture.[58] Then again it might not be. That is the nature of modern technology: its scale for good and destruction is so great that we do not want to take needless chances. Until we have considerably more knowledge of the impact of the warming of the atmosphere, we would be wise to take preventive steps.

We cannot reject modern technology. There are no golden ages in the past, and utopian visions of small scale community technologies in the future bear little relationship to reality. To reap the benefits of modern science and technology, we must act always carefully and intelligently. We must build in large margins of environmental safety in the same way that we build large margins of safety in our airplanes or our bridges. There is evidence in fact that we are doing more of this than critics concede. It is the affluence that technology brings that allows us to set aside large areas for conservation. As Aldo Leopold says in the famous conservationist work, *A Sand County Almanac,* "wild things ... had little value until mechanization assured us a good breakfast and until science disclosed the drama of where they came from and how they live."[59] The story is told (possibly it is apocryphal but nevertheless illustrative) of the physicist testifying before the Joint Congressional Committee set up after World War II to write legislation for the control of atomic power. After hearing of its enormous destructive powers, one of the senators asked if we couldn't destroy all bombs and the knowledge necessary to make them. The physicist answered, "Senator, the bomb is here to stay; the question is, Is Man?" Most of us would love to rid the world of destructive weapons and the knowledge to make them. We can't. But we can control them. We can't rid ourselves of modern science and technology because most people don't want to, and if we were to turn back our technology very far the globe would support far fewer of us. Nothing in this study is intended to deny the serious nature of the world's population and resource problems. I am in no way advocating complacency. However difficult our problems may be, there are no empirical grounds for apocalyptic visions of certain defeat. We could lose, but the bulk of the evidence indicates that we probably won't. There is a solid factual basis for cautious optimism. Success in solving these problems is a function of the extent to which human beings are willing to act with intelligence and not of inherent environmental limitations.

Of all the metaphors for our modern predicament, the one of Spaceship Earth seems most apt. It recognizes that we live together in a system and must work together cooperatively so that it functions for everyone's benefit. The Spaceship also symbolizes human beings' ability to use science and technology creatively to break barriers that were previously restraining. Mankind is capable of soaring toward the stars. John Dewey probably sums up my arguments better than I can:

Man who lives in a world of hazards is compelled to seek for security. He has sought to attain it in two ways. One of them began with an attempt to propitiate the powers which environ him and determine his destiny.... The other course is to invent arts and by their means turn the powers of nature to account; man constructs a fortress out of the very conditions and forces which threaten him.... This is the method of changing the world through action as the other is the method changing the self in emotion and idea.[60]

The choice is ours. Apocalypse did not happen yesterday. We need not give up on tomorrow or cower under visions of doom. Within broad limits, we are free to create a new tomorrow. To the question of whether man will continue, I answer with words from the Nobel Prize acceptance speech of William Faulkner, who is, as Professor Zamora has made clear in her essay on literature, generally more somber in his novelistic views: "I decline to accept the end of man.... I believe that man will not merely endure: he will prevail."[61]

Notes

[1] Robert L. Heilbroner, *An Inquiry Into The Human Prospect* (New York: Norton, 1974), p. 13.

[2] Paul R. Ehrlich, *The Population Bomb* (New York: Ballantine Books, rev. ed. 1971), p. xi.

[3] Ehrlich, p. 45. see also William and Paul Paddock, *Famine 1975! America's Decision: Who Will Surive* (Boston: Little, Brown, 1967), p. 61, quoting U.S. Secretary of Agriculture, Orville Freeman.

[4] See, for example, Stephen H. Schneider, *The Genesis Strategy: Climate and Global Survival* (New York: Plenum Press, 1976), pp. x-xi.

[5] "Vulnerability—the Strength of Science," in Garrett Hardin, *Stalking the Wild Taboo* (Los Altos, Ca.: William Kaufman, 1978), p. 77.

[6] Garrett Hardin, *The Limits of Altruism: An Ecologist's View of Survival* (Bloomington: Indiana Univ. Press, 1977), p. 1.

[7] Paul R. Ehrlich, "Eco-Catastrophe," *Ramparts*, 8, No. 3 (Sept. 1969), 24-29, reprinted in *Current* (3 (Oct. 1969), 23-32.

Apocalypse Yesterday   219

[8] Ehrlich, "Eco-Catastrophe," 30-31.
[9] Ehrlich, "Eco-Catastrophe," 30.
[10] Ehrlich, "Eco-Catastrophe," 24-28.
[11] Ehrlich, "Eco-Catastrophe," 30. Elsehwere, he finds a "net result of 1.2 billion deaths, one out of every three people, is not inconceivable." Ehrlich, *The Population Bomb*, p. 47.
[12] Paul R. Ehrlich, "World Population: Is the Battle Lost?" *Reader's Digest*, 94, No. 2 (Feb. 1969), 137-140, and Paul R. Ehrlich, "The Countdown to Disaster," *Wall Street Journal*, 3 Dec. 1968.
[13] William and Paul Paddock, *Famine, 1975! America's Decision: Who Will Survive* (Boston: Little, Brown, 1967) and Paul Ehrlich, "The Coming Famine," *Natural History*, 77, No. 5 (May 1968), 6-15.
[14] Paddock, p. 9.
[15] Paddock, pp. 82-84, 78, 20.
[16] Paddock, p. 8.
[17] Paddock, p. 61.
[18] William and Paul Paddock, *Time of Famines: America and the World Food Crises*, a new edition of *Famine 1975!* with a new introduction and postscript (Boston: Little, Brown, 1976), author's note.
[19] William and Paul Paddock, *Famine, 1975!*, pp. 207-209.
[20] Hardin, *Limits to Altruism*.
[21] William and Paul Paddock, *Time of Famines*, author's note.
[22] Paddock, *Time*, author's note.
[23] Paddock, *Time*, 252.
[24] Paddock, *Time*, 251.
[25] Paddock, *Time*, 252.
[26] Donella H. Meadows, Dennis L. Meadows, Jorgen Randers and William W. Behrens III, *The Limits to Growth: A Report for the Club of Rome's Project on the Predicament of Mankind* (1972; rpt. New York: Universe Books, A Potomac Associates Book, 1974).
[27] Meadows et al., p. 24.
[28] Ehrlich, "The Coming Famine."
[29] Ehrlich, "The Coming Famine," p. 8, and Ehrlich, *The Population Bomb*, pp. 179-80.
[30] Ehrlich, *The Population Bomb*, p. 2.
[31] Ehrlich, "World Population: A Battle Lost?" p. 140.
[32] John R. Madox, *The Doomsday Syndrome* (New York: McGraw-Hill, 1972), p. 60.
[33] Paul R. Ehrlich, review of Garrett Hardin's book, *The Limits of Altruism*, in *Human Nature* 1, No. 3 (Mar. 1978), 20.
[34] Garrett Hardin, "Ethical Implications of Carrying Capacity," and "Who Cares for Posterity?" in Hardin, *The Limits of Altruism*, pp 46-69, 81-84.
[35] Quoted by Harvey Simmons, "System Dynamics and Technocracy," in H.S.D. Cole, Christopher, Freeman, Marie Jahoda and K.L.R. Pavitt, eds., *Thinking About the Future: A Critique of the Limits to Growth* (London: Chatto & Windus for Sussex University Press, 1974), p. 200. (Reprinted in the United States as *Models of Doom: A Critique of the Limits to Growth*, New York: Universe Books, 1973.)
[36] Simmons, pp. 199, 201.
[37] Paul R. Ehrlich and Anne H. Ehrlich, "What Happened to the Population

Bomb?" *Human Nature*, 2, No. 1 (Jan. 1979), p. 70. The Ehrlichs are more cautious and subdued in this piece. In all modesty, they consider that "awareness" generated by books like *The Population Bomb* contributed to the decline in the birthrate in the U.S. Possibly people were so frightened after reading the book that they were unable to have sex. As a matter of fact, the birth rate in the U.S. began to fall in the late 1950s, and the absolute number of births began falling in the early '60s.

[38]See, among the many sources on current population and population trends, *Population Reports*, Series M., No. 3, July 1979, "The World Fertility Survey: Current Status and Findings," and *Population Reports,* Series M, No. 4 (Nov. 1979), "Age at Marriage and Fertility." These surveys also indicate that only about half of the women in the world are aware of modern birth control techniques giving considerable room for expansion of family planning programs and for further reductions in the birth rate.

[39] D.S. Miller, "What Food Crises?" A review of Mary Alice Caliendo, *Nutrition and the World Food Crises,* in *Nature,* 281, (Sept. 27, 1979), 323-324.

[40]Miller, 324.

[41]P. Buringh, H.D.J. van Heemst and G.J. Staring, *Computation of the Absolute Maximum Food Production of the World* (Wageningen, Netherlands: Department of Tropical Soil Science, Agricultural University, Wageningen, The Netherlands, 1975).

[42]Buringh, et al., p. 1.

[43]In some cases, their assumptions turn out to be too conservative. They assume that eighty per cent of the arable land in Asia is in use. Satellite data now indicate that in 1978 "only seventy-three percent of land was being used for production." *Our Magnificent Earth: A Rand McNally Atlas of Earth Resources* (Chicago: Rand McNally, 1979), p. 49.

[44]*World Food and Nutrition: The Potential Contributions of Research,* prepared by the Steering Committee, NRC Study on World Food and Nutrition of the Commission on International Relations, National Research Council (Washington: National Academy of Sciences, 1977), pp. 8-10.

[45]For example, on the possibility of making plants much more efficient in their photosynthesis, see Robert C. Cowen, "Coming: A Leap in Food Supply?" *Christian Science Monitor* (Dec. 12, 1979), p. 16, and Peter J. Vajk, *Doomsday Has Been Cancelled* (Culver City, CA.: Peace Press, 1978), pp. 76-77.

[46]Robert Solow, Lecture, University of Houston, Fall, 1976. General Data of Solow on crustal abundance is supported by Vajk, pp. 64-65, and Cole, p. 36. See also Nathan Rosenberg, "Innovative Response to Material Shortages," *The American Economic Review*, 63, No. 2 (May 1973), 111-118, and Scott Gordon, "Today's Apocalypses and Yesterday's," *The American Economic Review,* 63, No. 2 (May 1973), 106-110. A seminal work on the history of resource availability in the United States is H.J. Barnett and Chandler Morse, *Scarcity and Growth* (Baltimore: Johns Hopkins Univ. Press, 1963).

[47]David Morawetz, *Twenty-five Years of Economic Development 1950-1975* (Washington: The World Bank, 1977), p. 67. See also his article, same title, in *Finance and Development,* 14, No. 3 (Sept. 1977), 10-12.

[48]See *World Development Report 1979* (Washington: The World Bank, Aug. 1979), and *The Planetary Product: Progress Despite the Blues 1977-1978 (Washington:* Bureau of Public Affairs, U.S. Dept. of State, Special Report No. 58).

[49]*Health United States* (Washington: Office of Health Research, Statistics and Technology, Public Health Service, U.S. Dept. of Health, Education, and Welfare 1979), p. 115. See also Susan Previent Lee, "What's Needed is Affluence," *New York Times,* 4 Jan. 1980.

[50]See, for example, Keneneth S. Deffeyes and Ian D. MacGregor, "World Uranium Resources," *Scientific American*, 292, No. 1 (Jan. 1980), 66-76, or table above. On energy efficiency/conservation, see Robert Stobaugh and Daniel Yergin, eds.,

Energy Future: The Report of the Harvard Business School Energy Project (New York: Random House, 1979); James M. Griffin and Henry B. Steele, *Energy Economics and Policy* (New York: Academic Press, 1980), ch. 7, pp. 212-242.

[51]Meadows et al., p. 27.

[52]There is even a book with the title: Lester R. Brown, *The Twenty-Ninth Day: Accommodating Human Needs and Numbers to the Earth's Resources* (New York: W.W. Norton, 1978).

[53]Ehrlich, "Eco-Catastrophe," 32.

[54]T.C. Sinclair, "Environmentalism: A la recerche du temps perdu—bien perdu?" in H.S.D. Cole et al., p. 175.

[55]Any student of economic history knows that there were no golden ages in the past. There are a number of interesting popular and some scholarly works exploring the conditions of life in prior times, showing how unpleasant they were compared to the present. See, for example, the delightful book by Otto Bettman, *The Good Old Days—They Were Terrible* (New York: Random House, 1974).

[56]Rosenberg, 116.

[57]Nicholas Wade, "CO2 in Climate: Gloomsday Predictions Have No Fault," *Science* 206, No. 4421 (Nov. 23, 1979), 912-913, and Thomas H. Maugh, II, "The Threat to Ozone is Real, Increasing," *Science*, 206, No. 4423 (Dec. 7, 1979), 1167-1168.

[58]"Greenhouse Effect May Not Be Bad, Says Horticulturalist," *Houston Chronicle*, Jan. 6, 1980.

[59]Aldo Leopold, *A Sand County Almanac: With Essays on Conservation From Round River* 1949; rpt. New York: Sierra Club/Ballantine, 1966), p. xvii.

[60]John Dewey, *The Quest for Certainty: A Study of the Relation of Knowledge and Action* (New York: Putnam's Sons, Capricorn Books, 1960), p. 3.

[61]William Faulkner, *The Novel Prize Speech* (New York: Spiral Press, 1951). The speech was given on December 10, 1950; the prize was awarded for 1949.

Appendix

The Revelation of Saint John The Divine

CHAPTER 1

A Glorious Vision of Jesus Christ

The Revelation of Jesus Christ, which God gave unto him, to shew unto his servants things which must shortly come to pass; and he sent and signified *it* by his angel unto his servant John:

2 Who bare record of the word of God, and of the testimony of Jesus Christ, and of all things that he saw.

3 Blessed *is* he that readeth, and they that hear the words of this prophecy, and keep those things that are written therein: for the time *is* at hand.

4 John to the seven churches which are in Asia: Grace *be* unto you, and peace, from him which is, and which was, and which is to come; and from the seven Spirits which are before his throne;

5 And from Jesus Christ, *who is* the faithful witness, *and* the first begotten of the dead, and the prince of the kings of the earth. Unto him that loves us, and washed us from our sins in his own blood,

6 And hath made us kings and priests unto God and his Father; and him *be* glory and dominion for ever and ever. Amen.

7 Behold, he cometh with clouds; and every eye shall see him, and they *also* which pierced him: and all kindreds of the earth shall wail because of him. Even so, Amen.

8 I am Alpha and Omega, the beginning and the ending, saith the Lord, which is, and which was, and which is to come, the Almighty.

9 I John, who also am your brother, and companion in tribulation, and in the kingdom and patience of Jesus Christ, was in the isle that is called Patmos, for the word of God, and for the testimony of Jesus Christ.

10 I was in the Spirit on the Lord's day, and heard behind me a great voice, as of a trumpet,

11 Saying, I am Alpha and Omega, the first and the last: and, What thou seest, write in a book, and send *it* unto the seven churches which are in Asia; unto Ephe-sus, and unto Smyrna, and unto Perga-mos, and unto Thy-a-tira, and unto Sardis, and unto Philadelphia, and unto La-od-i-cea.

12 And I turned to see the voice that spake with me. And being turned, I saw seven golden candlesticks;

13 And in the midst of the seven candlesticks *one* like unto the Son of man, clothed with a garment down to the foot, and girt about the paps with a golden girdle.

14 His head and *his hairs were* white like wool, as white as snow; and his eyes *were* as a flame of fire;

15 And his feet like unto fine brass, as if they burned in a furnace; and his voice as the sound of many waters.

16 And he had in his right hand seven stars: and out of his mouth went a sharp twoedged sword: and his countenance *was* as the sun shineth in his strength.

17 And when I saw him, I fell at his feet as dead. And he laid his right hand upon me, saying unto me, Fear not: I am the first and the last:
18 I *am* he that liveth, and was dead; and, behold, I am alive for evermore, Amen; and have the keys of hell and of death.
19 Write of the things which thou hast seen, and the things which are, and the things which shall be hereafter;
20 The mystery of the seven stars which thou sawest in my right hand, and the seven golden candlesticks. The seven stars are the angels of the seven churches: and the seven candlesticks which thou sawest are the seven churches.

CHAPTER 2
Christ's Messages to the Churches

Unto the angel of the church of Ephe-sus write; These things saith he that holdeth the seven stars in his right hand, who walketh in the midst of the seven golden candlesticks;
2 I know thy works, and thy labour, and thy patience, and how thou canst not bear them which are evil: and thou hast tried them which say they are apostles, and are not, and hast found them liars:
3 And hast borne, and hast patience, and for my name's sake hast laboured, and hast not fainted.
4 Nevertheless I have *somewhat* against thee, because thou hast left thy first love.
5 Remember therefore from whence thou art fallen, and repent, and do the first works; or else I will come unto thee quickly, and will remove thy candlestick out of his place, except thou repent.
6 But this thou hast, that thou hatest the deeds of Nic-o-lai-tanes, which I also hate.
7 He that hath an ear, let him hear what the Spirit saith unto the churches; To him that overcometh will I give to eat of the tree of life, which is in the midst of the paradise of God.
8 And unto the angel of the church in Smyrna write; These things saith the first and the last, which was dead, and is alive;
9 I know thy works, and tribulation, and poverty, (but thou art rich) and *I know* the blasphemy of them which say they are Jews, and are not, but *are* the synagogue of Satan.
10 Fear none of those things which thou shalt suffer: behold, the devil shall cast *some* of you into prison, that ye may be tried; and ye shall have tribulation ten days: be thou faithful unto death, and I will give thee a crown of life.
11 He that hath an ear, let him hear what the Spirit saith unto the churches; He that overcometh shall not be hurt of the second death.
12 And to the angel of the church in Perga-mos write; These things saith he which hath the sharp sword with two edges;
13 I know thy works, and where thou dwellest, *even* where Satan's seat *is*: and thou holdest fast my name, and hast not denied my faith, even in those days wherein Antipas *was* my faithful martyr, who was slain among you, where Satan dwelleth.
14 But I have a few things against thee, because thou hast there them that hold the doctrine of Balaam, who taught Balac to cast a stumblingblock before the children of Israel, to eat things sacrificed unto idols, and to commit fornication.
15 So hast thou also them that hold the doctrine of the Nic-o-lai-thanes, which thing I hate.
16 Repent; or else I will come unto thee quickly, and will fight against them with the sword of my mouth.
17 He that hath an ear, let him hear what the Spirit saith unto the churches; To him that overcometh will I give to eat of the hidden manna, and will give him a white

stone, and in the stone a new name written, which no man knoweth saving he that receiveth *it*.

18 And until the angel of the church in Thy-a-tira write; These things saith the Son of God, who hath his eyes like unto a flame of fire, and his feet *are* like fine brass;

19 I know thy works, and charity, and service, and faith, and thy patience, and thy works; and the last *to be* more than the first.

20 Notwithstanding I have a few things against thee, because thou sufferest that woman Jez-e-bel, which calleth herself a prophetess, to teach and to seduce thy servants to commit fornication, and to eat things sacrificed unto idols.

21 And I gave her space to repent of her fornication; and she repented not.

22 Behold, I will cast her into a bed, and them that commit adultery with her into great tribulation, except they repent of their deeds.

23 And I will kill her children with death; and all the churches shall know that I am he which searcheth the reins and hearts: and I will give unto every one of you according to your works.

24 But unto you I say, and unto the rest in Thy-a-tira, as many as have not this doctrine, and which have not known the depths of Satan, as they speak; I will put upon you none other burden.

25 But that which ye have *already* hold fast till I come.

26 And he that overcometh, and keepeth my works unto the end, to him will I give power over the nations:

27 And he shall rule them with a rod of iron; as the vessels of a potter shall they be broken to shivers: even as I received of my Father.

28 And I will give him the morning star.

29 He that hath an ear, let him hear what the Spirit saith unto the churches.

CHAPTER 3
Christ's Messages to the Churches

And unto the angel of the church in Sardis write; These things saith he that hath the seven Spirits of God, and the seven stars; I know thy works, that thou hast a name that thou livest, and art dead.

2 Be watchful, and strengthen the things which remain, that are ready to die: for I have not found thy works perfect before God.

3 Remember therefore how thou hast received and heard, and hold fast, and repent. If therefore thou shalt not watch, I will come on thee as a thief, and thou shalt not know what hour I will come upon thee.

4 Thou hast a few names even in Sardis which have not defiled their garments; and they shall walk with me in white: for they are worthy.

5 He that overcometh, the same shall be clothed in white raiment; and I will not blot out his name out of the book of life, but I will confess his name before my Father and before his angels.

6 He that hath an ear, let him hear what the Spirit saith unto the churches.

7 And to the angel of the church in Philadelphia write; These things saith he that is holy, he that is true, he that hath the key of David, he that openeth, and no man shutteth; and shutteth, and no man openeth;

8 I know thy works: behold, I have set before thee an open door, and no man can shut it: for thou hast a little strength, and hast kept my word, and hast not denied my name.

9 Behold, I will make them of the synagogue of Satan, which say they are Jews, and are not, but do lie; behold, I will make them to come and worship before thy feet, and to know that I have loved thee.

10 Because thou hast kept the word of my patience, I also will keep thee from the hour

Appendix 225

of temptation, which shall come upon all the world, to try them that dwell upon the earth.

11 Behold, I come quickly: hold that fast which thou hast, that no man take thy crown.

12 Him that overcometh will I make a pillar in the temple of my God, and he shall go no more out: and I will write upon him the name of my God, and the name of the city of my God *which is* new Jerusalem, which cometh down out of heaven from my God: and *I will write upon him* my new name.

13 He that hath an ear, let him hear what the Spirit saith unto the churches.

14 And unto the angel of the church of the La-od-i-ceans write; These things saith the Amen, the faithful and true witness, the beginning of the creation of God;

15 I know thy works, that thou art neither cold nor hot: I would thou were cold or hot.

16 So then because thou art lukewarm, and neither cold nor hot, I will spue thee out of my mouth.

17 Because thou sayest, I am rich, and increased with goods, and have need of nothing; and knowest not that thou art wretched and miserable, and poor, and blind, and naked:

18 I counsel thee to buy me gold tried in the fire, that thou mayest be rich; and white raiment, that thou mayest be clothed, and *that* the shame of thy nakedness do not appear; and anoint thine eyes with eye salve, that thou mayest see.

19 As many as I love, I rebuke and chasten: be zealous therefore, and repent.

20 Behold, I stand at the door, and knock: if any man hear my voice, and open the door, I will come in to him, and will sup with him, and he with me.

21 To him that overcometh will I grant to sit with me in my throne, even as I also overcame, and am set down with my Father in his throne.

22 He that hath an ear, let him hear what the Spirit saith unto the churches.

CHAPTER 4
John's Vision of God's Throne

After this I looked, and, behold, a door *was* opened in heaven: and the first voice which I heard *was* as it were of a trumpet talking with me; which said, Come up hither, and I will shew thee things which must be hereafter.

2 And immediately I was in the spirit: and, behold, a throne was set in heaven, and *one* sat on the throne.

3 And he that sat was to look upon like a jasper and a sardine stone: and *there was* a rainbow round about the throne, in sight like unto an emerald.

4 And round about the throne *were* four and twenty seats: and upon the seats I saw four and twenty elders sitting, clothed in white raiment; and they had on their heads crowns of gold.

5 And out of the throne proceeded lightnings and thunderings and voices: and *there were* seven lamps of fire burning before the throne, which are the seven Spirits of God.

6 And before the throne *there was* a sea of glass like unto crystal: and in the midst of the throne, and round about the throne *were* four beasts full of eyes before and behind.

7 And the first beast *was* like a lion, and the second beast like a calf, and the third beast had a face as a man, and the fourth beast *was* like a flying eagle.

8 And the four beasts had each of them six wings about *him*; and *they were* full of eyes within: and they rest not day and night, saying, Holy, holy, holy, Lord God Almighty, which was, and is, and is to come.

9 And when those beasts give glory and honour and thanks to him that sat on the throne, who liveth for ever and ever,

10 The four and twenty elders fall down before him that sat on the throne, and worship him that liveth for ever and ever, and cast their crowns before the throne,

saying,

11 Thou are worthy, O Lord, to receive glory and honour and power: for thou hast created all things, and for thy pleasure they are and were created.

CHAPTER 5
The Scroll with the Seven Seals

And I saw in the right hand of him that sat on the throne a book written within and on the backside, sealed with seven seals.

2 And I saw a strong angel proclaiming with a loud voice, Who is worthy to open the book, and to loose the seals thereof?

3 And no man in heaven, nor in earth, neither under the earth, was able to open the book, neither to look thereon.

4 And I wept much, because no man was found worthy to open and to read the book, neither to look thereon.

5 And one of the elders saith unto me, Weep not: behold, the Lion of the tribe of Juda, the Root of David, hath prevailed to open the book, and to loose the seven seals thereof.

6 And I beheld, and, lo, in the midst of the throne and of the four beasts, and in the midst of the elders, stood a Lamb as it had been slain, having seven horns and seven eyes, which are the seven Spirits of God sent forth into all the earth.

7 And he came and took the book out of the right hand of him that sat upon the throne.

8 And when he had taken the book, the four beasts and four *and* twenty elders fell down before the Lamb, having every one of them harps, and golden vials full of odours, which are the prayers of saints.

9 And they sung a new song, saying, Thou art worthy to take the book, and to open the seals thereof: for thou wast slain, and hast redeemed us to God by thy blood out of every kindred, and tongue, and people, and nation;

10 And hast made us unto our God kings and priests: and we shall reign on the earth.

11 And I beheld, and I heard the voice of many angels round about the throne and the beasts and the elders: and the number of them was ten thousand times ten thousand, and thousands of thousands;

12 Saying with a loud voice, Worthy is the Lamb that was slain to receive power, and riches, and wisdom, and strength, and honour, and glory, and blessing.

13 And every creature which is in heaven and on the earth and under the earth, and such as are in the sea, and all that are in them, heard I saying, Blessing, and honour, and glory, and power, *be* unto him that sitteth upon the throne, and unto the Lamb for ever and ever.

14 And the four beasts said, Amen. And the four *and* twenty elders fell down and worshipped him that liveth for ever and ever.

CHAPTER 6
The Opening of Six of the Seals

And I saw when the Lamb opened one of the seals, and I heard, as it were the noise of thunder, one of the four beasts saying, Come and see.

2 And I saw, and behold a white horse: and he that sat on him had a bow; and a crown was given unto him: and he went forth conquering, and to conquer.

3 And when he had opened the second seal, I heard the second beast say, Come and see.

4 And there went out another horse *that was* red: and *power* was given to him that sat thereon to take peace from the earth, and that they should kill one another: and there was given unto him a great sword.

5 And when he had opened the third seal, I heard the third beast say, Come and see.

Appendix 227

And I beheld, and lo a black horse; and he that sat on him had a pair of balances in his hand.

6 And I heard a voice in the midst of the four beasts say, A measure of wheat for a penny, and three measures of barley for a penny; and *see* thou hurt not the oil and the wine.

7 And when he had opened the fourth seal, I heard the voice of the fourth beast say, Come and see.

8 And I looked, and behold a pale horse: and his name that sat on him was Death, and Hell followed with him. And Power was given unto them over the fourth part of the earth, to kill with sword, and with hunger, and with death, and with the beasts of the earth.

9 And when he had opened the fifth seal, I saw under the altar the souls of them that were slain for the word of God, and for the testimony which they held:

10 And they cried with a loud voice, saying, How long, O Lord, holy and true, dost thou not judge and avenge our blood on them that dwell on the earth?

11 And white robes were given unto every one of them; and it was said unto them, that they should rest yet for a little season, until their fellowservants also and their brethren, that should be killed as they *were*, should be fulfilled.

12 And I beheld when he had opened the sixth seal, and, lo, there was a great earthquake; and the sun became black as sackcloth of hair, and the moon became as blood;

13 And the stars of heaven fell unto the earth, even as a fig tree casteth her untimely figs, when she is shaken of a mighty wind.

14 And the heaven departed as a scroll when it is rolled together; and every mountain and island were moved out of their places.

15 And the kings of the earth, and the great men, and the rich men, and the chief captains, and the mighty men, and every bondman, and every free man, hid themselves in the dens and in the rocks of the mountains;

16 And said to the mountains and rocks, Fall on us, and hide us from the face of him that sitteth on the throne, and from the wrath of the Lamb:

17 For the great day his wrath is come; and who shall be able to stand?

CHAPTER 7
The Servants of God Sealed

And after these things I saw four angels standing on the four corners of the earth, holding the four winds of the earth, that the wind should not blow on the earth, nor on the sea, nor on any tree.

2 And I saw another angel ascending from the east, having the seal of the living God: and he cried with a loud voice to the four angels, to whom it was given to hurt the earth and the sea,

3 Saying, Hurt not the earth, neither the sea, nor the trees, till we have sealed the servants of our God in their foreheads.

4 And I heard the number of them which were sealed: *and there were* sealed an hundred *and* forty *and* four thousand of all the tribes of the children of Israel.

5 Of the tribe of Juda *were* sealed twelve thousand. Of the tribe of Teuben *were* sealed twelve thousand. Of the tribe of Gad *were* sealed twelve thousand.

6 Of the tribe of Aser *were* sealed twelve thousand. Of the tribe of Nephtha-lim *were* sealed twelve thousand. Of the tribe of Ma-nasses *were* sealed twelve thousand.

7 Of the tribe of Simeon *were* sealed twelve thousand. Of the tribe of Levi *were* sealed twelve thousand. Of the tribe of Issa-char *were* sealed twelve thousand.

8 Of the tribe of Zabu-lon *were* sealed twelve thousand. Of the tribe of Joseph *were* sealed twelve thousand. Of the tribe of Benjamin *were* sealed twelve thousand.

9 And this I beheld, and, lo, a great multitude, which no man could number, of all

nations, and kindreds, and people, and tongues, stood before the throne, and before the Lamb, clothed with white robes, and palms in their hands;
10 And cried with a loud voice, saying, Salvation to our God which sitteth upon the throne, and unto the Lamb.
11 And all the angels stood round about the throne, and *about* the elders and the four beasts, and fell before the throne on their faces, and worshipped God,
12 Saying, Amen: Blessing, and glory, and wisdom, and thanksgiving, and honour, and power, and might, *be* unto our God for ever and ever. Amen.
13 And one of the elders answered, saying unto me, What are these which are arrayed in white robes? and whence came they?
14 And I said unto him, Sir, thou knowest. And he said to me, These are they which came out of great tribulation, and have washed their robes, and made them white in the blood of the Lamb.
15 Therefore are they before the throne of God, and serve him day and night in his temple: and he that sitteth on the throne shall dwell among them.
16 They shall hunger no more, neither thirst any more; neither shall the sun light on them, nor any heat.
17 For the Lamb which is in the midst of the throne shall feed them, and shall lead them unto living fountains of waters: and God shall wipe away all tears from their eyes.

CHAPTER 8
Seven Angels with Seven Trumpets

And when he had opened the seventh seal, there was silence in heaven about the space of half an hour.
2 And I saw the seven angels which stood before God; and to them were given seven trumpets.
3 And another angel came and stood at the altar, having a golden censer; and there was given unto him much incense, that he should offer *it* with the prayers of all saints upon the golden altar which was before the throne.
4 And the smoke of the incense, *which came* with the prayers of the saints, ascended up before God out of the angel's hand.
5 And the angel took the censer, and filled it with fire of the alter, and cast *it* into the earth: and there were voices, and thunderings, and lightnings, and an earthquake.
6 And the seven angels which had the seven trumpets prepared themselves to sound.
7 The first angel sounded, and there followed hail and fire mingled with blood, and they were cast upon the earth: and the third part of trees was burnt up, and all green grass was burnt up.
8 And the second angel sounded, and as it were a great mountain burning with fire was cast into the sea: and the third part of the sea became blood;
9 And the third part of the creatures which were in the sea, and had life, died; and the third part of the ships were destroyed.
10 And the third angel sounded, and there fell a great star from heaven, burning as it were a lamp, and it fell upon the third part of the rivers, and upon the fountains of waters;
11 And the name of the star is called Wormwood: and the third part of the waters became wormwood; and many men died of the waters, because they were made bitter.
12 And the fourth angel sounded, and the third part of the sun was smitten, and the third part of the moon, and the third part of the stars; so as the third part of them was darkened, and the day shone not for a third part of it, and the night likewise.
13 And I beheld, and heard an angel flying through the midst of heaven, saying with a loud voice, Woe, woe, woe, to the inhabiters of the earth by reason of the other voices of the trumpet of the three angels, which are yet to sound!

Appendix

CHAPTER 9
The Sounding of the Fifth Angel

And the fifth angel sounded, and I saw a star fall from heaven unto the earth: and to him was given the key of the bottomless pit.

2 And he opened the bottomless pit; and there arose a smoke out of the pit, as the smoke of a great furnace; and the sun and the air were darkened by reason of the smoke of the pit.

3 And there came out of the smoke locusts upon the earth: and unto them was given power, as the scorpions of the earth have power.

4 And it was commanded them that they should not hurt the grass of the earth, neither any green thing, neither any tree; but only those men which have not the seal of God in their foreheads.

5 And to them it was given that they should not kill them, but that they should be tormented five months: and their torment *was* as the torment of a scorpion, when he striketh a man.

6 And in those days shall men seek death, and shall not find it; and shall desire to die, and death shall flee from them.

7 And the shapes of the locusts *were* like unto horses prepared unto battle; and on their heads *were* as it were crowns like gold, and their faces *were* as the faces of men.

8 And they had hair as the hair of women, and their teeth were as *the teeth* of lions.

9 And they had breastplates, as it were breastplates of iron; and the sound of their wings *was* as the sound of chariots of many horses running to battle.

10 And they had tails like unto scorpions, and there were stings in their tails: and their power *was* to hurt men five months.

11 And they had a king over them, *which is* the angel of the bottomless pit, whose name in the Hebrew tongue *is* A-bad-don, but in the Greek tongue hath *his* name A-polly-on.

12 One woe is past; *and*, behold, there come two woes more hereafter.

13 And the sixth angel sounded, and I heard a voice from the four horns of the golden altar which is before God,

14 Saying to the sixth angel which had the trumpet, Loose the four angels which are bound in the great river Euphrates.

15 And the four angels were loosed, which were prepared for an hour, and a day, and a month, and a year, for to slay the third part of men.

16 And the number of the army of the horsemen *were* two hundred thousand thousand: and I heard the number of them.

17 And thus I saw the horses in the vision, and them that sat on them, having breastplates of fire, and of jacinth, and brimstone: and the heads of the horses *were* as the heads of lions; and out of their mouths issued fire and smoke and brimstone.

18 By these three was the third part of men killed, by the fire, and by the smoke, and by the brimstone, which issued out of their mouths.

19 For their power is in their mouth, and in their tails: for their tails *were* like unto serpents, and had heads, and with them they do hurt.

20 And the rest of the men which were not killed by these plagues yet repented not of their works of their hands, that they should not worship devils, and idols of gold, and silver, and brass, and stone, and of wood: which neither can see, nor hear, nor walk:

20 Neither repented they of their murders, nor of their sorceries, nor of their fornication, nor of their thefts.

CHAPTER 10
A Strong Angel with a Little Book

And I saw another mighty angel come down from heaven, clothed with a cloud: and a rainbow *was* upon his head, and his face *was* as it were the sun, and his feet as pillars of fire:

2 And he had in his hand a little book open: and he set his right foot upon the sea, and *his* left *foot* on the earth,

3 And cried with a loud voice, as *when* a lion roareth: and when he had cried, seven thunders uttered their voices.

4 And when the seven thunders had uttered their voices, I was about to write: and I heard a voice from heaven saying unto me, Seal up those things which the seven thunders uttered, and write them not.

5 And the angel which I saw stand upon the sea and upon the earth lifted up his hand to heaven,

6 And sware by him that liveth for ever and ever, who created heaven, and the things that therein are, and the earth, and the things that therein are, and the sea, and the things which are therein, that there should be time no longer:

7 But in the days of the voice of the seventh angel, when he shall begin to sound, the mystery of God should be finished, as he hath declared to his servants the prophets.

8 And the voice which I heard from heaven spake unto me again, and said, Go *and* take the little book which is open in the hand of the angel which standeth upon the sea and upon the earth.

9 And I went unto the angel and said unto him, Give me the little book. And he said unto me, Take *it*, and eat it up; and it shall make thy belly bitter, but it shall be in thy mouth sweet as honey.

10 And I took the little book out of the angel's hands, and ate it up; and it was in my mouth sweet as honey: and as soon as I had eaten it, my belly was bitter.

11 And he said unto me, Thou must prophesy again before many peoples, and nations, and tongues, and kings.

CHAPTER 11
The Two Witnesses Prophesy

And there was given me a reed like unto a rod: and the angel stood, saying, Rise, and measure the temple of God, and the altar, and them that worship therein.

2 But the court which is without the temple leave out, and measure it not; for it is given unto the Gentiles: and the holy city shall they tread under foot forty *and* two months.

3 And I will give *power* unto my two witnesses, and they shall prophesy a thousand two hundred *and* threescore days, clothed in sackcloth.

4 These are the two olive trees, and the two candlesticks standing before the God of the earth.

5 And if any man will hurt them, fire proceedeth out of their mouth, and devoureth their enemies: and if any man will hurt them, he must in this manner be killed.

6 These have power to shut heaven, that it rain not in the days of their prophecy: and have power over waters to turn them to blood, and to smite the earth with all plagues, as often as they will.

7 And when they shall have finished their testimony, the beast that ascendeth out of the bottomless pit shall make war against them, and shall overcome them, and kill them.

8 And their dead bodies *shall lie* in the street of the great city, which spiritually is called Sodom and Egypt, where also our Lord was crucified.

9 And they of the people and kindreds and tongues and nations shall see their dead bodies three days and an half, and shall not suffer their dead bodies to be put in graves.

10 And they that dwell upon the earth shall rejoice over them, and make merry, and shall send gifts one to another; because these two prophets tormented them that dwelt on the earth.

Appendix 231

11 And after three days and an half the Spirit of life from God entered into them, and they stood upon their feet; and great fear fell upon them which saw them.
12 And they heard a great voice from heaven saying unto them, Come up hither. And they ascended up to heaven in a cloud; and their enemies beheld them.
13 And the same hour was there a great earthquake, and the tenth part of the city fell, and in the earthquake were slain of men seven thousand: and the remnant were affrighted, and gave glory to the God of heaven.
14 And the second woe is past; *and*, behold the third woe cometh quickly.
15 And the seventh angel sounded; and there were great voices in heaven, saying, The kingdoms of this world are become *the kingdoms* of our Lord, and of his Christ; and he shall reign for ever and ever.
16 And the four and twenty elders, which sat before God on their seats, fell upon their faces, and worshipped God,
17 Saying, We give thee thanks, O Lord God Almighty, which art, and wast, and art to come; because thou hast taken to thee thy great power, and hast reigned.
18 And the nations were angry, and thy wrath is come, and the time of the dead, that they should be judged, and that thou shouldest give reward unto thy servants the prophets, and to the saints, and them that fear thy name, small and great; and shouldest destroy them which destroy the earth.
19 And the temple of God was opened in heaven, and there was seen in his temple the ark of his testament: and there were lightnings, and voices, and thunderings, and an earthquake, and great hail.

CHAPTER 12
A Woman Clothed with the Sun

And there appeared a great wonder in heaven; a woman clothed with the sun, and the moon under her feet, and upon her head a crown of twelve stars:
2 And she being with child cried, travailing in birth, and pained to be delivered.
3 And there appeared another wonder in heaven; and behold a great red dragon, having seven heads and ten horns, and seven crowns upon his heads.
4 And his tail drew the third part of the stars of heaven, and did cast them to the earth: and the dragon stood before the woman which was ready to be delivered, for to devour her child as soon as it was born..
5 And she brought forth a man child, who was to rule all nations with a rod of iron: and her child was caught up unto God and *to* his throne.
6 And the woman fled into the wilderness, where she hath a place prepared of God, that they should feed her there a thousand two hundred *and* threescore days.
7 And there was war in heaven: Michael and his angels fought against the dragon; and the dragon fought and his angels,
8 And prevailed not; neither was their place found any more in heaven.
9 And the great dragon was cast out, that old serpent, called the Devil, and Satan, which deceiveth the whole world: he was cast out into the earth, and his angels were cast out with him.
10 And I heard a loud voice saying in heaven, Now is come salvation, and strength, and the kingdom of our God, and the power of his Christ: for the accuser of our brethren is cast down, which accused them before our God day and night.
11 And they overcame him by the blood of the Lamb, and by the word of their testimony; and they loved not their lives unto the death.
12 Therefore rejoice, *ye* heavens, and ye that dwell in them. Woe to the inhabiters of the earth and of the sea! for the devil is come down unto you, having great wrath, because he knoweth that he hath but a short time.
13 And when the dragon saw that he was cast unto the earth, he persecuted the woman which brought forth the man *child*.

14 And to the woman were given two wings of a great eagle, that she might fly into the wilderness, into her place, where she is nourished for a time, and times, and half a time, from the face of the serpent.
15 And the serpent cast out of his mouth water as a flood after the woman, that he might cause her to be carried away of the flood.
16 And the earth helped the woman, and the earth opened her mouth, and swallowed up the flood which the dragon cast out of his mouth.
17 And the dragon was wroth with the woman, and went to make war with the remnant of her seed, which keep the commandments of God, and have the testimony of Jesus Christ.

CHAPTER 13
The Beast With Seven Heads and Ten Horns

And I stood upon the sand of the sea, and saw a beast rise up out of the sea, having seven heads and ten horns, and upon his horns ten crowns, and upon his heads the name of blasphemy.
2 And the beast which I saw was like unto a leopard, and his feet were as *the feet* of a bear, and his mouth as the mouth of a lion: and the dragon gave him his power, and his seat, and great authority.
3 And I saw one of his heads as it were wounded to death; and his deadly wound was healed: and all the world wondered after the beast.
4 And they worshipped the dragon which gave power unto the beast: and they worshipped the beast, saying, Who *is* like unto the beast? who is able to make war with him?
5 And there was given unto him a mouth speaking great things and blasphemies; and power was given to him to continue forty *and* two months.
6 And he opened his mouth in blasphemy against God, to blaspheme his name, and his tabernacle, and them that dwell in heaven.
7 And it was given unto him to make war with the saints, and to overcome them: and power was given him over all kindreds, and tongues, and nations.
8 And all that dwell upon the earth shall worship him, whose names are not written in the book of life of the Lamb slain from the foundation of the world.
9 If any man have an ear, let him hear.
10 He that leadeth into captivity shall go into captivity: he that killeth with the sword must be killed with the sword. Here is the patience and the faith of the saints.
11 And I beheld another beast coming up out of the earth; and he had two horns like a lamb, and he spake as a dragon.
12 And he exerciseth all the power of the first beast before him, and causeth the earth and them which dwell therein to worship the first beast, whose deadly wound was healed.
13 And he doeth great wonders, so that he maketh fire come down from heaven on the earth in the sight of men,
14 And deceiveth them that dwell on the earth by *the means of* those miracles which he had power to do in the sight of the beast; saying to them that dwell on the earth, that they should make an image to the beast, which had the wound by a sword, and did live.
15 And he had power to give life unto the image of the beast, that the image of the beast should both speak, and cause that as many as would not worship the image of the beast should be killed.
16 And he causeth all, both small and great, rich and poor, free and bond, to receive a mark in their right hand, or in their foreheads:
17 And that no man might buy or sell, save he that had the mark, or the name of the beast, or the number of his name.

Appendix 233

18 Here is wisdom. Let him that hath understanding count the number of the beast: for it is the number of a man; and his number *is* Six hundred three score *and* six.

CHAPTER 14
The Fall of Babylon

And I looked, and, lo, a Lamb stood on the mount Sion, and with him an hundred forty *and* four thousand, having his Father's name written in their foreheads.

2 And I heard a voice from heaven, as the voice of many waters, and as the voice of a great thunder: and I heard the voice of harpers harping with their harps:

3 And they sung as it were a new song before the throne, and before the four beasts, and the elders: and no man could learn that song but the hundred *and* forty *and* four thousand, which were redeemed from the earth.

4 These are they which were not defiled with women; for they are virgins. These are they which follow the Lamb whithersoever he goeth. These were redeemed from among men, *being* the firstfruits of God and to the Lamb.

5 And in their mouth was found no guile: for they are without fault before the throne of God.

6 And I saw another angel fly in the midst of heaven, having the everlasting gospel to preach unto them that dwell on the earth, and to every nation, and kindred, and tongue, and people.

7 Saying with a loud voice, Fear God, and give glory to him; for the hour of his judgment is come: and worship him that made heaven, and earth, and the sea, and the fountains of waters.

8 And there followed another angel, saying, Babylon is fallen, is fallen, that great city, because she made all nations drink of the wine of the wrath of her fornication.

9 And the third angel followed them, saying with a loud voice, If any man worship the beast and his image, and receive *his* mark in his forehead, or in his hand,

10 The same shall drink of the wine of the wrath of God, which is poured out without mixture into the cup of his indignation; and he shall be tormented with fire and brimstone in the presence of the holy angels, and in the presence of the Lamb:

11 And the smoke of their torment ascendeth up for ever and ever: and they have no rest day nor night, who worship the beast and his image, and whosoever receiveth the mark of his name.

12 Here is the patience of the saints: here *are* they that keep the commandments of God, and the faith of Jesus.

13 And I heard a voice from heaven saying unto me, Write, Blessed *are* the dead which die in the Lord from henceforth: Yea, saith the Spirit, that they may rest from their labours; and their works do follow them.

14 And I looked, and behold a white cloud, and upon the cloud *one* sat like unto the Son of man, having on his head a golden crown, and in his hand a sharp sickle.

15 And another angel came out of the temple, crying with a loud voice to him that sat on the cloud, Thrust in thy sickle, and reap: for the time is come for thee to reap; for the harvest of the earth is ripe.

16 And he that sat on the cloud thrust in his sickle on the earth; and the earth was reaped.

17 And another angel came out of the temple which is in heaven, he also having a sharp sickle.

18 And another angel came out from the altar, which had power over fire; and cried with a loud cry to him that had the sharp sickle, saying, Thrust in thy sharp sickle, and gather the clusters of the vine of the earth; for her grapes are fully ripe.

19 And the angel thrust in his sickle into the earth, and gathered the vine of the earth, and cast *it* into the great winepress of the wrath of God.

20 And the winepress was trodden without the city, and blood came out of the

winepress, even unto the horse bridles, by the space of a thousand *and* six hundred furlongs.

CHAPTER 15
Seven Angels with Seven Vials of Wrath

And I saw another sign in heaven, great and marvellous, seven angels having the seven last plagues; for in them is filled up the wrath of God.

2 And I saw as it were a sea of glass mingled with fire: and them that had gotten the victory over the beast, and over his image, and over his mark,*and* over the number of his name, stand on the sea of glass, having the harps of God.

3 And they sing the song of Moses the servant of God, and the song of the Lamb, saying, Great and marvellous *are* thy works, Lord God Almighty; just and true *are* thy ways, thou King of saints.

4 Who shall not fear thee, O Lord, and glorify thy name? for *thou* only *art* holy: for all nations shall come and worship before thee; for thy judgments are made manifest.

5 And after that I looked, and, behold, the temple of the tabernacle of the testimony in heaven was opened:

6 And the seven angels came out of the temple, having the seven plagues, clothed in pure and white linen, and having their breasts girded with golden girdles.

7 And one of the four beasts gave unto the seven angels seven golden vials full of the wrath of God, who liveth for ever and ever.

8 And the temple was filled with smoke from the glory of God, and from his power; and no man was able to enter into the temple, till the seven plagues of the seven angels were fulfilled.

CHAPTER 16
The Angels Pour Out Their Vials

And I heard a great voice out of the temple saying to the seven angels, Go your ways, and pour out the vials of the wrath of God upon the earth.

2 And the first went, and poured out his vial upon the earth; and there fell a noisome and grievous sore upon the men which had the mark of the beast and *upon* them which worshipped his image.

3 And the second angel poured out his vial upon the sea; and it became as the blood of a dead *man*: and every living soul died in the sea.

4 And the third angel poured out his vial upon the rivers and fountains of waters; and they became blood.

5 And I heard the angel of the waters say, Thou art righteous, O Lord, which art, and wast, and shalt be, because thou hast judged thus.

6 For they have shed the blood of saints and prophets, and thou hast given them blood to drink; for they are worthy.

7 And I heard another out of the altar say, Even so, Lord God Almighty, true and righteous *are* thy judgments.

8 And the fourth angel poured out his vial upon the sun; and power was given unto him to scorch men with fire.

9 And men were scorched with great heat, and blasphemed the name of God, which hath power over these plagues: and they repented not to give him glory.

10 And the fifth angel poured out his vial upon the seat of the beast; and his kingdom was full of darkness; and they gnawed their tongues for pain,

11 And blasphemed the God of heaven because of their pains and their sores, and repented not of their deeds.

12 And the sixth angel poured out his vial upon the great river Eu-phrates; and the water thereof was dried up, and the way of the kings of the east might be prepared.

13 And I saw three unclean spirits like frogs *come* out of the mouth of the dragon, and

Appendix 235

out of the mouth of the beast, and out of the mouth of the false prophet.
14 For they are the spirits of devils, working miracles, *which* go forth unto the kings of the earth and of the whole world, to gather them to the battle of that great day of God Almighty.
15 Behold, I come as a thief. Blessed *is* he that watcheth, and keepeth his garments, lest he walk naked, and they see his shame.
16 And he gathered them together into a place called in the Hebrew tongue Ar-ma-geddon.
17 And the seventh angel poured out his vial into the air; and there came a great voice out of the temple of heaven, from the throne, saying, It is done.
18 And there were voices, and thunders, and lightnings; and there was a great earthquake, such as was not since men were upon the earth, so mighty an earthquake, *and* so great.
19 And the great city was divided into three parts, and the cities of the nations fell: and great Baby-lon came in remembrance before God, to give unto her the cup of the wine of the fierceness of his wrath.
20 And every island fled away, and the mountains were not found.
21 And there fell upon men a great hail out of heaven, *every stone* about the weight of a talent: and men blasphemed God because of the plague of the hail; for the plague thereof was exceeding great.

CHAPTER 17
The Woman Arrayed in Purple and Scarlet

And there came one of the seven angels which had the seven vials, and talked with me, saying unto me, Come hither; I will shew unto thee the judgment of the great whore that sitteth upon many waters:
2 With whom the kings of the earth have committed fornication, and the inhabitants of the earth have been made drunk with the wine of her fornication.
3 So he carried me away in the spirit into the wildernss: and I saw a woman sit upon a scarlet beast, full of names of blasphemy, having seven heads and ten horns.
4 And the woman was arrayed in purple and scarlet colour, and decked with gold and precious stones and pearls, having a golden cup in her hand full of abominations and filthiness of her fornication:
5 And upon her forehead *was* a name written, MYSTERY, BABYLON THE GREAT, THE MOTHER OF HARLOTS AND ABOMINATIONS OF THE EARTH.
6 And I saw the woman drunken with the blood of the saints, and with the blood of the martyrs of Jesus: and when I saw her, I wondered with great admiration.
7 And the angel said unto me, Wherefore didst thou marvel? I will tell thee the mystery of the woman, and of the beast that carrieth her, which hath the seven heads and ten horns.
8 The beast that thou sawest was, and is not; and shall ascend out of the bottomless pit, and go into perdition: and they that dwell on the earth shall wonder, whose names were not written in the book of life from the foundation of the world, when they behold the beast that was, and is not, and yet is.
9 And here *is* the mind which hath wisdom. The seven heads are seven mountains, on which the woman sitteth.
10 And there are seven kings: five are fallen, and one is, *and* the other is not yet come; and when he cometh, he must continue a short space.
11 And the beast that was, and is not, even he is the eighth, and is of the seven, and goeth into perdition.
12 And the ten horns which thou sawest are ten kings, which have received no kingdom as yet; but receive power as kings one hour with the beast.
13 These have one mind, and shall give their power and strength unto the beast.

14 These shall make war with the Lamb, and the Lamb shall overcome them: for he is Lord of lords, and King of kings: and they that are with him *are* called, and chosen, and faithful.
15 And he saith unto me, The waters which thou sawest, where the whore sitteth, are peoples, and multitudes, and nations, and tongues.
16 And the ten horns which thou sawest upon the beast, these shall hate the whore, and shall make her desolate and naked, and shall eat her flesh, and burn her with fire.
17 For God hath put in their hearts to fulfil his will, and to agree, and give their kingdom unto the beast, until the words of God shall be fulfilled.
18 And the woman which thou sawest is that great city, which reigneth over the kings of the earth.

CHAPTER 18
The Fall of Babylon

And after these things I saw another angel come down from heaven, having great power; and the earth was lightened with his glory.
2 And he cried mightily with a strong voice, saying, Babylon the great is fallen, is fallen, and is become the habitation of devils, and the hold of every foul spirit, and a cage of every unclean and hateful bird.
3 For all nations have drunk of the wine of the wrath of her fornication, and the kings of the earth have committed fornication with her, and the merchants of the earth are waxed rich through the abundance of her delicacies.
4 And I heard another voice from heaven, saying, Come out of her, my people, that ye be not partakers of her sins, and that ye receive not of her plagues.
5 For her sins have reached unto heaven, and God hath remembered her iniquities.
6 Reward her even as she rewarded you, and double unto her double according to her works: in the cup which she hath filled fill to her double.
7 How much she hath glorified herself, and lived deliciously, so much torment and sorrow give her: for she saith in her heart, I sit a queen, and am no widow, and shall see no sorrow.
8 Therefore shall her plagues come in one day, death, and mourning, and famine; and she shall be utterly burned with fire: for strong *is* the Lord God who judgeth her.
9 And the kings of the earth, who have committed fornication and lived deliciously with her, shall bewail her, and lament for her, when they shall see the smoke of her burning,
10 Standing afar off for the fear of her torment, saying, Alas, alas that great city Babylon, that mighty city! for in one hour is thy judgment come.
11 And the merchants of the earth shall weep and mourn over her; for no man buyeth their merchandise any more:
12 The merchandise of gold, and silver, and precious stones, and of pearls, and fine linen, and purple, and silk, and scarlet, and all thyine wood, and all manner vessels of ivory, and all manner vessels of most precious wood, and of brass, and iron, and marble,
13 And cinnamon, and odours, and ointments, and frankincense, and wine, and oil, and fine flour, and wheat, and beasts, and sheep, and horses, and chariots, and slaves, and souls of men.
14 And the fruits that thy soul lusted after are departed from thee, and all things which were dainty and goodly are departed from thee, and thou shalt find them no more at all.
15 The merchants of these things, which were made rich by her, shall stand afar off for the fear of her torment, weeping and wailing,
16 And saying, Alas, alas that great city, that was clothed in fine linen, and purple, and scarlet, and decked with gold, and precious stones, and pearls!

17 For in one hour so great riches is come to nought. And every shipmaster, and all the company in ships, and sailors, and as many as trade by sea, stood afar off,
18 And cried when they saw the smoke of her burning, saying, What *city* is like unto this great city!
19 And they cast dust on their heads, and cried, weeping and wailing, saying, Alas, alas that great city, wherein were made rich all that had ships in the sea by reason of her costliness! for in one hour is she made desolate.
20 Rejoice over her, *thou* heaven, and *ye* holy apostles and prophets; for God hath avenged you on her.
21 And a mighty angel took up a stone like a great millstone, and cast *it* into the sea, saying, Thus with violence shall that great city Babylon be thrown down, and shall be found no more at all.
22 And the voice of harpers, and musicians, and of pipers, and trumpeters, shall be heard no more at all in thee; and no craftsman, of whatsoever craft *he be*, shall be found any more in thee; and the sound of a millstone shall be heard no more at all in thee:
23 And the light of a candle shall shine no more at all in thee; and the voice of the bridegroom and of the bridge shall be heard no more at all in thee: for thy merchants were the great men of the earth; for by thy sorceries were all nations deceived.
24 And in her was found the blood of prophets, and of saints, and of all that were slain upon the earth.

CHAPTER 19
The Marriage of the Lamb

And after these things I heard a great voice of much people in heaven, saying, Alleluia; Salvation, and glory, and honour, and power, unto the Lord our God.
2 For true and righteous *are* his judgments: for he hath judged the great whore, which did corrupt the earth with her fornication, and hath avenged the blood of his servants at her hand.
3 And again they said, Alleluia. And her smoke rose up for ever and ever.
4 And the four and twenty elders and the four beasts fell down and worshipped God that sat on the throne, saying, Amen; Alleluia.
5 And a voice came out of the throne, saying, Praise our God, all ye his servants, and ye that fear him, both small and great.
6 And I heard as it were the voice of a great multitude, and as the voice of many waters, and as the voice of mighty thunderings, saying, Alleluia: for the Lord God omnipotent reigneth.
7 Let us be glad and rejoice, and give honour to him: for the marriage of the Lamb is come, and his wife hath made herself ready.
8 And to her was granted that she should be arrayed in fine linen, clean and white: for the fine linen is the righteousness of saints.
9 And he saith unto me, Write, Blessed *are* they which are called unto the marriage supper of the Lamb. And he saith unto me, These are the true sayings of God.
10 And I fell at his feet to worship him. And he said unto me, See *thou do it* not: I am thy fellowservant, and of thy brethren that have the testimony of Jesus: worship God: for the testimony of Jesus is the spirit of prophecy.
11 And I saw heaven opened, and behold a white horse; and he that sat upon him *was* called Faithful and True, and in righteousness he doth judge and make war.
12 His eyes *were* as a flame of fire, and on his head *were* many crowns; and he had a name written, that no man knew, but he himself.
13 And he *was* clothed with a vesture dipped in blood: and his name is called The Word of God.
14 And the armies *which were* in heaven followed him upon white horses, clothed in

fine linen, white and clean.

15 And out of his mouth goeth a sharp sword, that with it he could smite the nations: and he shall rule them with a rod of iron: and he treadeth the winepress of the fierceness and wrath of Almighty God.

16 And he hath on *his* vesture and on his thigh a name written, KING OF KINGS, AND LORD OF LORDS.

17 And I saw an angel standing in the sun; and he cried with a loud voice, saying to all the fowls that fly in the midst of heaven, Come and gather yourselves together unto the supper of the great God;

18 That ye may eat the flesh of kings, and the flesh of captains, and the flesh of mighty men, and the flesh of horses, and of them that sit on them, and the flesh of all *men, both* free and bond, both small and great.

19 And I saw the beast and the kings of the earth, and their armies, gathered together to make war against him that sat on the horse, and against his army.

20 And the beast was taken, and with him the false prophet that wrought miracles before him, with which he deceived them that had received the mark of the beast, and them that worshipped his image. These both were cast alive into a lake of fire burning with brimstone.

21 And the remnant were slain with the sword of him that sat upon the horse, which *sword* proceeded out of his mouth: and all the fowls were filled with their flesh.

CHAPTER 20

Satan Bound for a Thousand Years

And I saw an angel come down from heaven, having the key of the bottomless pit and a great chain in his hand.

2 And he laid hold on the dragon, that old serpent, which is the Devil, and Satan, and bound him a thousand years.

3 And cast him into the bottomless pit, and shut him up, and set a seal upon him, that he should deceive the nations no more, till the thousand years should be fulfilled: and after that he must be loosed a little season.

4 And I saw thrones, and they sat upon them, and judgment was given unto them: and *I saw* the souls of them that were beheaded for the witness of Jesus, and for the word of God, and which had not worshipped the beast, neither his image, neither had received *his* mark upon their foreheads, or in their hands; and they lived and reigned with Christ a thousand years.

5 But the rest of the dead lived not again until the thousand years were finished. This *is* the first resurrection.

6 Blessed and holy *is* he that hath part in the first resurrection: on such the second death hath no power, but they shall be priests of God and of Christ, and shall reign with him a thousand years.

7 And when the thousand years are expired, Satan shall be loosed out of his prison,

8 And shall go out to deceive the nations which are in the four quarters of the earth, Gog and Magog, to gather them together to battle: the number of whom *is* as the sand of the sea.

9 And they went up on the breadth of the earth, and compassed the camp of the saints about, and the beloved city: and fire came down from God out of heaven, and devoured them.

10 And the devil that deceived them was cast into the lake of fire and brimstone, where the beast and the false prophet *are*, and shall be tormented day and night for ever and ever.

11 And I saw a great white throne, and him that sat on it, from whose face the earth and the heaven fled away; and there was found no place for them.

Appendix 239

12 And I saw the dead, small and great, stand before God; and the books were opened: and another book was opened, which is *the book* of life: and the dead were judged out of those things which were written in the books, according to their works.
13 And the sea gave up the dead which were in it; and death and hell delivered up the dead which were in them: and they were judged every man according to their works.
14 And death and hell were cast into the lake of fire. This is the second death.
15 And whosoever was not found written in the book of life was cast into the lake of fire.

CHAPTER 21
A New Heaven and a New Earth

And I saw a new heaven and a new earth: for the first heaven and the first earth were passed away; and there was no more sea.
2 And I John saw the holy city, new Jerusalem, coming down from God out of heaven, prepared as a bride adorned for her husband.
3 And I heard a great voice out of heaven saying, Behold, the tabernacle of God *is* with men, and he will dwell with them, and they shall be his people, and God himself shall be with them *and be* their God.
4 And God shall wipe away all tears from their eyes; and there shall be no more death, neither sorrow, nor crying, neither shall there be any more pain: for the former things are passed away.
5 And he that sat upon the throne said, Behold, I make all things new. And he said unto me, Write: for these words are true and faithful.
6 And he said unto me, It is done. I am Alpha and Omega, the beginning and the end. I will give unto him that is athirst of the fountain of the water of life freely.
7 He that overcometh shall inherit all things: and I will be his God, and he shall be my son.
8 But the fearful, and unbelieving, and the abominable, and murderers, and whoremongers, and sorcerers, and idolaters, and all liars, shall have their part in the lake which burneth with fire and brimstone: which is the second death.
9 And there came unto me one of the seven angels which had the seven vials full of the seven last plagues, and talked with me, saying, Come hither, I will shew thee the bride, the Lamb's wife.
10 And he carried me away in the spirt to a great and high mountain, and shewed me that great city, the holy Jerusalem, descending out of heaven from God,
11 Having the glory of God; and her light *was* like unto a stone most precious, even like a jasper stone, clear as crystal;
12 And had a wall great and high, *and* had twelve gates, and at the gates twelve angels, and names written thereon, which are *the names* of the twelve tribes of the children of Israel:
13 On the east three gates; on the north three gates; on the south three gates; and on the west three gates.
14 And the wall of the city had twelve foundations, and in them the names of the twelve apostles of the Lamb.
15 And he that talked with me had a golden reed to measure the city, and the gates thereof, and the wall thereof.
16 And the city lieth foursquare, and the length is as large as the breadth: and he measured the city with the reed, twelve thousand furlongs. The length and the breadth and the height of it are equal.
17 And he measured the wall thereof, an hundred *and* forty *and* four cubits, *according to* the measure of a man, that is, of the angel.
18 And the building of the wall of it was *of* jasper: and the city *was* pure gold, like unto clear glass.

19 And the foundations of the wall of the city *were* garnished with all manner of precious stones. The first foundation was *jasper,* the second, sapphire; the third, a chalcedony; the fourth, an emerald.

20 The fifth, sardonyx; the sixth, sardius; the seventh, chrysolyte; the eighth, beryl; the ninth, a topaz; the tenth, a chrysoprasus; the eleventh, a jacinth; the twelfth, an amethyst.

21 And the twelve gates *were* twelve pearls; every several gate was of one pearl: and the street of the city *was* pure gold, as it were transparent glass.

22 And I saw no temple therein: for the Lord God Almighty and the Lamb are the temple of it.

23 And the city had no need of the sun, neither of the moon, to shine in it: for the glory of God did lighten it, and the Lamb *is* the light thereof.

24 And the nations of them which are saved shall walk in the light of it: and the kings of the earth do bring their glory and honour into it.

25 And the gates of it shall not be shut at all by day: for there shall be no night there.

26 And they shall bring the glory and honour of the nations into it.

27 And there shall in no wise enter into it any thing that defileth, neither *whatsoever* worketh abomination, or *maketh* a lie: but they which are written in the Lamb's book of life.

CHAPTER 22
The River and Tree of Life

And he shewed me a pure river of water of life, clear as crystal, proceeding out of the throne of God and of the Lamb.

2 In the midst of the street of it, and on either side of the river *was there* the tree of life, which bare twelve *manner of* fruits, *and* yielded her fruit every month: and the leaves of the tree *were* for the healing of the nations.

3 And there shall be no more curse: but the throne of God and of the Lamb shall be in it; and his servants shall serve him:

4 And they shall see his face; and his name *shall be* in their foreheads.

5 And there shall be no night there; and they need no candle, neither light of the sun; for the Lord God giveth them light: and they shall reign for ever and ever.

6 And he said unto me, These sayings *are* faithful and true: and the Lord God of the holy prophets sent his angel to shew unto his servants the things which must shortly be done.

7 Behold, I come quickly: blessed *is* he that keepeth the sayings of the prophecy of this book.

8 And I John saw these things, and heard *them*. And when I had heard and seen, I fell down to worship before the feet of the angel which shewed me these things.

9 Then saith he unto me, See *thou do it* not: for I am thy fellowservant, and of thy brethren the prophets, and of them which keep the sayings of this book: worship God.

10 And he saith unto me, Seal not the sayings of the prophecy of this book: for the time is at hand.

11 He that is unjust, let him be unjust still: and he which is filthy, let him be filthy still: and he that is righteous, let him be righteous still: and he that is holy, let him be holy still.

12 And, behold, I come quickly; and my reward *is* with me, to give every man according as his work shall be.

13 I am Alpha and Omega, the beginning and the end, the first and the last.

14 Blessed *are* they that do his commandments, that they may have right to the tree of life, and may enter in through the gates into the city.

15 For without *are* dogs, and sorcerers, and whoremongers, and murderers, and idolaters, and whosoever loveth and maketh a lie.

Appendix 241

16 I Jesus have sent mine angel to testify unto you these things in the churches. I am the root and the offspring of David, *and* the bright and morning star.
17 And the Spirit and the bride say, Come. And let him that heareth say, Come. And let him that is athirst come. And whosoever will, let him take the water of life freely.
18 For I testify unto every man that heareth the words of the prophecy of this book, If any man shall add unto these things, God shall add unto him the plagues that are written in this book:
19 And if any man shall take away from the words of the book of this prophecy, God shall take away his part out of the book of life, and out of the holy city, and *from* the things which are written in this book.
20 He which testifieth these things saith, Surely I come quickly. Amen. Even so, come, Lord Jesus.
21 The grace of our Lord Jesus Christ *be* with you all. Amen.

General Bibliography and Author Index

This list contains works of general relevance to the study of American apocalyptic attitudes within the parameters of the disciplines represented in this volume. It does not include all of the works mentioned in the foregoing essays: more complete bibliographical data for each discipline is found in the footnotes of the respective essays.

Alter, Robert. "The Apocalyptic Temper." In *After the Tradition.* New York: E. P. Dutton and Co., Inc., 1969. Following the argument of Martin Buber in "Prophecy, Apocalyptic, and the Historical Hour," this essay compares the premises of prophecy and apocalypse and their uses in literature.

Altizer, Thomas J.J. "Imagination and Apocalypse." *Soundings,* 43 (1970), 398-412. An analysis of the dualistic character of apocalypse.

Andrews, Edward D. *The People Called Shakers.* Rev. ed. New York: Dover Publications, Inc., 1963. The classic exposition of Shaker belief and practice.

Asimov, Isaac, *A Choice of Catastrophes: The Disasters That Threaten Our World.* New York: Simon and Schuster, 1979. Excellent survey of five classes of possible catastrophes from the first class, destruction of the universe, to the fifth, elimination of the human species. He concludes that they are unlikely to occur except in the very distant future.

Aspinwall, William. *A Brief Description of the Fifth Monarchy, or Kingdome That Shortly Is to Come Into the World.* London: Printed by M. Simmons, 1673. A Puritan millennialist tract; expects the apocalypse in 1673.

Bailey, Paul. *Wovoka, the Indian Messiah.* Los Angeles: Westernlore Press, 1957. Explores the life of the prophet of the Ghost Dance.

Barkun, Michael. *Disaster and The Millennium.* New Haven: Yale University Press, 1974. A study of millenarian movements and the relationship between catastrophe and conversion in such movements. An interesting combination of psychological, sociological and historical approaches to the phenomenon of millenarianism.

Barnett, H.J. and Chandler Morse. *Scarcity and Growth.* Baltimore: Johns Hopkins University Press, 1963. Important study of resources in the United States demonstrating that the real costs of all "natural" resources (except wood) had been steadily falling in the 19th and 20th centuries. As a consequence, resource costs as a percentage of GNP were also falling. The book thereby challenges the basic doctrine of classical economics that resource costs would rise through time, eventually limiting economic growth. This view of classical economics expected a "steady state" and was in some ways a harbinger of the limits to growth theories.

Beckerman, Wilfred. *In Defense of Economic Growth.* London: J. Cape Publishers, 1974. An optimistic extension of current economic and social patterns, based on traditional notions of progress.

Bercovitch, Sacvan. *The American Jeremiad.* Madison, Wisconsin: University of Wisconsin Press, 1978. A study of literary and religious conventions of the Puritan "doomsday" discourse.

———. "The Typology of America's Mission." *American Quarterly,* 32 (Summer 1978),

General Bibliography and Author Index 243

135-155. Biblical indications of America's divinely directed destiny.

Bestor, Arthur E., Jr. *Backwoods Utopias: The Sectarian Origins and the Owenite Phases of Communitarian Socialism in America, 1663-1829.* 2nd ed. Philadelphia: University of Pennsylvania Press, 1970. The apocalyptic dimension in major utopian experiments.

Bowman, J.T. "Eschatology of the New Testament." *The Interpreter's Dictionary of the Bible.* Vol. II. New York: Abingdon Press, 1962. A short overview of New Testament eschatology by a scholar in the field. Very good on providing basic categories of apocalyptic.

Braden, Charles S. *These Also Believe.* New York: Macmillan Co., 1949. A dated, but basic guide to American sectarian groups.

Brauer, Ralph. *The Horse, The Gun and The Piece of Property: Changing Images of the TV Western.* Bowling Green, Ohio: Bowling Green University Popular Press, 1975. Relevant to a consideration of the apocalyptic elements of the Western.

Brodie, Fawn M. *No Man Knows My History: The Life of Joseph Smith.* New York: Alfred A. Knopf, 1945. Remains a standard biography of the founder of Mormonism.

Brown, Ira V. "Watchers for the Second Coming: The Millenarian Tradition in America." *Mississippi Valley Historical Review,* 39 (1952), 441-58. Argues the centrality of millennialism in American religion.

Brown, William and Herman Kahn. *The New Two-Hundred Years:* London: J. Cape Publishers, 1974. An optimistic extension of current economic and social patterns, based on traditional notions of progress.

Buber, Martin. *The Prophetic Faith.* New York: Harper Torchbook, 1960. A prominent Jewish theologian's discussion of the prophetic eschatological tradition.

_____. "Prophecy, Apocalyptic, and the Historical Hour." In *Pointing the Way: Collected Essays.* Ed. and trans. Maurice Friedman. Baltimore: Johns Hopkins Press, 1957. A comparative discussion of the prophetic and apocalyptic vision of history: Buber is very critical of the apocalyptic vision.

Calvin, John. *The Institutes of the Christian Religion.* Translated by Ford Lewis Battles. The Library of Christian Classics, Vols. XX, XXI. Philadelphia: Westminister Press, 1960.

Campbell, B.G. *Humankind Emerging.* 2nd ed. Boston, Toronto: Little, Brown and Co., 1979. A comprehensive and well-illustrated text giving a general account of the physical and cultural aspects of human evolution.

Case, Shirley Jackson. *The Millennial Hope.* Chicago: University of Chicago Press, 1918. History and doctrine of apocalyptic expectation in Christianity.

Cawelti, John G. *The Six-Gun Mystique.* Bowling Green, Ohio: Bowling Green University Popular Press, 1970. University of Chicago English professor Cawelti has written much in the area of popular culture studies. This work is the holy scripture of the western as cultural value drama.

Chapman, Walker. *The Golden Dream: Seekers of El Dorado.* New York: Bobbs-Merrill Co., Inc., 1967. A complete study of the mythical projection of the golden New Jerusalem by the early explorers of the Central and South America.

Charles, R.H. *A Critical and Exegetical Commentary on the Revelation of St. John.* Edinburgh: T. & T. Clark, 1920. A commentary by the acknowledged authority on eschatology.

_____. *A Critical and Exegetical Commentary on the Book of Daniel.* Oxford: Clarendon Press, 1929. A commentary on an apocalyptic of the archetype.

_____. *Eschatology: The Doctrine of a Future Life in Israel, Judaism and Christianity.* 1899; rpt. New York: Schocken Books, 1963. Considered the standard work on eschatology, Charles traces the development of "visions of the end" from their Biblical beginnings to the early Christian writings.

Cherry, Conrad, ed. *God's New Israel: Religious Interpretations of American Destiny.* Englewood Cliffs: Prentice-Hall, 1971. A sourcebook linking perceptions of American destiny with apocalyptic hopes.

Cohn, Norman. *The Pursuit of the Millennium.* Rev. ed. New York: Oxford University Press, 1970. A study of medieval millenarianism important for theory and method.

Columbus, Christopher. *The Four Voyages of C. Columbus.* Trans. J. M. Cohen. Baltimore: Penguin Books, 1969. See in particular the letter to Dona Juana de la Torre and the narrative of the third voyage for Columbus's apocalyptic sense of his enterprise.

Cole, H.S.D., Christopher Freeman, Marie Jahoda, and K.L.R. Pavitt, eds. *Thinking About the Future: A Critique of the Limits to Growth.* London: Chatto and Windus for Sussex University Press, 1974. (Reprinted in the U.S. as *Models of Doom: A Critique of the Limits to Growth.* New York: Universe Books, 1973.) Systematic, interdisciplinary scientific point by point critique of the *Limits to Growth.* Does not advocate complacency but generally argues that resource problems are serious but not beyond our capability to solve. Probably the best single book on the subject

Commoner, Barry. *The Closing Circle: Nature, Man, and Technology.* New York: Bantam Books, 1971. A powerful argument for the potentially disastrous relationships between population pressure, declining natural resources and business expectations. Written for the layman during the early days of the ecological revolution in America.

Conrad, Peter. *Imagining America.* New York: Oxford University Press, 1980. A survey of several nineteenth-century and twentieth-century European literary figures' visits to America which confirms the continuing attraction of the New World as the potential site of human redemption and historical renewal.

Cotton, John. *The Churches Resurrection.* London: Printed by R.O. and G.D. for Henry Overton, 1642. An exposition of the apocalypse by a leading American Puritan.

———. *An Exposition Upon the Thirteenth Chapter of the Revelation.* London: Printed for Livewel Chapman, 1655. A Puritan approach to the New Testament Apocalypse.

———. *The Pouring Out of the Seven Vials.* London: Printed by R.S. for Henry Overton, 1642. A Puritan argument that the Papacy must fall before the apocalyptic dawn.

Court, John M. *Myth and History in the Book of Revelation.* Atlanta: John Knox Press, 1979. An exhaustive reading of The Book of Revelation, with special focus on the sources of that apocalypse. A useful reference.

Cox, Harvey. *Turning East: The Promise and Peril of the New Orientalism.* New York: Simon and Schuster, 1977. A survey of the "new religions" which sees them as revitalizing rather than threatening the Christian world view.

Cross, Whitney R. *The Burned-Over District: The Social and Intellectual History of Enthusiastic Religion in Western New York, 1800-1850.* Ithaca: Cornell University Press, 1950. On revivalistic and millennial fervor in the nineteenth century.

Darlington, C.D. *The Little Universe of Man.* London, Boston, and Sydney: Allen and Unwin, 1978. A superbly written and fascinating account of diverse aspects of the nature of contemporary man. The strong emphasis on genetics warrants the attention of the serious scholar as well as the general public.

Davidson, James W. *The Logic of Millennial Thought: Eighteenth-Century New England.* New Haven: Yale University Press, 1977. Analyzes late Puritan

General Bibliography and Author Index 245

apocalypticism.

Diamond, Stanley, ed. *Primitive Views of the World*. New York: Columbia University Press, 1964. Includes discussion of ancient man's "cosmic" view of time as cyclical and endlessley recurring.

Dobzhansky, Theodosious. *The Biology of Ultimate Concern*. New York: New American Library, 1967. A philosophy of prophetic eschatology based on the thought of Teilhard de Chardin by a Nobel prize geneticist.

Dwight, Timothy. *The Duty of Americans, at the Present Crisis*. New Haven: Thomas and Samuel Green, 1798. Sees the destruction of Roman Catholicism as the precursor of the Apocalypse.

———. *A Sermon Delivered in Boston, September 16, 1813*. Boston: S.T. Armstrong, 1813. Predicts the coming of the Apocalypse around 2000 A.D.

Eckholm, Eric P. *Losing Ground: Environmental Stress and World Food Prospects*. New York: W.W. Norton, Inc., 1976. A prediction of increasing problems in feeding the growing populations of third world countries.

Edelson, Edward. *Great Science Fiction From the Movies*. New York: Archway 1976. A brief paperback history of science fiction in films. Popularly written, skimming of the surface, with some slightly in-depth critical analysis.

Edwards, Jonathan. *Apocalyptic Writings*. Ed. Stephen J. Stein. Vol. V of *The Works of Jonathan Edwards*, New Haven: Yale University Press, 1977. Sermons and other writings on the Apocalypse by America's leading eighteenth century divine.

———. *The Great Awakening*. Ed. C.C. Goen. Vol. IV of *The Works of Jonathan Edwards*. New Haven: Yale University Press, 1972. In some of this collection, Edwards sees the revivals as bringing the apocalyptic kingdom to America.

———. "History of the Work of Redemption." Ed. Sereno E. Dwight. In Vol. III of *The Works of President Edwards*. New York: S. Converse, 1829. Casts the whole of history as a prelude to the Apocalypse.

Ehrlich, Paul R. *The Population Bomb. 1971;* Rev. ed. New York: Ballantine Books, 1976. A well-known prediction of global disaster resulting from over-population.

Elden, Frederick. *Crisis in Eden: A Religious Study of Man and His Environment*. Nashville and New York: Abingdon Press, 1970. Elden argues that the Christian view of man's relation to his environment has been one of domination over nature, with far-reaching and potentially dangerous consequences.

Eliade, Mircea. *Cosmos and History: The Myth of The Eternal Return*. Ed. Willard Trask. New York: Pantheon Books, 1954. Eliade develops the thesis that human consciousness may articulate its sense of being-in-the-world in archaic-cyclical, biblical-historical or secular-historicist symbols. He describes each of these understandings of reality and in the last chapter urges a rejection of historicity and a return to the Christian vision of the meaning of history.

———. *Death, Afterlife, and Eschatology*. Part 3 of *From Primitives to Zen*. New York: Harper and Row, 1967. A comparative mythographical approach to eschatology.

Ellul, Jacques. *The Technological Society*. New York: Alfred Knopf, 1964. Should be required reading in every university. An argument that technology is irrefutably self-perpetuating, will bring a prophetic eschaton, whether we like it or not, and that we won't. An absolutely brilliant work by a leading anti-theological doom-sayer.

Ellwood, Robert S., Jr. *One Way: The Jesus Movement and Its Meaning*. Englewood Cliffs: Prentice-Hall, 1973. Shows the apocalyptic element in youth-oriented Jesus groups.

Enroth, Ronald M., Edward E. Ericson, Jr., and C. Breckenridge Peters. *The Jesus*

People: *Old-Time Religion in the Age of Aquarius.* Grand Rapids: William B. Eerdmans Publishing Co., 1972. Evangelical sociologists discuss the apocalyptic character of the Jesus Movement.

Fackenheim, Emil. *Quest for Past and Future.* Boston: Beacon Press, 1968. A gathering of Fackenheim's essays which explore the significance of Jewish thought in the modern world.

Farrar, Austin. *A Rebirth of Images: The Making of St. John's Apocalypse.* Boston: Beacon Press, 1963. A discussion of the symbolic content of the most complete example of conventional apocalyptic archetypes, St. John's Apocalypse.

Festinger, Leon, Henry W. Riecken, and Stanley Schachter. *When Prophecy Fails: A Social and Psychological Study of a Modern Group that Predicted the Destruction of the World.* Minneapolis: University of Minnesota Press, 1956. A specific study in a narrative mode which details the reactions of individuals to the disconfirmation of the apocalyptic predictions of their appointed seer. Very interesting and perceptive in both psychological and sociological observations.

Fiedler, Leslie. *The Return of the Vanishing Americans.* New York: Stein and Day, 1968. See, in particular, the chapter entitled "The World without a West" for a discussion of the impact of America on Renaissance Europe.

──── *Waiting for the End.* New York: Stein and Day, 1964. A discussion of the author's vision of the end of our current literary tradition.

Fishwick, Marshall, and Ray Browne, eds. *Icons of Popular Culture.* Bowling Green, Ohio: Bowling Green University Popular Press, 1970. A series of brief studies of American values as they manifest themselves in three-dimensional form, i.e., the symbols of values as object or icon. About half of the articles investigate methodology, half focus on the objects themselves, from oars to coke bottles. Relevant to a consideration of apocalyptic icons in contemporary culture.

Folsome, C.E. *The Origin of Life. A Warm Little Pond.* San Francisco: W.H. Freeman and Company, 1979. A good, brief summary of the modern evidence for the origin of life. For the less technically minded reader.

Frankel, Charles. *The Case for Modern Man.* Boston: Beacon Press, 1959. This book defends the doctrine of progress, the idea that history is controlled by human beings and is a record of the betterment of humanity, as well as the notion that human beings are essentially moral and rational.

Franklin, H. Bruce. *Future Perfect.* New York: Oxford University Press, 1970. Franklin suggests the relationship of the vision of the New Jerusalem in apocalypse to the visions of the future in science fiction.

Frederickson, George M. *The Inner Civil War: Northern Intellectuals and the Crisis of the Union.* New York: Harper & Row, Publishers, 1965. A study in intellectual history, examining the impact of the Civil War on American ideology.

Fritsch, C.T. "Apocrypha." *The Interpreter's Dictionary of the Bible.* Vol. IV. New York: Abingdon Press, 1962. A biblical scholar's general description of the intertestamental books known as the Apocrypha.

Frye, Northrup. *Anatomy of Criticism: Four Essays,* Princeton, New Jersey: Princeton University Press, 1957. The third essay, "Archetypal Criticism: Theory of Myths," contains a useful discussion of apocalyptic and demonic imagery, asserting that Revelations comprises a mythical conclusion for the Bible as a whole.

Gaster, T.H. "Satan." *The Interpreter's Dictionary of the Bible.* Vol. IV. New York: Abingdon Press, 1962.

Gaustad, Edwin S., ed. *The Rise of Adventism.* New York: Harper and Row, 1975. Essays on the background of modern American millennialism.

George, Frank H. *Science and the Crisis in Society.* London and New York: John Wiley and Sons, Ltd., 1970. An expert in cybernetics looks at the recent

General Bibliography and Author Index 247

period of "world-wide social unrest" and the rapid change in social standards and values.

Gilsdorf, Joy B. "The Puritan Apocalypse: New England Eschatology in the Seventeenth Century." Unpublished Ph.D. dissertation, Yale University, 1964. The most thorough study of early Puritan apocalyptic thought.

Glock, Charles Y., and Robert N. Bellah, ed. *The New Religious Consciousness.* Berkeley and Los Angeles: University of California Press, 1976. A collection of essays which explores various aspects of the "new" religious consciousness.

Greeley, Andrew J. "Varieties of Apocalypse in Science Fiction." *Journal of American Culture,* 2, 2 (1979), 279-287. A brief look at the ways in which the myth of apocalypse has recently dominated science fiction, particularly in the relatively unknown writer, R.A. Lafferty.

Gribbon, John. *Forecasts, Famines and Freezes.* New York: Walker, 1976. A discussion of recent climatic changes and the problem of food production on an overcrowded planet.

Gronigen, B.A. von. *In the Grip of the Past: An Essay on an Aspect of Greek Thought.* Leiden: E.J. Brill, 1953. An analysis of Greek language, grammar and thought which asserts that the Greeks were a past rather than present or future oriented people.

Groseclose, Barbara S. *Emanuel Leutze, 1816-1868: Freedom Is the Only King.* Washington, D.C.: Smithsonian Institution Press, 1975. Published for the National Collection of Fine Arts. The only full-length study of the painter to date, serving as the catalogue for an exhibition of Leutze's work held in 1975. The study includes, in addition to catalogue entries, a chronology, biography, and discussions of individual paintings.

Guardini, Romano. *The End of the Modern World: A Search for Orientation.* Trans. Joseph Theman and Herbert Burke. New York: Sheed and Ward, 1956. A foremost European theologian comments on the contemporary crisis in religion and culture.

———. *The Last Things.* Trans. Charlotte E. Forsyth and Grace B. Branham. New York: Pantheon Books, Inc., 1954. A theological discussion of Christian eschatological belief.

Gunnell, John. *Political Philosophy and Time.* Middletown, Connecticut: Wesleyan University Press, 1968. A study of the nature of the relationship between political visions and the sense of time and history.

Hammell, William M., ed. *The Popular Arts in America: A Reader.* New York: Harcourt Brace Jovanovich, Inc., 1972. One of the better readers in popular culture studies. Includes four essays on the popular arts in general, and groups the rest of the studies under the categories of movies, radio and television, music, and print (magazines, genre fiction). Contributions by academics, creators of popular culture works, and reprints of classic essays in the field.

Hanson, Paul D. *The Dawn of Apocalyptic.* Philadelphia: Fortress Press, 1975. A discussion of the origins of apocalyptic thought.

Hardin, Garrett. *The Limits of Altruism: An Ecologist's View of Survival.* Bloomington, Indiana: Indiana University Press, 1977. One of the many books and articles by the author famous (or infamous?) for his arguments in support of abortion and the lifeboat ethic.

Harrison, John F.C., *The Second Coming: Popular Millenarianism 1780-1850.* New Brunswick, N.J.: Rutgers University Press, 1979. The world of popular Millenarianism is rich in unusual characters and extreme doctrines and raises wider issues of historical analysis: the social forms in which beliefs relate to social action; attitudes toward, and expectations of social change.

Hassan, Ihab. "Beyond a Theory of Literature: Intimations of Apocalypse." *Compar-*

ative *Literature Studies*, 1 (1964), 261-71. A consideration of the formal nature of literature, with a suggestion of an apocalypse in the style of contemporary prose fiction.

Hatch, Nathan O. *The Sacred Cause of Liberty: Republican Thought and the Millennium in Revolutionary New England.* New Haven: Yale University Press, 1977. Relates political ideology and symbols to apocalyptic expectation.

Heilbroner, Robert. *An Inquiry into the Human Prospect.* New York: W.W. Norton, Inc., 1974. An eminent economist's pessimistic analysis of the future, based on the stated assumption that the reader shares with him "an awareness of the oppressive anticipation of the future" current in America.

Heschel, Abraham. *The Prophet, 1955 rpt.* New York: Harper and Row, 1962. A study of the lives and words of the prophets, intended to clarify the ideas of the prophets and the meaning of prophecy.

Hopkins, C. Howard. *The Rise of the Social Gospel in American Protestantism, 1865-1915.* New Haven: Yale University Press, 1940. Still the standard exposition of the Social Gospel and its optimism for the future.

Hopkins, Mark. *Miscellaneous Essays and Discoveries.* Boston: T.R. Marvin, 1847. Regards nineteenth century revivalism and the missionary impulse as forerunners of the Apocalypse.

Hopkins, Samuel. *A Treatise on the Millennium.* Boston: Isaiah Thomas and Ebenezer T. Andrews, 1793. Develops the position first advanced by Jonathan Edwards.

Hoyle, F. *Ten Faces of the Universe.* San Francisco: W.H. Freeman and Company, 1977. A popular account of the recent advances in modern astronomy by the highly controversial but well-respected British astronomer.

Huit, Ephraim. *The Whole Prophecie of Daniel Explained.* London: Printed for H. Overton, 1644. A Puritan interpretation of the Old Testament Apocalypse.

Husserl, Edmund. *The Phenomenology of Internal Time Consciousness.* Trans. S. Churchill. Ed. Martin Heidegger. Bloomington: Indiana Univesity Press, 1964. A phenomenological approach to the nature of psychic and mythic time.

Jacob, Edmond. *The Theology of the Old Testament.* New York: Harper and Bros., 1958. A helpful discussion of Old Testament prophetic and apocalyptic modes.

Jenni, E. "Eschatology of the Old Testament." *The Interpreter's Dictionary of the Bible.* Vol. II. New York: Abingdon Press, 1962. An overview of Old Testament eschatology (particularly apocalyptic) by a scholar in the field.

Jewett, Robert. *The Captain America Complex.* Philadelphia: Westminster Press, 1973. A New Testament Professor looks at popular culture with an eye to political ramifications in American foreign policy. Somewhat dated now, this is still a very readable study of Kennedy-Johnson-Nixon diplomacy at its cultural base.

Kahn, Herman, and Anthony J. Wiener. *The Year 2000.* New York: MacMillan, 1967. The results of the future studies of the Hudson Institute by the men who run it. The pro-technology prophetic eschatological vision of the future, it includes very stimulating scenarios of possible futures.

Kaul, A.N. *The American Vision: Actual and Ideal Society in Nineteenth-Century Fiction.* New Haven: Yale University Press, 1963. See especially Kaul's chapter on Hawthorne, pp. 139-213, in which he relates Hawthorne's utopian vision to the millennialism of his Puritan forebears.

Kermode, Frank. *The Sense of An Ending.* New York: Oxford University Press, 1966. An exploration of the relationship between fiction and the human understanding of crisis, especially terminal crisis.

Ketterer, David. *New Worlds for Old: The Apocalyptic Imagination, Science Fiction, and American Literature.* Garden City, New York: Anchor Press/Doubleday, 1974. A discussion of apocalypse and science fiction, particularly in the works of nineteenth-century writers such as Hawthorne and Poe.

Kitses, Jim. *Horizons West*. Bloomington: Indiana University Press, 1970. An analysis of the films of Anthony Mann, Budd Boetticher, and Sam Peckinpah, with literary/historical methodology of aesthetic criticism.

LaBarre, Weston. *The Ghost Dance*. New York: Dell Publishing Co., 1972. Remains the best study of a variant apocalypticism among the Sioux.

Landsman, Gail. "Science Fiction: The Rebirth of Mythology," *The Journal of Popular Culture*, V, 4 (Spring 1972), 989-995. A provocative and convincing attempt to view science fiction as the philosophical theology of American culture.

Lawrence, D.H. "Apocalypse." In *Phoenix: The Posthumous Papers of D.H. Lawrence*. Ed. Edward D. McDonald. New York: The Viking Press, 1964. Lawrence comments on the astrology of apocalypse, which he feels to be the real interest of the myth: it is, for him, a "magnificent cosmic and starry drama" that provides an "imaginative infusion" into our perception of space.

_____.*Studies in Classic American Literature*. 1924; rpt. New York: The Viking Press, 1964. Lawrence points to the apocalyptic attitudes of nineteenth-century writers of American fiction and poetry.

Lee, R.B. and I. Devore, eds. *Kalahari Hunter-Gatherers: Studies of the !Kung San and their Neighbors*. Cambridge: Harvard University Press, 1976. A classic study of a fast-disappearing tribe of hunter-gatherers who, we believe, have retained the traditional life-style of our ancestors.

Levine, Lawrence. "Songs and Slave Consciousness." *Anonymous Americans: Explorations in Nineteenth-Century Social History*. Ed. Tamara K. Hareven. Englewood Cliffs: Prentice-Hall, 1971. Notes the present aspect of apparent futuristic symbolism in slave religion.

Lewis, R.W.B. "Day of Wrath and Laughter," in *Trials of the Word: Essays in American Literature*. New Haven: Yale University Press, 1965. A discussion of the "comic apocalypse" in contemporary American fiction.

_____. *The American Adam: Innocence, Tragedy, and Tradition in the Nineteenth-Century*. Chicago: The University of Chicago Press, 1955. A study of the myth of Adam and the Garden of Eden in nineteenth century American literature.

Lindsey, Hal, with C.C. Carlson. *The Late Great Planet Earth*. Grand Rapids, Michigan: Zondervan, 1970. All of Lindsey's novels depend specifically on his uses of the myth of apocalypse.

_____. *The Liberation of Planet Earth*. Grand Rapids, Michigan: Zondervan.

_____. *Satan is Alive and Well on Planet Earth*. New York: Bantam, 1974.

_____. *The Terminal Generation*. New York: Bantam, 1977.

_____. *There's a New World Coming*. New York: Bantam, 1975.

Lippy, Charles H. "John Thomas and the Christadelphians in America." Unpublished M. Div. thesis, Union Theological Seminary, 1968. The most comprehensive analysis of the unusual apocalypticism of this sect.

Löwith, Karl. *Meaning in History*. Chicago: Phoenix Books, 1949. A philosophical discussion of the patterns imposed on time by man in his search to endow history with human and divine significance.

Lowance, Mason I., Jr. "Increase Mather's 'New Jerusalem' Manuscript and Millennialism in Late Seventeenth-Century New England." *Proceedings of the American Antiquarian Society*, Vol. 88, (1977). A study of Puritan typological exegesis.

Luce, Henry R., ed. *The National Purpose*. New York: Holt, Rinehart and Winston, 1960. A remarkable collection of statements by American politicans (including Billy Graham) on America's mission to save the world.

Luther, Martin. First and Second Prefaces to *The Book of Revelation* (1522 and 1546). In Vol. XXXV of *Luther's Works*. Ed. E. Theodore Bachman. Philadelphia: Fortress Press, 1960.

Maclear, James F. "The Republic and the Millennium." In *The Religion of the Republic.* Ed. Elwyn A. Smith. Philadelphia: Fortress Press, 1971. The apocalyptic framework of much nationalistic sentiment.

Maddox, John. *Beyond the Energy Crisis.* New York: McGraw-Hill, 1975. An optimistic appraisal of future sources of energy by a much respected "futurologist."

———. *The Doomsday Syndrome.* New York: McGraw-Hill Company, 1972. A convincing argument against the "prophets of doom" whose arguments are based on "pseudo-scientific" data.

Mannheim, Karl. *Ideology and Utopia.* Trans. Louis Worth and Edward Shils. London: Kegan Paul, Trench, Trubner, 1936. A historical discussion of the theory and practice of utopian communities.

Manuel, Frank E. *Shapes of Philosophical History.* Stanford: Stanford University Press, 1965. A discussion of the metaphoric patterns which have been applied to history as man has tried to conceptualize the nature of time.

Marcuse, Herbert. *One Dimensional Man.* Boston: Beacon Press, 1964. A critique of contemporary western culture which describes it as unable to transcend the limits of materialistic, empiricist thought and warns of the dehumanizing effects of modern society.

Marx, Leo. *The Machine in the Garden: Technology and the Pastoral Ideal in America.* New York: Oxford University Press, 1964. Marx examines the contradiction between the Romantic vision of America as a pristine wilderness and the development of machines in the nineteenth century.

Mather, Increase. *A Discourse Concerning...the Glorious Kingdom of Lord Jesus Christ, on Earth, Now Approaching.* Boston: Printed by B. Green for Benj. Eliot, 1710. Puritan emphasis on the imminence of the end.

———. *The Mystery of Israel's Salvation Explained and Applyed.* London: Printed for John Allen, 1669. Views the conversion of Jews to Christianity the necessary precursor of the Apocalypse.

May, John R. *Toward a New Earth: Apocalypse in the American Novel.* Notre Dame and London: University of Notre Dame Press, 1972. Interpreting the myth of apocalypse as primarily millennial in its projection of the future, May discusses several nineteenth and twentieth century novelists as using the myth to suggest a better future.

McCormick, John. *Catastrophe and Imagination.* London: Folcroft, 1958. A discussion of the ways in which English and American fiction has dealt with the catastrophic nature of reality.

McGinn, Bernard. *Vision of the End: Apocalyptic Traditions in the Middle Ages.* New York: Columbia University Press, 1979. A monumental scholarly study of many apocalyptic texts, with the texts included in their entirety, from 400 A.D. to 1500 A.D.; Professor McGinn surveys a vast rage with great knowledge and insight.

McLoughlin, William C. *Revivals, Awakenings, and Reform.* Chicago: University of Chicago Press, 1978. The most recent study of the revival tradition, noting its frequent apocalyptic character.

Meadows, Donella H., Dennis L. Meadows, Jorgen Randers, and William W. Behrens, III. *The Limits to Growth: A Report for the Club of Rome's Project on the Predicament of Mankind.* New York: Universe Books, A Potomac Associates Book, 1972. Study using computers and systems dynamics approach seeking to demonstrate rapid collapse of the world economy about 100 years hence owing to resource exhaustion unless steps are taken to limit growth.

Melcher, Marguerite Fellows. *The Shaker Adventure.* Princeton: Princeton University Press, 1941. An old, but valuable semi-popular study of the Shakers and their millennialism.

Merleau-Ponty, Maurice. *The Phenomenology of Perception.* New York: Humanities Press, 1962. A phenomenological consideration of temporal constructs, among other such perceptual constructs.

Miller, David H. *Ghost Dance.* New York: Duell, Sloan and Pearce, 1959. A monograph on Sioux millennialism.

Miller, Perry, ed. *The American Puritans, Their Prose and Poetry.* Garden City, New York: Doubleday, 1956. A broad collection of Puritan prose and poetry, with very useful introductions to each selection.

_____.*Jonathan Edwards.* Toronto: William Sloane Associates, 1949. A general treatment of the life and works of Edwards.

_____."The End of the World." *William and Mary Quarterly,* 3rd ser., 8 (1951): 171-91. (Reprinted in *Errand into the Wilderness.* Cambridge: Harvard University Press, 1956, pp. 217-239). The only published analysis of seventeenth century Puritan apocalypticism.

Miller, William. *Evidence from Scripture and History of the Second Coming of Christ About the Year 1843.* Troy, N.Y.: Kemble and Hooper, 1836. The nub of Miller's imminent apocalypticism.

Mishan, E.J. *Pornography, Psychedelics and Technology.* Winchester, Mass: Allen and Urwin, 1980. A pessimistic prognosis of the transformation being wrought by the "gathering momentum of science and technology." The author is critical of uncontrolled technology and growth.

Mooney, James. *The Ghost-Dance Religion and the Sioux Outbreak of 1890.* Ed. Anthony F.C. Wallace. Chicago and London: University of Chicago Press, 1965. Reprinted of the earliest study of the social impact of the Dance and the military response.

Morawetz, David. *Twenty-five Years of Economic Development 1950-1975.* Washington, D.C.: The World Bank, 1977. Good corrective to overly pessimistic prophecies in that the book shows the significant progress that has been made in Third World countries.

Morse, Jedidiah. "An Address to the Christian Public." *Panoplist and Missionary Magazine United,* 4 (1811): 244. Sees the potential global extension of Christianity as a precondition of the Apocalypse.

Napier, David. "Prophets and Prophecy." *The Interpreter's Dictionary of the Bible.* Vol. III. New York: Abingdon Press, 1962. A short overview of the more extreme eschatology of the apocalypse and its influence on biblical materials.

Nichol, Francis D. *The Midnight Cry.* Washington, D.C.: Review and Herald Publishing Assoc., 1944. An apologetic exposition of Millerite apocalypticism by a Seventh-Day Adventist.

Niebuhr, H. Richard. *The Kingdom of God in America.* New York: Harper and Brothers, 1937. A classic study of religious visions of American destiny.

Niebuhr, Reinhold. *Faith and History.* New York: Charles Scribner's Sons, 1939. A twentieth-century theologian considers the nature of historical meaning in the context of Christianity.

O'Gorman, Edmundo. *The Invention of America: An Inquiry into the Historical Nature of the New World and the Meaning of History.* Bloomington: Indiana University Press: 1961. A fascinating study of Renaissance Europe's reception of the idea of a new world to the west.

Paddock, William and Paul Paddock. *Famine—1975! America's Decision: Who Will Survive.* Boston: Little, Brown & Co., 1967. Reprinted in 1976 as *Time of Famines: America and the World Food Crises.* Controversial prophecy of famine. Book advocates triage whereby food aid is withheld from hopeless nations as a strategy to minimize inevitable mass death from overpopulation and malnutrition.

Palmer, Peter. "Eschatology and Foreign Policy in the Thought of Reinhold Niebuhr, William Ernest Hocking, and John Courtney Murray." Unpublished Ph.D. dissertation, The University of Chicago, 1965.

Parker, Thomas. *The Visions and Prophecies of Daniel Expounded*. London: Printed for E. Paxton, 1646. A Puritan understanding of Old Testament apocalypticism.

Perrin, Norman. *Jesus and the Language of the Kingdom*. Philadelphia: Fortress, Press, 1976. An analysis of Jesus's apocalypticism.

Pieper, Josef. *Hope and History*. New York: Herder and Herder, 1969. A historiographic discussion of positive eschatological visions of time.

Poulet, Georges. *Studies in Human Time*. Trans. Elliott Coleman. Baltimore: Johns Hopkins Press, 1956. An excellent general study of the temporal structures of literature in various historical periods, although the temporal structure of apocalyptic literature *per se* is not discussed.

Rauschenbusch, Walter. *Christianity and the Social Crisis*. Ed. Robert D. Cross. New York: Harper and Row, 1964. Places the Social Gospel in an apocalyptic cast.

Reed, C.A., ed. *Origins of Agriculture*. The Hague: Mouton, 1978. An up-to-date and thorough review of the theories on the origin of agriculture in the Old and New World.

Ricoeur, Paul. *The Symbolism of Evil*. Trans. Emerson Buchanan. New York: Harper and Row, 1967. A hermeneutic interpretation of the development of the symbolism of sin, evil, from archaic cultures to Christian times.

Rist, M. "Apocalypticism." *The Interpreter's Dictionary of the Bible*. Vol I. New York: Abingdon Press, 1962. An overview of the biblical meaning of prophecy by the Dean of the Pacific School of Religion.

Rose, Stephen, and Lois Rose. *The Shattered Ring: Science Fiction and the Quest for Meaning*. Richmond: John Knox, 1970. Seminary graduate Stephen Rose and his wife review the classics of science fiction for their philosophical and theological ideas, and find the literature remarkably productive at that level.

Rovit, Earl. "On the Contemporary Apocalyptic Imagination." *The American Scholar*, 37, 3 (Summer, 1968), 458-63. A discussion of the versions and perversions of apocalypse in contemporary literature and politics.

Rowley, H.H. *The Relevance of Apocalyptic: A Study of Jewish and Christian Apocalypse from Daniel to the Revelation*. New York: Association Press, 1963. A theological discussion of the forms of apocalypse and their significance.

Russell, D.S. *The Method and Message of Jewish Apocalyptic*. Philadelphia: Westminster Press, 1964. A useful exposition of the basic forms and content of traditional Judaic apocalyptic writing.

Sandeen, Ernest R. *The Roots of Fundamentalism: British and American Millenarianism, 1800-1930*. Chicago: University of Chicago Press, 1970. Locates the origins of fundamentalism in millennial expectation.

Sauer, C.O. *Agricultural Origins and Dispersals*. 2nd ed. Cambridge: M.I.T. 1962. A rather old-fashioned presentation of unusual arguments of the origin of agriculture in the Far East. Now superseded by more modern texts, this author still has some interesting and, as yet unrefuted, original ideas.

Schechter, Harold and Charles Molesworth. "It's Not Nice to Fool Mother Nature: The Disaster Movie and Technological Guilt." *The Journal of American Culture*, I, i (Spring 1978), 45-50. An analysis of the rash of disaster movies in the 1970s.

Schneider, Stephen H., with Lynne E. Mesirow. *The Genesis Strategy: Climate and Global Survival*. New York: Plenum, 1976. Schneider believes that global starvation is imminent unless certain measures are taken: a prescriptive approach to the problem of limited food supplies in the world.

Schweitzer, Albert. *The Quest for the Historical Jesus*. New York: Macmillan, 1961.

General Bibliography and Author Index 253

One of the most amazing single volume works of the history of ideas ever written, it destroys a century of scholarship which interpreted Jesus without reference to his eschatological consciousness. All contemporary interpretation of Jesus is post-Schweitzer.

Shepard, Thomas. *The Parable of the Ten Virgins Opened and Applied.* London: Printed for John Rothwell and Samuel Thomson, 1660. Notes the unexpected timing of the Apocalypse within the framework of Puritan thinking.

_____. *God's Plot: The Paradoxes of Puritan Piety, Being the Autobiography and Journal of Thomas Shepard.* Edited and introduced by Michael McGiffert. Amherst, Massachusetts: The University of Massachusetts Press, 1972. Shepard rivals Jonathan Edwards in his lurid descriptions of God's apocalyptic wrath; McGiffert's introduction is very useful in placing Shepard in the Puritan apocalyptic tradition.

Sherwin, Martin J. *A World Destroyed: The Atomic Bomb and the Grand Alliance.* New York: Knopf, 1976. A historical view of the first decision to use atomic weapons, and the implications of that decision.

Shuler, John L. *Is the End Near?* Nashville and Atlanta: Southern Publishing Association, 1928. The Apocalypse from the view of a Jehovah's Witness

Simon, Julian L. *The Ultimate Resource.* Princeton, N.J.: Princeton University Press, 1981. Economist Simon draws on the work of many researchers to refute theories of the depletion of natural resources, the population explosion, etc. A very optimistic stance.

Skinner, B.F. *Beyond Freedom and Dignity.* New York: Vintage Books, 1971. A definitive account by America's most famous behavioral psychologist of the principles of behaviorism and of the ways in which the application of these principles to social problems could avert impending disaster.

Stehle, Raymond Louis. " 'Westward Ho!': The History of Leutze's Fresco in the Capitol." *Records of the Columbia Historical Society of Washington, D.C., 1960-62.* Ed. F.C. Rosenberger. Washington, D.C.: Columbia Historical Society, 1963. A history of Leutze's mural based on available documents, and also telling contemporary newspaper reviews and descriptions of the painting.

Stiles, Ezra. *The United States Elevated to Glory and Honour.* New Haven: Thomas and Samuel Green, 1783. A late Puritan view on the place of the early Republic in the coming Apocalypse.

Strong, Josiah. *The New Era or the Coming Kingdom.* New York: Baker and Taylor, 1893. An early Social Gospel work stressing the primacy of the United States in advancing the Apocalypse.

_____. *Our Country.* Ed Jurgen Horbst, 1885; rpt. Cambridge: Harvard University Press, 1963. The rise of Anglo-Saxon, industrial America as a sign of the proximity of the Apocalypse.

_____. *The Twentieth Century City.* New York: Baker and Taylor, 1898. Urbanization as a precondition of the Apocalypse.

Strout, Cushing. *New Heavens and New Earth: Political Religion in America.* New York: Harper and Row, 1974. An important study of the ways in which apocalyptic attitudes have been translated into the secular political sphere.

Teilhard, De Chardin. *The Divine Milieu.* New York: Harper and Row, 1965. A full-fledged contemporary prophetic eschatology, merging Thomistic philosophy and paleontological research into a mystic vision of the development of all life toward personal community in consciousness.

Thomas, John. *Elpis Israel: Being an Exposition of the Kingdom of God.* New York: Fowlers and Wills, 1851. The major Christadelphian work on the Apocalypse.

Tichi, Cecelia. *New World, New Earth.* New Haven: Yale University Press, 1979. A comment on the eschatological optimism inherent in American history and culture.

Tsanoff, Radoslav. *Civilization and Progress.* Lexington, Kentucky: University Press of Kentucky, 1971. The first part of the book is an intellectual history of the idea of progress. The second part takes the position that the idea of progress is a viable schema of history only if we recognize that progress depends on human choices, that these choices may thwart as well as advance the improvement of humanity.

Turner, Justin G. "Emanuel Leutze's Mural *Westward the Course of Empire Takes Its Way.*" *Manuscripts,* Vol. 18, no. 2 (Spring 1966), pp. 4-16. Contains a transcription of notes left by Leutze describing and explaining his mural.

Tuveson, Ernest L. *Millennium and Utopia: A Study in the Background of the Idea of Progress.* Berkeley: University of California Press, 1949. An intellectual history of secular and religious millennialist thinking.

―――. *The Redeemer Nation: America's Millennial Role.* Chicago: University of Chicago Press, 1968. An appraisal of visions of American destiny and their apocalyptic overtones.

Warshovsky, Fred. *Doomsday.* New York: Pocket Books, 1977. A look at the various political and environmental crises of our times.

Washington, Joseph R. Jr. *Black Religion: The Negro and Christianity in the United States.* Boston: Beacon Press, 1964. Contains a good discussion of the meaning of the images in Black spirituals.

Whisenhunt, Donald W. *The Environment and the American Experience: A Historical Look at the Ecological Crisis.* Port Washington, New York: Kennikat Press, 1974. A summary of the various "revolutions"—religious, intellectual, political, population—which America has passed through since its inception.

Wigglesworth, Michael. *The Day of Doom; or a Poetical Description of the Great and Last Judgment.* New York: American News Co., 1867. Reprinted in *The American Puritans: Their Prose and Poetry.* Ed. Perry Miller. Garden City, New York: Doubleday, 1956, pp. 282-294. The Apocalypse in Puritan verse.

Wilson, Bryan R. *Sects and Society.* Berkeley: University of California Press, 1961. A sociological analysis of the role of sectarian ideology, with emphasis on the Christadelphians.

Wollheim, Donald A. *The Universe Makers.* New York: Harper and Row, 1971. A series of humanistic studies in science fiction as philosophy of life, with brief discussion of classic works and authors.

Wood, B.A. *Human Evolution.* London: Chapman and Hall, 1978. A slim volume with a wealth of condensed information on the physical evolution of man.

Youngs, Benjamin S. *The Testimony of Christ's Second Appearing.* Lebanon, Ohio: From the Press of John M'Clean, 1808. The most comprehensive of Shaker apocalypticism.

Notes on the Contributors

DEBRA BERGOFFEN, Associate Professor of Philosophy at George Mason University, received her education at Syracuse and Georgetown Universities. Her areas of interest are the philosophy of history, the work of Nietzsche, and the philosophical implications and dimensions of Freud's thought. She has published articles on contemporary western culture and philosophy.

ERNEST CASSARA has been Professor of History at George Mason University since 1970. He has previously taught at Tufts University, Albert Schweitzer College in Switzerland, where he also served as Director of the College, and Goddard College in Vermont, where he also served as Dean. Professor Cassara's most recent books are *The Enlightenment in America* and *History of the United States of America: A Guide to Information Sources.*

THOMAS R. DEGREGORI, Professor of Economics, University of Houston, is the author of books and numerous articles and papers, mainly on the issues of technology and development or on the economic development of Africa. He is currently working on a book on science, technology, and economic development which will include a revised form of the essay in this collection. He has consulted on technology projects in Africa and Asia, where he has also lectured on technology transfer.

MICHAEL EMSLEY received his undergraduate and graduate degrees in zoology from London University. He has taught at the University of the West Indies, Trinidad, the Academy of Natural Sciences of Philadelphia, has served as Director of the William Beebe Tropical Research Station, Trinidad, and is currently Professor of Biology at George Mason University. He is editor of *Biotropica,* the journal of the Association for Tropical Biology. His most recent book is *Rain Forests and Cloud Forests.*

DAWN GLANZ, Assistant Professor of Art History in the School of Art at Bowling Green State University in Ohio, received her graduate training at Columbia University and the University of North Carolina at Chapel Hill. Her research has included studies of the iconography of westward expansion in American art of the nineteenth century, Daniel Boone and the iconography of national heroism, and images of the fur trapper in nineteenth-century American art.

CHARLES H. LIPPY, Associate Professor of History and Religion at Clemson University, was educated at Union Theological Seminary and Princeton University. He has written articles on various American religious sects and movements, and a book, *Seasonable Revolutionary: The Mind of Charles Chauncy.*

JOHN WILEY NELSON is the author of various studies of popular culture and American values: his book on this topic is *Your God is Alive and Well and Appearing in Popular Culture.* He has taught at Pittsburgh Theological Seminary, where he was Associate Professor of Systematic Theology; he is now the Minister of the First Presbyterian Church of Trenton, New Jersey. Dr. Nelson is a well-known country-and-western musician.

LOIS PARKINSON ZAMORA is Assistant Professor of English at the University of Houston. She received her education in Comparative Literature at Stanford University and at the University of California at Berkeley. Her area of interest is contemporary North American and Spanish American fiction; she has published studies of several contemporary writers, including Gabriel Garcia Marquez, Julio Cortazar, Mario Vargas Llosa, Thomas Pynchon, and John Barth, as well as translations of contemporary Mexican fiction.

Index

Abraham, 19, 20, 45
Absalom, Absalom! (Faulkner), 119-22
Adam, as symbol of American pioneer, 108, 114
Adams, Henry: belief in entropy of, 123; vision of future of, 122. Works: *Education of Henry Adams, The,* 123; *Mont-Saint-Michel and Chartres,* 123
Adams, John, 83
Africa, emergence of man in, 187-88
Age of Iron, 17
Age of Reason, 77
Agricultural Revolution, 193, 198
Agriculture: development of, in Central America, 194; development of, in Mediterranean, 193-94; invention of, 193; potential for development in, 211-12; slash-and-burn technique of, 195-96; in temperate and tropical areas, 194
Airport, 172
Alamo, Tony and Sue, 56
Altman, Robert, 170; *McCabe and Mrs. Miller,* 169, 170-71
Amadis de Gaula, (Montalvo), 99
America: concept of messianic role in history, 141; contemporary doomsday mentality of, 11; early system of education, 84; entry of man into, 190; as focus for apocalyptic vision, 1; genetic diversity of, 197; protestantism, 52, 53
"America, a Prophecy," (Blake), 107
American Dream, An (Mailer), 131
American Revolution, 76, 91; flowering of patriotism in, 107; social impact of, 83-84
Andes Mountains, 194
Angkor Wat (Cambodia), 194
Angel City (Shepherd), 110
Anglicans, 66, 76
Antichrist, 4, 39, 43; European alliance under, 163; in work of Hawthorne, 116; metaphoric opposition to Christ in Book of Revelation, 98
Anti-historicism: of archaic peoples, 14; distinctions between apocalyptic and cosmic, 16; Greek, 14
Apocalypse: American sense of, 1, 11; anti-historical motifs of, 14, 25; appeal during times of oppression of, 4, 28-29; artistic embodiments of, 8; dating of, 158; definition of, 2; determinism of, 4; dualism of, 3, 4, 98; existential-phenomenological perspective of, 12; Hebrew and Christian canons of, 3; as myth of transformation, 97-98; optimism of, 25; scientific and technological usage, 8; temporal sequence of, 2, 11-12, 13; tradition, 13; use of symbols in, 5, 11
Apocalypse, Four Horsemen of, 5, 206
Apocalyptic eschatology, as opposed to prophetic eschatology, 158-60
Apocalyptic symbols: archetypes, 5; in Book of Revelation, 3; use of, 11-12; meaning of, 12; hermeticism of, 5; the whore and the bride, 98; numerology of, 131; Northrup Frye's discussion of, 125-126, 128
Apocrypha, 73
Aquarian Age, 33
Arbella, the, 66, 74
Arcadia, as image for New Jerusalem, 108
Aristotle, 154
Armageddon, Battle of, 179; according to Lindsey, 163-64; in *Absalom, Absalom!,* 121; Civil War as, 111, 143; whale as symbol for in Melville, 117; in *The Universal Baseball Association,* 131
As I Lay Dying (Faulkner), 118
Asimov, Isaac, 167, 174. Works: *Foundation Trilogy, The,* 167; *I, Robot,* 174
Aspinwall, William, 39, 40
Autobiography (Franklin), 109
Autumn of the Patriarch, The (Garcia Marquez), 4

Babylon, 23, 98
Bad Day at Black Rock, 169
Bancroft, George, *History of the United States,* 85; "The Progress of Mankind," 134, n. 23.
Baptists, 55, 68, 75
Baldwin, James, racially apocalyptic prose

256

of *The Fire Next Time,* 111, 135, n.26.
"Battle Hymn of the Republic, The" 111
Battlestar Galactica, 166, 176, 177, 203
Bay Staters, 69
"Bear, The" (Faulkner), 119
Beatus of Liebana, illuminated manuscripts of, 139
Bellow, Saul, *Mr. Sammler's Planet,* 131
Beneath the Planet of the Apes, 173
Berg, David, 56
Bering Straits, 190
Berkeley, George (Bishop), 100, 108; "Versus on the Prospect of Planting Arts and Learning in America," 100, 145
Billy Jack, 166
Bingham, George Caleb, depiction of archetypal pioneers by, 142-43; *Emigration of Daniel Boone into Kentucky, The,* 142
Bionic Woman, The, 167
Birth rate, decline in, 202, 210-11
Birth control: by !Kung tribe, 192; in Third World countries, 193
Blake, William, "America, a Prophecy," 107
Blithedale, Romance, The (Hawthorne), 115-16
Boone, Daniel: as archetypal pioneer, 142; as depicted in Leutze mural, 144
Boone, Rebecca, as nineteenth-century, American Madonna, 142-43
Born Again Movement, 37
Bradford, William (Governor): as author of first piece of American literature, 102, 108; *History of Plymouth Plantation,* 65, 102
Brook Farm, as utopian community, 115
Browne, Ray, 154, 155
Bruno, Giordano, 130
Buber, Martin, designation of "prophetic eschatology" by, 23, 158
Bullinger, Henry, 183
Burroughs, William, 123
Butch Cassidy and the Sundance Kid, 169

Calafa, mythical queen of the Amazons, 100
California, as setting for modern pessimistic fiction, 109, 129; as symbol of utopia for Cortes, 100; for Whitman, 109
Campbell, Alexander, 45
Campbellites, 45
Canticle for Liebowitz, A (Miller), 173
Cawelti, John, *Six-Gun Mystique, The,* 154, 156

Casablanca, as American western, 166
cataclysm, 1, 117
Catal Huyuk (Turkey), 194
"Celestial Railroad, The" (Hawthorne), 112
Central Intelligence Agency, 92
Cervantes, Miguel de, 100
Chateaubriand, Francois Rene de, portrayal of "Red Indian" by, 107
Chicen Itza (Mexico), 194
Childhood's End (Clarke), 168
Children of the Damned, 178
Children of God, 56
Chlorofluorocarbons, effect on atmosphere of, 216-17
Christ, 37, 46, 48; early appeal of, 3; metaphoric opposition in Revelation of, 98; as new Adam, 114
Christadelphians, 39, 45, 46
Christian Foundation, 56
Christian World Liberation Front, 56
Church of England, separation of Puritans from, 65, 67
"City Upon a Hill," as Puritan vision of America, 71, 74, 77, 101
Civil War, American, 7, 85, 88; effect on Whitman of, 113-114; millennialist expectation after, 149
Clark, Elmer T., 47
Clark, George Rogers, as depicted in Leutze mural, 144
Clarke, Arthur, 168; Works: *Childhood's End, 2001: A Space Odyssey,* 168
Close Encounters of the Third Kind, 203
Club of Rome, 216; Meadows Report on human predicament to, 208, 209, 211
Coal. *See* Energy
Cohn, Norman, 42; *Pursuit of the Millennium, The,* 37
Cold War, the, 91
Columbus, Christopher, 1, 64, 99
Common Sense, (Paine), 78-79
Communism, American dedication to containment of, 92
Connecticut Valley, 69
Cooper, James Fenimore: themes of, male companionship, 109; themes of, war with nature, 111; use of apocalyptic setting, 109; *Pioneers, The,* 111
Coover, Robert: apocalyptic novels of, 130. Works: *Origins of the Brunists, The,* 129; *Universal Baseball Association, Inc., J. Henry Waugh, Prop., The,* 130-131
Cortes, Hernan, 100

Cosmic time (Archaic temporality), 14-16
Cotton, John, 39
Crevecoeur, J. Hector St. John de, 111, 118; apocalyptic use of "new man" by, 109; idea of American melting pot of, 86; *Letters from an American Farmer*, 111
Crying of Lot 49, The (Pynchon), 109

Daniel, The Book of, 27, 46; as apocalyptic writing, 3; interpretation by Lindsey of, 165; tradition of apocalyptic eschatology in, 157
Darby, John Nelson, 54
Darwin, Charles, 163
Darwinism, 52, 95, n.21
Daumier, Honore, 128
"Day of Doom, or a Poetical Expression of the Great and Last Judgment, A" (Wigglesworth), 40
Day of Judgment, the, 2; imagery of, 104; as negative side of apocalypse, 110
Day the Earth Caught Fire, The, 173
Day of the Locus, The (West), 110, 124, 126-29
Declaration of Independence, 78, 79
Deliverance (Dickey), 165
"Demographic transition," definition of, 197
Demon Seed, 174
Desiderio, Monsu, 128
Deutero-Isaiah, 157
Dewey, John, 218
Diamond, Stanley, 15
Dickey, James, *Deliverance*, 165
Dictionary (Webster), 84
Didion, Joan, 109, 110, 123. Works: *Play it as it Lays*, 109; *Slouching Towards Bethlehem*, 110
Diet, adaptation of man to chemicals in, 202-203
Disciples of Christ. See Campbellites
Dispensationalism, 54
Dissenters, migration to America of, 75-76
Dr. Strangelove, 173
Don Quixote, 100
Donne, John, sermon on corruption of Europe by, 100-01
Drayton, Michael, 100
"Drum Taps" (Whitman), 113
Durer, Albrecht, woodcut illustrations of Book of Revelation by, 140, 147-48
Dwight, Timothy, 141
Dylan, Bob, 155

Earth: emergence of man on, 186-88; origin of, 185-86
Earthquake, 172
Eden: as mirror image of New Jerusalem, 108; view of American West as new, 151
Education of Henry Adams, The (Adams), 123
Edwards, Jonathan, 38, 41, 42, 140; doomsday sermons by, 104; medieval mind of, 105. Works: *History of the Work of Redemption, A*, 41, 105, 106; "Sinners in the Hands of an Angry God," 104; *Some Thoughts Concerning the Present Revival of Religion in New England*, 41
Egypt, 51
Ehrlich, Paul, 208, 214; advocacy of triage during famine by, 209; prophesies of, 206-07; *Population Bomb, The*, 206
El Dorado, 1, 145
Eliade, Mircea, 97
Elijah, as Messiah, 26
Eliot, John, 73
Ellison, Ralph, 111
Elpis Israel; Being an Exposition on the Kingdom of God (Thomas), 45
Ely, Richard T., 52
Emerson, Ralph Waldo, 151; exploration of individualism by, 113; use of railroad as symbol of chaos by, 112. Works: "Man the Reformer," 113; "Society and Solitude," 113
Emigration of Daniel Boone into Kentucky, The (Bingham), 142
Energy: American over-consumption of, 199-200; effect of climate on, 201; exploitation of, 213; use of coal for, 201-02; use of nuclear power for, 201; use of solar power for, 201
Energy Crisis, American underestimation of, 200-02
Enlightenment, The, 66, 77, 80, 81
"Entropy" (Pynchon), 124
Entropy, law of, as metaphor for end of culture, 123-25
Erhard, Werner, as false prophet, 162
Eschatology: humanistic interpretation of, 165; naturalistic interpretation of, 165-66
Eschatology, contemporary apocalyptic: as anti-Western, 168; humanity versus natural world in, 172-73; humanity versus technology in, 174-78; political conspiracy

paranoia in, 178. *See* Apocalypse, Apocalyptic eschatology.
Eschatology, contemporary prophetic: as evolutionary humanism, 167-68; as humanistic pro-science, 166-67. *See* Prophetic eschatology.
est, 162
European Age of Exploration, 178
Ezekiel, 27, 157, 163

"Facing West from California's Shores" (Whitman), 109
Fail Safe, 33
Famine 1975! America's Decision: Who Will Survive (Paddock and Paddock), 207
Famine, in America, 207
Fascism, American, struggle against, 91
Faulkner, William, 218; apocalyptic themes in novels of, 118-22; cosmic pessimism of, 118-19. Works: *Absalom, Absalom!,* 119-22; *As I Lay Dying*, 118; "Bear, The," 119; *Go Down, Moses*, 119; *Hamlet, The*, 118; *Light in August*, 118; *Sound and the Fury, The*, 118
Fire Next Time, The (Baldwin), 111
Fishwick, Marshall, 154
Fitzgerald, F. Scott, *Great Gatsby, The*, 110
Food additives. *See* Diet
Food and Drug Administration, 202
Food of the Gods, 173
Food production. *See* Agriculture
Forbidden Planet, 174-75
Forbin Project, The 174
Forests, world, disappearance of, 196
Forrester, Jay, 208
Fosdick, Harry Emerson, 55
Foundation Trilogy, The (Asimov), 167
Frankenstein (Shelley), 174
Franklin, Benjamin, 75, 108; attitude toward Europe of, 81; dismissal of original sin by, 109; *Autobiography*, 109
Fredrickson, George, 143
French Revolution, the, 43
Freud, Sigmund, 163
Frye, Northrup, 125, 128
Fundamentalism, 55, 95, n.21; "Fundamentalist-Modernist Controversy; 55
Futureworld, 178

Galileo, 77
Gans, Herbert, 156
Garcia Marquez, Gabriel, *Autumn of the Patriarch, The*, 4
Genesis, Book of, 45
Germany, immigrants from, 87
Ghost Dance, 37, 39, 50, 59
Gladden, Washington, 52
"Global Report to the President—Entering the Twenty-First Century, The," 203
Glorious Revolution, the, 74
Go Down, Moses (Faulkner), 118
"God's American Israel," 141
"God's Controversy with New England" (Wigglesworth), 40
Golden Calf, the, 20
Gomorrah, 67
Goodall, Jane, 192
Goya y Lucientes, Francisco, 128
Graham, Billy, 57
Grapes of Wrath, The (Steinbeck), 127
Great Awakening, The, 39, 41, 42, 105, 141
Great Gatsby, The (Fitzgerald), 110; Compared to Tod in West's *The Day of the Locust*, 127
Greek: anti-historicism, 13, 14, 22, 25, 28, 33; orientation toward reality, 32; perception of history, 20; theme of historical degeneration, 26
Greening of America, The (Reich), 32
Guardi, Francesco, 128

Hakluyt, Richard, 100
Half-Way Covenant, 70
Hall, David D., 40
Hamlet, The (Faulkner), 118
Hardin, Garrett, 206, 207, 208, 209; *Limits to Altruism, The*, 209
Hartford, Connecticut, 69
Hawthorne, Nathaniel, 112; article on Leutze mural by, 150; dialectic between millennial and cataclysmic visions in, 115; end of American innocence in, 114; treatment of Civil War by, 114; use of apocalyptic characters by, 109. Works: *Blithedale Romance, The*, 115-16; *Scarlet Letter, The*, 115; "The Celestial Railroad," 136, n.33; "Earth's Holocaust," 136, n.33; "The New Adam and Eve," 136, n.33.
Heart is a Lonely Hunter, The (McCullers), 131
Hebrew Scriptures, 25-26
Hegel, Georg Wilhelm Friedrich, 31, 35, 163
Heilbroner, Robert, *Inquiry into the Human Prospect, An*, 206

Herron, George, 52
Herodotus, 17
Heschel, Abraham, 22
Hesiod, anti-historicism of, 16, 17, 18
Hicks, Edward, reliance on vision of Isaiah of, 140; *Peaceable Kingdom, The*, 140
High Noon, 169
High Plains Drifter, 169-70, 171
Hines, Joshua V., 46
History of Plymouth Plantation (Bradford), 65
History of the Work of Redemption (Edwards), 105-06
Hombre, 169
Homo erectus, 188, 189
Homo sapiens, 189, 190, 203
Hopkins, Samuel, 41
Huguenots, French, as dissenters, 75
Huit, Ephraim
Husserl, Edmund, 9, 180, n.9
Hutchinson, Anne, 67-68, 69

I, Robot (Asimov), 174
Indians, American, 49, 196-97
Industrialization: reduction in birth rate during, 197; religious opposition to, 214-15
Inquiry into the Human Prospect, An (Heilbroner), 206
Invasion of the Body Snatchers, 178
Ireland, immigration from, 87
Irving, Washington: "Rip Van Winkle," 112
Isaiah, The Book of, 1; as text for Leutze mural, 147
Israel, 51; apocalyptic response to fall of, 24; covenant of, with Yahweh, 66; invasion of, by Russia, 163; situation of, after destruction of Jerusalem, 27, 31
Israelites, 67, 72

Jefferson, Thomas, 76, 78, 80, 84; attitude toward Europe of, 81, 82
Jehovah's Witnesses, 39, 58; admixture of historical time and apocalypse time of, 48, 49;
apocalypticism of, 43; social context in emergence of, 52
Jeremiah, 23, 24
Jericho, 194
Jerusalem, 23, 27, 163
Jesus, 27, 158
Jesus Movement, 39, 56-57
Jesus People, 33, 35, 59
Jewett, William S., allusions to Old Testament in work of, 142; *Promised Land, The*, 142
Judaic prophetic tradition, 4
Judaism, 27, 45

Kali Yuga, 33
Kant, Immanuel, 163
Kennedy, John F., 93
Kennedy, Robert F., 93
Kermode, Frank, 9, 132; *Sense of an Ending, The*, 9
Kierkegaard, Soren, 163
King, Martin Luther, Jr., 93
Kikuyu, the, 192
Korea, American involvement in, 92
Korean War; effect of, on American Dream, 169
Krishna Consciousness, 33
Kubrick, Stanley, 168, 173, 174. *Dr. Strangelove*, 173; *2001: A Space Odyssey*, 168, 174
!Kung, 192-93

Last Judgment, the, 55, 77; imagery of, in painting and sculpture, 140; imagery of, in Leutze mural, 140; transcendence of time of, 105-06
Late Great Planet Earth, The (Lindsey), 154, 161, 163
Lathe of Heaven, The (LeGuin), 175-76
Latin America, U.S. involvement in, 92
Lawrence, D.H., 116, 117
Lazarus, Emma: "New Colossus, The," 88
Leakey, Louis, 187
Leaves of Grass (Whitman), 113
Lee, Ann, 44
LeGuin, Ursula, *Lathe of Heaven, The*, 175-76
Leopold, Aldo: *Sand County Almanac, A*, 217
Letters from an American Farmer (Crevecoeur), 86, 111
Leutze, Emmanuel, 100; mural by; analogy between pioneers and Israelites in, 146; appeal to contemporary audiences of, 151; choice of Golden Gate as goal of emigration in, 145; depiction of Westward expansion of America in, 143, 144, 145; as evidence of Millennial Kingdom, 152; image of Promised Land and Chosen People in, 146-47; interpretation by Anne Brewster of, 149; Old Testament history of, 146; religious imagery of, 144-45; as synopsis of progress of history, 146
Life expectancy, increase in, 197-98, 213
"Life Without Principle" (Thoreau), 110

Index   261

Lifeboat Ethic, in dealing with famine, 207
Light in August (Faulkner), 118
Limits to Altruism, The (Hardin), 209
Limits to Growth, The, 208, 213-214
Lincoln, Abraham, apocalyptic conception of Civil War, 135, n.25
Lindsey, Hal, 179, 154, 162, 163; description of heaven by, 164; interpretation of Book of Revelation by, 161, 163, 164-65. Works: *Late Great Planet Earth, The,* 154, 161, 163; *Satan is Alive and Well on Planet Earth,* 161, 162; *Terminal Generation, The,* 161
Lonely are the Brave, 169
"Long, Too Long America" (Whitman), 113
Louisiana Purchase, the, 89
Luther, Martin, 183

Maddox, John R., 209
Magnalia Christi Americana (Mather), 71, 74, 102-03
Magnasca, Alessandro, 128
Maharishi Mahesh Yogi, as false prophet, 162
Mailer, Norman, 123, 131; *American Dream, An,* 131
Malraux, Andre, 132
Man: cultural advances of, in art, 190; in religion, 189; in tool-making, 189; in use of fire, 188-89; development of agriculture by, 191-92; development of technology by, 188; emergence of, 186-88; life expectancy of early, 192; predatory nature of, 191
"Man the Reformer" (Emerson), 113
Manifest Destiny, 43, 89
Marcuse, Herbert, 31
Marx, Karl, 31, 35, 163
Masai, 192
Massachusetts Bay Colony, 68, 79-80; failure of charter of, 74; as haven for dissenters, 75
Mather, Cotton, 71, 74, 103; *Magnalia Christi Americana,* 71, 74, 102-03
Mather, Increase, 39, 103-04; "New Jerusalem," 103
Matthew, The Book of, 162
Mauser, Ulrich, 158
Mayflower Compact, 79
McCabe and Mrs. Miller, 169, 170-71
McCarthy Hearings: effect of, on American Dream, 169
McCullers, Carson, *Heart is a Lonely Hunter, The,* 131

McGuffey, William Holmes, readers by 85
Meadows, Dennis and Donella, 208
Meadows Report, 209, 211
Meigs, Montgomery, 149-50
Melville, Herman: apocalyptic versions of paradise and hell of, 116; theme of male companionship by, 109; treatment of Civil War by, 114; use of Ahab as Christ and Antichrist by, 117; use of apocalyptic characters by, 109; use of whale as symbol of Armageddon by, 117. Works: *Moby Dick,* 116; *Typee,* 116.
Messiah: as eschatological term, 25; role of, 25-26; Jesus as, 27
Messianic Age, 23, 25; apocalyptic interpretation of, 24-25; deterministic sense of history of, 24; imminent beginning of, 24; inauguration of, 26; Kingdom of, 28; as reward, 21
Methodists, 55, 75
Mexican War: as part of nineteenth-century American conception of manifest destiny of America, 89
Millenarianism, 39
Millennial Kingdom: as American West, 142, 144; as invisioned by Leutze mural, 151-52
Miller, D.S., *Nutrition and the World Food Crisis,* 211
Miller, Walter, *Canticle for Liebowitz, A.,* 173
Miller, William, 46, 47, 58
Millerites, 39, 47, 48, 49
Miss Lonelyhearts (West), 124-25
Mississippi, state of, 49
Mr. Sammler's Planet (Bellow), 131
Moby Dick (Melville), 117
Mohammedanism, 139
Molesworth, Charles, 172, 173
Monroe Doctrine, the, 92
Mont-Saint-Michel and Chartres (Adams), 123
Montalvo, Garci-Rodriguez de, 99, 100; *Amadis de Gaula,* 99;
Moody, Dwight L., 57
More Than Human (Sturgeon), 168
Mormons, 43
"Mother Ann's Work," 44

Nantes, Edict of, 75
National Research Council, U.S. National Academy of Sciences, 211-212

Natural resources: American consumption of world store of, 199-200; use of economic model to determine exhaustion of, 216
"New Colossus, The" (Lazarus), 88
New Deal, the 89
New England, 71; Puritan migration to, 65; symbolic association with Old Testament Israel of, 103
New Jerusalem, 1, 3, 5, 35, 139; as descending from heaven, 103; description of, in early American literature, 102; failure of, to appear, 104; metaphoric opposition of, in Revelation, 98; supplantation of image of, 108; as urban ideal, 102
"New Jerusalem" (Mather), 103
New World, 7, 69, 184, 200; Black Americans in, 51; migration to, 64
Newton, Isaac, 77
Night of the Lepus, 173
Nightwings (Silverberg), 178
1984 (Orwell), 33
Nixon, Richard M., 93
Noyes, John Humphrey, 43
Nuclear power. *See* Energy
Nutrition and the World Food Crisis (Miller), 211
Nye, Russel, 154, 156

O'Connor, Flannery, 136, n.41
Oil, discovery of, 198
On the Beach, 33, 173
One-Eyed Jacks, 169
One Flew Over the Cuckoo's Nest, 155
Oneida Perfectionists, 43
Orient, the, 64
Origin of the Brunists, The (Coover), 129
Orvieto, Cathedral of, 140
Ox Bow Incident, The, 155

Paddock, Paul and William, 207, 208; *Famine 1975! America's Decision: Who Will Survive*, 207
Paine, Thomas, 78-79; *Common Sense*, 78-79
Panama Canal Treaty, 92
Papacy, The, 39
Parallax View, The, 178
Parker, Thomas, 39
Parousia, 41, 43, 46, 54, 55, 58; belief in imminence of, 47, 59; definition of, 37
Pascal's Wager, 208-209
Peaceable Kingdom, The (Hicks), 140

Penn, William, 75
Pennsylvania: as haven for dissenters, 75; universal education in, 84
Percy, Walker, 131; *Second Coming, The*, 131, 134, n.41.
Peru, 194
Pilgrims, 65
Pioneers, The (Cooper), 111
Piscean Age, 33
Pisgah, Mount, 102, 142
Planet of the Apes, 173
Plato, 18
Play It as It Lays (Didion), 109
Plymouth Brethren, 54
Plymouth Colony, 65, 75
Poe, Edgar Allan, 110, 134, n.22
Popular culture: American Western in, 166; elitist view of, 155; rejection of Marxist contentions of, 156; stereotyping of, 156
Population Bomb, The (Ehrlich), 206
Porter, Katherine Anne, 136, n. 41
Poseidon Adventure, The, 172
Presbyterians, 55, 75
Professionals, The, 169
Promised Land, the, as depicted in Leutze mural, 148
Promised Land, The (Jewett), 142
Prophetic eschatology, 158-60, 161
Pseudepigrapha, 73
Puritan: apocalyptic sense, 108; belief in promise of future, 97; belief in retributive justice, 105; puritans, 39, 140; histories: depiction of struggle on earth of, 101; leaders, goal of, 67; literature, 98, 101 ff; theory of conversion, 70
Puritans, 79, 184; apocalyptic mentality of, 6; appearance of apocalyptic visions to, 4; attitude toward Indians of, 73-74; concern with dissent of, 69-70; disapproval of Quakers by, 68; first generation struggle of, 71; intolerance of, by English Puritans, 74; as models for others, 75; God of, 76; strict moral code of, 76; Calvinistic belief of 77
Purdy, James, 123
Pursuit of the Millennium, The (Cohn), 37
Pynchon, Thomas, 109, 123, 124. Works: *Crying of Lot 49, The*, 109; "Entropy," 124

Quakers, 68, 74

Raleigh, Walter (Sir), 100

Rauschenbusch, Walter, 52, 53
Reforming Synod of 1679, 67, 71
Reich, Charles, 32; *Greening of America, The,* 32
Revelation, The Book of, 3, 27, 103, 139, 157, 158; destruction of "third part" of world in, 164; numerology of, 131; passages of, quoted by Columbus, 1; similarity of, to Puritan histories, 101; symbolism in, 5; symbolic opposites in, 98. *See* Saint John.
Rhode Island, state of, 68, 75
"Rip Van Winkle" (Irving), 112
Roman Catholic Canon, tradition of apocalyptic eschatology in, 157
Roman Catholic Church, 43
Roman Empire, 163
Romanticism: influence of, on myth of pioneer, 107; conception of American wilderness, 107
Rosa, Salvator, 128
Rosseau, Jean-Jacques, 107
Rush, Benjamin (Dr.), 78, 83, 84
Russell, Charles Taze, 48
Russia, 163
Rutherford, Joseph (Judge), 48

Sabbath, the 47
St. Foy, Church of (at Conques), 140
Saint John of Patmos, 120-21, 143; Revelation of, 129, 139, 140. *See* Revelation, The Book of
Saint Paul, 73, 95, n.21, 158
Salem, Massachusetts, witch trials in, 73
Sand County Almanac, A (Leopold), 217
Sargeant pepper's Lonely Hearts Club Band, 155
Satan, 3, 4, 48, 164; as apocalyptic contrary, 108; influence on false prophets of, 163; role of in *Absalom, Absalom!,* 121
Satan is Alive and Well on Planet Earth (Lindsey), 162
Sauer, Carl, 191
Scarlet Letter, The (Hawthorne), 115
Schechter, Howard, 172, 178
Schofield, C.I., 54
Schurz, Carl, 87
Scott, George C., 155
Searchers, The, 169
Second Coming, the, 37, 45, 48, 58
Second Coming, The (Percy), 131
"Second Coming, The" (Yeats), 110
Sense of an Ending, The (Kermode), 9
Separatists, as left wing of Puritan movement, 65
Sergas de las Esplandian, Las, 100
Sermon on the Mount, the, 66
Seventh-Day Adventists, 37, 43, 47, 48, 49, 52
"Seward's Icebox," as part of manifest destiny, 89
Shakers, 39, 43-45, 46, 58
Shamans, 49-50
Shane, 166
Shape of Things to Come, The (Wells), 167
Shelley, Mary, 174; *Frankenstein,* 174
Shootist, The, 155
Shepherd, Sam, *Angel City,* 110
Shepherd, Thomas, 39, 104
"Sight in Camp in the Daybreak Gray and Dim, A" (Whitman), 113
Signorelli, Luca, 140
Silverberg, Robert, *Nightwings,* 178
Simmons, Harvey, 210
Simon, Paul, 155
Simple Cobler of Aggawam, The (Ward), 69
Sinclair, T.C., 214
"Sinners in the Hands of an Angry God" (Edwards), 104
Sinyavsky, Andrei, 4-5
Six-Gun Mystique, The (Cawelti), 154
Six Million Dollar Man, The, 167
Slan (Van Vogt), 167
Slouching Towards Bethlehem (Didion), 110
Social Gospel, 52, 53-54
"Society and Solitude" (Emerson), 113
Sodom, 67
Solar power. *See* Energy
Solow, Robert, estimation of mineral resources by, 212
Some Thoughts Concerning the Present Revival of Religion in New England (Edwards), 41
Sioux, 49, 59
Sound and the Fury, The (Faulkner), 118
South Pacific, 155
Spanish-American War, part in national expansion of, 90
Sparks, "Daddy" Jack, 56
Stagecoach, 169, 172
Star Trek, 166, 174, 176; as prophetic eschatology, 168
Star Wars, 166, 176-77, 203
Steinbeck, John, *Grapes of Wrath, The,* 127
Stiles, Ezra, 43
Stowe, Harriet Beecher, James Baldwin's

comments on, 135, n.26; *Uncle Tom's Cabin*, 111
Strong, Josiah, 52, 53
Sturgeon, Theodore, *More Than Human*, 168
Sumner, William Graham, 88
Sun Myung Moon, as false prophet, 162

Tawney, R.W., 214-15
Taxi Driver, 169, 171-72
Terminal Generation, The (Lindsey), 161
Them, 173
Thomas, John, 45, 46; *Elpis Israel; Being an Exposition of the Kingdom of God*, 45
Thoreau, Henry David, 109, 110, 112
Time: apocalyptic concept of, 13, 14, 19; archaic (cosmic) concept of, 14-16; Greek sense of, 13, 16, 19; structuring of, 15-16
Tocqueville, Alexis de, 113
Towering Inferno, The, 172
Transcendental Meditation, 162
Tuveson, Ernest, 143
Twain, Mark, 109
2001: A Space Odyssey, 174
Typee (Melville), 116
Tyson, Cicely, 155

Uncle Tom's Cabin (Stowe), 111
Unification Church, 162
Unitarians, as dissenters, 75
United Nations, 91, 92
United Society of Believers in Christ's Second Coming. *See* Shakers
United States National Academy of Sciences, 211, 216
Universal Baseball Association, Inc., J. Henry Waugh, Prop., The (Coover), 130-31
Universalists, as dissenters, 75
Universe, calculation of age of, 185
Ussher, John (Bishop), 185

Van Vogt, A.E., *Slan*, 167
Vega, Garcilaso de la, 100
"Verses on the Prospect of Planting Arts and Learning in America" (Berkeley), 101, 145
Vietnam, American involvement in, 92
Vietnam War, 179
Village of the Damned, 178
Virginia Company, the, 79

Walking Tall, 166
Ward, Nathaniel, *Simple Cobler of Aggawam, The*, 69

Washington, Joseph R., Jr., 51
Watergate Scandal, 93, 179
Weber, Max, 37
Webster, Noah, 84, 85; *Dictionary*, 84
Wells, H.G., 167; *Shape of Things to Come, The*, 167
West, Benjamin, 140
West, Nathanael, 110, 123, 124, 125-29. Works: *Day of the Locust, The*, 110, 124, 125-29; *Miss Lonelyhearts*, 124-25
Western movies, apocalyptic elements in, 166
White, Ellen G., 47
Whitman, Walt: description of loss of innocence by, 114; effects of Civil War on, 113-14; nostalgia for mythic territory by, 109; temporal nature of poetic vision, 135, n.32; treatment of individualism by, 113. Works: "Drum Taps," 113; "Facing West from California's Shores," 109; *Leaves of Grass*, 113; "Long, Too Long America," 113; "Sight in Camp in the Daybreak Gray and Dim, A," 113. *See also* 135-36, n.32
Wild Bunch, The, 169
William of Normandy (William the Conqueror), 79
Wilson, Woodrow, 81, 90
Wigglesworth, Michael: calendaring of day of doom by, 106-07; description of impending cosmic disaster by, 106. Works: "Day of Doom, or a Poetical Expression of the Great and Last Judgment, The," 40, 72, 106; "God's Controversy with New England," 40, 106.
Winnebago, 15
Williams, Roger, 67, 68
Winthrop, John, 66, 71, 74, 76, 101; "Modell of Christian Charity, The" 71
Wise, Isaac Mayer, 87
Wittwer, Sylvan, 216
World Bank, the 213
World Fertility Surveys, 210
Wounded Knee, Battle of, 50
Wright, Richard, 111
Wythe, George, 82-83

Yahweh, 2, 66
Yeats, W.B., "Second Coming, The," 110
Yuha, 190

Zechariah, 162
Zion, 71